THE SEEDS WE PLANTED

THE SEEDS WE PLANTED

PORTRAITS OF A NATIVE HAWAIIAN CHARTER SCHOOL

Noelani Goodyear-Kaʻōpua

University of Minnesota Press
Minneapolis | London

FIRST PEOPLES
New Directions in Indigenous Studies

Publication of this book was made possible, in part, with a grant from the Andrew W. Mellon Foundation.

Published by the University of Minnesota Press
111 Third Avenue South, Suite 290
Minneapolis, MN 55401-2520
http://www.upress.umn.edu

LIBRARY OF CONGRESS CATALOGING-IN-PUBLICATION DATA
Goodyear-Ka'opua, Noelani, author.
The seeds we planted : portraits of a native Hawaiian charter school / Noelani Goodyear-Ka'opua
(First peoples: new directions in indigenous studies)
Includes bibliographical references and index.
ISBN 978-0-8166-8047-4 (hardback)
ISBN 978-0-8166-8048-1 (pb)
1. Charter schools—Hawaii—Case studies. 2. Place-based education—Hawaii—Case studies. 3. Indigenous peoples—Education—Hawaii—Case studies. I. Title.
LB2806.36.G68 2013
371.0509969—dc23   2012043828

Printed in the United States of America on acid-free paper

The University of Minnesota is an equal-opportunity educator and employer.

20 19 18 17 16 15 14 13   10 9 8 7 6 5 4 3 2 1

*In memory of George Terry Kanalupilikokoamaʻihuʻi Young
and all nā kumu aloha ʻāina who preceded us and reminded us
who we are*

E iho ana o luna
E pi'i ana o lalo
E hui ana nā moku
E kū ana ka paia

What is above will come down
What is below will rise up
The islands will come together
The walls will stand again

Contents

Preface

The year 1998 marked one hundred years of U.S. control of Hawaiʻi, which the international community of nations had recognized as an independent country—the Hawaiian Kingdom—since the 1840s. I spent that summer teaching a course in applied English for Kanaka Maoli students about to enter their senior year in high school.[1] The course was part of a state community college summer bridge program founded to address the underrepresentation of Native Hawaiians in higher education. Through a suite of courses, the students were to develop skills for navigating the postsecondary transition to a career or college. My friend and high school classmate Keola Nakanishi worked alongside me as a coteacher. Young educators fresh out of college, we were told that students should learn how to create résumés, write cover letters, complete job application forms, and practice other basic skills young people need in order to apply for college or enter the work force. We, however, were eager to teach literacy as a liberatory praxis rather than as just an economic expedient.

I had recently completed a bachelor's degree in Hawaiian studies at the University of Hawaiʻi at Mānoa, a program that encouraged students to analyze the political stakes of knowledge and to blend scholarship with robust community engagement. Like women's studies, ethnic studies, and Native studies programs elsewhere, Hawaiian studies grew out of social movements for justice. Our teachers approached education as part of a larger political project of Hawaiian self-determination and nationhood. Like them, I wanted to help my own students see their paths as embedded in larger terrains of collective struggle and survival. Keola and I titled our class Mana Maoli (True Power or Native Power), signifying what we wanted our students to recognize in themselves and in our people.

We opened that summer with a conversation about how our ʻŌiwi ancestors of the kingdom era had produced a level of popular literacy comparable to, if not exceeding, most nations in the world.[2] Within

a generation after the introduction of a printing press in 1822, nearly
the entire adult population had attended school and learned to read
and write.[3] Amid waves of foreign-introduced diseases and imperialist designs on their country, nineteenth-century Kānaka wrote
and published copious pages of histories, letters, songs, lamenta-
tions, and political commentary, particularly through the Hawaiian-
language newspapers but also as books, personal correspondences,
and legal documents.[4] In fact, the millions of pages of documents in
the Hawaiian language comprise a unique treasure among Indigenous
peoples worldwide, whose languages, cultures, and knowledge bases
have been assaulted by processes of imperialism and colonialism. Literacy provided new avenues for articulating Hawaiian nationhood. It
became a practice of Hawaiian survivance, a term which emphasizes
"renewal and continuity into the future" rather than loss and mere survival "through welcoming unpredictable cultural reorientations."[5] As
Vizenor writes, "Survivance is the continuance of stories, not a mere
reaction, however pertinent."[6]

I have written this book as a twenty-first-century story of Hawaiian
survivance. This uniquely Hawaiian story addresses broader concerns
about what it means to enact Indigenous cultural-political resurgence
while working within and against settler colonial structures. Contemporary Indigenous education seeks to rearticulate schooling (historically aimed at our assimilation to settler society) within projects of
collective renewal and continuity.

Through our conversations on that first day of class, I was stunned
to learn that none of our students, except the two who had been enrolled in Hawaiian-language immersion schools for the previous twelve
years, were aware that our kūpuna (ancestors) exponentially and en-
thusiastically spread the skills of print literacy in the early 1800s. Powerful pedagogies of erasure caused such disconnection. For the bulk of
the twentieth century, the settler state government in Hawai'i failed to
support or fund any form of Indigenous education. Young people were
severed from the legacy of Hawaiian literacy, as not a single school in
the islands made the Native Hawaiian language or culture central to
its curriculum until the advent of language-immersion schools in the
mid-1980s.[7]

Kanaka social movements of the 1970s had successfully pressed for change in various aspects of life in the islands. Riding this wave of so-cial movement, delegates to the 1978 state constitutional convention included provisions for a Hawaiian education program consisting of language, culture, and history in the public schools, and they affirmed Hawaiian as an official language of the state. Finally, in 1986 the ninety-year ban on Hawaiian language–medium instruction in public schools was defeated, and the first publicly funded Hawaiian-language immer-sion schools of the twentieth century began to emerge.

Yet there I found myself in a classroom twenty years after major constitutional change, and still a vast majority of my students were unfamiliar with the works of any of the most famous Hawaiian writers and scholars of the nineteenth century. Having entered kindergarten the year after the landmark 1978 constitutional convention, I had an ex-perience in school that was quite similar to the students in front of me. Still, I was shocked that little had changed in the ensuing years. Prior to entering our classroom in their final summer of high school, most of our students had never been assigned literature by any Kanaka Maoli author, in Hawaiian or English. They had been taught little if anything of the richness of Hawaiian geography, chant, agriculture, aquaculture, navigational arts and science, or moʻolelo (stories/histories).

Through our conversations during the rest of the summer, I learned about another disturbing aspect of this group's educational experi-ences: besides the two Hawaiian-immersion students, most of the oth-ers could not remember having Kanaka Maoli teachers in their regular schools. Native Hawaiians are indeed underrepresented in Hawaiʻi's teaching force, comprising roughly 10 percent, as compared with more than a quarter of the public school student enrollment.[8] I believe our students' experiences and recollections were also shaped by a histori-cally rooted racial construction of Kānaka as pupils in need of tutelage rather than as teachers and intellectual leaders. In dominant narratives of the nineteenth-century explosion in Hawaiian literacy, white Amer-ican Protestant missionaries are typically represented as the agents of change, the teachers who brought and bestowed literacy. When Kanaka teachers are mentioned at all with regard to the phenomenal growth of mass literacy, popular and academic histories typically dismiss them as ill prepared or unqualified.[9] The existing historiography of education in Hawaiʻi generally ignores the fact that Kānaka Maoli comprised a majority of the islands' teachers throughout the nineteenth century, right up until the 1893 U.S.-backed coup against Queen Liliʻuokalani.

Such erasures and misrepresentations are common in settler colonial discourses that work to legitimize the seizure of land and political sovereignty from Indigenous nations by infantilizing them.[10] For instance, simultaneous with the explosion of literacy in Hawaiʻi, American political leaders were justifying their policies of Indian removal by publicly describing Indians as children. Schneider observes that in the early decades of the 1800s, "Native nations stopped being hailed as external and sovereign, and in their inaugural addresses presidents began describing them as internal to the state . . . as eternally childlike, playing around the knees of a colonizing state."[11] Settler colonial schooling continues the imperial domesticating projects of subsuming the lands and peoples of independent and sovereign nations within the internal, or domestic, sphere of an imperial occupier.

The impact that a century-long disconnection from legacies of literacy, teaching, and educational excellence had on the group of passionate and intelligent young Hawaiians I had the privilege of teaching and learning from back in 1998 was clearly apparent to me. These were ʻōpio ʻōiwi (Native youth) who had succeeded through to the twelfth grade and were still considering higher education despite their less-than-empowering experiences with schools. Though they had powerful stories to tell and profound insights to make, they generally did not see themselves as writers or intellectuals, as eloquent and articulate with important things to say. Schooling had largely blinded them to their own brilliance. It failed to cultivate in them a strong sense of their own voices and the connections of those voices to a deeper, collective ancestral well. Against that backdrop, this book works against the deeply entrenched notion that intellectual rigor is incompatible with Indigenous cultures. As will become apparent, excellence in education is a Hawaiian cultural value, and Kānaka ʻŌiwi have demonstrated an enduring love for self-directed learning.

Against enduring racist, colonial constructions of Indigenous nations as children in the patriarchal family of a settler state, as perpetual pupils in the classrooms of empire, this book explores the work of contemporary Native Hawaiian educators who have struggled to articulate self-determined notions of education and nationhood. In this book I offer a story about twenty-first-century Hawaiian-focused public charter schools, a movement I became involved in shortly after teaching that literacy course in 1998. The opportunity to open public charter schools afforded local communities limited autonomous school governance, yet under the framework of a settler state system subject to Hawai'i state and U.S. federal laws such as the No Child Left Behind Act (NCLB). Although Kānaka Maoli make up only about one-fifth of Hawai'i's current population, more than half of the charter schools that have been founded since 1999 are the initiatives of predominantly 'Ōiwi communities. Hawaiian culture–based charters tend to be community oriented, small scale, and staffed by a significantly larger percentage of Kanaka Maoli teachers than mainstream schools. In the context of significant budget constraints, they negotiate dominant knowledge regimes that alternately devalue and exploit Hawaiian culture.

The seeds for this book were planted during my involvement in the early years of the charter schools' emergence. In 1999 Keola and I became part of the core group of young educators and parents who founded Hālau Kū Māna (HKM), a secondary school that remains one of the only Hawaiian culture–based charter schools located in urban Honolulu. Like the other communities throughout the islands, we aimed to make Hawaiian cultural knowledge and practices—such as navigation, sailing, fishpond restoration, and taro cultivation—centerpieces for cultural revival, community building, and academic excellence. This was no small task, given that our schools were receiving significantly less per-pupil funding from the state than conventional public schools while also lacking the provision of adequate facilities and serving a significantly higher percentage of students eligible for free and reduced lunch and special education services.[12]

This book charts some of HKM's struggles, genealogies, and educational practices. It takes HKM educators as cultural-political actors who have used schools to sustain and reimagine the lāhui Hawai'i, the Hawaiian nation. How do an Indigenous people use educational institutions and technologies introduced as colonizing forces to maintain and transform their collective sense of purpose and interconnection—of peoplehood and nationhood? In the face of ongoing forces of imperialism, settler colonialism, and white supremacy, how can the practices and struggles that emerged in our school inform education for the future? One way HKM educators have done this is through *land-centered literacies* that form the basis of a pedagogical praxis of *aloha 'āina*. By land-centered literacies, I mean a range of critically engaged observational, interpretive, and expressive practices that put land and natural environment at the center. Land-centered literacies can include narrower definitions of literacy that refer specifically to working with printed text, but they can also include reading the patterns of winds or the balance of water in a stream. Moreover, the Hawaiian land-centered literacies I discuss in this book include study of and engagement with historical and contemporary relations of power.

The central problem for Indigenous Hawaiian charter schools operating under the existing settler state is that although we have begun to reclaim kuleana (responsibility, authority) for educating our youth, the ultimate authority for determining what children should learn and when they should learn it still remains with the settler state government.[13] The success, funding, and survival of these schools are determined by authorities that do not necessarily value Indigenous cultural knowledge or values. The regimes of knowledge supported, for example, by the existing Hawaii Content and Performance Standards and the U.S. national Common Core State Standards focus on conventional literacies that marginalize important Indigenous knowledge practices and reify constructions of literacy that exclude the kinds of land-based literacies that have enabled Indigenous survivance for generations. Yet the struggle to assert and practice these knowledges and the bonds that connect Kānaka Maoli to the 'āina (land that feeds) have always been tempered by the struggle to survive as an institution within a settler-dominant system.

One of the ironies of Hawai'i's charter school law was that although charters were intended to give communities some autonomy from the state's board of education (BOE), the BOE was the only body authorized to grant a charter.[14] In other words, the centralized educational authority that groups were trying to get out from under was the very body evaluating applications and granting permission to operate. The centralized nature of the state's system is both a remnant of the colonial past and evidence of the colonial present.

In December 2000 Keola and I pulled into the well-lit suburban middle school parking lot in Mililani on the night HKM's charter was up for consideration by the Hawai'i state BOE. It was a forty-five-minute drive from HKM's urban Hawaiian neighborhoods to this middle-class suburb, and as it was a weeknight, no other members of our community were able to attend. When our item came up on the agenda, Keola and I were instructed to sit at a tiny desk with one microphone in front of the board members who sat along the full length of a long table at the front of the room. Over the PA system, someone instructed us to "go ahead and speak."

Our presentation was an exercise in delicate rhetorical maneuvering. On one hand, we had to demonstrate a need for a school like ours, basically telling the board members that they and the Department of Education have been unsuccessful in addressing the needs of Native Hawaiian youth. I briefly discussed the educational status of Native Hawaiian students in the public school system, using safe words like "culturally inappropriate" rather than "racist" or "colonial." There we were, approaching the very agency we were criticizing—in an arena where they clearly had the upper hand—and saying that we could do a better job through a Hawaiian culture–driven program. Keola elaborated on what the actual program would look like, stating our goal of educational self-determination yet also explaining how we would maintain accountability to the board.

As we talked, few of the board members looked directly at us. When we finished our presentation and the board opened its discussion, they spoke only to each other. Instead of engaging with our proposed curriculum or governance structure, they debated whether they had the authority to grant our charter. After twenty minutes of contemplating their own authority, they exercised it and granted us the first charter to a start-up school on O'ahu. Keola and I spontaneously embraced each other in relief, elation, and hopefulness. It felt a joyous moment, a moment of victory. Still, I felt the board members silently watching us in our moment of celebration. By the time we left the meeting, I felt more conscious of how my own words and emotions had been shaped by the relations of force and authority around us.

Later that evening when I returned home, the sheer happiness was tempered by reflection and questioning. Why should a board comprised wholly of settlers be the sole authority to tell us, as Indigenous educators, whether we are worthy and capable of schooling our own children? Why does their approval make us so happy? Why should they have the exclusive authority and control of resources such that their approval is required in the first place? As more Hawaiian-focused schools like ours were authorized, would our efforts to create alternatives to the mainstream system absolve the rest of the Department of Education from their responsibilities to Hawaiian youth and other marginalized people? What does it mean to "exercise educational self-determination" in these contexts?

In exploring some of these questions, this book draws on my own participation and observation at HKM over ten years, as well as conversations and more formal interviews with cofounders, teachers, students, and alumni. The book elaborates the ways educators navigate these often competing forces of state accountability, self-determination, and a received sense of kuleana. I posit Hawaiian engagements with schooling and Hawaiian social movements not as homogenous monoliths whose characteristics are dictated by a static political or cultural trajectory but as a discursive field in which individuals, communities, ideas, and practices are deeply genealogically tied while always fertilizing new genealogical connections.

Over the past thirteen years, I have watched and worked alongside committed educators and families tirelessly laboring to grow Hālau Kū Māna and other "New Century" Hawaiian culture–based public charter schools against all odds. I have never ceased being amazed that a people can see so much hope and possibility in institutions that have been forcefully assimilative and deeply inadequate. The story of HKM and Indigenous Hawaiian charter schools that I tell in this book is, like all stories, situated, partial, and unfinished. It is offered with the hope that it will inspire not only further innovation in Indigenous education but also the transformation of the deep structures of settler colonialisms and imperialisms. Will more people—both Indigenous and settler—join together in the coming decades to further transform the educational systems that have marginalized Indigenous people and our knowledges? The lyrics that form the introduction's second epigraph, written by an early group of HKM students, remind us that the coming generations of Native youth will be a force to be reckoned with, one way or another.

Acknowledgments

This book is the product of the collective mana, action, and thoughts of many, many people. I can only begin to thank some of them here, and I apologize in advance to those I have not specifically named. Nui koʻu mahalo iā ʻoukou pākahi a pau.

I must first mahalo the ʻāina that have inspired and sustained my work on this book over the past ten years: Waʻahila, ʻAihualama, Mānoa, Maunalaha, Makiki, Heʻeia, Kaʻalaea, Kualoa, Lāʻau, Keawanui, Honouliwai, Puna, and especially the great Moana Nui as it touches the shores of Waikīkī and Santa Cruz. I am deeply grateful to nā kūpuna, nā ʻaumākua, and nā kupaʻāina of these places for guiding and moving me and so many others.

To my beloved kūpuna, Dorothea Sui Kum Chun Kaʻōpua, Lyman David Kaʻai Kaʻōpua, Marjorie Wood Goodyear, and Stanley Goodyear, your love continues to surround me and give me the strength to do what I can to serve others.

I am forever indebted to my parents, Brian Goodyear and Lana Kaʻōpua, for not only supporting me throughout my life thus far but also reading various parts of this book at different stages of its growth and evolution. Mom, mahalo for walking with me through the processes of developing a meaningful research agenda and going up for tenure. Dad, it has been so rewarding and comforting to have been simultaneously writing this book as you finished yours. Thank you for your detailed reading and for sharing your work with me. I could not ask for more amazing parents. Mahalo, as well, to my dear kaikaina, Vanessa Kulamanu. You are always close to my heart. The time that you spent serving HKM is not forgotten.

Mahalo a nui to the kumu, administrative support staff, alakaʻi, haumāna, and families of Hālau Kū Māna. This book would not be possible without the courage, fortitude, and hana nui you have put forth to keep the dream alive. My intent is that this book carry your stories to future generations of Kānaka who will draw strength, wisdom, and hope from your efforts. Since there isn't room enough to name every single person who has contributed to Hālau Kū Māna over its first decade, I want to recognize the four kumu who have persevered in giving the ʻōpio of HKM their energies on a daily basis for nearly the entirety of the school's existence up to this point: Bonnie Kahapeʻa-Tanner, Kāwika Mersberg, Kalaukia Kekoa, and Kekama Amona. You are my heroes. I also acknowledge and thank the three people who served as HKM's Poʻo over the first decade of the school's life: Keola Nakanishi, NormaDeene Musick, and Mahinapoepoe Paishon Duarte. May your tireless efforts of love and sacrifice be rewarded tenfold.

I hope this book honors the many amazing kumu with whom I have had the privilege of learning over the years. My life, my work, and this book have been profoundly shaped by the influence of teachers like Kanalu Young, Haunani-Kay Trask, Jonathan Kamakawiwoʻole Osorio, Lilikalā Kameʻeleihiwa, Kekuni Blaisdell, Kīhei Nīheu, Terrilee Kekoʻolani, John Lake, and Davianna McGregor. E nā kumu, you have all shown me that writing, teaching, and research must be grounded in community movement. I am also deeply thankful to have had the mentorship of James Clifford and Neferti Tadiar while I was completing my dissertation, which provided a foundation for this book.

The transformation of my dissertation into this book was made possible by the Mellon-Hawaiʻi postdoctoral fellowship funded by the Andrew W. Mellon Foundation, Kamehameha Schools, and the Kahiau Foundation and administered by the Kohala Center. Mahalo to Matthews Hamabata and Cortney Hoffman, as well as the members of the selection committee, for organizing the fellowship and supporting us so wholeheartedly. My fellow fellows, I admire and treasure each of you. Most especially, I am deeply grateful to my mentor, Charles R. Lawrence III, for his seemingly endless supply of encouragement, stories, wisdom, delicious food, and willingness to share his beautiful family with me and my ʻohana. Chuck, you and Mari both epitomize the kind of scholar and human I hope to become, and your guidance on this book has made it what it is.

Many colleagues and friends have read and offered invaluable feedback on this text, as well as providing tremendous moral support along the way. Mahalo nui to Hokulani Aikau, Leilani Basham, Candace Fujikane, Noenoe Silva, Dean Saranillio, Kāwika Tengan, Kahunawai

Wright, and the two readers secured by the University of Minnesota Press for reviewing this book at various stages in its development. I am also grateful to the students in my fall 2011 POLS 777 course, especially Kara Miller, Aiko Yamashiro, and Adam Chang for their close reading and helpful suggestions. I also thank my colleagues who read early versions of the book proposal and who encouraged me to keep up a regular writing schedule to get it all done: Noelani Arista, Kapā Olivera, Kuʻualoha Hoʻomanawanui, Jon Goldberg-Hiller, Michael Shapiro, Katharina Heyer, and Ehito Kimura. Many of the ideas in this book have been greatly enriched by ongoing exchanges between our Indigenous politics program at the University of Hawaiʻi at Mānoa and the University of Victoria's Indigenous governance faculty and students. To Taiaiake Alfred, Jeff Corntassel, and Waziyatawin, I send my great aloha, respect, and hope that we will continue to aloha ʻāina together. Mahalo to my fellow participants in the 2009–10 junior faculty seminar for your support with writing and teaching. And I cannot extend enough thanks to the friends who supported me through the very early stages of this project by helping me survive graduate school at the University of California–Santa Cruz, especially Darshan Campos, Deb Vargas, April Henderson, Nicole Santos, David Shorter, and Kim Christen.

I thank everyone at the University of Minnesota Press who has helped with the production of this book, especially Jason Weidemann for the generous amounts of time given to encouraging the development of this project.

Tanya Mailelani Naʻehu and Hanohano Naʻehu, you two never cease to inspire and encourage me in your hana nui as educators, parents, storytellers, beloved friends, and caretakers and defenders of sacred ʻāina. My hope for the lāhui Hawaiʻi and my understandings of aloha ʻāina also continue to be renewed by my friends in MANA (Movement for Aloha no ka ʻĀina). May we all raise our children and someday our moʻopuna alongside each other to carry on the struggle. Last but not in any way least, mahalo piha to my kāne, ʻĪmaikalani, and my two girls, Kaiakahinaliʻi and Laʻilaʻikūhonua, who bring me endless joy and fulfillment. You inspire me to get up and try to make the world a better place every day. I am so proud to watch you do the same. Your patience, love, songs, hugs, kisses, and accomplishments sustain me. Ke aloha pau ʻole iā ʻoukou, e kuʻu mau lei onaona.

Indigenous Education, Settler Colonialism, and Aloha 'Āina

I maika'i ke kalo i ka 'ohā.
(The health of the taro is observed in the offspring it produces.)

- Traditional Hawaiian proverb

You tried to take it all away, but we have our pride that will stay.
We may look like a bunch of kids, but you better watch out we're
closing in.
Took our queen and locked her away, now you'll deal with us the
present day.

As the seventh generation, we must all become a nation.
Keep the land prosperous, rise above, above all the rest.
We won't take it for granted, 'cuz that is the seed you planted.
We will not take it for granted, 'cuz that is the seed we planted.

- Lyrics from "Seventh Generation," written and performed in
  2002 by Hālau Kū Māna students Ku'ulei Freed, Shari Kapua
  Chock, Kaleiali'i Baldwin, and Ka'apuni Asaivao

As the 2010–11 school year was coming to a close, I sat with Kau'i Onekea—a 2006 Hālau Kū Māna (HKM) graduate—at the wooden picnic tables under the two white twenty-by-twenty-foot tents where HKM students ate lunch. Kau'i was never a student on this, the current and hopefully permanent campus. She had returned, however, to HKM as an assistant Hawaiian language teacher two years after her 2006 graduation. When the four trailer-classroom spaces behind us were full, she sometimes held classes outside at these tables.

Kau'i had walked across the stream from her home in Maunalaha, where her 'ohana (extended family) has lived for generations back as far as they can remember. Maunalaha remains one of the only places in

Honolulu where a small community of Hawaiian families have been able to maintain continuous residence on the land since 'Ōiwi Wale Nō (Natives only) times.[1] A nineteenth-century port town, Honolulu eventually became the governmental and commercial center of the islands. As the city grew up around them and a haole (white foreigner) oligarchy actively displaced Kanaka and Asian settler subsistence farmers from various parts of Honolulu throughout the twentieth century, the 'ohana of Maunalaha became what Davianna McGregor likens to a "cultural kīpuka." Kīpuka are stands of old-growth trees and plants that survive the destruction of volcanic flows and then "regenerate life on the barren lava that surrounds them."[2] Maunalaha and its people similarly survived the flow of concrete and steel that created the hundreds of high-rise buildings within walking distance, living evidence of Hawaiian survivance amid settler colonial structures.

Unlike McGregor's kīpuka, Maunalaha and Hālau Kū Māna—a Hawaiian culture–based secondary school operating since 2001—are in close proximity to the centers of urban life. Just above us, on Makiki Heights and Round Top Drive, sit some of the most expensive luxury homes in town. On my way to meet with Kau'i, I drove past two of the top private schools in Honolulu, each less than three miles from HKM's well-hidden campus. After our meeting I made the five-minute drive down Ke'eaumoku Street to Ala Moana, a beach park sitting across the street from the world's largest outdoor shopping mall, which is over two million square feet and regularly charting over a billion dollars in annual sales—a monument to global capitalism and consumerist culture residing upon our land. But Kānaka are here too, in the city, maintaining connections to 'āina (land that produces sustenance) and to each other. This was precisely why those of us who were involved in the founding of Hālau Kū Māna specifically chose to locate the school in Honolulu rather than in other parts of the island that were well known as areas with high concentrations of Native Hawaiian people.

Kau'i and I talked about her high school years at HKM and her return as a staff member and teacher. Over the span of those eight years, she saw it all: each of the school's four campuses and three executive directors, the birth of the school's sailing canoe, the restoration of ancient lo'i kalo (taro fields), the school restructuring under the No Child Left Behind Act (NCLB), a few of her peers' pregnancies, the deaths of

FIGURE I. *The Hālau Kū Māna class of 2006 chants to begin their graduation ceremonies on the ʻIolani Palace grounds in Honolulu. Visible from back left to front right are Aaron Tui, Christian Nahoopii-Hose, Shari Kapua Chock, Kipeni Aldosa, and Kauʻi Onekea. Photograph courtesy of Hālau Kū Māna New Century Public Charter School.*

kūpuna (elders) who gifted their knowledge to her teachers and class-mates, the transfer of a handful of friends and relatives back to "main-stream" Department of Education schools, and the successful gradua-tion of many more from Hālau Kū Māna. Kauʻi served on HKM's local school board as a student representative and then again later as an in-structional staff representative. Reflecting on what motivated her com-mitment to the school throughout those years and various struggles, she recalled the story of how she, her classmates, and teachers helped build a traditional hālau waʻa (a style of house for sheltering canoes as well as people) out of mangrove wood and pili grass at Kānewai, where the school was located for the first two years of operation.

The construction of this house of learning, made in traditional fashion but with a combination of indigenous and introduced plant materials, epitomized for her the collection of experiences she was a part of as a former student and teacher at Hālau Kū Māna. It was a joint project spearheaded by the University of Hawai'i at Mānoa's Center for Hawaiian Studies and Ka Papa Lo'i o Kānewai. The primary kūpuna who served as cultural advisors for the hale included 'Anakala Eddie Kaanana of Miloli'i, respected fisherman, farmer, and language advocate; and Captain Clay Bertelmann of Nā Kālai Wa'a Moku o Hawai'i, builder of the Makali'i voyaging canoe. The collective labor allowed Kau'i to interact with college students and to be near treasured masters of Indigenous knowledge. She emphasized that physical proximity to kūpuna was essential because "you never know when they're going to spill out this knowledge and all this mana. You just gotta be around." Hālau Kū Māna, she reflected, allowed her to participate in the active creation of history, the affirmation of ancestral knowledge, and the practice of a living Hawaiian culture.

> When we have grandkids, we can tell them we were there. We were a part of it. Being there and being a part of it is something that you cannot replace with anything. You cannot just read about it in a book; you actually live it. And that's what I *love* about Hālau Kū Māna. You are actually put in the situations that you read about and learn about, not just sit in class. That is something that is always going to be a part of my life now. I mean, everything that we do . . . I will pass on. I will teach other people and tell the stories of what I did when I was young: when I was young, we helped build a hale pili. When I was young, we helped put together a double-hulled sailing canoe. All these big moments in my life, and in the Hawaiian, the Hawaiian world, the movement of the Hawaiian people, it is just amazing to learn when you're so young. Our parents and grandparents didn't even get the opportunity to even *read* about Hawaiian things. They couldn't even read about [our people] in school, and here we are living it! We're *doing* it, not just reading about it. And that's the big thing about Hālau Kū Māna that I loved and made me stick around. We didn't have a fancy school [campus] or the best lunch . . . and I'm grateful for what we've been through. It teaches you a lot, you know? Teaches you to work with what you got and

be appreciative of what you have. We didn't need the best school on the mountain ... to keep us there. [We] just needed the desire to be there and learn the culture.[3]

Kauʻiʻs words speak not only about the transformative potential of Indigenous culture–based, place-based, and project-based learning, which form the core of HKM's educational approach. Embedded within her story is an articulation of the continuing need for Kānaka Maoli and other autochthonous people—so long construed as marginal figures, victims, or anachronistic natives frozen within history—to be educated as builders and shapers of pasts, presents, and futures. By understanding her kuleana in the context of a larger, intergenerational movement for self-determination and aloha ʻāina, Kauʻi has a foundation from which to resist powerful forces of elimination, alienation, and belittlement. Indigenous people living alongside, within, and against settler colonial societies experience such forces daily. And against those forces, we tell our stories of persistence, reaffirming our collective presence and permanence. We rebuild structures that nurture our collective strength and health.

Sovereign Pedagogies and Settler Colonial Structures

This book follows the work of educators reclaiming public K–12 education as a form of Hawaiian self-determination and sovereign practice in the first decade of the twenty-first century. After a century of assimilationist schooling, Kanaka Maoli communities seized the opportunity to assert a limited measure of autonomy in the settler state's public education system by starting charter schools that made Hawaiian culture, including ʻāina-based knowledge and language, the foundation of their educational programs. Several of the schools, including Hālau Kū Māna, explicitly describe their work as the exercise of "educational self-determination," and they collectively aim to address the historically embedded inequalities observed in the mainstream school system. The efforts to build Indigenous Hawaiian culture–based charter schools have been about not only educational reform but also the restoration of the holistic health of Hawaiian communities and nationhood. They are projects of survivance.[4]

Over the ten years I variously worked alongside and observed teachers at Hālau Kū Māna, I saw them striving to practice what I call *sovereign pedagogies.* I do not use this term to suggest that the teachers or the school were wholly autonomous. Rather, I use it to reference an ongoing collective struggle to support ʻŌiwi survivance and to end colonial relations of power and knowledge. My usage is influenced by Robert Allen Warrior's notion of a process-oriented "intellectual sovereignty," which calls scholars and educators committed to Indigenous freedom to allow "the definition and articulation of [sovereignty] to emerge" through critical reflection on the struggles of our peoples to exercise their collective power.[5] For Warrior the struggle for sovereignty "is not a struggle to be free from the influence of anything outside ourselves, but a process of asserting the power we possess as communities and individuals to make decisions that affect our lives."[6] His notion of sovereignty echoes the words of Kanak (New Caledonian) independence leader Jean-Marie Tjibaou, who said, "It's sovereignty that gives us the right and the power to negotiate interdependencies.... Independence means reckoning interdependencies well."[7] To practice sovereign pedagogies then is to recognize that sovereignty at both the personal and the collective levels is critical for the health and the optimal learning of Indigenous people, as it is for all people. In fact, in the Hawaiian language one can use the same word to indicate life *and* sovereignty: *ea.* The two are that crucial to one another. Indigenous scholars have shown that the power to define what counts as knowledge and to determine what our people should be able to know and do is a fundamental aspect of peoplehood, freedom, collective well-being, and autonomy.[8] Moreover, I intend the term *sovereign pedagogies* to signal that the continuing socioeconomic and educational inequalities Kānaka Maoli face within the settler school system and broader society can never be fully remedied without addressing the continued suppression of Hawaiian political sovereignty. In other words, education that celebrates Indigenous cultures *without* challenging dominant political and economic relations will not create futures in which the conditions of dispossession are alleviated.

In this book I situate the Hawaiian charter school movement and the specific work of classroom teachers at one school in the context of longer genealogies of Hawaiian survivance. Focusing on community strengths without ignoring systems of power and oppression, I chart connections between Hālau Kū Māna and broader Hawaiian struggles for cultural persistence, political power, and land. Hawaiian charter school operators agree to work within settler state educational systems in order to reach students and plant the huli (stalks) of change.[9] But for Kanaka Maoli educators, like other aboriginal peoples who work within settler state institutions, choosing to exist as a state public charter school influences the ways in which culture is created, taught, and practiced. Under a state system made possible by the seizure of Hawaiian national lands and institutions a century earlier, educators need to be sanctioned by settler authorities in order to produce cultural knowledge within our own communities. What struggles emerge when teaching Indigenous culture within institutions built to marginalize and displace Indigenous knowledges and relations? What bases of power allow people to persist despite hurdle after hurdle? In what ways are Indigenous and settler teachers working together to transform settler-colonial relations of power, knowledge, and wealth? What educational possibilities are produced out of these contexts when teachers and students try to reside in and learn from these tensions rather than ignore or attempt to transcend them?

As a settler-colonial school system, the Hawai'i state public education system is the only system in the United States in which Indigenous students comprise the largest proportion, more than a quarter, of the total enrollment. It is also the most centralized system in the United States, and Hawai'i is the only state with a single board that governs all schools across diverse communities.[10] Additionally, the proportion of Native charter schools in relation to all public schools in Hawai'i exceeds that of all state public education systems in the United States—a sign of the demand among predominantly Native Hawaiian communities for schools controlled by the communities themselves. Given these circumstances, Hawai'i provides a rich context for considering the successes and the problems of setting up semiautonomous Native educational spaces within settler state frameworks.

Two significant dangers arise that deserve mention right from the outset. First, settler state forces constantly work to inscribe these educational kīpuka, or zones of Indigenous cultural growth, as *safety zones*. Educational historians and theorists Tsianina Lomawaima and

Teresa McCarty observe that U.S. federal educational policy with respect to Indian nations has worked to produce and police safety zones,
state-enforced spaces for containing potentially threatening Indigenous cultural difference. Just enough "culture" is allowable, so long as
it does not threaten or undermine settler-colonial relations of power.
They write, "The federal government has not simply vacillated between
encouraging or suppressing Native languages and cultures but has in a
coherent way . . . attempted to distinguish safe from dangerous Indigenous beliefs and practices."[11] Thus, instead of looking at Indigenous
educational initiatives as either self-determining or assimilationist,
Lomawaima and McCarty encourage us to pay attention to the ways
cultural differences are marked, contained, and marginalized in safety
zones, as well as at the ways educators, students, and their communities contest and/or reify those boundaries. Throughout this book
I attend to the tensions between asserting Indigenous educational
self-determination and working within a settler state school system
by invoking the metaphors of *safety zones* and *cultural kīpuka* (stands
of continued Indigenous cultural growth). For kīpuka to be able to
regenerate life, they must grow. Trees and ferns find and expand cracks
in the hard, dry lava, thus expanding and changing the conditions of
possibility. If the function of a safety zone is to contain, marginalize,
stagnate, and strangle, the function of the kīpuka is to transform conditions of death and destruction and to renew the potential for life.
How do educators work to protect and proliferate kīpuka without
being constrained as mere safety zones?

The second danger is directly linked to Hālau Kū Māna's existence
not only as a state-sanctioned space but specifically as a charter school.
In a U.S. national context, charter schools are perhaps the most visible
and popular type of reform linked to the privatization of public schools.
On the one hand, Native Hawaiian community-based charter schools
are explicitly aiming to decentralize the authority of a settler state over
our educational destinies, our human and land-based resources. This
is an anticolonial project. On the other hand, the larger U.S. national
charter school reform movement is often linked to forces that also aim
to decentralize state authority because of a faith in the market model
and the logics of capitalism. This is a neocolonial project. Indigenous
decolonizing projects that seek to erode settler state authority must be

self-critically aware of the possibilities of becoming linked with privatization schemes that deepen inequalities and uphold fundamental values that run counter to our own.

In many states, schools opened and/or managed by large nonprofit and for-profit corporations—educational management organizations (EMOs)—have come to dominate the charter school landscape. In the decade since charter school legislation was enacted in Hawaiʻi, the governance of charter schools has largely remained at the community level, and approximately half of the thirty-one charter schools in the islands are run by predominantly Native Hawaiian communities that continue to assert the importance of ʻŌiwi cultural values and practices. In comparison with the mainstream public education system, these Hawaiian schools are doing significantly better at addressing some of the most persistent facets of educational inequality, improving students' socioemotional health, test scores, and community and family engagement and the underrepresentation of Native teachers and school leaders.[12] That said, this book is not a wholesale endorsement of or argument for charter schools as a general remedy to addressing issues of educational and social inequality and injustice. Although the U.S. national charter school movement has touted charters as a method of school reform that can address achievement gaps, there is significant evidence to show that this rhetoric is not always followed by results.[13]

In the Hawaiʻi case, though, we can see that the most glaring and persistent gaps for Native people are being effectively addressed when those communities themselves are empowered with educational control. Hawaiʻi charter school law specifically restricts such schools from being operated by for-profit entities, and the opening of new charter schools was limited from the beginning. This measured approach to enacting charter school reform under the State of Hawaiʻi was due in part to the influence of strong public sector unions. The strength of labor in Hawaiʻi historically emerged through the interracial organizing of Asian settler and Native Hawaiian laborers against a white supremacist plantation oligarchy in the islands.[14] I gesture toward this history as a way to signal the importance of strategic alliance. Even though some Hawaiian educators have expressed frustration about the limited number of charter school slots under the existing law, I argue that precisely because the charter reform wave was limited in part by organized labor, it inadvertently held open the space for Hawaiian communities rather than a rush of for-profit EMOs. Thus, I want to make clear that by writing about the strengths and challenges of Hawaiian culture–based charter schools, I do not intend to elide the problematics of privatizing public schooling. Instead, I hope to disarticulate decolonizing efforts to decentralize settler state control of education from market-based arguments for decentralization through privatization. The Hawai'i case calls us to consider how social movements can assure that those who are most disempowered and marginalized gain power over their communities' educational futures. In that sense this book supports the idea that historically rooted injustices can be allayed only when the people most negatively impacted by systems of power/knowledge realize control over the means to change those systems.

This theme of people realizing their own power by taking action to collectively build the structures that nurture their preferred futures struck me as one of the most powerful points of Kau'i's story about the hale pili. It wasn't just the existence of this Indigenous structure that sustained her but the very process of building it. What empowered her and many others was the collective work, the ability to see their hana (labor) in the context of larger cultural, political, and intergenerational fields. Kau'i shared that the excitement about building the hale pili was heightened at the time by a song some of her peers had written called "Seventh Generation."[15] As quoted in the epigraph, the song expresses the writers' perceptions of themselves as a seventh generation—a generation that will remedy old injustices and raise the Hawaiian people and culture to renewed levels of health and excellence. They borrowed the metaphor from a Native American ally, Ardy Sixkiller, who shared with staff and students a story from her tradition about a generation that would rise up against a long period of oppression. Students saw parallels between this story and a prophecy within Hawaiian oral tradition that they regularly chanted with fellow students from other Hawaiian culture–based charter schools of the Nā Lei Na'auao alliance: "E iho ana o luna; e pi'i ana o lalo. E hui ana nā moku a kū ana ka paia!" (What was above will come down; what was below will rise. The islands will unite and the walls will stand again!). At the time the students were recording the song and performing it live at various public events, the last A-frame of the hale's skeleton was ready to be raised. Kauʻi remembered that the students of HKM were given the kuleana of raising the seventh frame, which completed the structure of the hālau and has in the ensuing years allowed it to stand firm against some of the most intense storms and floods in recent Mānoa history.

This cross-cultural sharing of stories in solidarity exemplifies the reasons I choose in this book to use the term Indigenous, which I see as an always already historically situated category of alliance rather than a static, ahistorical category of identity.[16] For me use of the terms Kānaka ʻŌiwi and Kānaka Maoli indicates the specificity of Native Hawaiians' relationship to our genealogical homeland—the place where the bones of hundreds of generations of our ancestors are buried and have thus become one with the ʻāina. To use the term Indigenous is not only to speak from that grounding but also to emphasize our relationality to other Native peoples who similarly maintain their connection to their lands and aboriginal ancestors, often against forces seeking to sever those ties. It is a category that not only distinguishes us from settlers but, perhaps more important, connects those constituting ourselves as Indigenous to one another across the specificities of our histories and experiences.

Indigenous educational researchers have underscored that each expression of Indigenous education is unique and shaped by the land and community from which it grows.[17] That said, it should be clear from the outset that as a case study, this book is not meant to be representative of all Hawaiian or Indigenous culture–based schools. Rather, my aim is to explore persistent questions about Indigenous-settler relations, education, and power while also elaborating uniquely ʻŌiwi concepts and practices that may help create postimperial futures.

While HKM educators have tried to establish and maintain cultural kīpuka, they have been simultaneously pressured by forces aiming to constrain the school as a safety zone, a settler state–sanctioned space in which Indigenous culture can be practiced as long as it remains unthreatening to settler society. Chapter 1 establishes the ways this fundamental tension has been embedded in Hawaiian culture–based charter schools from the start. I chart the ways these schools were produced out of the intersection of two social movements with very distinct aims—a Hawaiian cultural/political nationalist movement and the U.S.-based charter school movement, which advocates

educational reform based on school choice. Though these two movements produced a space of overlap, they also continue to be incommen-
surate in many ways. I situate the Hawaiian charter school movement
within the broader struggles for land and sovereignty that accelerated
Hawaiian cultural and political resurgence from the 1970s onward,
showing that this genealogy of struggle opened the space for schools
like HKM to exist in the first place.

Chapter 2 highlights an example of this incommensurability, showing the ways school restructuring under the stipulations of the No
Child Left Behind Act worked to reinscribe HKM's educational program within mainstream American notions of proper schooling. The
2001 law shifted the federal government's historic emphasis on redis-
tributing money for public education to monitoring student, school,
and district performance through a standardized accountability and
assessment system.[18] I argue that NCLB and the associated State of
Hawai'i's educational standards worked as disciplining and reassimilating forces. For example, their narrow focus on conventional literacy
marginalized important Indigenous land–centered literacies and other
knowledge practices. School restructuring under NCLB limited some
of the early forms of innovative Indigenous education practiced at
HKM, and it was particularly poignant because HKM educators took
this on as a program of self-restructuring required for school survival.
Yet as the fences of the safety zone went up, educators continued to
talk about self-determination. This chapter highlights the gap between
the ways HKM educators understood *self-determination* and the ways
the term has been defined within U.S. policy toward the Indigenous
peoples it recognizes.

In chapters 3, 4, and 5, I elaborate the ways Hawaiian educators are
rebuilding Indigenous structures or vessels that contest settler-colonial
structures, specifically the 'auwai (irrigation ditch), the wa'a (canoe),
and the leo (voice). Turning to what has worked well and remained
strong in HKM's curriculum before and after NCLB restructuring, I
highlight contemporary Hawaiian practices of aloha 'āina that expand
dominant notions of academic excellence and literacy. Chapters three
and four offer portraits of two of the multidisciplinary 'āina-based Projects that have remained consistent pillars of HKM's sovereign pedagogies throughout the school's first decade.[19] Chapter 3 tells a story of

HKM's ongoing efforts to revitalize kalo cultivation, and chapter 4 narrates students' training to sail wa'a. Through these complementary rooted and routed practices, kumu (teachers) provided students with opportunities to cultivate kuleana and enlarge their own worlds, thus resisting confinement within an imposed safety zone. These chapters also discuss some of the gendered dynamics of revitalizing these cultural practices within the context of contemporary schooling.

In chapter 5, I return to an explicit focus on social movement, looking at the ways HKM members have explicitly engaged in Hawaiian social movement and cultural practice as political expression by cultivating students' voices. This chapter features the reflections and insights of HKM graduates more than the preceding chapters. In order to highlight the point that cultural practice is always political, I provide portraits of HKM 'ōpio performing diverse forms of cultural expression as acts of political expression. Their words and actions illustrate the multiple ways in which active engagement with timely and often controversial political issues produce meaningful learning. This chapter uses the Hawaiian concept of ho'omana to describe the ways students come to see themselves as important actors within a genealogically situated movement for self-determination and sovereignty. I argue that it is through continued articulation with the social movements that opened the space for the birth of institutions like Hawaiian charter schools—and Indigenous education more broadly—that we can push the bounds of settler safety zones that manifest both externally and internally.

While the portraits in this book primarily focus on what is good and what is working in Hawaiian education, it is necessary to set the backdrop by spending some time outlining the historically rooted and ongoing conditions of settler colonialism in Hawai'i. In the remaining sections of this introduction, I provide context for the portraits of Hālau Kū Māna offered in the chapters to come, laying the foundations and sketching the environment in which this hale was built. First, I show that the work of twenty-first-century Hawaiian educators had historical predecessors in the nineteenth-century kingdom era. I then discuss current understandings of settler colonialism in critical Indigenous studies, arguing that both a logic of elimination and a corresponding logic of containment are evident in Hawai'i's settler state school system. In conversation with those seeking to end colonialist relations through enacting Indigenous resurgence and education, I introduce a Hawaiian concept and ethical practice that has been central to HKM educators, aloha 'āina, and that might provide hope for more just and sustainable futures. The introduction concludes with a discussion of my methods and positionality in this study.

Independent Hawaiian Schools and the Emergence of a Settler State

In Hawaiʻi, public schools did not always function as part of a settler state system. How did schools become part of the infrastructure of settler colonialism? Kānaka Maoli are among the few aboriginal nations living under U.S. empire who built a national school system under the laws of a Native-led government in the nineteenth century.[20] Within that system, until the end of the 1890s, ʻŌiwi Hawaiʻi also comprised a majority of the teachers in the kingdom. This history has been largely overlooked, as existing histories of schooling in Hawaiʻi focus almost exclusively on the role haole missionaries and settlers played in teaching literacy and developing the islands' educational system.[21] Contrary to these narratives that suggest Hawaiian public education was made in the image of American public schooling and that ignore the role of Kanaka leaders and teachers in establishing literacy and schooling in the Hawaiian Kingdom, in this section I emphasize the agency of ʻŌiwi educators to show that Kanaka school reformers of the twentieth and twenty-first centuries had historical antecedents. The achievements of literacy and the establishment of a public school system in the kingdom might be more accurately seen as resulting from a partnership between Kānaka and haole as hoa (companions, colleagues, or peers) or as hoa paio (opponents or antagonists in battle).[22] Much more research needs to be done to uncover the history of Kanaka Maoli agency in building, governing, and teaching in the public school system, which is beyond the scope of this book.[23] This section will at least provide, however, evidence that schooling was not simply imported by missionaries and imposed upon Hawaiians. In other words, Hawaiʻi's schools were not always settler-colonial structures.

In the wake of American missionary arrival in 1820, early schooling projects were closely tied to developing literacy among Kānaka. Although American missionaries are largely credited with establishing a written form of the Indigenous language and then teaching Hawaiians to read, it is clear that the achievements of printing and literacy were a result of the joint efforts of Native Hawaiians and foreigners. The first company of American missionaries who arrived in Hawai'i in 1820 were accompanied by four Kānaka Maoli who had made their way to the U.S. East Coast years earlier. These men helped teach the missionaries elements of the Hawaiian language and translated for them upon arrival in the islands. Schütz notes that one of them, Thomas Hopu, was writing letters utilizing spellings that more closely mirrored the modern, standardized Hawaiian orthography well before the American Calvinist mission established its official orthography.[24]

Mission station schools became points of access to the new skills of reading and writing. Protestant missionaries wanted Kānaka to be able to read the Bible, in the hope of converting them to Christianity.[25] Kānaka were enamored with the technologies of the printed word. Enrollment at the mission station schools grew at an incredibly rapid pace, and Kānaka quickly took on the majority of the teaching roles. Educational historian Benjamin Wist writes that for Hawaiians, "'going to school' was a form of recreation."[26] He recounts that from the mid-1820s to the early 1830s, nearly the whole adult population went to schools to learn to read, although he downplays the role Kānaka played in this popular-literacy boom. The numbers clearly indicate, however, that it would have been impossible for missionaries alone to have taught all or even most of the pupils counted. At the height of school enrollment in 1832—when there were more than 53,000 pupils in 900 schools—only four missionary companies had arrived to the islands, including just over fifty American men and women, plus eleven Native Hawaiians and Tahitians.[27] Between 1820 and 1848, only 140 American Protestant missionaries came to Hawai'i, and they were not all present on the islands at the same time. They could not have possibly overseen 900 schools or managed a ratio of one thousand Native students to each missionary.[28] The vast majority of teachers in these schools were 'Ōiwi.

Adult Kānaka came to schools for what they wanted—to learn to read and write—and then they left, some taking on Christian teachings and a Christian identity and many others discarding them. Only five years after the high enrollment of 1832, the number of pupils dropped to about two thousand.[29] Kānaka maintained their passion for reading, writing, and publishing in the following decades, however, when literacy was used not only as a tool for accessing or creating social capital but also as an important tool of resistance.[30]

As the number of willing adult pupils in missionary schools waned through the 1830s, the focus shifted toward schooling children as proper national subjects for an evolving Hawaiian nation-state. The codification and institutionalization of public schooling in 1840 was adjunct to the creation of the first Hawaiian constitution under King Kamehameha III (Kauikeaouli), who declared, "He aupuni palapala koʻu; ʻo ke kanaka pono ʻo ia koʻu kanaka." In the authoritative text on Hawaiian proverbs, ʻŌlelo Noʻeau: Hawaiian Proverbs & Poetical Sayings, Pukui translates his words as, "Mine is the kingdom of education; the righteous man is my man."[31] An additional interpretation could also include that the king was indicating that his government would be one based on documents (palapala), for which literacy was necessary. Both interpretations suggest that education and literacy were seen as critical elements of a modern Hawaiian nationhood and subjecthood.

King Kamehameha III established the kingdom as a constitutional monarchy in which literacy and an emergent national public school system became key features in forming and formalizing the modern Hawaiian state. Hawaiian leaders made schooling part of a self-modernizing project, in tension but sometimes articulating with the continuing missionary project of "civilizing" Kānaka. By 1842 elementary-level education in reading, writing, geography, and arithmetic was required for anyone to be married or hold high office.[32] Hawaiian was the predominant language of instruction in schools, and any attempts to teach English were within the context of a robust literacy within the Indigenous language.

For the aliʻi class, King Kamehameha III passed an 1840 law establishing a school for chiefly children in which they would learn English, history, geography, higher-level math, and philosophy, among other things.[33] The government did not begin any broader allocation of funds to English-medium schooling until 1851. Even then, Hawaiian-medium instruction remained predominant for the next three decades. Throughout the second half of the nineteenth century, the struggle between Hawaiian and English in government schools and in the law reflected the struggles for power in the kingdom between 'Ōiwi statesmen and haole businessmen.[34]

'Ōiwi leaders used compulsory schooling as an indispensable part of the production of modern, Hawaiian national subjects. The two comprehensive historical accounts of public education in the Hawaiian Kingdom overlook those Kānaka who led the kingdom's public education system (most likely because they did not draw on Hawaiian-language sources), so it is worth summarizing the contributions of those education leaders here.[35] The Hawaiian Kingdom's legislature appointed Hawaiian scholar, author, and ordained minister Davida Malo as the first luna (superintendent) of public instruction for the kingdom in 1841—a post he held for four years. Under Malo they also appointed five kahu kula (school agents or inspectors) who oversaw all government schools on each of the five major islands. All five appointees were Kānaka: John 'Ī'ī for O'ahu, Pāpōhaku for Kaua'i, Kanakaokai for Moloka'i, David Malo for Maui, and Kanakaahuahu for Hawai'i.[36] These leaders had the power to grant teaching certificates and oversee teachers, to monitor the progress of students, to be the judges of the school law, and to provide for teachers' salaries.[37] Malo was a staunch advocate for Native teachers and their adequate compensation.[38]

The development of the public school system throughout the second half of the nineteenth century was embedded in a larger struggle for hegemony between rival visions of Hawai'i's national future. Whereas white men representing the nexus of missionary and sugar business interests were attempting to build the kingdom's public school system as a way of sorting and segregating racialized citizen-subjects for an oppressive plantation society, Native Hawaiian statesmen and community leaders were separating public schools from church affiliation, promoting literacy in the Hawaiian language, and increasing funding for the "common" schools—those serving primarily working-class Hawaiian and Asian pupils. Schooling supported economic shifts away from extended family living and natural resource management and toward the patriarchal nuclear family unit within a capitalist economy. These economic transformations relied upon an increasing centralization of both natural resources and educational control in the hands of a white, male corporate business elite. For instance, haole sugar planters financed the construction of elaborate networks of irrigation tunnels and ditches that collected water, diverting it from natural watershed areas to their fields, often on opposite sides of the islands. Early efforts to privatize water coincided with the shifting of financial resources away from Hawaiian-medium common schools toward English select schools.

For many years, however, the kingdom's public schools also served as spaces where Hawaiian educators could transmit older stories in new ways, strengthening a sense of peoplehood among their mostly Native students, until the resources were gradually diverted in the 1870s and then decisively cut off after the 1893 illegal coup against the Hawaiian Kingdom's government. Mataio Kekūanāo'a led the kingdom's public school system for eight years as president of the board of education from 1860 until his death in 1868.[39] Descended from high chiefs of O'ahu and Hawai'i islands, Kekūanāo'a was an experienced statesman who accompanied King Kamehameha II to London from 1823 to 1824 to strengthen diplomatic ties between Hawai'i and Britain, and he served as the governor of O'ahu from 1839 to 1863. Kekūanāo'a's predecessor as head of public education, the American Protestant Rev. Richard Armstrong, is often credited as bringing stability and developing the "public" character of the educational system—abolishing sectarian schools and introducing a tax-supported economic base.[40] In reviewing the reports of various heads of the kingdom's board of education made to the legislature from 1840 to 1893, however, it is clear that Kekūanāo'a articulated the most explicit concern for distancing government schools from church powers and providing an adequate appropriation of public funds to support that separation. For example, in Kekūanāo'a's report of 1866, he spent a significant amount of time discussing his concern for the lack of adequate school facilities resulting from insufficient funding. He advocated moving schools out of churches and mission stations, thus strengthening an inclusive national character:

> In many places the schools, for want of special buildings, are kept in the meeting houses or chapels of [the] Protestant or Catholic population residing on the land. . . . The result is that in almost all of these places, the public schools are merely tenants at the will of this or that religious denomination. . . . Another result

of this absence of proprietary right on the part of Government
is that these houses being looked upon as really and especially
religious edifices, and not as national school houses, are avoided
by parents and children of denominations different from that
one which owns the building. It is necessary to provide as far
as possible for *all* the people the advantage of a common school
education. . . . The common schools should come to be regarded
as strictly neutral ground in religious matters.[41]

In addressing the problems of inadequate facilities, Kekūanāo'a proposed that the national board of education match the funds of local
districts in which parents wanted to build or thoroughly renovate a
schoolhouse.[42] This enabled independence from mission and church.
Although Kekūanāo'a identified as Protestant, his arguments show he
was able to keep his religious affiliation separate from his leadership of
public education, unlike his predecessor.

In the debates over language in the schools, Kekūanāo'a firmly articulated the importance of the Hawaiian language in affirming Hawaiian
national identity. While advocates for what legal historian Paul Nahoa
Lucas calls an "English-mainly" system of education and government
pushed to reduce the status of the Hawaiian language,[43] Kekūanāo'a
asserted the importance of government support for Hawaiian-medium
education:

> The theory of substituting the English language for the
> Hawaiian, in order to educate our people, is as dangerous to
> Hawaiian nationality, as it is useless in promoting the general
> education of the people. If we wish to preserve the Kingdom of
> Hawaii for Hawaiians, and to educate our people, we must insist
> that the Hawaiian language shall be the language of all our Na-
> tional Schools, and that English shall be taught whenever practi-
> cable, but only as an important branch of Hawaiian education.[44]

He urged the legislature to increase funding for schools taught in
Hawaiian, and it wasn't until after his administration that enrollment
in English-medium schools grew significantly vis-à-vis the Hawaiian-
medium schools.

Hawaiian nationalist educators struggled against the white supremacist educational approaches that were gaining dominance prior
to formal U.S. imperial control of the islands. White supremacist and
assimilationist models of schooling did not become hegemonic in the
Hawaiian Kingdom until the late 1870s and early 1880s, as haole sugar
barons and financiers increased their economic and political power. As
mentioned, the development of the sugar irrigation ditch structures
was coeval with the white supremacist oligarchy's ascendance to power,
including taking control of the educational system. In the immediate
wake of the 1876 Treaty of Reciprocity, which allowed Hawai'i-grown
sugar to enter U.S. markets duty free, one of the Big Five sugar companies formed the first private water company.[45] That same year also included the beginning of the movement of funds from common schools
for the multitudes to select schooling for a smaller elite. Select English-
medium schools received more than 4.5 times more per student than
Hawaiian-medium common schools.

Unlike Kekūanāo'a, Charles R. Bishop, who served as president of
the board of education throughout the 1870s and early 1880s, significantly increased funding for English-language schools while cutting
funding from Hawaiian-language common schools.[46] Bishop directed
a turn toward industrial education, emphasizing labor over literacy, articulated in this way:

> The rising generation [of Hawaiians] are not as industrious as
> their ancestors were; that they—and especially those educated
> in the higher schools and in the English language—have wrong
> ideas about labor; in short, are lazy and idle, and have much
> more of pride and conceit than is good for them.[47]

Four years later, he again argued to the Hawaiian legislature that it was
important to prepare students in the common schools for industrial
and agricultural labor, and "hence the instruction of our youth should
have for its object, not only mental culture, but also the development of
those faculties which most facilitate industrial effort."[48] While serving
on the board of education and working to create policies that would
train students for work in sugar and its related industries, Bishop held

large investments in the industry and was intimately involved in the
push to import Asian laborers, who could be paid cheaply.[49]

By the time Bishop vacated his position at the helm of public education, the select, English-medium schools were receiving more than
seven times the funding of the common schools, even though they had
far fewer students. Teachers' salaries at English schools—positions
filled by non-Natives—were markedly higher, and the availability of
teachers in the Hawaiian language was curtailed when the courses
of study at Lahainaluna Seminary and Hilo Boarding School, which
trained many of the Native teachers, were changed from Hawaiian to
English. Although some English advocates argued that rising enrollments demonstrated that Kānaka wanted to embrace English and
move away from their own mother tongue, it is clear that this was no
simple matter of abandoning one language for another. As Benham
and Heck point out, the choices became unequal as the government
(heavily influenced by the sugar industry) increased funding support
for English select schools over Hawaiian common schools. For instance, "most of the teacher professional development was conducted
for English-speaking education, and many of the texts and materials
brought from the United States were not translated for usage in the
common schools."[50]

In 1883 King Kalākaua and his privy council forced Bishop to resign
from his position as head of the board of education. Four years later, a
group of haole sugar businessmen known as the Hawaiian League forced
the king to sign a constitution stripping him of crucial powers, allowing
white foreigners to vote, instituting property and income requirements,
and completely disenfranchising Asians.[51] Subsequently, Bishop was
reappointed to lead the kingdom's board of education until 1893. Under
his and subsequent white, male business-affiliated leadership, schools
were used to help build and reinforce a hierarchical plantation society.
U.S. military and diplomatic officials collaborated with local sugar plantation elites in intensifying their encroachment on Hawaiian sovereignty
over the national lands of the internationally recognized kingdom. After
Bishop's business associates conspired to overthrow Native rule in
Hawai'i, they cut *all* funding for Hawaiian-language education, leaving
the vast majority of Kanaka teachers without teaching positions and keiki

'Ōiwi (Native children) without schooling in their ancestral language.[52] This effective ban on publicly supported Hawaiian-language education remained in effect until the 1980s, when the first Hawaiian-language immersion schools were founded.[53] State funding for Hawaiian-language education remains, however, only a tiny fraction of English-language education. Moreover, since the 1887 Bayonet Constitution, proportional representation of Kānaka Maoli to public school governance has not been achieved to this day.

By 1898, as part of the expansion of the American empire after the Spanish-American War, the U.S. Congress unilaterally claimed possession of Hawai'i through a joint resolution enforced by the continued and swelling presence of its armed forces. As Hawai'i solidly became, under the finger of its military occupation, a U.S. territory, the cultural work of masking the violent means of coercion and producing consent to U.S. rule began in earnest.[54] On a policy level the aim was to fracture the historical precedent of recognizing Hawai'i as an autonomous nation-state and instead establish a subordinate relationship between the U.S. government and the Kānaka 'Ōiwi, without their aupuni (government). On an ideological level the goal was to transform Kanaka Maoli collective understanding of themselves from a self-governing political body to a small and relatively powerless racial minority domesticated under the United States. These dual forces have shaped public education in the islands ever since.

This brief overview of public education in the Hawaiian Kingdom shows that in the earlier period schooling was not simply a colonial imposition. Kānaka and settlers together engaged in building popular literacy and a Hawaiian national school system. Ali'i and foreigners both folded visions for schooling into competing projects of modernization and nation building. Sometimes, they worked in collaboration as interlocutors embedded in complicated relations of power and, at other times, as political opponents articulating and acting on very different visions of education. The suppression of Hawaiian political sovereignty at the end of the nineteenth century caused a rupture in the ability of Kānaka to govern and direct the educational system. Throughout the next century, assimilatory education propped a plantation economy and worked to legitimize American settler colonialism. From the onset of the U.S. occupation of Hawai'i in 1893 to the present day, the occupying state's educational system has functioned to reproduce a society not only unequal but largely blind to its own coloniality. Invasion is a structure that like the sugar ditches continues to siphon wealth from Indigenous people and lands to enrich and enable settler society. The lāhui Hawaiʻi (the Hawaiian people/nation) has been forcefully parched by such structures.

Indigenous Studies and Settler Colonialisms

In this book I refer to the current Hawaiʻi public education system as a settler-colonial or settler state school system. My usage of this language follows the analysis of noted Hawaiian political scholar Haunani-Kay Trask, who describes twentieth-century Hawaiʻi as "a settler society . . . in which the indigenous culture and people have been murdered, suppressed, or marginalized for the benefit of settlers who now dominate."[55] More recently, Fujikane and Okamura have extended this analysis to further interrogate Asian settler practices that maintain the structures of a U.S. settler state. They cite the Hawaiʻi public school system as a primary institutional example of dynamics of settler colonialism and structural inequality in the islands.[56]

As Indigenous studies scholars have established, settler colonialisms seek to rid the land of collective Native presence and permanence in order to make way for and legitimize settler societies.[57] Settler colonialisms are historically rooted, land-centered projects that are never fully complete, thus requiring constant effort to marginalize and extinguish Indigenous connections so as to secure control of land. As Alyosha Goldstein writes, settler colonialism refers not so much to "a static relationship as a condition of possibility that remains formative while also changing over time."[58] In short, such conditions persist in the present. In Hawaiʻi's case a prolonged military occupation enables ongoing settlement and the dominance of a settler society.[59] The public school system functions to naturalize these relations of power.

Hawaiʻi's public school system is built on and funded by the revenues from lands illegally seized from the Hawaiian Kingdom government at the time of the 1893 invasion. While the State of Hawaiʻi derives a significant portion of its revenues from those seized lands, its mainstream educational system continues a history of inequality and underservice to Kānaka Maoli.[60] In addition to comprising the largest group within the public education system, the number of Native Hawaiian students attending public schools is growing faster than the islands' other major ethnic groups.[61] Within the system our youth are more often labeled "special ed" or "behaviorally handicapped."[62] Furthermore, conventional public schools that have a predominantly Native Hawaiian population have a larger proportion of uncertified, untenured teachers and have a higher frequency of being in restructuring or corrective action status under the conditions of No Child Left Behind.[63] As compared with non-Hawaiian students in Hawai'i and all public high school students in the United States, Native Hawaiian youth have the highest rates of self-reported drug use and almost all other high-risk behaviors measured on the state's biennial Youth Risk Behavior survey.[64] It is worth noting that year after year the Hawai'i survey's results show that Native Hawaiian high school students attempt suicide at least twice as often as non-Hawaiian students, and Native Hawaiian high school females are raped at roughly twice the rate of non-Hawaiians.[65]

These are not just conditions of inequality but of genocide and the heteropatriarchal logics of elimination characteristic of settler colonialisms and white supremacy. Here, genocide refers to the extinguishment of a group not only through mass killing but also through the elimination of their sense of being a people, through the obstruction of a collective group's ability to maintain their bonds with one another.[66] As Indigenous studies scholars point out, settler-colonial relations of power operate on logics of elimination whereby Indigenous connections to land and to each other are supposed to disappear. Patrick Wolfe explains:

Settler colonialism has both negative and positive dimensions. Negatively, it strives for the dissolution of native societies. Positively, it erects a new colonial society on the expropriated land base—as I put it, settler colonizers come to stay: invasion is a structure not an event. In its positive aspect, elimination is an organizing principal of settler-colonial society rather than a one-off (and superseded) occurrence. The positive outcomes of the logic of elimination can include officially encouraged

miscegenation, the breaking-down of native title into alien-
able individual freeholds, native citizenship, child abduction,
religious conversion, resocialization in total institutions such
as missions or boarding schools, and a whole range of cognate
biocultural assimilations. All these strategies, including frontier
homicide, are characteristic of settler colonialism. . . . Settler
colonialism destroys to replace.[67]

Such structural violences are committed both through formal settler
state structures and what Candace Fujikane calls "*settler practices*,
ranging from colonial administration to the routines of every day
life."[68] U.S. imperialism and settler colonialism have been sustained
and reproduced through gendered grammars of race.[69] Accordingly,
white supremacy should not just be understood as a set of beliefs in
the superiority of those groups constituted as "white" but as a nexus
of "separate and distinct, but still interrelated, logics" that undergird
U.S. empire and that require the systematic death and/or assimilation
of particular groups.[70] As Zeus Leonardo puts it, white supremacy is
"forged in the historical process. It does not form out of random acts of
hatred, although these are condemnable, but rather out of a patterned
and enduring treatment of social groups."[71]

Settler-colonial school systems are built upon seized lands and resources, and they work to legitimize and reproduce the broader settler
society and its political economic order. They naturalize the use and
governance of those lands and resources within those orders, to the
detriment of Native peoples. They enact the logic of elimination by
suppressing Native histories and contemporary realities, by discount-
ing Indigenous epistemologies and knowledge bases, and by individu-
alizing and disciplining Native bodies.

The logic of elimination is fundamental to settler-colonial operations. The history of schooling for Indigenous people under U.S. empire shows, however, that settler states also maintain their authority
through a corresponding *logic of containment*. We Natives stubbornly
persist. The pragmatic acknowledgement by settler authorities that
despite efforts to remove and assimilate us, Natives will *not* just disappear necessitates the kind of safety zones about which Lomawaima
and McCarty write. These zones contain Indigenous relations and

knowledge within particular ideological and physical boundaries. Such containment can manifest in geographic forms as reservations or small school spaces, in political forms as legal-recognition frameworks that seek to subsume sovereignty within the settler state's domestic laws, and in ideological forms as school curricula that allow a sprinkling of Indigenous history and culture only to maintain its marginality.

The logic of containment is clearly apparent in Hawai'i. Over the past thirty-five years notable gains have been made to carve niches for Hawaiian language and culture–based education within the settler state system, including Hawaiian studies programs in K–12, tertiary, and enrichment education. However, the valuable work these programs do with students has not yet resulted in changing the deep and persistent inequalities of power, wealth, and well-being in the school system and the broader society. Writing in 2003, Hawaiian educator Kū Kahakalau critiques programs made possible through Article X of the Hawai'i State Constitution, which states, "The State shall promote the study of Hawaiian culture, history and language and provide for a Hawaiian education program consisting of language, culture and history." She argues that locally governed, Native-controlled schools are necessary precisely because the settler state had reneged on its own constitutional mandate and continued to subordinate Native Hawaiians and our knowledge bases. As she finds:

> No data exist indicating that any of the programs initiated by the DOE in response to Article X have had any noteworthy impact on Hawai'i's 50,000 public school students of Hawaiian ancestry, or their over 150,000 non-Hawaiian counterparts. As a matter of fact, nearly 25 years after the passage of Article X, the vast majority of Hawai'i's public school graduates, whether Native or non-Native still do not know even the very basics about Hawaiian history, our Native culture or language, certainly not enough to perpetuate Hawai'i's Native traditions into the next millennium.[72]

Although the Hawaiian language is one of the two official languages of the State of Hawai'i, there is still no significant effort within the state's Department of Education to widely institute bilingual education, even though delimited zones of Hawaiian cultural education are permitted. Furthermore, Kahakalau asserts that many state-initiated programs for Hawaiian students have been remedial in nature and have "created the perception that culturally and environmentally-based education . . . cannot be academically rigorous."[73]

The conditions of genocide and the logics of elimination and containment that I have sketched remain largely unchanged because the power relations remain largely unchanged. Institutional power matters. At the top of the existing institutional hierarchy in the Hawaiʻi public education system are a single statewide board of education appointed by the governor and a superintendent that govern the entire system across eight islands. There have been few if any Native Hawaiians, Filipinos, or Pacific Islanders in these top-level positions of power over the past 120 years, even though those groups make up a significant share of the islands' and the school system's population. Below those top-level positions are layers of district-level and complex-area administrators and then school-based administrators, followed by the teachers and the noninstructional staff. At the student level Native Hawaiians and other socioeconomically subordinated ethnic or racial groups, including Filipinos, Samoans, and Latinos, comprise a substantial majority of Hawaiʻi's public school enrollment. But the representation of these groups sharply declines as one looks up the institutional hierarchy, whereas the representation of socioeconomically privileged groups— Japanese, white, and Chinese—increases.[74] Members of those groups also comprise a majority of the private school enrollments in a state where there is a marked gap between the quality of public and private school education. Though the phenotype of white supremacy and settler colonialism in Hawaiʻi has shifted over the last century, deep structures remain. U.S. settler colonialism continues to sustain itself in Hawaiʻi through a grammar of race—albeit one that differs from racial dynamics on the U.S. continent.

Critical scholarship in queer Indigenous studies also calls us to look at the ways heteropatriarchy—"the normalizing and privileging of patriarchal heterosexuality" based on binary gender systems—is also a fundamental logic and organizing force within settler colonialisms.[75] As Finley writes, "Colonialism needs heteropatriarchy to naturalize hierarchies and unequal gender relations."[76] Indeed, one of the first

efforts of missionary-run schools in Hawai'i was to inculcate bour-
geois Euro-American gender roles and replace the extended 'ohana
with the heteropatriarchal nuclear family unit.[77] Finley goes on to add
that Indigenous communities have sometimes taken on the limiting
and violent logics that exclude a multiplicity of Native expressions of
gender and sexual identity and practice: "Heteropatriarchy has become
so natural in many Native communities that it is internalized and institutionalized as if it were traditional."[78] Thus, any move away from
settler-colonial relations requires challenging such discourses. In this
book, particularly in chapters 3 and 4, I look at the ways the revitalization of Hawaiian cultural practices sometimes contests and at other
times remains complicit with heteropatriarchal norms. If Indigenous
education does not build in the opportunity for critical analysis and
deconstruction of the logics and structures of settler colonialism, we
risk replicating the very relations we hope to overcome.

One of my hopes is that this book will provoke more thoughtful debate and action against the intersecting forms of subordination under
settler colonialism. As such, it should be clear that I do not simply
advocate equality for Kānaka Maoli within the existing school system
or settler society. Following Sandy Grande, I believe that "unless educational reform happens concurrently with analyses of the forces of
colonialism, it can only serve as a deeply insufficient (if not negligent)
Band-Aid over the incessant wounds of imperialism."[79] What educational practices can help us overcome and provide viable alternatives to
those violent systems?

Indigenous Resurgence

How can education ensure Indigenous survivance and hasten the end
of settler colonialism? The field of Indigenous education has pushed
beyond finding ways to help Native students achieve within schools
by identifying cultural learning styles or "infusing" Indigenous histories or cultural practices into existing curricula. Rather, a growing
international community of Native educators and scholars are designing and implementing schools and systems, highlighting the political stakes of Indigenous education, and creating the epistemological
space for Indigenous knowledges and social relations to flourish.[80]

Such educators aim not only to improve schools but to strengthen and grow Indigenous communities, acknowledging that this broader social agenda requires transformation in the hierarchies of knowledge and power within and beyond schools. Indigenous scholars have shown that the power to define what counts as knowledge and to determine what our people should be able to know and do—what Linda Tuhiwai Smith calls "epistemic self-determination"—is a fundamental aspect of peoplehood, freedom, collective well-being, and autonomy.[81]

This book explores one community's efforts to enact epistemic self-determination and to articulate sovereign pedagogies, working within settler state structures but also trying to imagine and create futures beyond those structures. It looks at how people work to grow and proliferate a cultural kīpuka while being interpellated (or hailed by) settler state authorities as a state-sanctioned safety zone. What has enabled transformative pedagogies is a conscious awareness that opening space within the settler state's educational system is not enough in and of itself. It is not enough to exist as a charter school and to simply maintain an institutional presence in which Hawaiian culture can be taught, recognized, and sanctioned by the settler state. Rather, the larger goal and purpose is to create and maintain opportunities for community members to constantly renew personal and collective obligations to the land and to each other. It is the process of recognizing our own power to control the educational futures of our peoples that is transformative. Glen Coulthard reminds us that when Indigenous movements become enraptured with seeking settler state recognition for our ability to govern and make decisions for ourselves, we do not tranform the colonial relationship but rather reaffirm it. Instead, he and other Indigenous politics scholars argue that Indigenous resurgence should "be fashioned toward our own on-the-ground practices of freedom."[82]

Similarly, Jeff Corntassel offers the notion of *sustainable self-determination* as a distinct alternative to previous strategies of Indigenous political mobilization that have focused on seeking rights and entitlements from dominant states or within the international system of states.[83] He argues that framing our movements in rights-based terms can actually be harmful to Indigenous communities because doing so reinvests power within settler state apparatuses. Instead, sustainable self-determination shifts the focus of Indigenous mobilization from state-centric approaches to practices that enable Indigenous economic independence (or at least less dependence on transnational corporate capitalism), spiritual regeneration, and social health through a continual renewal of relational obligations. The hallmarks of sustainable self-determination include focusing on individual, family, and community responsibilities, regenerating local and regional Indigenous economies, and recognizing the interconnection of social, spiritual, environmental, and political aspects of self-determination. The ultimate goal is for Indigenous people to have

> the freedom to practice indigenous livelihoods, maintain food security, and apply natural laws on indigenous homelands in a sustainable manner. Critical to this process is the long-term sustainability of indigenous livelihoods, which includes the transmission of these cultural practices to future generations.[84]

This orientation to long-term future survival through connection to ancestral practices and narratives is, after all, a primary goal of Indigenous education. The notion of sustainable self-determination centers the renewal of Indigenous collective capacities to feed and sustain ourselves from our lands, requiring widely disseminated, land-centered literacies and diverse bodies of collective knowledge on our terms, as opposed to the highly centralized, standardized, and dominant approach to education in the United States today. The sustainable self-determination framework underscores the importance of seeing Indigenous educational endeavors as economic and ecological health initiatives, as well. As we seek the language and literate practices to provide a foundation for long-term health and sustainable self-determination we can look to the innovations of our ancestors, which have profound relevance for our lives today and into the future.

Indigenous education can furthermore be beneficial to all people because, to return again to Coulthard, "our cultures have much to teach the Western world about the establishment of relationships within and between peoples and the natural world that are profoundly non-imperialist."[85] How can Indigenous and settler peoples work in solidarity to transform structures of invasion? How might we live in "constructive engagement" with one another?[86] One way might be for

Indigenous and settler peoples to work at replacing the logics of settler colonialism with logics and ethical practices that nurture Indigenous survivance. Speaking about the Hawaiian case from her own positionality, Candace Fujikane suggests, for example, that "Asian settlers . . . will continue to benefit from and be a part of the larger system of U.S. settler colonialism until Hawaiians regain their lands and nation. Only by achieving such justice can Asian settlers liberate themselves from their roles as agents in a colonial system of violence."[87]

Like these and other scholars and activists who are concerned with building solidarity to end colonialism and support just and sustainable life, this book addresses questions of how to "make the road by walking" because it tells a story that is not exclusively about Kānaka Maoli.[88] Rather, it is about how an educational community comes to understand and define itself as a collective that makes Hawaiian culture foundational to its day-to-day life, including both ʻŌiwi and settlers as valuable members within this ʻohana without glossing over the differences between them. At Hālau Kū Māna, Kanaka ʻŌiwi and settler educators together attempt to transform the culture and purpose of mainstream schooling by articulating an ʻŌiwi ancestral ethic within the limits of the very institution they hope to change. As a community of learners, teachers and students alike must learn to deal with the tensions of firmly asserting who Hawaiians are and what Hawaiian culture is while leaving open the productive space to ask, Who are we? and, What is my distinct responsibility as it relates to my position at this time and place?[89] Through the portraits in this book, I elaborate contemporary Hawaiian ethical practices that present powerful alternatives to the logics of settler colonialism. In the following section, I briefly introduce some of the ways Kānaka have historically understood and mobilized around aloha ʻāina, in order to contextualize this book's discussion of the ways HKM educators ground their sovereign pedagogies in this ethical practice.

Aloha ʻĀina: A Multiplicity of Land-Centered Literacies

The concept of aloha ʻāina has been a root of Hawaiian resistance to imperialism for over one hundred years, and it was one of the primary recurring ethics and practices articulated by the twenty-first-century educators discussed in this study. HKM educators have sought to make aloha ʻāina the foundation of an intellectually rigorous project-based and place-based educational program. Aloha ʻāina expresses an unswerving dedication to the health of the natural world and a staunch commitment to political autonomy, as both are integral to a healthy existence. Although it is often imperfectly translated as both "love for the land" and "patriotism," the *aloha* part of this phrase is an active verb, not just a sentiment. As such, it is important to think of aloha ʻāina as a practice rather than as merely a feeling or a belief.

Aloha ʻāina has been a practice of Kanaka Maoli survivance for generations. Pukui and Elbert describe aloha ʻāina as "a very old concept, to judge from the many sayings (perhaps thousands) illustrating deep love for the land."[90] In *Place Names of Hawaiʻi*, the authors further explain that sayings praising the land are themselves called *aloha ʻāina* and that such sayings reinforce familial ties, links to the past, and connections to the land and sea as sources of life.[91]

As a political philosophy and praxis, aloha ʻāina is often glossed as patriotism or nationalism. In her groundbreaking study of Hawaiian resistance to annexation by the United States, however, Noenoe K. Silva points out that aloha ʻāina

> encompasses more than nationalism and is not an exact fit with the English word "patriotism," the usual translation. Where nationalism and patriotism tend to exalt the virtues of a people or a race, aloha ʻāina exalts the land. It refers to the appreciation of the beauty of this land . . . but aloha ʻāina goes beyond love of beauty as well. The Kanaka Maoli have a genealogical, familial relationship to the land.[92]

Kānaka ʻŌiwi, like many Indigenous peoples throughout the world, recognize all beings—birds, rocks, insects, plants, winds, waters—as familial relations. All are part of interrelated, living systems. Kameʻeleihiwa notes that within the familial system described by Hawaiian cosmogonic genealogies, Kānaka are younger siblings and, thus, of a lower rank compared with relatives such as the coral polyp, the fern shoot, or the kalo. Our aloha (loving, caring action) for the

land is required by this familial relationship.[93] Kānaka also recognize
our connection to 'āina as genealogical because we are composed of
'āina; the organic material of which we are made literally comes from
the earth and is constantly returning to it. Our stories come from and
are layered upon the land. Thus, many 'Ōiwi assert that we are not only
related to the land but also a part of what is referenced when one talks
about 'āina.[94] It is through action, through practicing aloha 'āina, that
we produce ourselves in relation to and as a part of 'āina.

Unlike the root words *nation* and *patriot*, which are both etymologi-
cally tied to European notions of family, tribe, and country that have
historically been gendered male, *aloha 'āina* does not connote a male-
dominant familial structure. Feminist scholars and activists have long
pointed out the need to challenge masculinist nationalisms and to his-
toricize "the family" since the archetypal patriarchal family has so often
been an organizing metaphor and institution that renders nationalist
movements dismissive of or directly hostile to healthy and just gender
relations and sexual practices.[95] Native feminists have further argued
that decolonizing gender and sexuality is a fundamental part of the
struggle for sovereignty and social health.[96] About U.S. colonialism,
Hall writes:

> The deliberate destruction of non-heteronormative and
> monogamous social relationships, the indigenous languages
> that could conceptualize these relationships, and the cultural
> practices that celebrated them has been inextricable from
> the simultaneous colonial expropriation of land and natural
> resources.[97]

The educational recovery of the language and practices of aloha 'āina
can potentially open, then, possibilities for broader conceptualizations
of familial and national relationships. *Patriot*, derived from Ancient
Greek, refers to connection through male lines—of fathers or clans—
and is closely related to the word *patriarch*, which specifically refers to
the male head, ruler, or progenitor of a tribe, clan, or religious institution. 'Ōiwi genealogies are traced, however, along both male and female lines, with more attention to birth order than gender.[98] Moreover,

Hawaiian cosmological traditions feature many powerful female deities and ancestors who create earth, navigate vast ocean distances, lead
their families, battle, give birth, and govern.[99]

As an intervention against dominant educational paradigms, I suggest thinking about aloha ʻāina as a multiplicity of literacies. Here, I
use the plural term *literacies* to include a range of critically engaged observational, interpretive, and expressive skills that encompass but are
not limited to human linguistic and social practices. The recognition
of what I am calling *land-centered literacies* extends upon the work to
broaden older, outmoded understandings of literacy as simply about
reading and writing printed text. Land-centered literacies include the
ways Kānaka ʻŌiwi developed practices of reading the stars and other
celestial bodies and events; offering chants in our own human language
and then observing and finding meaning in the responses of winds,
rains, birds, waves, or stones; and writing ourselves into the landscape
by drawing water through irrigation ditches to loʻi kalo and then back
to streams. Particularly in the era of NCLB, in which only certain literacies are validated and assessed, it is important for Indigenous people to
assert our own reading and expressive practices as equally valuable.[100]

I specifically choose the term *literacies* to frame my discussion of
aloha ʻāina for a few reasons. First, the term signals the critical importance that Kanaka mastery of reading, writing, and printing played in
the formation of a Hawaiian nationalist consciousness in the 1800s,
as well as the ongoing importance of conventional literacy for survival and survivance today. In the first half of the nineteenth century,
the Kānaka who survived epidemics of foreign-introduced diseases
mourned our dead and took up a practice of hope and power: reading
and writing. Although many Kānaka had become familiar with documents over several decades of intercourse with foreigners, it wasn't
until after the first press was brought to the islands in 1821 that popular
literacy proliferated throughout the archipelago. American missionaries maintained dominance in publishing for the next forty years, and
they promoted literacy as part of their mission to Christianize Hawaiians. The desire to read and write moved, however, across every level of
Hawaiian society so quickly that everyday Kānaka became teachers for
their own communities, far exceeding the number of missionaries who
were teaching Hawaiians. With this technology people could capture

older knowledge forms—stories, chants, genealogies, celestial and geo-graphical mappings, practical instructions and prayers—that may have otherwise been lost if they remained only in their oral manifestations amid the waves of depopulation. Writing became a new way to repro-duce the nation and to express aloha ʻāina in new contexts.

Second, thinking about aloha ʻāina as an unbounded set of com-municative practices reminds us that we are constituted by our actions as much as by our genealogy. Aloha ʻāina centers the cultivation and protection of the relationship of Kānaka to all elements of our natural world. If healthy relationships entail communication, then the prac-tice of aloha ʻāina must include facility in multiple languages, human and nonhuman. Pedagogies grounded in aloha ʻāina recognize that hu-mans do not have a monopoly on language.[101] They also encourage people to recognize and discover patterns, transmissions of informa-tion, attempts to commune, and acknowledgements of kinship from our nonhuman relatives. They require and reaffirm multiple ways of knowing.[102] We become poʻe aloha ʻāina through our actions of aloha ʻāina. In this sense the category opens up larger systemic possibilities for change by not limiting these practices to ʻŌiwi Hawaiʻi alone but allowing settlers to take on the ethics and practices of aloha ʻāina. This was an important point for the non-ʻŌiwi teachers at HKM who have found a place for themselves within Hawaiian culture–based educa-tion by engaging in practices of aloha ʻāina alongside their students and colleagues.

Third, I use the term *literacies* in describing Kānaka practices of aloha ʻāina precisely because that conventional form of literacy is still hegemonic within schools. Universal K–12 education in the United States has widely disseminated some literacies, although quite un-evenly, while marginalizing other literacies entirely, such as Indigenous land-centered literacies. In general, mainstream school systems train students to see the lands and natural resources upon which we survive as incidental to rather than generative of core standards for learning. Although education researchers and practitioners are now acknowl-edging a wider range of "new literacies" that are certainly valuable, for the most part they still frame literacies as forms of communication and meaning making between humans, even if through different media.[103] That is, human languages and relationships remain at the center. In contrast, Indigenous peoples have developed forms of reading and writing the world that are not as anthropocentric, yet these have been systematically subordinated within dominant knowledge regimes.[104]

The pedagogical praxis of aloha ʻāina this book advocates shares strong affinities with many of the central aims of critical pedagogy and critical literacy. As critical literacy scholars have long asserted, literacies are not politically neutral technical skill sets but social practices embedded within cultural and historical contexts.[105] Literate practices as forms of knowledge are imbricated with power. Allan Luke puts it crisply, "Literacy and education are means for access to cultural knowledge and social power. . . . One always reads and writes in cultural contexts and social situations—and it is in these contexts and situations where relations of power are constructed, deployed and waged."[106] A critical literacy praxis involves learning reading and writing as part of what Freire calls the *conscientização* (conscientization) process, which is not only about becoming conscious of one's experience as shaped within specific relations of power and hegemonic discourses but also about actively resisting and transgressing those relations and discourses.[107] Branches of critical pedagogy push further to expand its previously anthropocentric frame and to include Indigenous epistemologies and analyses. For example, Grande's notion of "Red pedagogy" goes beyond "the incorporation of indigenous knowledge and praxis in schools . . . [and] the development of Native curricula" to include theorizing and disrupting the specific forms of power and domination that marginalize and dispossess Indigenous peoples.[108] Additionally, an emergent "ecopedagogy" movement calls critical educators to analyze and oppose the spread of neoliberalism and imperialism that has precipitated monumental ecological crises and to simultaneously "foment collective ecoliteracy."[109]

Aloha ʻāina includes land-centered literacies and is based on an intimate connection with and knowledge of the land, and like critical literacy and critical pedagogy, it should also be clearly understood as a political praxis. As Trask, Silva, and Basham have all elaborated, Kānaka have at various times articulated aloha ʻāina as a Hawaiian form of anticolonial, anti-imperialist resistance and critique.[110] When American political leaders and the white oligarchy in Hawaiʻi were attempting to annex Hawaiʻi to the United States in the 1890s, aloha ʻāina was "the cornerstone of resistance." Silva explains that this phrase and identification (as poʻe aloha ʻāina) expressed "the desire that makaʻāinana and aliʻi shared for self-rule as opposed to rule by the colonial oligarchy of settlers or the military rule of the United States."[111] Her widely influential book *Aloha Betrayed: Native Hawaiian Resistance to American Colonialism* shows that the phrase *aloha ʻāina* was used in countless places, including political speeches, newspapers (as well as the actual title of a newspaper), and the names of organizations that initiated mass petitions and successfully lobbied against annexation for several years. Basham's research on the period from 1893 to 1898, the initial phase in which Native rule was usurped, goes further to document and discuss over three hundred mele lāhui (songs and chants for the Hawaiian nation) composed and published in protest of foreign takeover, many of which specifically used the phrase *aloha ʻāina*. Basham identifies the most popular mele that recounted the Kaua Kuloko—an organized and armed attempt to throw off the undemocratic rule of a white supremacist oligarchy—titled "Ke Aloha ʻĀina Paʻa Mau Loa" (My Love for the Land Is Secured Forever).[112] Together, Silva's and Basham's research demonstrate that Kānaka used a broad range of expressive practices to fight for their national independence and political autonomy. Silva argues that even after the United States assumed control of the islands, Kānaka "continued to create and recreate the inner domain of spiritual and cultural identity based on their love for the land, even while operating within the U.S. political arena."[113] Similarly, the educators featured in this book find ways to cultivate and articulate aloha ʻāina even while working within the context of a settler-colonial schooling system. In chapter 5, I discuss the ways an explicit engagement with the politics of aloha ʻāina has been a crucial part of their work.

Approximately eighty years after the antiannexation movements, Kānaka and their allies used the concept of aloha ʻāina to describe and inspire the movement to stop the U.S. military's bombing and desecration of the island of Kahoʻolawe.[114] Most recognize George Jarrett Helm Jr., an early leader of the movement and of Protect Kahoʻolawe ʻOhana (PKO), as the person who did the most to bring the term back to popular consciousness. Helm was a musician and scholar (although not located within an academic institution) who moved between various literate practices to forge a powerful style of community organizing for aloha ʻāina. Many perceived him as a radical, elders in particular, until they heard him sing and spoke to him in person. His fluency with old-style Hawaiian music opened them to his eloquent speeches and less formal conversations about how the defense of Kahoʻolawe against further destruction by the U.S. Navy was a form of aloha ʻāina.[115] Helm has also been described by siblings, friends, and colleagues as a voracious reader and deep thinker who always urged people to do their "homework"—that is, to do the research and reading that would put their activism on solid ground. Moreover, his connection to ʻāina and kūpuna was sustained through frequent prayer. Important to note, the PKO's practice also emphasized (and continues to emphasize) the need to honor and use ancestral sacred places on the island, thus re-viving and perpetuating literacies, in the broad sense of the term, that strengthen the relationships between humans and ʻāina.[116]

Helm was among the handful of men and women who aimed to protect and resuscitate this living island by placing their own lives and bodies between the bombs and the ʻāina. Walter Ritte, who was among the "early warriors" who landed on Kahoʻolawe without the U.S. Navy's sanction, wrote that Helm's "love for these islands made him commit his life to protecting the land. He would cry in sadness when he was unable to explain to the military the concept of *Aloha Aina*. It was his heart that allowed him to give all of himself to *aloha aina*."[117] During these landings, he and others kept journals to write their reflections and experiences. On one of his last occupations of the island before his disappearance, Helm wrote the following entry:

> Last Sunday of the month/day of Kahoʻolawe occupation—using flashlight to write this note—much has been done in preparation for this protest (spiritually especially). Without the spiritual element, life would be like an empty breath, no substance. Piʻilani is guiding us through this adventure as we offered hoʻokupu and mohai aloha to the kupuna of the past at Hale o Piʻilani. The occupation of the military reservation is not so much a defiance as it is a responsibility to express our legitimate concern for the land of the Hawaiian. Kahoʻolawe is a part of my culture. . . . We are against warfare but more so against imperialism.[118]

My own process of writing this book might be seen as a product of the tensions between rather than the synergistic blending of a multiplicity of literacies.

My Role as Activist Researcher and Storyteller

This book grows out of the long-term relationships between myself and the people, ʻāina, and dynamic vision that comprise Hālau Kū Māna. This book draws on the stories, words, and observed practices of many HKM educators and graduates, and it cannot be extricated from my own position as the teller of this particular collection of stories and experiences. Thus, my role as an Indigenous researcher, student, and educator should be made transparent. In keeping with the knowledge practices of both Indigenous narrative making and ethnography, it is important to briefly situate myself at the outset of this story.

By the time I graduated from a selective, private K–12 school built for Hawaiian youth, I had become highly proficient in conventional literacy in the English language and, to a much lesser extent, in the Hawaiian language. I could read texts of various levels and had become a fairly decent writer for someone my age. I scored high on the SATs, earned entrance into elite universities, and was given access to the kinds of social capital that allow for a professional, middle-class lifestyle. I was and, in many ways, still am a privileged Kanaka. I also had a healthy dose of the sort of "reading the world" (a la Friere) that came from being raised by activist, intellectual parents who taught me to be attentive to power and injustice.

But at the same time, I had never been taught the names of the winds and rains of the lands on which I lived. My schooling had never brought me to physically encounter and learn from a sailing canoe or loʻi kalo based on ancestral design. We did not learn about the water resources of the district in which my school was located. I did not know the names of the moon or even that each phase of the moon had its own name, which would have been common knowledge for the smallest of children in the days of my ʻŌiwi ancestors. My illiteracy would have been laughable at another time in history. Yet in my own schooling experience, that kind of ignorance was encouraged. (I can recall my AP English teacher getting upset and expressing her utter disapproval that I had chosen for our assigned research paper on a classic poet's work a Māori writer. How shameful that such an advanced student would ignore the canonical authors of European and American verse! The collection I had chosen was the only book of poetry by a Pacific Islander that I could find in our library.) By the time I was ready to move into higher education, I was deeply aware of the limits of my own education.

I believe it was this imbalance in the kinds of literacies cultivated at school that led me to the nascent Hawaiian charter school movement. Simply put, as I became an educator I did not want other young people to be denied the kinds of Indigenous, land-centered literacies that thousands of young Kānaka like myself were being denied each year. I also knew it was still important for them to have access to the kinds of literacies in which my colleagues and I had been schooled.

I should note that I did not begin my dissertation research (which forms a basis for this book) intending to study and write about charter schools or even about schooling more generally. But as the Hawaiian movement, Hawaiʻi state charter school legislation, and my immediate intellectual community converged in the historical moment at which most of the Hawaiian culture–based charter schools were born, I happened to become part of a group that saw a need for and thus opened a school. My academic research followed that initiative, in the wake of the collective identification of this need. In that sense, this project began as and continued to be what has become known in anthropology as activist research. As Hale describes, activist research "is predicated on alignment with a group of people organized in struggle, and on the collaborative relations of knowledge production with members of that group."[119] Activist research explicitly aims to contest existing relations of power and to envision and live new relations. This book can be seen as an activist ethnography produced out of the collective struggle of a community, although told here by a single author.

As I understand it, activist ethnography involves building relationships based on continual dialogue with people in struggle and being attentive to relations of power between those engaged in the research rather than simply identifying whether the researcher is an insider or outsider to the communities studied. In the case of my work on this book, I have moved within a spectrum of insiderness to this changing school community and the larger Hawaiian charter school movement. Over the past ten years, I have sometimes been right in the thick of things at HKM and at other times have played more marginal roles within the community. In some cases my position as a professional academic and cofounder carried a certain amount of authority and privilege to speak when others could not, and in other cases, these titles meant very little.

In terms of the content and time frame within which this study took place, there were two main periods of my focused research: 2001–4, during which time I was completing a dissertation, and 2010–11, when I was updating that earlier work for this current form. During my dissertation research I alternated between paid and voluntary work at HKM as a teacher and a local school board member. This meant that I regularly was in the classroom and the boardroom, as well as at staff meetings and social gatherings. During that period I conducted in-depth interviews primarily with teachers but also with a handful of founding parents and students. Immediately after completing my PhD in 2005, I took a leadership position as HKM's program director for two years. This job included primary oversight of the instructional faculty and staff, as well as the school's curriculum and assessment system, professional development program, and overall student well-being. At that time, the countless mundane things needed to sustain a school eclipsed my role as a researcher and writer, even though I saw my role as a leader to be founded on continuous observation, review of data from many sources, assessment, and action. I was no longer taking formal ethnographic field notes, although I did maintain a walk-through journal as part of my supervisory duties. The demands of leadership did not, however, allow me to spend as much time in the classroom as I believe was necessary for close ethnographic research. Rather, my work was more about program evaluation. Report writing was a process of constant translation and of finding ways to quantify the qualitative growth we were seeing in our students. I cannot say that I was doing critical, cultural research during that period. What those years did give me was an embodied knowledge of the day-to-day struggles of operating a school that tried to make Indigenous culture its foundation within a system that could not even fathom what that meant or understand why it was valuable. My colleagues and I were living the tensions daily, with the weight of our students' well-being constantly on our shoulders. This impressed upon me, far more than any university course could, the importance of attending to the stakes of one's scholarship and teaching. As I gained kuleana at HKM the experience also allowed me to more fully internalize the Indigenous research ethics of allowing the research questions to be shaped by the needs of the community, sharing knowledge, attending to the protocols of what kinds of knowledge could and could not be made public, and maintaining long-term relationships beyond the length of a particular research project.[120]

The people and places of Hālau Kū Māna allowed me to embrace the notion of method as practice and process.[121] For example, my understanding of aloha ʻāina was deepened not only by my classroom observations and interviews but by practicing with my colleagues and friends customs that recognized our living connection to ʻāina, ancestors, and each other in the context of our lives in and beyond school. We marked many milestones of the life cycle together, especially those relevant to our generation as new mākua (parents): researching and relearning our genealogies, planting our children's ʻiewe (afterbirths), mourning the passing of our elders, and engaging in hoʻoponopono (a familial process of resolving conflicts) to heal our relationships. We deepened the bonds between us by naming and feeding each others' children, by celebrating and grieving together, by planting together, and by standing on the ʻāina together.

In that sense, the relationships forged during this research were, to use Colectivo Situaciones' terms, about *composition*. Their research collective argues that a condition of transformative research is the creation of the ties that are not limited to utilitarian or intellectual purposes. Comparing research to love and friendship, they call us to reimagine research as a process in which all "emerge from the experience reconstituted" and are "pierced by this shared experience" rather than in terms of a subject-object relation.[122] Given such relationships with colleagues, students, and families at HKM, I have seen many of the issues that the school and individual members of the school community have faced in depths that a researcher with a less-extended connection to the school would not have. All of these experiences and relationships provided opportunities for insight. But that kind of intimate access and deep connection to the school community also necessitated that I vigilantly reflect on the kinds of things that could and could not be included in this written form of our stories. It also meant that I needed to sometimes find ways to distance myself in order to think and write with perspective.

It was not until I left full-time employment at HKM in fall 2007 and later my position as chair of the local school board in 2010 that I could fully make that step back. By stepping out of these positions of kuleana, I was actually able to spend much more time going back into the classrooms, to engage a new crop of faculty in informal conversations and semiformal interviews about their work, and to talk-story with HKM alumni. It was during this time that I was introduced to Lawrence-Lightfoot's portraiture method and the critical race methodology of counterstorytelling, both of which move away from deficits-oriented approaches to educational research.

Lawrence-Lightfoot and Davis elucidate five key features of portraiture: (1) close attention to context; (2) balancing the writer's voice with the voices of the actors; (3) developing good relationships throughout the research process; (4) culling important themes, patterns, and metaphors; and (5) creating an authentic and evocative, aesthetic whole.[123] I hope these elements are apparent in the portraits of Hālau Kū Māna I offer in this book. Portraiture appealed to me for a number of reasons, the first of which was its beauty. Portraiture acknowledges that scholarly writing is an art form that takes a situated perspective and should include attentiveness to the aesthetics of the finished piece. Yet at the same time, it demands detailed observation and rigorous documentation and analysis—marks of good, empirical science. Reading Lawrence-Lightfoot's *A Good High School* was like listening to my favorite contemporary Hawaiian music.[124] I thought of singer-songwriters like Liko Martin, Israel Kamakawiwoʻole, or Kapali Keahi, who are able to express the struggles and strengths, the pain and persistence of Kānaka in ways that touch your naʻau and make you think. They mellifluously call injustice as it is, in tones round as the full moon, smooth as a day on the ocean with light winds, and anchored always by an undercurrent of love. This was the style I wanted to emulate.

I was further drawn to portraiture because it calls the portraitist to focus on what makes schools good—on what is working—without ignoring the challenges, struggles, and imperfections that make humanity beautiful, rich, and worth studying. This focus on strengths is particularly important for communities that have been pathologized, minimized, and marginalized by researchers in the past.[125] Additionally, like the era in which Lawrence-Lightfoot first developed this method, current educational policy and popular common sense have arguably become even more intensely focused on identifying and labeling failure among schools, teachers, students, and their communities.

Against those currents this book presents a counternarrative. Within critical race methodologies, counternarratives decenter dominant racializations and relations of power by focusing on and valuing the experiences of those who have been subordinated by prevailing regimes of power.[126] They can include personal narratives, biographical stories, or composite narratives that draw on various data to weave a single story representative of many people's experiences. In all cases, these counterstories speak back to master narratives that reproduce unjust social relations.[127] Such stories and the struggles they capture are seen as sources of strength and, in Yosso's terms, as forms of "community cultural wealth."[128] Although this book offers a counternarrative composed of the stories of many teachers and former students, it does not follow the practice used in some critical race theory narratives and in most school ethnographies of obscuring the name of the school or changing the names of the actors. From an ʻŌiwi perspective names bear mana, and they tell part of the story. Sources should be credited for the contribution of their thoughts and actions and should be accountable for them, as well. All of the HKM educators and graduates interviewed for and quoted in this study consented to have their names used. Many of them explicitly expressed that it was important to identify themselves to show that they were proud of their school and the work they were doing. I do, however, use pseudonyms for students who were minors at the time of the classroom observations described in various scenes within this book.

As I engaged people in interviews, or kūkākūkā (conversations), over the years I noticed kumu frequently talking about their genealogies—their actual ancestors, the kumu who trained them, and the intellectual/cultural lineages in which they situated themselves—and how these genealogies shaped them. For instance, Kumu Bonnie

Kahapeʻa-Tanner framed her kuleana as a kumu in relation to the larger waʻaʻohana (family of voyaging canoes) and the lineage of navigators in whose wake she followed. In the early years I was not explicitly asking about genealogy. But the patterns of speaking about education in terms of genealogy and genealogical responsibility were so persistent that I began paying close attention to the ways that genealogy was more than just contextual information but was still a form of Hawaiian intellectual production. It was when people spoke of their moʻokūʻauhau that they often became most clear about their own kuleana, their learning objectives, and their visions of potential futures.

Hawaiian genealogical narratives remind us to always be concerned with power and the ways it is exercised, for they have historically been used to justify and legitimize the mana of our leaders and teachers. Yet Kanaka Maoli genealogical practices also rely on stories and metaphors rather than static, prescriptive models. That is, they leave open the space for new action in the present, informed by the past. Perhaps most important for Kānaka Maoli and other Indigenous people today, our genealogies can serve as anticolonial tools while also reminding us that the colonial experience, however harrowing, is only a blip on the time line of the collective experience of our peoples. This book might be seen as one moʻokūʻauhau in that tradition, written in the hope that many more will be recorded, crafted, disputed, and debated.

ONE

The Emergence of Indigenous Hawaiian Charter Schools

The mission of liberatory Hawaiian education is to promote, protect and nurture Hawaiian culture in the next millennium, in an ever-changing modern society and work towards future political, economic, social and cultural Hawaiian self-determination.

■ Kū Kahakalau, founder of Kanu o ka ʻĀina public charter school and Nā Lei Naʻauao Hawaiian charter school alliance

It could be argued that the establishment, against all odds, of Hawaiian culture–based charter schools in urban and rural communities across the islands was the most visible and significant accomplishment of the Hawaiian movement in the first decade of the twenty-first century. The post–World War II and poststatehood democratic revolution in Hawaiʻi neither brought revolutionary changes in land usage nor upset existing settler colonial structures of power and logics of domination.[1] Rather, it replaced some white settler elites with local Japanese and Chinese settler elites. In much the same way, the political ascendance of Asian settlers within the public education sector to the ranks of Department of Education decision making has not led to a significant upset in the regimes of knowledge and power that maintain the suppression of Hawaiian sovereignty and the social inequalities in which Native people and more recent and/or less assimilated immigrants remain at the bottom.[2]

Kānaka Maoli, in alliance with non-Hawaiian educators and families who support Hawaiian education, created charter schools as preferred alternatives to an unresponsive and unequal mainstream school system. This chapter explains how an Indigenous movement based on aloha ʻāina came to dominate or, at least, play a major role in the establishment of charter schools in Hawaiʻi. I look at the emergence of

Indigenous Hawaiian culture–based charter schools at the intersection of two distinct movements: the late twentieth- and early twenty-first-century Hawaiian nationalist movement and the U.S. charter school movement.

The articulation of these two movements was in some ways odd given that the charter school model of school reform has often been linked to neoliberal, market-based ideologies, whereas Hawaiian movements have mobilized against the fragmentation and destruction that unregulated market expansion has often caused on our lands. The U.S. charter school phenomenon has proved able, however, to include space for an array of groups with varying social, political, and economic aims. This chapter addresses the historical and political context within which such an articulation was possible in the Hawaiian case. I particularly attend to the ways Kānaka Maoli who founded charter schools understood this work. I begin with an overview of some of the struggles for land, water, cultural practice, and sovereignty that created the conditions of possibility out of which Hawaiian charter schools could emerge. My discussion highlights aspects of aloha ʻāina that would later become central to the educational practices at Hālau Kū Māna and other Hawaiian charters. Throughout the chapter I show the ways twenty-first-century Hawaiian charter schools operate in the spaces of tension between naturalized structures of racism and settler colonialism and the ongoing assertion of Hawaiian self-determination and peoplehood.

Education and Aloha ʻĀina in Post-1959 Hawaiian Social Movements

The dominant narrative about Hawaiʻi's transition from territory to fiftieth state has remained largely unchanged from the mid-twentieth century to the present. The myth centers on the trope of equality and democracy arising out of a formerly racially stratified plantation society, a triumph of civil rights over white supremacy. In his ground-breaking critical study of Hawaiʻi statehood discourses, Dean Sara-nillio describes this hegemonic historical narrative as a "tale about a long struggle to oppose *haole* (white) racism and an expression of self-determination that was democratically and definitively settled" with the passage of the 1959 Hawai'i Admission Act and the rise of a new historic bloc led by the descendants of Asian plantation laborers.[3] He observes that whereas the statehood movement "made racism against Asian Americans visible, statehood proponents made invisible (by naturalizing) another form of oppression, a primitivist (and American modernist) notion that viewed Native Hawaiians, like other indigenous peoples, as permanently 'unfit for self-government.'"[4]

Although a critical mass of Hawaiian history scholars have shown that the process by which Hawai'i became incorporated as a state violated international law and perpetuated the denial of Hawaiian political self-determination and sovereignty, the idea that statehood brought an end to racism and U.S. colonial rule over the islands, ushering in an era of new equality, continues.[5] Myths of equality and multicultural harmony foreclose contemporary public debate about the ongoing inequality evident in Hawai'i's school system and the dynamics of settler colonialism therein. As I indicated in the introduction, collectively Kānaka Maoli have been failed by Hawai'i's public school system. Even though public education was hailed as an important equalizer by those who rose to power seeking to overturn the haole-led plantation society of the territorial era, Hawai'i's Indigenous people remain in a position of disempowerment with respect to the system. Moreover, the pernicious myth that Indigenous Hawaiian knowledge is less rigorous and less valuable than more recently introduced knowledges is bolstered by existing school systems in Hawai'i.

Despite the lack of institutional power over Hawai'i's school system, Kānaka 'Ōiwi have arguably invested more time and energy into designing and implementing educational initiatives than in any other aspect of our movement in the poststatehood era. Late twentieth- and early twenty-first-century Hawaiian social movements have been consciously and explicitly pedagogical, including popular-consciousness raising, community-based educational programs, and formal school-based reform initiatives. Many Kānaka have recognized that sovereignty and self-determination involve the ability to decide what future generations should be able to know and do. Collective knowledges constitute nations. Thus, control of our educational futures remains crucially important for Indigenous people; it is a matter of our survival.[6]

In the wake of the U.S. Congressional act declaring Hawai'i a state, a vision of integration and assimilation was proffered by an extensive plan for remaking the Kamehameha Schools (KS)—a private school serving students of Native Hawaiian ancestry since 1887. In 1960 the KS board of trustees contracted Booz, Allen and Hamilton, a management consulting firm based in Chicago, to conduct the most comprehensive evaluation and planning survey completed on the schools up until that time.[7] The survey team included seven non-Hawaiian men: three consultants with the contracted firm's Educational Administration Division and four professors of education from Stanford University, the University of Chicago, and the University of Illinois. The authors emphasized that any vision for KS's future had to account for the changing social and political landscape of Hawai'i. Thus, they made several predictions about poststatehood Hawai'i. Some of their predictions were correct: The population would continue to grow at a rapid rate and the proportion of students with Hawaiian ancestry would increase. The economy of the state would grow and expand, particularly in service industries like tourism, with major shifts in employment patterns from an agricultural to a service-based economy. They reasoned that these economic shifts would require rethinking vocational education programs, like the agricultural and industrial training programs at Kamehameha. They also predicted these shifts would have tremendous impact on the value of the estate, with its vast land holdings, and recommended the trustees capitalize on those changes. Within the next decade local residents would be protesting the development of high-priced housing on KS trust lands formerly in agricultural use.

The American educational experts who produced the Booz report also made several forecasts that would prove to be simplistic and wrong. In particular, they believed that Hawaiian assimilation to American culture would accelerate in the wake of statehood and that Hawaiian culture would have less and less meaning and importance. They wrote, "Hawaii is becoming increasingly similar to other states ... social and cultural patterns of the state can be expected to become more typically American in the decades ahead. At the same time, Hawaiian culture will tend to have less influence than in the past decades."[8] In light of this forecasted assimilation, they surmised that "the educational needs of children of Hawaiian ancestry [would] become less different from those of other children" and that Hawai'i's public school system would "be increasingly able to meet the educational needs of children of Hawaiian ancestry."[9]

The Booz report's predictions were wrong on both counts. First, the settler state's public school system has never adequately met the needs of Native students, as evidenced by the inequalities described in the introduction. Second, rather than allowing our culture to fade away quietly, Hawaiians of the 1960s onward have recommitted to ancestral cultural practices of all kinds, including language, voyaging, dance, chant, scholarship, healing, and martial arts, to name a few. As ethnic studies scholar Davianna McGregor writes, "Rather than leading to fuller assimilation of Native Hawaiians into American society, statehood sparked a reassertion of Native Hawaiian rights and revitalization of Native Hawaiian language, culture, and spirituality."[10] Education has been central to these revitalization movements, as the perpetuation of cultural knowledge requires teaching and learning across generations.

The Hawaiian nationalist movement—both cultural and political—has also been motivated by resistance to exactly the kind of land development and profit making that KS trustees took up following the Booz report. In fact, Haunani-Kay Trask, Hawaiian political scholar and KS graduate, argues that it was the fight against evictions of Kanaka Maoli and other local farmers from Kalama Valley by the KS/Bishop estate in 1970 that was "the birth of the modern Hawaiian movement."[11] Trask notes that the socioeconomic conditions of Native Hawaiians actually worsened as a result of the poststatehood shift from an agriculturally driven plantation economy in the first half of the twentieth century to an economy dependent on tourism and land speculation in the second half: "Pushed from their rural enclaves by the developer's bulldozer, many of these Hawaiians took up residence in crowded urban highrises or in makeshift beach villages. Others moved to one of the dwindling farming valleys, like Kalama, in the hopes of staving off the end to their slow, rural lifestyle."[12] Kalama Valley evictees like Moose Lui and George Santos were supported by Kānaka like Kīhei "Soli" Nīheu, Kehau Lee, Kalani 'Ohelo, Larry Kamakawiwo'ole, Joy Ahn, and Pete Thompson, and together they pointed out the irony that an institution founded for Hawaiian students by a Hawaiian ali'i was evicting

Hawaiians and other local farmers in order to build high-priced sub-urban homes that most Kānaka could not afford. Education was an important part of their struggle. In addition to raising consciousness about the evictions by publishing pamphlets and interfacing with local news media, members of the Kōkua Kalama Committee—which later became Kōkua Hawaiʻi—also conducted regular study sessions during their occupation of the valley. These sessions became a way to teach themselves the kinds of things they hadn't learned or been exposed to in school and was described by participants as their own process of decolonization.[13]

Although the resistors were not able to stop the transformation of Kalama Valley into an upper-middle-class suburb, their struggle posed an early challenge to the discourses of progressive change in post-statehood Hawaiʻi. Trask notes that "as the first prolonged resistance effort in the post-Statehood era, Kalama Valley undercut the eu-phoric characterizations of 'The New Hawaiʻi' as an enlightened post-plantation society governed by consensus politics where pluralism rather than oligarchy reigned."[14] In the decades that followed, the social dislocations and continued inequality that resulted from rapid over-development and the accompanying erosion of Indigenous land-based lifestyles were countered by a rising cultural and political Hawaiian nationalist movement based on aloha ʻāina.

The struggle at Kalama was a powerful pedagogical moment. For the first time in the twentieth century, landless Kānaka who had been pushed around from place to place decided that they would stand up to the largest private landowner in Hawaiʻi, in a very public and vis-ible way. Their occupation of the valley, against bulldozers and snip-ers, taught other communities that they could similarly organize to maintain their connections to ʻāina. As Kōkua Hawaiʻi member Pete Thompson recalls:

> Here's this estate set up for the benefit of Hawaiians. Here's Hawaiians being evicted. Here's young Hawaiian activists getting arrested standing up for the pressing needs and the Hawaiian community, and here's the landlord sending people in to arrest them and drag them off the property. [Kalama Valley] was a pivotal struggle and a lot of things sprouted after

that, which eventually led to a number of other struggles. Some were more successful in terms of actual settlements or developments stopped. . . . [Kalama] was poignant. . . . It was serious . . . and it gave rise to decades of activism.[15]

The formation and work of Kōkua Hawaiʻi—the primary activist group that arose out of the Kalama struggle—crystallized the importance of Hawaiian leadership in Hawaiian struggles for justice. It was a moment when Hawaiian leaders made clear to supporters of other ethnicities that Kānaka needed to take the kuleana to speak for themselves and the ʻāina. Thompson's own community-organizing work reached its height when he became involved in supporting the Waiāhole-Waikāne Community Association against eviction by their landlord, the Marks family. In the early 1970s, the landowner planned to evict approximately 120 families living between the two rural windward Oʻahu valleys in order to make way for 7,000 condominium units.[16] The successful struggle against that proposed development led to a longer protracted fight, beginning in the 1990s, over the water that would feed healthy ecosystems and taro fields.

The Waiāhole water struggles that ostensibly began in the 1990s actually stretched back to at least 1916, when the Waiāhole ditch system, built to divert water from windward valleys to the drier plains of central Oʻahu for sugar cultivation, first opened. Under King Sugar and the territorial regime, the territorial courts in Hawaiʻi commodified water resources, and it wasn't until the social movements of the 1970s that water was once again recognized as a public good.[17] In the 1990s a windward Oʻahu coalition of farmers and grassroots community associations led the charge in pressuring the state to actually enforce and practice the legal mandates passed years earlier. Taro farmers and cultural practitioners made explicit the connection between free-flowing streams, subsistence, community health, and education. Some of them later became involved with charter schools: the Hoeʻohana were core founders of Hakipuʻu Learning Center (HLC), and Meaala Bishop became one of HLC's teachers. Her husband, Danny Bishop, assisted the loʻi class at Hālau Kū Māna in the creation of the loʻi system under their care, in addition to hosting and teaching students from various other Hawaiian charter schools on his own Waiāhole farm. In the struggles to protect natural stream flow and Indigenous forms of taro farming, non-Native allies have also played key roles. In Waiāhole, for example, the Reppun ʻohana has been instrumental in practicing and sharing their knowledge of building and maintaining loʻi kalo. Evan Beachy, a member of the Reppun ʻohana, helped in the writing of Hālau Kū Māna's initial start-up application. Because of Waiāhole and similar struggles for water and healthy loʻi kalo, restoration of loʻi and stream monitoring projects have been woven into the curriculum of many Hawaiian charter schools, particularly those located in ahupuaʻa with perennially running streams and a historical tradition of kalo production. Chapter 3 discusses this aspect of HKM's curriculum.

Land struggles of the 1970s aimed not only at protecting ʻāina that was in active cultivation or upon which people were residing. The movement to stop the U.S. Navy's use of Kahoʻolawe island as a target brought the revitalization of traditional Hawaiian religious practices and cultural protocols to the forefront. Leaders of this struggle galvanized support around the ethics and praxis of aloha ʻāina, which presupposed that ʻāina is living and imbued with spirit. Members of the grassroots organization formed to stop the bombing and regreen the island, the Protect Kahoʻolawe ʻOhana (PKO), learned the heavy responsibilities that came with their decision to reinvigorate their relationship with the island. Their kuleana to the island included multiple facets. As McGregor, a longtime PKO organizer, explains:

> Aloha ʻāina embodied several layers of responsibility. At one level, it meant protecting the physical sustainability of Hawaiian lands and natural resources. At another level, it meant organizing and rallying for Hawaiian native rights and sovereignty to achieve political standing necessary to protect the ʻāina. At the deepest level, it meant a spiritual dedication to honor and worship the gods who were the spiritual life of these forces of nature.[18]

In January 1976 during the Hawaiian season of Makahiki, honoring peace, a group of resistors landed on Kahoʻolawe. Over the next few years, nine known landings were made in defiance of the U.S. military's usage of and authority over the island. Over time the PKO's strategy morphed to include an extensive and multipronged popular education campaign that included community concerts, school visits and speaking engagements, meetings with Hawaiian elders on various islands, and eventually, supervised trips to the island. Just as Kōkua Hawai'i had taken up self-education in political theory and strategy a decade earlier, the PKO took on their own process of filling gaps in their generation's knowledge of how to properly perform cultural ceremonies. Because of the potential and actual loss of life that occurred in attempting to stop the bombing and reestablish a Kanaka presence on the island, PKO members felt it was essential to access and honor the island in a culturally and spiritually appropriate way. The restoration and re-creation of such ceremonies and protocols became central to the forms of aloha 'āina practiced by the PKO.

According to McGregor, in 1981 the 'Ohana asked Kumu Hula Edith Kanaka'ole and Nālani Kanaka'ole of Hālau o Kekuhi "to train them in how to conduct a Makahiki ceremony," so as to seek the god Lono's guidance and care in healing and regreening the island.[19] A year later, the 'ohana held the first publicly known Makahiki ceremonies of the twentieth century. This publicly visible revitalization of Hawaiian spiritual practice can be both directly and indirectly linked to the resurgence of Hawaiian oli and protocol in various settings, including contemporary Hawaiian charter schools. The practices revitalized by the Kaho'olawe movement inspired the use of chant and ceremony in contexts other than hula practice and performance. Many of the Hawaiian charter schools use chants that honor specific places and ancestral figures, tell particular stories, or serve certain cultural functions, such as showing that the student is prepared and ready to enter into a space of learning. Whereas the regular (nonspectacle) usage of oli was practically unheard of in schools in the 1960s, 1970s and 1980s, in many twenty-first-century Hawaiian charter schools traditional-style chants are used for a variety of purposes, including opening and closing the school day, welcoming visitors, planting, and asking for permission to enter the forest or the ocean. The Kanaka'ole family and the Edith Kanaka'ole Foundation are the primary founders and leaders of Ke Ana La'ahana public charter school on Hawai'i Island (or the Big Island). They have also influenced numerous teachers who pass on the practice of oli at various charter schools throughout the islands, and many of the Hawaiian culture–based charter schools employ kumu who are culturally sanctioned to train students in oli and hula.[20]

The same year that a handful of poʻe aloha ʻāina made their first landing on Kahoʻolawe, the double-hulled waʻa (canoe) named *Hōkūleʻa* made its first voyage from Hawaiʻi to Tahiti. The *Hōkūleʻa* was, from its inception, meant to challenge colonial knowledge regimes that cast doubt on whether Kānaka Maoli and our relatives across Oceania could make intentional, long-distance voyages across the vast Pacific Ocean. Proof that Indigenous Oceanic maritime accomplishments far surpassed their European contemporaries threw a wrench into discourses that cast Native islanders as dumb and lazy and Native knowledge as worthless. When Satawalese master navigator Mau Piailug led a Hawaiʻi crew on *Hōkūleʻa*'s first voyage, the waʻa became an icon for the renewal of Hawaiian pride and a renewed faith in the value of ancestral knowledges. Hawaiian navigators like Nainoa Thompson, Billy Richards, Shorty and Clay Bertlemann, and many others became students of "Papa" Mau and created a rebirth of Indigenous Oceanic voyaging traditions that inspired the rebuilding of canoes in various islands across Polynesia.[21]

The *Hōkūleʻa* and the waʻa kaulua that were built in the ensuing years have all made education a central part of their work. Education occurs not only in the training of new crews and navigators to sail and maintain the canoes but through the development of curriculum, the satellite communication between voyagers and various publics on land, and the opening of the waʻa to student and community groups. The waʻa are seen as moving classrooms that can teach not only the skills of how to sail but also important cultural values and environmental awareness. The focus of the Polynesian Voyaging Society (PVS) on education is reflected throughout the rest of the waʻa ʻohana.[22] In the PVS's first decade, this educational focus included partnering to publish numerous children's books and curriculum guides for teaching schoolchildren about the waʻa.[23] Over the years college-level courses in Hawaiian navigation and voyaging have been developed in conjunction with university faculty, and there are now classes offered at five campuses within the University of Hawaiʻi system. The dawn of the Internet age also made real-time access to accounts from voyagers accessible to international audiences, such that the experience of long-distance voyaging could be vicariously lived by students in hundreds of schools in Hawai'i and beyond.[24] A number of the Hawaiian-focused charter schools have partnerships with various wa'a, such as the *Makali'i* on Hawai'i Island. Chapter 4 describes the role that the wa'a program has played at HKM, which has its own sailing wa'a, *Kānehūnāmoku*, that serves as an ocean-based classroom. Lead teacher and captain Bonnie Kahape'a-Tanner, who has trained under some of the aforementioned navigators, considers *Kānehūnāmoku* to be a genealogical descendant of *Makali'i* and *Hōkūle'a*.

Hawaiian charters founded in the first decade of the twenty-first century also built from the foundation of an earlier movement to implement Hawaiian-language immersion programs within the mainstream public education system. In place of the model in which Hawaiian was taught as a foreign language, in 1983 a handful of families and educators founded the 'Aha Pūnana Leo (APL) to support 'ohana-based Hawaiian-language immersion education. The APL began opening independent preschools, and then as the first preschoolers graduated, members of the APL pushed the state to live up to its 1978 constitutional mandate by supporting Hawaiian-medium instruction in public schools. Each year, Hawaiian-language teachers and families had to return to the statewide board of education in order to petition for approval of the next grade level until the board finally approved a K–12 program in 1992.

Some of the founding leaders and teachers at Hawaiian charter schools came directly out of the language-immersion movement and now use charters as a vehicle for continuing the immersion pedagogical model. Both Makalapua Alencastre and Kauanoe Kamanā were parents of children in Department of Education immersion schools, board members of APL, and language teachers before becoming the founding directors of Hawaiian-language immersion charter schools, Ke Kula 'o Samuel M. Kamakau and Ke Kula 'o Nāwahīokalani'ōpu'u, respectively.[25] Other charter school founders have used the opportunity for curricular innovation to offer the option of bilingual (Hawaiian and English) education in addition to either English-medium or Hawaiian-medium education.[26]

By the 1980s many Hawaiian movement leaders were articulating an explicitly nationalist agenda calling for Hawaiian sovereignty.

Earlier land struggles had challenged overdevelopment of 'āina by large private landowners and had brought to light the state and federal governments' historical neglect and abuse of their responsibilities to Native Hawaiian beneficiaries under the Department of Hawaiian Homelands trust and the Ceded Lands trust—both composed of Hawaiian Kingdom crown and government lands that were seized at the start of the American occupation. Building consciousness about the national lands of the Hawaiian Kingdom provided a critical piece in the development of Hawaiian sovereignty discourse. In 1921 the U.S. Congress set aside 200,000 acres—a tiny fraction of the seized Hawaiian national lands—for an arbitrary beneficiary class based on a "50 percent blood quantum."[27] These lands were generally considered the least productive of that larger corpus of lands, the remainder of which remained in the hands of the U.S. Department of Defense and, after 1959, the State of Hawai'i.[28] Movement leaders called for an even deeper historical reexamination of the state and U.S. federal governments' legitimacy and authority over those lands in the first place. Hawaiian homesteaders pushed for the right to sue the government for breech-of-trust obligations, and this initiative morphed into one of the largest Hawaiian sovereignty organizations—Ka Lāhui Hawai'i.[29]

The massive organization of the lāhui (nation/people) in the 1990s required popular education and consciousness raising based on sound scholarly research. Not only academics but people of all vocations were striving to remedy a century of historical miseducation and misinformation. Following their gross power grab in 1893, the haole elite actively worked to legitimize their political usurpation and to naturalize U.S. imperial control through schools and textbooks, among other things. In 1992, a year before the centennial observance of the coup against Queen Lili'uokalani and the ongoing suppression of independent Hawaiian government, forty Hawaiian organizations joined together with the goal of reeducating themselves and the broader public about the historical basis for Hawaiian claims of sovereignty and independence. Taking the name Hui Na'auao (a group seeking wisdom or enlightenment), they led hundreds of educational workshops on Hawaiian history, self-determination, and different models of sovereignty. Ku'ulei Maunupau, who became a grant writer and parent at Hālau Kū Māna public charter school in 2002, recalls the importance of one Hui Naʻauao educational session in her own political awakening. After graduating from a Hawaiʻi public school, she immediately enlisted in the U.S. military. When Kuʻulei returned home, she attended one of Hui Naʻauaoʼs educational workshops.

> I still remember it . . . basically I learned for the first time that our queen was overthrown. And this was at twenty [years old]! All these emotions came out. I was pissed, like "wait, I've been lied to for twenty years?" I really believed that Captain Cook had saved the Hawaiian people and made us civilized. For that to turn around at twenty, it's almost life-shattering because you feel like you've been living a lie.[30]

A decade later, it became important for her to enroll her daughter in a school that would provide the kind of cultural and political learning that she was denied in her own schooling. "Because I came from the public school system, we lacked any knowledge of our history and culture. The deepest appreciation I have for [HKM] is they can give her that. . . . She will carry the knowledge of our ancestors." Kuʻuleiʼs story is emblematic of one of the greatest achievements of the Hawaiian sovereignty movement: the removal of the historical blinders from the eyes of countless people in the islands and beyond. The pedagogical aspects of the 1990s movements included films, marches, community education initiatives, an archipelago-wide peopleʼs international tribunal, street theater, public television shows, websites, and museum showcases, as well as an explosion of scholarship directly related to Hawaiian nationhood, land, and sovereignty by a rising generation of Hawaiian researchers.[31]

Although incredible advances were made in shifting the terms of popular debate in Hawaiʻi, in peeling back decades of misinformation, and in winning some localized struggles, the collective lāhui ʻŌiwi Hawaiʻi has still not seen any significant gain in terms of the fundamental aspects of collective, political sovereignty: land and autonomous governance. These movements shaped, however, the conditions of possibility in which Hawaiian communities initiated charter schools as forms of self-determination at the turn of the twenty-first century.

The U.S. Charter School Movement and
Hawai'i's Charter School Law

In the United States, charter schools have become the most robust and fastest-growing element of school reform efforts centered on the notion of school choice. The national charter school movement cannot be claimed by a particular segment of the political spectrum, as both its history and its current forms are linked with a diverse range of political perspectives and visions for school reform. Charters and school choice are too often credited solely to the neoliberal model of deregulation (a la Milton Friedman) and market-based educational reform. However, it is clear that the roots of the charter and school choice movements are more complicated. James Forman Jr. shows that the school choice movement can be linked both to groups that aimed to sidestep mandatory desegregation in the wake of the *Brown v. Board of Education* decision *and* to a much longer tradition, going back to Reconstruction, of black communities building community-run schools in order to provide a preferred alternative to the mainstream school system.[32] He recovers the role of progressive proponents of choice that preceded the contemporary rhetoric of school choice, connecting post–Civil War African American–sustained schools (when there simply was no other choice) to the Freedom Summer schools of 1964 and the free school, community control, and progressive vouchers movements of the late 1960s to mid-1970s. These movements were all about providing preferred educational alternatives that emerged from within a community, that were democratically governed, and that explicitly challenged the structural inequalities that were not only embedded in but also perpetuated by mainstream educational establishments and government bureaucracies.

Research focusing on contemporary policy makers also reveals a range of political values and reasons for supporting charter school reform. As Amy Stuart Wells and her colleagues write, "The diversity of political support for charter school reform has been apparent since the birth of the movement, which is simultaneously part of a larger, global phenomenon of deregulating, privatizing, and marketizing public education and a distinctly American phenomenon of the reoccurring demand for local and community control of schools."[33] One policy maker they interviewed referred to charter schools as an "empty vessel" into which different groups pour their own visions for educational and social reform.[34]

The specific notion of charters is often credited to Ray Budde, a New England educator who in the 1970s proposed that school districts be restructured by allowing small groups of teachers to receive contracts, or charters, from their local school boards in order to explore innovative educational approaches.[35] The idea gained momentum after its introduction in 1988 by the president of the American Federation of Teachers (AFT), Albert Shanker. The idea was that groups of teachers and parents could submit research-based proposals and, if approved, form publicly funded schools that would be freed from certain curricular, budgetary, and collective-bargaining provisions. These schools would still be held to the standards of student achievement and fiscal accountability of any public school, but the hope was that they could test innovations that might then inform broader change among their conventional counterparts. By 1988 the idea was already beginning to be tested out as a new paradigm in radically restructuring urban high schools in Philadelphia. The goal was to "dismantle the urban high school as we knew it—large, anonymous, and filled with more cracks than safety nets—and to nourish in its place, many small, intellectually intimate communities of learners called charters."[36] The Philadelphia Schools Collective defined their vision of charters as schools that are small, developed, and led by the teachers who work within them, as well as collaboratively taught, student centered, and heterogeneous.

The first charter school law was passed by the Minnesota legislature in 1991, based on the central values of choice, opportunity, and responsibility for results. Several states followed suit in the 1990s, and at present forty states and the District of Columbia have distinct charter school laws that govern the ways charters are implemented within each of them. Within the first decade of the twenty-first century, total U.S. enrollments in charters grew from about half a million in 1,600 schools to approximately 1.7 million in almost 5,000 schools.[37] Charter school advocates also measure growth according to market share, the percentage of public school students who are enrolled in public charter schools, and these numbers have been steadily growing over the decade, as well.[38] The numbers reveal why charter schools have been described as "the most rapidly growing force within the school choice movement" and, thus, why they were a readily available vehicle through which Hawaiian communities could concretely address long-standing dissatisfaction with the assimilatory, highly centralized Hawai'i public school system.[39]

The Hawai'i State Department of Education (HIDOE) is in fact *the* most centralized system in the United States, and Hawai'i is the only state in which a single district comprises the entire state system. A single board of education governs 256 conventional (noncharter) schools across the entire archipelago. Even though Hawai'i has a relatively small population, the Hawai'i Department of Education is, given its centralized nature, the tenth-largest school district in the United States. It has been argued that this centralization allows for a more equitable distribution of funding, since the HIDOE receives general funds directly from the state government, as opposed to counties supporting district schools through property taxes or other means. But it has also meant a large, expensive central bureaucracy and a hierarchical decision-making structure that has not historically nurtured robust community-level governance of neighborhood schools. Initial legislation in 1994 permitted twenty-five existing HIDOE schools to convert to "student-centered" schools that had a degree of flexibility in budgetary matters and could request exemption from certain Department of Education regulations. Even this step, which extended earlier efforts to implement school/community-based management in some schools, avoided the label *charter schools*.[40] Only two schools out of 253 in the state converted, both in affluent and predominantly white and Asian communities.[41] It wasn't until the law was modified in 1999 to allow for start-up schools that a more diverse range of communities became involved, as it would allow them to build schools from scratch rather than trying to change existing ones.

For more than fifty years, Hawai'i residents have solidly voted for Democrats, and a strong legacy of union organizing and public sector unions remains. Since the national charter school movement has been associated with Republican moves to privatize various governmental functions and to circumvent unions and collective bargaining, it is not surprising that the Democratic and Department of Education establishments in Hawai'i were wary of charter school reform at first. Thus, the Hawai'i state legislature passed in 1999 a moderate charter school law, relative to those of some other states and to the benchmarks set by the National Alliance for Public Charter Schools' model charter law. For the first ten years the key features of the Hawai'i law that demonstrated this more cautious position included (1) a cap on the number of charter schools that could exist at any given time; (2) a single authorizing (charter-granting) authority, which was originally the Hawai'i State Board of Education and then from 2007–12 the Charter School Review Panel under the authority of the board of education; (3) that collective bargaining agreements applied to charter school employees but that individual charter school boards were able to enter into supplemental agreements with specific unions; and (4) that the state did not provide access to equitable funding for facilities and capital improvement for charter schools, either in a per-pupil allocation or a separate grants program.

In 2012 the Hawai'i legislature overhauled the existing law by passing Senate Bill 2115, Relating to Charter Schools, which repeals chapter 302b of the Hawai'i Revised Statutes. The new law is specifically aimed at tightening state oversight of charter schools. As of this writing, it is too early to predict its impacts. Some of the significant changes include the following: (1) It mandates the dissolution of the Hawai'i Charter School Administrative Office (HCSAO), which provided administrative support to charter schools across the state and served as both an advocate and a monitoring body. In its place the law creates the new Public Charter School Commission, under the board of education's authority, to authorize and oversee all existing charter schools in the state. The law does not provide, however, for the new commission to have staff that supports the schools, as the HCSAO did. (2) Although the commission is the only authorizing agent as of fall 2012, the law also allows postsecondary institutions, nonprofit organizations, and state and county agencies to apply to become charter school authorizers, subject to approval by the board of education. Charter schools will now be evaluated under the terms of performance contracts made with their authorizer, and the section of the law dealing with these contracts is heavily focused on compliance. Rather than emphasizing institutional support, professional development, or community empowerment, the law emphasizes the authorizer's power to institute corrective action or school closure. (3) The law significantly alters the composition of local school boards. The intention of the 1999 law was to allow school communities to govern themselves by including representation of various constituent groups—including parents, school administrators, students, and both instructional and noninstructional staff—on a school's board. In contrast, the 2012 law requires professionalization of local charter school boards and restricts board membership to no more than 30 percent employees or relatives of employees of the school.

As of the 2011–12 school year, the size of Hawai'i's charter school system was average in comparison with those of other states and school districts.[42] The Hawai'i system, with its thirty-two start-up and conversion charter schools, seems quite modest in relation to states with the largest number of schools—numbering several hundred—such as California, Arizona, Florida, and Texas. When compared as a district, however, the Hawai'i system is ranked thirtieth among all school districts in the United States, based on the total number of students enrolled in charter schools. With over nine thousand charter school students, Hawai'i is on par with districts such as the Oakland Unified School District in California, the Denver Public School District in Colorado, Indianapolis Public Schools in Indiana, and St. Paul Public Schools in Minnesota.[43]

The Emergence of Hawaiian Culture–Based Charter Schools: The Difference between Choice and Kuleana

Whereas the broader U.S. charter school movement has largely been framed around the notion of choice, which is a market-oriented concept that centers the individual, the movement to establish and maintain Hawaiian culture–based charter schools has been framed around the notion of kuleana, which is oriented toward relational obligations as shaped by genealogy and land. The concept of kuleana permeates Kanaka 'Ōiwi society past and present. Contemporary Kanaka Maoli educator and economist Guy Kaulukukui suggests that although aloha is perhaps the most popularly recognized Hawaiian value, kuleana may be the most centrally important.[44] Often translated by combining the definitions of *rights*, *responsibilities*, and *authority* in English, the 'Ōiwi concept of kuleana also fundamentally implies genealogy and place.[45]

It not only suggests obligations and privileges but also can name the very relationship out of which such obligations and privileges might grow. A person might call a specific volcanic crater, bay, animal, or human relative their kuleana.

Nineteenth-century Kanaka historian Samuel Kamakau stresses the significance of familial lineage in determining one's kuleana.[46] Kuleana also came to be associated with rights of ownership of, access to, and private interest in land after the incorporation of Western private property norms into Hawaiian governance in the mid-1800s. For instance, the 1850 Kuleana Act allowed maka'āinana (common people of the land) to secure allodial title to lands, and these small parcels of land were and still are referred to as kuleana.[47]

Respected Hawaiian educators Eddie Kaanana and Ilei Beniamina both emphasize the continued importance of land and place to the concept of kuleana into the twentieth and twenty-first centuries. Blaich writes that when she interviewed 'Anakala (Uncle) Eddie about the meaning of kuleana, he talked immediately about the lands of an 'ohana, or extended family: "Feeding one's family, caring for one's children, and all other kuleana depended on one's ability to mālama that primary kuleana, to care for that piece of land and to make it productive."[48] Based on 'Anakala Eddie's description, Blaich argues that "in Hawaiian philosophy, rights and responsibilities are one and the same. Rights are earned only by first fulfilling responsibilities and every right or privilege comes with increased levels of responsibility. . . . All rights and responsibilities, are inextricably rooted in the land itself and in how well we care for it."[49]

From a Hawaiian point of view, kuleana is also tied to the wellbeing of the 'ohana or learning community. Becoming a contributing member of the extended family and community is an essential part of the learning process.[50] Thus, learning and knowledge are forms of privilege that come with attendant responsibilities to a larger collective. As learners master new skills they take on more complex responsibilities within the context of their learning community or 'ohana. In turn, it is through the fulfillment of more challenging duties in caring for the land and the community that they learn.

The creation of Hawaiian culture–based schools was not just an attempt to provide more choices for individual families as consumerist

units. Rather, the movement emerged out of a fundamental affirmation of the concept of kuleana as it applies to governance and education. Beniamina explains that knowing what is *not* one's kuleana is
the equally important, corresponding side of being clear about what *is*
one's kuleana:

> There is always kuleana attached to learning: sometimes one
> needs to know when to step back. If it is not your ahupua'a
> (land division usually extending from the uplands to the sea),
> not your 'ili (subdivision of an ahupua'a), not your moku (dis-
> trict), it is not even your mokupuni (island), don't maha'oi. You
> need to respect the kuleana enough to leave it be.[51]

It should not be surprising then that Hawaiian communities looked to
a decentralizing model, such as charter school reform, to disrupt the
highly centralized nature of the Hawai'i public school system.

In fact, the charter school reform movement in Hawai'i was dominated early on by predominantly Native Hawaiian communities designing Indigenous culturally based schools. The Hawai'i system is
the only state or district system in the United States in which more
than half of all charter schools are Indigenous culturally based schools.
Additionally, more than half of all charter schools in Hawai'i are on
islands other than O'ahu, by far the most populous island and the primary site of central decision making for the settler state Department
of Education bureaucracy. Thus, the movement has been shaped by
these dual efforts to decentralize and relocate local control to socially
and geographically distinct areas removed from the center of power
and to recognize the kuleana of Hawai'i's Indigenous people to design and control our own educational institutions.[52]

Given the weak embrace among Hawai'i public school administrators, union leaders, and legislators of the charter school model, Native
Hawaiian communities' support proved crucial in assuring this reform would survive as more than a passing fad. Former director of the
Hawai'i Charter Schools Administrative Office Jim Shon writes that
the charter school movement in Hawai'i "might not have taken hold as
strongly if not for the decision by leaders in the native Hawaiian community to hop on the charter bandwagon and create, for the first time,

Hawaiian-designed, Hawaiian-run schools."[53] (Apparently, Shon was unaware of nineteenth-century Hawaiian-run schools in the Hawaiian Kingdom.) Through the twentieth-century Hawaiian movements discussed, Kānaka Maoli had proved the ability to organize large numbers and to shape popular political debate. Once thirteen predominantly Hawaiian communities across four islands had invested their energies into starting charter schools, it became much less politically desirable for Hawaiʻi legislators to explicitly oppose charter school reform.[54]

The intersection of the U.S. charter school movement and the movement for Hawaiian self-determination can be tracked back to Hawaiian educators Kū and Nālei Kahakalau. Kū Kahakalau's dissertation recounts the story of their move to a rural part of Hawaiʻi Island, where they began to blend their kuleana of teaching at a local high school and of restoring and maintaining loʻi kalo in Waipiʻo Valley.[55] Several years of conducting Hawaiian-language and cultural immersion summer camps led them to create a school within a school at the local district public school. The limits of that model became apparent relatively quickly, however, and by 1998 the Kahakalaus had come together with a group of other families who were "dissatisfied with the present choices [in schools]" and formed the Kanu o ka ʻĀina Learning ʻOhana (KALO).

By that time, Hawaiʻi state law did allow for conversion charter schools, but the notion of charters was still virtually unknown by the general public in Hawaiʻi or by most Hawaiian educators. Kū was introduced to the model of charters—with their relative curricular and budgetary autonomy—by a member of her dissertation committee. She then pursued the idea through her own research. She saw freedom and possibility in the idea of a start-up charter school that would allow KALO to

> implement a multi-age, K–12 model similar to our Kūkulu
> Kumuhana Immersion camps. At the same time, Department
> of Education funding would give us long-term stability and
> assure that all our employees would be State employees with
> union wages and full benefits.[56]

Within the year the Kahakalaus would successfully lobby for start-up charter school legislation, receive board of education approval for the first start-up Hawaiian-focused charter school, and travel to numerous Hawaiian communities on multiple islands to share their ideas and inspire others to start their own schools. If not for their efforts in sharing and disseminating the knowledge about the legislation and about the mechanics of how to apply for a charter and start a school, many of the communities who founded Hawaiian-focused charter schools would not have made the small window in which to apply for charters before the cap of twenty-five schools was reached.[57] Kū Kahakalau became the founding director of Kanu o ka 'Āina, the first Hawaiian culture–based charter school, and Nā Lei Na'auao, the Native Hawaiian charter school alliance.

What was apparent in the early crossings of the Hawaiian movement with the charter school reform movement was that Hawaiian charter school founders were not driven by a passion for the charter school model as an educational reform, per se. Rather, founding educators and families repeatedly described their work as part of a kuleana to find better ways to nurture the well-being of 'Ōiwi youth, communities, and culture into the future. Many also highlighted the failure of the state's mainstream public education system to live up to its kuleana to provide meaningful and equitable educational experiences for its students, particularly its Indigenous students.

Many Hawaiian charter school founders articulated our entry into charter school reform as an exercise in Indigenous self-determination and liberation, a process of developing and implementing Hawaiian-designed and Hawaiian-controlled education. Kahakalau connected the movement to establish Hawaiian charter schools and to articulate "liberatory Hawaiian education" with transnational Indigenous movements for educational self-determination and sovereignty:

> While in Indian Country, Indian control of Indian education is already decades old, here in Hawai'i the notion that Hawaiians should and can create and eventually control our own comprehensive system of Hawaiian education has only recently surfaced. . . . Nā Lei Na'auao members are actively pursuing this quest, joining Indigenous educators from around the world, in declaring that different nations have different conceptions of things, and that our ideas of education are different from those

of the haole colonizers. Furthermore, we are asserting that as
Native educators, it is not only our Indigenous right, but our
duty, to both our ancestors and our descendants, to contribute
to the collective struggle for Hawaiian self-determination, by
working towards the liberation of Native Hawaiian students
from the present system of education, which is based entirely
on Western paradigms and Western traditions. Most importantly, by establishing Hawaiian charter schools throughout
the archipelago, Hawaiians are actually proving that Native
Hawaiians can create, implement and evaluate our own models
of education, that we can design and utilize our own research
methodologies, and define our own epistemologies, and that
we can work together to establish our own, comprehensive,
Native-controlled system of education, as we assert out Indigenous right as Hawai'i's Native people.[58]

Kahakalau's language, even when using English, demonstrates these
interconnected notions of rights, responsibilities, and authority embedded in the concept of kuleana.

It is also important to note that Kahakalau and others have taken,
as part of their kuleana to Hawaiian education, the responsibility of
standing in solidarity with other Indigenous people asserting their
powers over education. In 1999, the same year the Hawai'i settler state's
legislature passed the law opening the door to start-up charter schools,
Indigenous educators from around the world gathered in Hilo, Hawai'i,
at the World Indigenous Peoples' Conference on Education (WIPCE).
At that meeting Indigenous educators, including Kahakalau, formally
finalized and endorsed the *Coolangatta Statement on Indigenous Peoples'
Rights in Education*, which is based on the central principle that "Indigenous Peoples have the inalienable right to be Indigenous, which includes the right to self-determination."[59] The statement affirms that
the reclamation and revitalization of Indigenous educational systems is
a crucial part of self-determination and decolonization.

Just as Hawaiian charter schools were first being initiated, the 2000
U.S. Supreme Court's *Rice v. Cayetano* decision made stunningly clear
the stakes and importance of asserting Hawaiian self-determination
and status as a political, not a racial, group. Harold F. Rice, descendant

of a white American missionary settler family, had challenged the constitutionality of Hawaiian-only voting in Office of Hawaiian Affairs (OHA) elections. The OHA was established by the State of Hawai'i in 1978 to hold title to all property set aside or conveyed to it through the 1959 Admission Act and to use the income derived from public trust lands for the benefit of native Hawaiians. Participation in OHA elections had previously been restricted to anyone who could trace their ancestry to the Indigenous people who resided in Hawai'i prior to 1778—the arrival of Captain James Cook. The plaintiff, represented by attorney John Goemans, framed Hawaiians as a racial minority rather than an Indigenous people or a national group with collective rights, and he argued that the voting provisions were racially discriminatory under the U.S. Constitution. As the defendant, the State of Hawai'i argued that the limitation on the right to vote was based not on race but on the unique status of Hawaiian people as legally defined beneficiaries of the trust. The U.S. Supreme Court found in Rice's favor and opened elections for trustees of the OHA to all Hawai'i residents.[60] But as Hawaiian scholar Kēhaulani Kauanui argues, one of the primary problems was that neither the United States nor the State of Hawai'i recognized the political sovereignty of the Hawaiian nation.[61] The decision thus perpetuated a long history of settler state laws imposing definitions of Hawaiian identity upon Kānaka Maoli. Among the key aspects of the ruling, the court's majority discounted Hawaiian cultural reckonings of identity based on genealogy. The law apprehended Hawaiians as a racial group rather than a national or Indigenous people with political standing. The decisions also powerfully reminded us that debates about Hawaiian collective identity and culture reflect contestations for control of lands and resources, as well as bodies and minds. With the Rice decision, the last vestige of electoral control over resources that Kānaka Maoli could collectively exercise within the settler state system was immediately dissolved.

The Birth of Hālau Kū Māna

Understanding the precarious and paradoxical nature of enacting educational self-determination within the context of settler state structures, those of us who participated in founding Hālau Kū Māna public charter school felt a deep sense of kuleana to address the conditions of our youth within the mainstream educational system. The status and health of our youth was too pressing to ignore, so a strategic move was made to work within settler state structures. Those of us who were part of the applicant group for HKM's charter saw our collective kuleana as twofold: to address the immediate needs of 'Ōiwi youth shamefully underserved by the mainstream system and to contribute toward a longer-term goal of building a comprehensive schooling system grounded in 'Ōiwi culture that could change the mainstream system, perhaps even rendering it obsolete. In short, we hoped to redefine schooling.

It was at the June 1999 forum on charter schools and liberatory Hawaiian education, led by Kū and Nālei Kahakalau, that Keola Nakanishi and I first learned about charter schools and their possibilities. In sharing their experiences building Kanu o ka 'Āina, Kū and Nālei Kahakalau gave voice to goals we had been thinking about as young, Native educators frustrated by what we saw among our people. They talked about local community control of our educational and cultural destinies, about the connections between education for 'Ōiwi youth and the health of our lāhui, and about the value of ancestral knowledges for present and future generations. They shared that their students were not only meeting and exceeding state and national standards but also developing a deep repertoire of Hawaiian cultural knowledges, practices, and protocols, as well as a love for learning.

Starting an Indigenous culturally based school would allow us to reach out to young people who were left thirsting for 'ike Hawai'i (Hawaiian knowledge) by both mainstream public and exclusive private schools. It would also be an opportunity, as the Kahakalaus showed, to demonstrate that Hawaiian cultural education was not remedial education and that academic and cultural rigor were intertwined. The parents and young educators who formed HKM's applicant group knew at an experiential level that our Native youth were generally being neglected, if not harmed, by the mainstream school system. For some members of our small hui (group), this kuleana was very personal and close to home. It was kuleana they felt as parents and as members of predominantly Hawaiian communities nestled just ma uka (mountainward) from the urban center of Honolulu. Whereas the majority of the other Hawaiian culture–based charter schools are located in more rural communities, Hālau Kū Māna is one of only two Hawaiian culture–based charter schools operating in urban Honolulu.

When Charlotte "Coco" Needham first heard about charter schools, she was serving as president of the Maunalaha Valley Community Association and already working on initiatives to address the needs of youth in her area. Her two children were at district high and middle schools, and as both a parent and a former staff member at two Department of Education schools, Coco had witnessed too many kids "who didn't quite fit fall through the system." While working in one elementary school's office, she watched a principal make students "stand in the corner with their nose against the wall." Her concern that schools were killing students' self-esteem and desire to learn heightened when she began working at the high school near her home. Although she attempted to initiate a Hawaiian cultural enrichment program there, she was shut down:

> For kids in about their sophomore or junior years, there's a gap. . . . The kids [are] trying to come to school, but they don't really fit into the mold . . . you know, read the book, do the lessons, be quiet in class. . . . But the attitude at the school was like, "Ok, yeah, we know that there are these kids falling through the cracks, and some of them are Native Hawaiian kids, *but* unfortunately, the numbers are small because the [total percentage of Hawaiians in the school's] population is small." So we were told the numbers couldn't justify additional funding for additional programs.[62]

Thus, Coco and others began doing small-scale Hawaiian cultural enrichment projects outside of the school environment, in partnership with the Queen Liliʻuokalani Children's Center. The program targeted ʻōpio residing in Maunalaha, which Coco describes as "one of the last intact Native Hawaiian communities where descendants of the original Kānaka still reside within urban Honolulu." The goal was to involve them in the care and revitalization of the ʻāina while also teaching them about the ancestral traditions of their area.

As we began the research for our initial start-up application the statistics we examined during the visioning and design process only confirmed Coco's experiences at a wider level.[63] We were surprised to find, for example, that Honolulu public high schools had the highest drop-out rates of all districts on Oʻahu, exceeding the more rural parts of the island, which were typically thought of as Hawaiian places with low academic performance.[64] We began to articulate the special issues facing urban Hawaiian communities, including a dispersed population with a lack of cohesive support networks, social services, or easy access to the landed, natural resources that often served as sources of sustenance and healing for families and communities. We believed a school would help to address some of these needs by providing a center for community gathering and an educational option for a limited number of youth and their families who were unsatisfied with existing schools in their districts.

HKM developers knew that our single school would not be enough to address the systemic problems that the majority of Kanaka youth would still have to face within the mainstream system, either in Honolulu or across the archipelago. But we hoped that by networking with other communities doing similar work, we could collectively lay some of the groundwork upon which future generations might build. The vision dovetailed with a community school initiative started several years earlier in the Hawaiian homestead communities of Papakōlea, Kewalo, and Kalāwahine.[65] The history of organizing in these communities stretches back to the 1920s and 1930s, when residents, particularly women leaders, successfully lobbied to have these areas protected as Hawaiian Homesteads under the Hawaiian Homes Commission Act in 1934.[66] Residents continued to struggle against racism and poverty for decades. In the early 1990s, a group of homesteaders, again led by women, initiated a community school. Under the sponsorship of the Papakōlea Community Association, Kula no nā Poʻe Hawaiʻi (School for the Hawaiian People, known as Kula, for short) was dedicated in May 1993 and included enrichment classes for children and adults of Papakōlea, Kewalo, and Kalāwahine communities.[67] By 1995 Kula had received nonprofit status and rearticulated its mission as a "community-based program, exist[ing] to provide educational activities to raise literacy, increase educational experiences and promote aspirations to contribute to community."[68] Its programs included teacher-apprenticeship classes, grant-writing seminars, and summer and weekend classes in art, marine studies, school readiness, and test prep. Funded largely by limited-term federal and state grants, Kula could provide supplementary educational programs, but youth from the Papakōlea, Kewalo, and Kalāwahine communities still primarily attended the large mainstream public schools nearby.[69]

The reach of both the Maunalaha and Papakōlea programs were limited by the fact that they were not full-blown public schools with stable sources of funding and enrollment. When the opportunity to develop a charter school arose, a handful of people from each of those communities joined with a small group of young Hawaiian educators seeking to fulfill their kuleana to the well-being of the lāhui Hawaiʻi by designing and implementing innovative project-based and place-based educational programs. HKM's founding director, Keola Nakanishi, and I had begun talking about our dreams and visions for a Hawaiian culture–based school while teaching together in the summer bridge program. We were inspired as much by those bright Hawaiian students with whom we had spent a summer as by our experiences attending an exclusive private school for Hawaiian students that taught us little about living, valuing, and practicing our Indigenous heritage. Thus, we were interested in creating an alternative to the assimilationist educational practices in both public and private schools in Hawaiʻi. Keola and I were both twenty-four years old at the time, hardly feeling like we had the knowledge and experience necessary to start a school from scratch but driven by a sense of kuleana.

Keola's story of becoming the central, leading force in the creation of HKM demonstrates the commonly understood idea among many Kānaka Maoli that most often you don't chose your kuleana; your kuleana chooses you. A child of two educators, Keola cites a series of events that revealed this responsibility to him. In 1999 he had been studying oli (chant) with Kumu John Keolamakaainanakalahuiokalaniokamehamehaekolu Lake and, through Kumu Lake, was selected to represent Hawaiian youth with the first Hawaiʻi delegation to attend the annual Sovereignty Symposium convened by Native American tribal and judicial leaders.[70] The theme of the conference that year was education. Listening to numerous Indian leaders speak about their schools gave concrete dimensions to a previously abstract dream:

I remember one man who was the superintendent of all the Native American schools in the southeast U.S. He gave a presentation that showed a lot of what he had done and gone through to build his kuleana and kūlana, and he described what these schools were able to achieve and accomplish. After the presentation he spent time talking to two of us who were the youngest participants, and he encouraged us to start our own schools. He was really dead serious about it.[71]

As Keola sat alone in the Tulsa airport awaiting his flight back to Hawai'i a tornado hit the runway, delaying his flight for eight hours and creating chaos in the airport. He says, however, that it gave him a prolonged period of solitude and calm amid the rush of strangers around him, during which the mana (power) and the mana'o (thoughts, ideas) shared by leaders at the Sovereignty Symposium could sink into his na'au (gut). His story was one of many I heard throughout my research that recognized natural events, such as storms, as a means by which ancestors and lands communicated and created the space for human reflection, response, and action.

After Keola's return flight, the pace of events at home quickened. Immediately upon arriving, he found a note I had left him telling him to meet me at a forum on liberatory Hawaiian education at the Center for Hawaiian Studies. It was the session hosted by Kū and Nālei Kahakalau. Keola remembers:

It was definitely no coincidence. . . . I didn't even put away my bags. . . . Literally upon arrival, I found myself in this forum surrounded by people of action and experience in Hawaiian education. And as I listened to Kū's message it was one that your mind and your na'au could not deny was resounding of truth and pono.

Within the month our small group of Native educators and community organizers, known as Mana Maoli, submitted a letter of intent to apply for a charter. Shortly thereafter, we met representatives from Maunalaha and Papakōlea, and these communities joined in support, becoming the home communities for Hālau Kū Māna. By the end of

FIGURE 2. *Founding HKM director Keola Nakanishi stands* (left) *holding a ti-leaf plant overhead for his kumu John Keola Lake* (center). *Nakanishi served as the director of Hālau Kū Māna from 2000 to 2008. Kumu Lake served as a member of the founding advisory board and helped establish some of the school's cultural protocols in the opening years. Photograph courtesy of Hālau Kū Māna New Century Public Charter School.*

the summer, we had outlined the educational program and governing structure of the school in our formal application for federal start-up monies.[72]

The next year and a half was devoted to more detailed planning, specifically the preparation of the Detailed Implementation Plan (DIP) that was the basis for the Hawai'i State Board of Education's decision on whether to grant us a charter. Months of work without pay went by, since there was a significant gap between the time our letter of intent was submitted and when the start-up monies were awarded. Even after those monies came through and a paid core group of planners was brought on board, resources were incredibly tight. Work was done out of a couple of people's homes. The same piece of chart paper was used for several meetings in a row. Keola and Kalama Cabigon volunteered their time to teach Hawaiian-language classes in Papakōlea as a way to reach out to and recruit potential students and families. Had it not been for the personal commitments and sacrifices of the early planners, the school would never have gotten off the ground.

The biggest challenge was, however, securing facilities for a school of approximately sixty-five sixth through twelfth graders, plus teachers and office staff. The Hawai'i charter law made (and still makes) no provision for facilities, and this was a huge hurdle for all the start-up schools. Two factors became crucial in allowing the school to come to fruition. First, the Center for Hawaiian Studies (CHS) at the University of Hawai'i at Mānoa agreed to partner with HKM, providing some offices and two covered spaces that could be used as classrooms until a permanent home could be secured.[73] CHS had won its own fight for a building only less than a decade before, and the facility, named Kamakakūokalani, had opened a few years prior to their offer to HKM. Second, HKM successfully applied for and received grant monies under the Native Hawaiian Education Act for a three-year project called Kilolani. The grant provided funding for curriculum development and for the construction of a double-hulled sailing canoe that would be used as an outdoor classroom in conjunction with the project's hands-on math and science-based curriculum focusing on Hawaiian navigation and voyaging. Thus, HKM developers were able to build directly from gains made by an earlier generation of educators who had fought for physical space and monetary resources to support Hawaiian education—work that had to be initiated before we could even know if we were going to receive the charter to operate.

The hope of building a school to strengthen Hawaiian communities, as well as foster individual student achievement through schooling, pervaded Hālau Kū Māna's opening ceremonies and 'aha'aina (feast) in 2001 at the Kamakakūokalani Center for Hawaiian Studies. Held on a Friday evening two weeks before the first day of school, the event was made possible through the planning, labor, and donations of parents and other community members who felt connected to and invested in the success of this new school.

Kumu John Keola Lake and his hālau led the opening protocols— a series of oli asking entrance for the procession of HKM staff, students, and 'ohana to the host campus, giving honor to the ancestors of that place, and publicly declaring the identity of the HKM group as

FIGURE 3. *In this photo from HKM's first year of operation, Pōmaikaʻi Freed (left) and Pono Batalona (right) discuss the story of George Helm and the Protect Kahoʻolawe ʻOhana with their kumu Keoni Wilhelm. They and their siblings were among the founding families of Hālau Kū Māna. The Kamakakūokalani Center for Hawaiian Studies provided space as an indoor learning site that year. Photograph by the author.*

a Hawaiian learning community. Hoʻokupu (offerings) were placed at the ahu (altar). The staff and students together planted forty stalks of kī and several loulu palms on the slope just outside Hālau o Haumea, the open-air hall that served as the space for the feast that night and would serve as a classroom throughout the rest of the year. When the last handful of soil had been patted firmly into the ground and each stalk stood without human support, music began. The parent committee had provided dinner for 300 people almost exclusively through their own personal donations of food, supplies, and labor, including the roasting of a 600-pound pig. Teachers, parents, and family friends donated several hours of live musical entertainment and DJ services at no cost to the school or any of the guests at the celebration.

As people lined up to make their plates at the buffet, I stood outside the hālau, looking on with Kumu Kanalu Young, professor of Hawaiian studies and a member of HKM's advisory council. From our vantage point just outside the main centers of action, we watched 'ōpio preparing plates for their kūpuna who could not stand in the long line. We heard animated conversations between people who sat at the long lū'au tables. And we smiled at seeing children running along the banks of the lo'i kalo below Haumea, chasing ducks and poking their toes into the water. In this stolen moment of repose, we caught our breaths and reflected on the stunning human reality that this event brought to months of discussion about and planning for the opening of Hālau Kū Māna.

"Tonight," he said, "I feel a deeper sense of community than I have ever felt before at the [Center for Hawaiian Studies]."

His comment surprised me. Kumu Kanalu had been working at the center years before they had a permanent building. He had witnessed firsthand the struggle to secure this building and to grow the university program. He had attended countless forums, workshops, classes, and parties in this very space. Yet this event was different, he told me, explaining that he'd felt it before even entering the building complex from the parking lot. Maybe it was all the teenagers hanging out on the steps at the front of the center, he laughed.

Kumu Kanalu mused that at its best, the hālau was made up of all the intergenerational relationships among everyone present that night. "From the youngest generation like [your daughter] Kaiakahinali'i to the eldest kupuna," he said, "*this* is what gives life to our work. You must be sure to include that in your writing."

He did not specify whether the hālau he was referring to was Hālau Kū Māna, the Center for Hawaiian Studies, or Kumu Lake's Hālau Mele (in which Kanalu was a student of oli). But I believed then and now that Kumu Kanalu was referencing all of these hālau—a brand new public secondary school, a state university, and an independent practitioner group—and the intersecting work among them. The connections and relationships constituted those hālau and enabled them, as institutions, to build community and contribute to Hawaiian survivance. Our conversation was abruptly interrupted by one of the many logistical details demanding my attention that evening. As the night wore on, many of the elders got tired and went home. Tables were cleared away; the lights dimmed; and the hālau began to fill with all the 'ōpio who had stayed primarily at the outskirts throughout the early part of the evening. This house of Hawaiian learning lit up with flashing red, green, and blue disco lights that blurred the boundary between school and community as the 'ōpio skanked to Hawaiian-style reggae deejayed by one of their fathers. The students and their families, most of whom had not previously spent a significant amount of time on the university campus, had completely taken ownership of the hālau with their presence. I felt overcome with joy. Kumu Kanalu's words danced at the back of my mind. They have never left me. A school, a hālau, is not constituted by its buildings but by the life in the relationships of the people and the place.

Conclusion

In this chapter I chart some of the genealogical connections—political, intellectual, and familial—between the efforts to build Hawaiian culture–based charter schools and larger Hawaiian struggles for land, cultural persistence, and political self-determination. Education has been a central part of poststatehood Hawaiian social movements, whether self-education aimed at filling gaps left by public and private schools, popular education to raise consciousness about the historical and contemporary injustices the Hawaiian nation has faced, or efforts to create alternatives to the islands' system of formal education. As in many nonviolent movements, Kānaka Maoli have looked to education as perhaps *the* primary way to organize and inspire. It is the interdependent relationships among social movements and formal institutions that in Kumu Kanalu's words, bring life to these schools. From an Indigenous perspective, it is important to acknowledge, celebrate, and continue to tell the stories of such births and multigenerational efforts.

At the same time, it is necessary to keep in view the tensions between the two movements, with such distinct trajectories, that came to be articulated in the emergence of Hawaiian culture–based charter schools. Both the Hawaiian movement and the U.S. charter school movement have valued local, community-based power and decision making. Space within the charter school framework has allowed predominantly Kanaka Maoli communities to found schools in which we can have some measure of autonomy over what is taught and how it is taught. At the same time, the U.S. charter school movement significantly differs from Hawaiian nationalist movements in that it does not in any significant way reckon with the historical and contemporary conditions of settler colonialism. Yet it is through such historically situated systems of power that inequalities within schools have been produced. If one of the primary goals of school reform debates in the U.S. charter school movement is to find ways to address persistent inequalities, then there must be a reckoning with ongoing settler-colonial relations. These conditions cannot continue to be ignored in debates about charter schools or school reform more generally. The Hawaiian movement, like the social movements of other Indigenous and oppressed peoples, has insisted that true change and justice requires confronting the ways history matters in the present.

If we do not maintain view of the tensions between these two movements, we risk reducing the contribution of Indigenous culture–based charter schools to a choice on a multicultural buffet of school options. The emergence of Hawaiian charter schools should not be seen simply as an expression of school choice, market diversity, or civil rights. Such collapsing of the complexities of these schools would parallel the kinds of master narratives surrounding the 1959 Hawai'i Admission Act.

Existing literature on charter schools circulating within a U.S. context frames schools like HKM and its sibling Hawaiian culture–based charter schools as "ethnocentric charter schools."[74] This terminology is both imprecise and inappropriate. At the most basic level, it is inappropriate because as Indigenous scholars have argued, self-definition is critical to our survival. Not a single Hawaiian culture–based school defines itself in any of its public documents as "ethnocentric." Such labeling ignores the fact that mainstream schooling is itself a cultural and a political process that maintains white privilege precisely through claims to a nonethnocentric universal. This is why it is necessary to pay closer attention to the tensions and incommensurabilities between the Hawaiian movements that birthed Hawaiian schools like HKM and the charter school framework, which remains squarely within a U.S.-national frame.

Moreover, as I show in subsequent chapters, Hawaiian charter school educators were striving to articulate deeper and more expansive cultural identities and collectives based upon a foundation of appreciating and practicing Hawaiian culture. It is simply inaccurate to see this cultural and educational work as isolationist retreat into ethnic enclaves or as separatist moves to hunker down into tribal forms of belonging and exclusion. In my research I saw teachers and students at HKM make cultural crossings every day, cultivating connections with Native peoples of Oceania and the Americas, as well as to non-Indigenous peoples, cultures, and epistemologies. By recentering Hawaiian genealogical connection and kuleana to ʻāina and to local, regional, and international communities, the work of HKM educators actually exposes the provincialism of American-style education under a settler state in Hawaiʻi. In chapter 2, I show that what limited the transformative power of Indigenous education at HKM was not the Hawaiian-cultural focus but the settler state's regimes of accountability that worked to contain and reassimilate educators' liberatory visions.

TWO

Self-Determination within the Limits of No Child Left Behind

Native Hawaiians and our communities have the right and the ability to create and implement our own systems of learning to fulfill our self-determined needs, values, priorities, and learning styles; to provide ourselves an equal opportunity to thrive and succeed according to our standards.

▪ Hālau Kū Māna's Detailed Implementation Plan,
prepared for the school's charter application

Policing and Resisting Settler State Safety Zones

In Hālau Kū Māna's second year of operation, I advised the first graduating class on the creation of a senior video documenting their reflections on their life journeys to that point. Each of the six ʻōpio grew up in different neighborhoods in Honolulu and spent the majority of their school years in the mainstream public system. Their most recent experiences prior to HKM had been at one of the large, public Honolulu high schools founded during the early territorial period and named for powerful white American men who were crucial in executing the U.S. annexation of Hawaiʻi and leading the newly formed settler state. For all of the students' families, moving to a brand-new school that did not yet have a proven record of success nor a permanent facility nor equitable state funding was a huge risk, but the potential rewards of becoming part of a small learning community that promised place-based and project-based education grounded in Native Hawaiian culture outweighed the risks for them. Five of the six seniors were joined at HKM by their siblings and/or cousins, and as such, their families formed a core of the school's first sixty-five students. Though HKM welcomed students of all ethnic backgrounds, it was the case that all of the first graduating seniors proudly claimed Kanaka Maoli ancestry.

Each week, the ʻōpio selected a location where we would film. The only parameter I gave them was to choose spots that had some significance to them and were within driving distance. Their choices of locations consistently demonstrated that urban Kanaka Maoli youth could be deeply connected to ʻāina even while surrounded by the traffic and built environment common to any large metropolis. One student took us to his favorite surf spot, known for its steep shore break. Another took our group to a ridgeline from which we could see the trails he and his dad hiked throughout his childhood. An upland oasis where one ʻōpio had constructed a shelter out of bamboo as a retreat from school, a little-known park that provided one ʻōpio and her friends with a perch to look down upon the city, a chilly mountain pool, a high coastal ledge good for launching one's body into the deep blue ocean below, these places were the ones they wanted to remember themselves in, and their familiarity with these places demonstrated the land-based relationships and literacies they had developed in spite of their schooling in institutions that did not value such knowledge and experience.

The only week they selected a set of buildings as their significant site was when they decided to return to the high school that four of them had attended prior to coming to Hālau Kū Māna. The school's fences, massive concrete structures, and security office functioned to contain and manage its over 2,500 students; these were physical manifestations of the settler state's disciplining and assimilationist practices. We did not schedule a formal appointment with the school, as I wanted our visit to happen organically. I wanted the ʻōpio's memories and experiences to shape the images they would capture. So I followed the students' lead into and through the institution, attentive to the way they entered and to what they highlighted and narrated during our journey. Their path highlighted the margins, the cracks, and the holes in the school's literal and figurative fences.

As I turned our vehicle down the highway exit ramp to their former school they asked if we could stop at the small park located immediately in front of the freeway cutoff and just behind the school. We parked, sat down at a picnic bench, and turned on the camera.

"This is Peter Buck park, where we used to go all da time fo cut school ʻcuz our school is only right there," one of the young men said.

"Yeah, I like to go over hea, but sometimes, the cops, they like boddah us. So we would jes go hide."

Two of the ʻōpio lived for most of their lives within walking distance from this park and the school. Ikaika and Napua recalled coming to play here as children and, later, taking smoke breaks here as adolescents.[1] And so we entered the school through the back gate, following the route students often took to escape the school grounds for such breaks. As the ʻōpio recalled the way security guards closely patrolled the campus borders and checked IDs, I felt a wave of nervousness wash over me. Would we be treated as truants, as trespassers? Kainalu, one of the boys (who during his last year enrolled at this large institution had 160 absences out of 180 instructional days), reassured us in his usual confident yet playful manner, "We jus tell ʻum what we really doing: we doin' it fo' school! We tell ʻum we graduating. Dey goin' be happy!" In my mind I was sure he was right; after all, I was a teacher. But at the same time, I felt the physical structures and threat of surveillance interpellating us as somehow delinquent.

It was midmorning as we walked through the campus, the students pointing out and recording various features. Passing a hole in the chain link fence, Kainalu demonstrated how a student might run through it. Ikaika narrated the reenactment, "Ho, ho, security! Run! Run!" A few minutes later, Ikaika slowed by an empty, fenced-off swimming pool. "That's our pool. *Their* pool," he corrected himself with extra emphasis. "But no more water. Nevah have water. It's all corroded."

We neared the first classroom building, but the ʻōpio were not interested in entering any classrooms or visiting any teachers, save their Hawaiiana class. As Kainalu crossed the field to see if anyone was in their old classroom—which looked exactly like the dozens of others in the building, except for a red and white floral-printed cloth hanging knotted in the open doorway—we stayed put. Napua zoomed in on the entryway from afar while she spoke, "This was our Hawaiiana class. This is the only class on the whole campus that teaches anything to do with Hawaiians. Only one class."

The one adult whom they were interested in visiting was Officer Chun, head of security, a man in his fifties who likely was of an ethnic mixture stemming from Hawaiʻi's plantation days and similar to the students and myself—Native Hawaiian and Chinese and, perhaps, some

Portuguese, Filipino, or Puerto Rican ancestry, as well. A student-created painting of a Hawaiian flag and the eight largest islands hung on his office wall, indicating that perhaps Officer Chun shared a pride in his Hawaiian identity similar to his interviewers'. Despite the fact that a couple of the 'ōpio vividly remembered being punished by Officer Chun for excessive tardies or other offences, they were genuinely happy to see him, and the feeling seemed mutual. Two students took the lead in interviewing him as Ikaika worked the camera, focusing on the photocopied images of weapons and small sacks of illegal drugs confiscated on campus, the group of mainly brown-skinned young men serving detention by cleaning up the school's front lawn, and, finally, the Hawaiian flag in the painting.

Before we left, Napua and I walked over to the school's large stone sign fronting the largest hall and facing the main street. We had finally worked our way from the back gates to the front of the campus. I started filming, and she looked directly into the camera and said, "Here we are at McCarthy High School. I don't know what else to say about this school. I went to McCarthy for three years, stayed in the same grade the whole time."[2] She paused, looking back at the buildings behind her. "Yup," she said, and looked straight into the camera and nodded, as though there was nothing else to say. Yet it seemed important for her to know that someone heard and captured this statement, evidence of both the institution's presence in her life and its utter inability to nurture meaningful, positive growth.

The journey we recorded together spoke volumes, however. School had been a place these students tolerated and survived. They experienced their former school as rundown, devoid of affirmation of their Hawaiian identities, and alienating because it was both boring and oppressive. The path they led me through into McCarthy High demonstrated that they were all too familiar with the institution's inadequacies. It was experienced more as a carceral space than as a place of learning. They knew they were required by law to be there. They saw themselves reflected in the security guards hired to keep them on campus. They often tried to get out anyway, coming in and out through the gaps at the margins.

This trip reminded me of the reasons why we created Hālau Kū Māna. In the short term, our small group of educators and parents wanted to break out of settler state–enforced zones that were neither safe nor stimulating for our Native youth. Instead, we aimed to build an educational space where students could feel nurtured yet challenged and where Kānaka would be as likely to be kumu (teachers, sources) and school leaders as we were to be security guards and bus drivers. In the long term, we aimed to intervene in the larger public education system, not just creating a single refuge in which to hide out but inciting and inspiring deep currents of change. Over its first decade, an average of 92 percent of HKM's enrolled students has been Kanaka Maoli. As written in HKM's original application for start-up federal funding:

> We, as the visionaries and planners of Hālau Kū Māna, aim for systemic change in the educational practices and institutions that service both Hawaiian and non-Hawaiian students. Hālau Kū Māna will develop not only individual students, but communities of lifelong learners who take active part in the control of their communities.[3]

The notion of self-determination as both collective and personal empowerment characterized this vision. We believed this required a radical departure from the fences, walls, and bell schedules that kept young people cut off from their ʻāina and other storehouses of ancestral knowledge. We found, though, that the settler state had other ways of policing its safety zones—not only chain link fences but also the No Child Left Behind Act, which was authorized just as start-up charter schools were opening in Hawaiʻi. This chapter explores the tensions between educators' assertions of self-determination and the settler-colonial forces that constrain them.

Safety Zones and Self-Determination

In chapter 1, I discuss the emergence of Native Hawaiian charter schools at the intersection of two distinct movements: (1) a constellation of Hawaiian mobilizations for aloha ʻāina, self-determination, and sovereignty and (2) educational reform initiatives based on the charter school model. The convergence of these movements produced a moment of new and radical possibility, as Indigenous communities could take direct, local control by starting their own charter schools. Predominantly Kanaka Maoli communities accounted for more than half of those groups who initiated public charter schools in Hawaiʻi, explicitly asserting Indigenous rights to educational self-determination. As some leaders of the Hawaiian charter school movement put it, these new schools provided spaces of liberation from the failures of assimilatory schooling, as well as the inadequacies of earlier models of Hawaiian studies education that included representations of Kānaka Maoli without disrupting dominant epistemologies and relations of power.[4]

In this chapter I explore some of the tensions and complexities of asserting liberatory education and educational self-determination while remaining within a settler state system. Public charter schools are equipped with a greater level of autonomy in fiscal and curricular matters than earlier state and federally funded programs in Hawaiian education, but they are hardly independent.[5] We might think of this work in terms of what Bevir and Rhodes, drawing on Foucault, describe as "agency without autonomy."[6] In doing so, we can recognize the creative ways in which educators function as social actors but are still influenced by discursive frames. What are, then, the implications of talking about self-determination and liberation when these schools receive only limited autonomy within existing state structures? In the course of describing how these tensions between self-determination and assimilation (often framed as accountability) played out at HKM, I provide an overview of the school's educational program and the way it changed over the period of my research, the first ten years of the school's existence. The impacts of the ongoing suppression of Hawaiians' political sovereignty and their control of the national lands fundamental to sovereignty also become evident in HKM's story as educators struggle to maintain the vision of educational self-determination against the forced reassimilation of these spaces of radical possibility opened a decade earlier. I highlight the practices and narrative strategies HKM educators use to sustain their work in the paradoxical terrains of doing Indigenous education within the settler state's public education system. On one hand, it is important to recognize and build upon the gains that Indigenous people have made in designing and controlling our own schools and educational systems over the past few decades. It is *also* important to maintain a critical perspective with respect to the discourse of educational self-determination and to the ways such language might suggest that the assimilatory policies of the settler state are over. Self-determination cannot simply be understood as "Natives making decisions about what is best for Natives" without keeping in view the structures of power within which such decisions are made.[7]

The U.S. government's policy related to Native education—including America Indian, Alaska Native, and Native Hawaiian education—has been officially characterized as a progression "from assimilation to self-determination."[8] Though there has been a shift toward greater autonomy, largely due to the pressure generated by Indigenous social movements, the era of assimilation has by no means been left securely in the past. Both the structural *possibility* for federally funded Native educational programs, as forms of self-determination, and the structural *reassimilation* of such initiatives to the dominant settler paradigm are enabled by the very same law: the No Child Left Behind Act of 2001 (U.S. Public Law 107–110). Earlier versions of the Elementary and Secondary School Act, which were later folded into NCLB, supported the creation of American Indian, Alaska Native, and Native Hawaiian educational programs and were part of the policy shift toward promoting self-determination. The U.S. Congress passed the Indian Education Act in 1972 and the Native Hawaiian Education Act in 1988.[9] Both were folded into Title VII of NCLB. Yet the provisions enacted in 2001—which entrench particular definitions about what counts as knowledge, student success, and acceptable qualifications for teachers—act as a reassimilating force. Since NCLB's implementation, educators throughout Indian country and Hawai'i have testified that it has severely impacted the use of Native-language and Native culture–based pedagogies in schools serving Native communities, thus directly contradicting the intent of educational self-determination and sovereignty.[10]

In recent years scholars studying Indian education have complicated the assimilation to self-determination theory in light of NCLB's implementation and tribal sovereignty. In looking at a Navajo case, Winstead and her colleagues argue that "NCLB further limits the already contested sovereignty tribes exercise over how, and in what language, their children are educated."[11] They point out that one of the complicating factors is the radical difference in theory and practice between self-determination and sovereignty. Federal policy has constructed self-determination as Native nations' power over particular domains (like education), but granted by and subject to the plenary power of the U.S. Congress. Sovereignty refers to the inherent power that resides within those nations and "thereby encompasses much more than federal definitions of self-determination."[12] Native nations insistently exercising this authority to create Indigenous schooling shouldn't be taken as evidence that the era of assimilation is over. Rather, there has been a shift in the strategies by which settler-colonial educational regimes work to assimilate, contain, or render innocuous Native communities.

This contradictory and variable policy environment—the purported exchange of assimilation for self-determination and the gap between self-determination and sovereignty—takes on another layer for Kānaka Maoli. The U.S. seized the national lands and governing power of the independent Hawaiian Kingdom at the end of the nineteenth century.[13] Though the U.S. government apologized for this "act of war" one hundred years later, not a single acre of land nor any power of government has been restored to the Hawaiian nation. Without the resources of a national land base and the political leverage of the recognition of our sovereignty, Kānaka Maoli are in a particularly vulnerable position, compelled to rely almost completely on grants from the settler state—U.S. federal and State of Hawai'i governments—in order to provide free public education programs. In the case of Hālau Kū Māna, for instance, federal grants under the Native Hawaiian Education Act (now part of NCLB) have allowed HKM to survive in a context of the State of Hawai'i's lack of provision of adequate facilities or equitable funding.

Lomawaima and McCarty's safety zone theory is helpful for thinking about this interplay of forces. They reject the pendulum metaphor for describing historical shifts in the relationship between U.S. educational policy and Indigenous people, which, for example, could be seen as swinging from assimilation to self-determination. Rather, they call us to see a continuous and ongoing cultural and political struggle. Put plainly, "the federal government has not simply vacillated between encouraging or suppressing Native languages and cultures but has in a

coherent way . . . attempted to distinguish safe from dangerous Indigenous beliefs and practices."[14] They suggest looking at the ways U.S. educational policy has produced and policed safety zones—state-enforced
spaces for containing potentially threatening Indigenous cultural difference. Instead of looking at Indigenous educational initiatives as either
self-determining or assimilationist, attention to safety zones encour-
ages us to examine the ongoing cultural struggles within and around
Indigenous educational initiatives.[15] In what ways are cultural differences being marked, contained, and marginalized in safety zones? In
what ways do Indigenous educators, students, and their communities
contest and/or reify those boundaries?

Like Lomawaima and McCarty, I am interested in the spaces of
educational opportunity that Hawaiian educators create in spite of
settler state containment strategies and safety zones. In the following
section, I explore the ways educators at Hālau Kū Māna have articulated practices of educational self-determination—through multiple
aspects of the school's organization and curriculum—that exceed U.S.
policy–based constructions of self-determination. But I am also interested in the forces that surveil and work to fence Indigenous education
within zones deemed safe by settler state power structures. Thus, I
analyze the assimilative forces enforced by the settler state and internalized by school personnel as HKM went into restructuring under
the No Child Left Behind Act. The chapter then returns to articulations of self-determination and sovereignty within HKM educators'
discourse to consider the sources of their resilience against such powerful, stifling forces.

Self-Determination in HKM Practice

The language of self-determination has been powerful for Indigenous
and other oppressed or subordinated people because it carries the dual
connotation of both individual and collective empowerment, both
"rooted in the inherent sovereignty of Native nations."[16] The health
of the self as individual and the self as a collective are intertwined and
reflected in one another. As Hokulani Aikau puts it, *self-determination*
is a term that "can encapsulate structural changes such as political
struggles for decolonization and independence as well as personal

struggles to perpetuate cultural practices."[17] This dual meaning is evidenced within native education to refer both to community control of programs, schools, research initiatives, and educational systems and to the decisions and behaviors of individual students who, for example, resist school environments hostile to their cultures and identities with an array of strategies.[18]

Throughout the first decade of Hālau Kū Māna's existence, teachers and school leaders consistently and across the board affirmed that they saw their personal and collective work as part of a broader movement for Hawaiian self-determination. The terms *self-determined* or *self-determination* appear consistently in the school's founding and governing documents. In my focused interviews with teachers over a ten-year span of the school's existence, almost every teacher affirmed that they understood HKM as an expression of Hawaiian self-determination, although it was not a term widely used in day-to-day interactions at the school. Rather, it was embedded in practice and emerged more explicitly when people were in reflective modes outside of the immediate demands of the school environment. In this section and the next, I discuss some of the ways self-determination emerged in practice throughout HKM's early years.

To emphasize the ways educators understood the collective sovereign self, this discussion is structured around a theorization of HKM's community offered by HKM's founding director, Keola Nakanishi. A tireless and charismatic leader, Keola frequently offered acronyms or mnemonic devices to articulate the school's mission and vision to staff, prospective parents, and partners (e.g., "the ABCs of Hālau Kū Māna—academics, behavior, culture," or "innoNative," pedagogies that offered new ways of teaching and learning based on ancestral, Indigenous practices). The weekend after HKM first opened for students, Keola and I sat on a quiet beach, debriefing each other on the first few days. After spending nearly two years in planning, it was surreal to finally have 'ōpio present! We marveled at how inexplicably wonderful and energizing the students were. Amid our discussions about the continued struggle to find out our total per-pupil allocation from the state and about some of the sharpening differences among the staff, Keola riffed on the aspects of community he thought would be essential to develop in building this school: paʻa, pilina, and pono.

Pa'a: Land and Facilities as a Foundation

Pa'a, or kumupa'a, were, for Keola, the necessary land-based foundations. He focused on the land and physical infrastructure that would
allow our young community to survive and grow. This was a particularly salient concern, since HKM did not have a permanent campus to
call home. The State of Hawai'i's charter school law contained no provision for facilities, and thus start-up schools were forced to dig into
the already less-than-equitable operations budgets to try to purchase
or lease and renovate facilities within the general real estate market.
While some schools were able to rent facilities from their first year
onward, many schools survived for multiple school years by holding
classes wherever they could do so for no cost, sometimes making agreements with nonprofit organizations to share space or sometimes just
holding classes at public parks. For HKM this meant a complete relocation of the central campus four times during the first six years, and at
each of the first three temporary sites, there was always the sense that
we would have to pick up and move again at a moment's notice, sometimes in the middle of the school year. These conditions evidenced not
only inequity for Hawai'i's charter schools but the ongoing ramifica-
tions of settler state control over the Hawaiian national land base.

During HKM's first several years, almost every teacher and alaka'i
saw the school's lack of a permanent home as the biggest hurdle and
hardship. For the first three years of operation, the temporary central
sites did not have enough space for all the students (an average of sixty-
five 'ōpio) to have class at the same time. Office, storage, and learning
spaces at various locations were pieced together. Vans transported students back and forth between primary and satellite classrooms five to
thirty-five minutes apart. The main office, a temporary offering from
the University of Hawai'i's Center for Hawaiian Studies, was located
in a modest space meant for independent student study. Shaped like
a Kūpau moon (a week into the moon's cycle), the area served as an
admissions and records office, a computer lab, a counseling office,
teachers' storage space, a library, and a mail and photocopying room.
A small closet on the dark side of the moon held files, hula costumes,
dusty donated books, and large and small tools of all sorts. Teachers
were allotted a single regular-sized carrel per pair for storing all of our

curriculum materials, instructional aids, student work, and personal belongings. The few offices where one could close a door for private meetings or quiet work time were the size of an average closet and could fit no more than a file cabinet and two chairs. More than fifteen people were daily packed into this tiny space, and sometimes a tech class would be squeezed in, as well. Kumu and haumāna (students) made the best of the situation, however, and regularly holding classes at various outdoor learning sites made sense in implementing the school's hands-on, place-based curriculum. Like other charter school leaders, Keola reminded state authorities about this problem year after year, writing in HKM's end-of-the-year report to the board of education:

> Imagine how far we could go, if as a public school we were granted both equal funding and facilities, as is automatically provided to other public schools? . . . We are a public school, our families pay taxes, and our keiki deserve the same safety, resources, and opportunities as other keiki at mainstream public schools, which are underfunded themselves.[19]

The situation of landlessness faced by many Hawaiian charter schools is an issue not only of needing to provide equal funding and facilities to Hawaiian schools because Native Hawaiians are part of the state's general public but also of the painful irony left out of HKM's reports to the state—so as not to threaten an already tense relationship—that the settler state itself functions on landed resources illegally seized from the internationally recognized, sovereign, and independent Hawaiian Kingdom and its people. Thus, the situation of landlessness faced by many Hawaiian charter schools mirrors the collective condition of Kānaka Maoli, who remain deprived of political control of our national land base.[20]

Securing a land base—a site—was Keola's priority in increasing the school community's capacity for self-determination. As Hawai'i's first decade of the charter school experiment wore on, many of the Hawaiian-focused schools were able to secure long-term agreements with private foundations, like the Kamehameha Schools, or with different state departments, such as the Department of Hawaiian Homelands or the Department of Land and Natural Resources (although rarely with the Department of Education) for central campus facilities, outdoor learning sites, and/or supplemental capital improvements funding. Owing largely to the leadership of Keola and HKM's former Alakaʻi Hoʻoulu Kaiāulu (ʻohana and community relations director) Lesley "Micky" Huihui, an agreement for the long-term usage of a parcel of Makiki land controlled by the Hawaiʻi State Department of Land and Natural Resources was finally secured in 2007. The area was identified as an underused public park that had actually become a site known for drug transactions and illegal dumping. It was a win-win situation for the HKM community to clean up and repurpose the strip of land that lay on the banks of a free-flowing stream between the two predominantly Kanaka Maoli communities that HKM had years earlier identified as its host communities, Maunalaha and Papakōlea. Securing this agreement was a major victory for HKM, yet the possibility still remains that the State of Hawaiʻi could terminate the school's lease without recourse, since it maintains ultimate authority.

Pilina: School and Community Relationships

Pilina was the network of human connections that would make up the HKM ʻohana—the extended family of students, families, school staff, and volunteers, as well as all people who might support Hawaiian culture–based education. HKM was built on the idea of disrupting the typical boundaries between school and community, and founders envisioned the hālau more like an ʻohana than like the large, impersonal industrial age institutions that were most public secondary schools. Throughout the first decade, school–community relationships were crucial to building and strengthening our new underresourced school. Thinking beyond the boundaries of the campus and actively cultivating relationships with diverse groups was integral to the hālau's culture.

Until 2012 local community control was structured into Hawaiʻi's charter school law, which stipulated that each charter school be governed by its own local school board comprised of representatives from the school's instructional faculty, noninstructional staff, student body, parents, and head of school, as well as additional community members as desired.[21] While each state has its own laws about charter school board powers and composition, the Hawaiʻi law reflected the broadly

FIGURE 4. *Students, teachers, and parents stand around* Kānehūnāmoku, *a* wa'a kaulua kiakahi, *at her first launch from Kualoa, O'ahu, in 2002. As part of the effort to push beyond the boundaries of classroom environments,* Kānehūnāmoku *has served as an integral learning site and source for HKM's educational program. Photograph courtesy of Hālau Kū Māna New Century Public Charter School.*

accepted general philosophy that charter schools should be governed by members of their learning and geographic communities.[22] Community involvement and integration at HKM went, however, far beyond the minimum requirement of the law.

Founders and early staff members attempted to build HKM as an 'ohana. In this vein, all people of parental age—whether staff or parents of current students—were referenced in school documents and formal communications as "mākua," whereas students were referred to as "'ōpio" (youths, adolescent members of the 'ohana). Since *makua* is not a typical term of address, in day-to-day school interactions 'ōpio routinely referred to teachers and support staff as "aunty" or "uncle" (terms of respect and affection in contemporary Hawai'i).[23] The 'ōpio were distinguished as kaikaina (younger siblings) and kua'ana (elder siblings). In addition to cultivating a sense of mutual obligation between elder and younger ʻōpio members of the school community, this terminology was seen as a way to avoid labeling students according to grade levels, which we were trying to move away from. We hoped to get away from the foundational assumption of grade levels that all students at any given age should be expected to know and do the same things at the same pace. In the early years ʻōpio were sometimes grouped according to ability within their larger multiage cohort (eleven to thirteen years or fourteen to seventeen years), and they were sometimes placed in groups that included both kaikaina and kuaʻana. The notion of grade levels was, however, so deeply ingrained in most students, teachers, parents, and the larger system to which we had to translate the program that within a few years the terms came to correspond both to roles within the ʻohana and to the conventional grade levels. Sixth through eighth graders continue to be collectively called kaikaina, and high schoolers, kuaʻana, but they are also divided by grade-level cohort.

For the first several years, students were not required to call any of their teachers "kumu," except those who had gone through the formal cultural protocols of becoming a recognized kumu, or master and teacher, in their field of knowledge. Some ʻōpio referred to one or more of their teachers as "kumu," but this was left to each ʻōpio's preference. In some years I observed that there was a general tendency for ʻōpio to address more male teachers as "kumu," whereas they more frequently addressed female teachers as "aunty." This problem was stemmed in the 2010–11 school year when a new Poʻo Kumu (principal/instructional leader), Mahinapoepoe Duarte, began asking that all adult staff be addressed using "kumu" and their first name (e.g., Kumu Noelani). This caused some teachers to question the ways such a blanket practice diluted the cultural importance and stature of the term *kumu*. It also helped avoid, however, unconsciously replicating gendered colonial hierarchies, such as referring to male teachers by a more authoritative title and female teachers by a more familial one. With the new practice, all staff regardless of ethnicity, gender, age, or experience were called kumu.

In the interest of making ʻohana and community relationships central to the school's culture, HKM's founders created an alakaʻi-level (leadership-level) position specifically responsible for organizing and strengthening relationships between community members, students' families, and school staff. This investment—particularly given that money was tight—demonstrated that integrating school and community was a major priority. From 2004 to 2010, Micky Huihui served in this position of Alakaʻi Hoʻoulu Kaiāulu. She carried out responsibilities typical to a school community coordinator, such as supporting the functioning of an ʻAha Mākua (parents' council); assuring regular communication between school and students' homes through newsletters, emails, and phone trees; and organizing special events to which families and other community members were invited, such as graduation or quarterly Lā ʻOhana (family days). She was also responsible for tracking the kōkua hours (service hours) to which all families and students enrolled at the school were obligated. The data she collected demonstrates a stunning level of parental involvement through service to the school. Families regularly gave more than twice the amount of required kōkua hours per ʻohana, a significant sign of close family–school partnership.[24]

Additionally, Micky describes two significant parts of her job that would have been out of the ordinary in a mainstream secondary school setting: coordinating Friday playshops as part of the regular curriculum and organizing volunteers in the building, improvement, and maintenance of the school's auxiliary and primary learning sites. Playshops were weekly opportunities for community members with specialized knowledges to teach, with the assistance of HKM kumu, and mentor multiaged groupings of the ʻōpio. These volunteers could share their experience as practitioners, and students could elect to take different playshops from semester to semester or continue with one in order to develop more advanced skills. The playshops included a diverse range of arts and cultural options, including lomilomi (massage), ceramics, aikido, contemporary Hawaiian art, guitar, waʻa maintenance, improvisational acting, surfing, spoken-word poetry, music production, ʻAha ʻŌpio (student leadership), and Pana Oʻahu (storied places of Oʻahu), to name a few. In some cases these playshops were the launching pad for lasting mentorship connections and significant achievement. For example, one student developed a long-term passion for spoken-word poetry and became part of an interscholastic slam team that participated in and eventually won the U.S. national slam championship. Additionally, many of the volunteer artists and practitioners became more invested in the school, in public education, and in the broader movement for Hawaiian cultural revitalization. As Micky puts it, "That mākua base grew ... that community base grew. They were moved. Even people that had previously had no connection to Hawaiian education were completely moved to the point that they kept coming back."[25] For instance, many came back to assist in the preparation and building of a permanent campus—an undertaking that according to Micky would have been a "mission impossible" to complete in the six months available.

She recalls that the state's lack of provision of land and facilities (the kumupaʻa that Keola talked about) became "an incredible motivation" to mobilize existing and new community relationships in the building of a primary campus and satellite sites. In December 2006, HKM leaders received notice that the school needed to immediately vacate its location. After intense negotiation with the private landowner, the leadership was given six months to move out. Micky and Keola had to coordinate the securing of a lease and building permits, the clearing and leveling of land, and the renovation of trailers as classrooms and offices, not to mention moving all the school's furniture, files, and equipment. This daunting project was made possible by literally thousands of hours of in-kind service by church groups, athletic teams, prison inmates, families, friends, and neighbors, which Micky organized and supervised.

A few years after the school's relocation to its permanent site, I sat with her on the HKM grounds as she reflected on the lasting relationships that were built along with the campus itself. These included countless individuals and groups that were not part of what would typically be construed as the community of a neighborhood school. Yet for her these broader networks of people became part of the self-determined community through shared labor. She specifically cited a partnership with a work group of local incarcerated men as particularly "clutch," or important, and she talked about how the relationship became familial. Micky and her site development assistant, Casey Gannon, had first seen the crew cutting grass at an adjacent state park as part of their normal rounds maintaining state property. By looking at the men, Casey and Micky surmised that most of them were Kānaka (Native Hawaiians). So the two women approached them and began to tell a few of the men and the officer in charge, "Uncle" Bolo, about Hālau Kū Māna, the school's mission, and their project of building a new campus from scratch. Uncle Bolo and his crew began coming regularly, often working side by side with Micky, HKM staff, families, and other volunteers to assist in the site development. Micky motioned in an 180-degree arc toward the patches of kalo, maiʻa, and other native and edible plants sitting between the stream and one of the classroom trailers and said:

> All of this was still trees. I have this specific memory of a tree that was right between this one and that one. Uncle Clarence had tied a rope to it and was trying to pull it with his truck, trying to pull it down, and his tires were spinning out. We just couldn't get this tree down, even though it looked like it wanted to fall. These guys—maybe eight deep—they tied that rope to the tree and they *pulled* that tree down. By themselves! [She laughed heartily.] It was incredible! Then, they cut it all up and cleared it out. Man! They were awesome Kanakas, *so* helpful! And they came back every month while [the site development] was happening. . . . I ran into Uncle Bolo the other day at Foodland. Amazing, lasting collaboration, and now he's like my uncle: "How's everything going, dear? How you doing? Where you living now?" . . . Their contribution was huge. It was huge.

Micky recalled that the partnership was mutually valuable and that working alongside these men gave HKM staff and families a different perspective on incarcerated people and on labor. "They showed us that it is a pleasure to work outside, and that was really good for us," she mused. Perhaps most important, Micky's story indicated the importance of seeing our people who have been imprisoned within the settler state's system as part of our ʻohana and community and that movements for self-determination and sovereignty cannot overlook the value and power of such relationships.

Pono: Moral Affinities and Collective Obligations

The third element in Keola's theorization of a self-determined community was pono. When we talked about HKM's opening week, he used the term *pono* to refer to the moral affinities that bring people together in a common vision, and he referenced a sense of intergenerational obligation. *Pono* also refers to the kind of well-being manifested in an individual, a community, or an environment when there are balanced and just conditions, and *pono* can mean "that which is necessary for life."

That day on the beach in 2001, Keola spoke of how all members of the HKM community would "have pono to the people who came before and will come after us." HKM could become a way to honor Kānaka of the past and to prepare new generations to continue and thrive long after we were gone. In committing to learn and practice Hawaiian cultural knowledges, community members could acknowledge their place in an intergenerational continuum. In that sense our genealogical precursors and descendants *are* our pono. Remembering them brings balance. Amid stressful and contentious times, members of the HKM 'ohana have found anchorage by staying focused on a broader vision of the self in the context of longer lineages of purpose.

These elements of pono are contained within HKM's 'Ae Like, a statement of collective values and commitments signed by every member of the learning 'ohana, from students to board members (see Figure 5). The 'Ae Like, literally "collective agreement," outlines some of the central purposes and corresponding actions to which all members commit. These shared commitments are seen as "essential ingredients for building and maintaining a thriving family-oriented, community-based place of learning." The 'Ae Like consistently frames all members of the school community as an 'ohana, and a functional 'ohana requires various values outlined in the document: mālama (caring for one another), makawalu (accepting and learning multiple perspectives), laulima (cooperating), mahalo (respecting and appreciating one another), and aloha (loving one another). In a school of HKM's size, it is actually possible to "demonstrate concern, care and understanding toward all members" of that 'ohana. The values are further operationalized by requiring mākua (parents and staff) to contribute kōkua hours to the school, knowing each individual student personally, and assuring regular, timely communication between home and school. These practices help maintain pono within the community, a balanced and healthy functioning of the collective self.

'Ae Like
Collective Values and Actions

As members of Hālau Kū Māna's learning 'ohana, we recognize the following values, traits, attitudes, and actions as essential ingredients for building and maintaining a thriving family-oriented, community-based place of learning:

'Ōpio:

+ Kū i ka māna, Kūlia i ka nu'u, Kūpono – Strive for māna, reach for your highest potential, and be pono!
+ Mālama – Demonstrate concern, care, and understanding toward all members of our learning 'ohana.
+ Makawalu – Always be open to new perspectives and new ways of learning.
+ Laulima – Accept responsibilities, contribute to the 'ohana.
+ Learn and actively perpetuate Hawaiian language, culture, and values.
+ Attend Hālau EVERY DAY scheduled and on time unless there is legitimate illness, injury, or emergency.
+ Communicate with a makua any problems or frustrations concerning the Hālau, other makua, 'ōpio, or your own life situations.
+ Kōkua, Mahalo, a Aloha kekahi i kekahi – Help, respect and appreciate, and show aloha to one another.

Mākua ('Ohana, Parent/Guardian):

+ All expectations and commitments mentioned above, except for attending Hālau every day!
+ Attend Hālau Kū Māna's quarterly pā'ina, Lā 'Ohana (at least one makua per 'ohana).
+ Attend quarterly 'Ohana Conferences with staff to review your 'ōpio's progress (at least one makua per 'ohana).
+ Read memos and initial your child's assignment book daily.
+ APPRECIATE YOUR CHILD'S DAILY SUCCESS!
+ Provide input and feedback on overall well-being of your child as necessary, and return calls from HKM staff promptly.
+ Participate fully in our main annual Hō'ike FUNdraiser, and participate as much as possible in any other fundraisers.
+ Kōkua a minimum of 16 hours per year, contributing to the needs of our 'ōpio and 'ohana overall (select a minimum of 2–3 things from the 'Pehea la e kōkua ai' list that you are willing to be called on as opportunities arise; Re-admission each year is contingent upon completion of all kōkua hours.
+ Join at least one committee (this counts toward kokua hours).
+ Be familiar with and abide by HKM's 'Ohana Handbook.

Makua A'o ('calabash' parent, a.k.a. HKM Staff):

+ All expectations and commitments mentioned above.
+ Maintain passion, commitment, perseverance, and professionalism in providing the highest quality learning experience for our 'ōpio.
+ Know each student personally as an individual – for their strengths, challenges, and specialties.
+ Engage in respectful collaboration with all members of the learning 'ohana.
+ Participate fully in all required professional development events and opportunities.
+ Written and verbal evaluations prepared for each makua/ 'ōpio conference, and as necessary to monitor progress of 'ōpio.
+ Initial response to 'ōpio or mākua concerns by the same or next day.

All who choose to become a part of Hālau Kū Māna share a collective vision and mission, and as core members of this learning 'ohana, we agree to strive for and participate in the above mentioned items in every way possible, to ensure the success of our Hālau in achieving our personal and collective goals.

FIGURE 5. *HKM's 'Ae Like (collective agreement) is a statement of values and commitments that is signed by every member of the learning 'ohana—from students to board members. It serves as an ethical foundation for the school's Hawaiian culture–based approach to education.*

A Self-Determined, 'Āina-Centered Curriculum: Nurturing a Kīpuka

HKM founders and early teaching staff used the limited autonomy of the charter school model to envision and develop a curriculum that centered place-based and project-based pedagogical approaches and that made Indigenous Hawaiian cultural knowledges the foundation for interdisciplinary and cross-cultural inquiry. Over the first ten years of HKM's existence, the school maintained this commitment and intent, but the extent to which place-based and project-based learning remained the organizing force of the curriculum diminished in the wake of school restructuring enforced under NCLB. As a case study, HKM illustrates that powerful forces of assimilation continue to operate within the framework of the limited self-determination offered by the settler state. This section describes the way the school's curricular framework evolved over the first five years, prior to entering restructuring status. The curriculum was aimed at nurturing students by encouraging them to see and cultivate the pilina between themselves, the 'āina, and their local and global communities. Projects allowed 'ōpio and kumu together to engage and address community needs.

Like many of the other Hawaiian-focused charter schools, HKM adopted a curriculum design that marked an explicit departure both from mainstream schools and from earlier versions of Hawaiian studies in K–12 schooling, which have been criticized for exoticizing without empowering, failing to include Kanaka community control, and decontextualizing selected cultural practices from history, land, and people.[26] HKM founders were not aiming at replicating a "cultural infusion" model, which is characterized by "superficially adding fragmented pieces of cultural knowledge to the existing structure."[27] Rather, Hawaiian-focused charter school operators were inspired by the vision of making Indigenous cultural practices, needs, and resources—specific to their local communities—the *foundation* of the curriculum. Mandatory state standards in subjects deemed by dominant educational discourses to be core could then be connected to the Projects.

This goal of making Hawaiian culture the foundation rather than the window dressing required not only a different set of lesson plans but a radical rethinking of the common characteristics of a school environment. As Mary Hermes writes, "To reflect the epistemology of the indigenous people, changes are needed in the organization of the school day, the language of instruction, the content, the pedagogy and the approach."[28] This was the kind of total overhaul that HKM founders and subsequent teachers set out to accomplish: to remake the typical school schedule, to move outside the four-walled classroom and provide new contexts for learning, to design new assessment systems, to include cultural experts as kumu whether or not they were state-certified school teachers, to rethink the staffing and organizational structure typical of schools, and to generally push the boundaries between school and community.

In its opening years, HKM operated with a modified-block schedule that broke the school day up into morning Focus Groups and afternoon Projects.[29] In the morning students with similar ability levels met in classes that focused on one of the subject areas school leaders deemed to be core, including math, language arts, and hula. (Hula also easily exceeded the state's minimum requirements for both physical education and fine arts.) After lunch, teams of teachers and students of all grade levels (six through twelve) assembled in groups that undertook semester-long collective Projects, such as building a dry-land māla or preparing for a nearshore sailing voyage. These Projects integrated skills from various fields but especially focused on social studies and science. At the end of each term, teachers met to discuss and prepare assessment reports on each individual student's cognitive, affective, and social development, as well as their demonstration of effort, participation, and mastery of course contents. Quarterly Lā ʻOhana and an annual hōʻike (performance) allowed the ʻōpio to demonstrate their learning to families, neighbors, legislators, funders, and other supporters, who were invited to these events to witness and celebrate the production of knowledge in which HKM students and faculty engaged.

By the school's fourth year of operation (2004–5), several factors had fallen into place to allow the curriculum to stabilize and blossom. The school had moved into what leaders believed would be a semi-permanent location that could accommodate everyone's basic needs; negotiations related to off-campus learning sites had solidified; and the relatively high faculty turnover of the first few years had given way to a core of teachers who would remain at HKM for five or more years. With these basics in place, Projects became a stronger organizing structure for the curriculum. Students spent every other day at one of the primary outdoor sites: lo'i restoration and land stewardship in Mānoa, fishpond maintenance and ocean ecology in He'eia and Kewalo, and canoe maintenance, navigation, sailing, and reef monitoring at Kualoa and Ka'alaea. Each of these Projects integrated science, math, history, and language arts in both classroom and field settings.

Teachers built the program around a prevalent Hawaiian land division: the ahupua'a. As a political, social, familial, ecological, and economic system, the ahupua'a is a way of organizing resources. By scaffolding the curriculum around a deepening understanding of this system and the particular ahupua'a in which students resided and attended school, multiple fields of inquiry could be integrated. At the Kaikaina level (sixth through eighth grade), students were introduced to the foundational concepts of the ahupua'a. One year was spent in the Ko Kula Uka Project, focusing on the resources of the upland and integrating multiple subjects around a quarterly theme. For example, a unit on housing allowed students to participate in building traditional hale pili, study Pacific migration patterns, and use geometry and consumer math to look at home construction and maintenance. A second middle school year was devoted to Ko Kula Kai, focusing on the coastal and nearshore ocean environments. One sample unit included studying about and working at a man-made canal in Waikīkī, the Ala Wai. Students could learn the history of the canal's development and see the impacts of pollution and improper management on the waters of the entire ahupua'a. They were also able to learn how native plants could be used to address those problems through phytoremediation. Another sample unit was driven by the guiding question, How did traditional Hawaiian fishing methods sustain life for both Kānaka (humans) and i'a (fish, marine animals)? The general framework of the middle school program has remained constant since 2005. Additionally, in the 2008–9 school year a separate sixth-grade Project was introduced in which the students spent a semester each studying and interacting with uka (upland) and then kai (sea) resources.

The Kua'ana (ninth- through twelfth-grade) program went through more change than the Kaikaina program during the period of school restructuring (discussed in the next section), but it too maintained an organization around upland and coastal resources. Initially, students were assigned to one of three yearlong Projects: Waʻa, which focused on the canoe as the principal vessel of travel for Kānaka Hawaiʻi; Loko Iʻa, which focused on the fishpond as the principal technology for protein production in traditional Hawaiian society; and Loʻi, which focused on the production of kalo, the staple food of Hawaiian society. Eventually, the Waʻa and Loko Iʻa Projects were combined such that ninth and tenth graders comprised a Kai-focused course and eleventh and twelfth graders comprised Papa Loʻi. (These Projects are described in more detail in subsequent chapters.) The Kuaʻana-level Projects were designed to take inquiry deeper and to give the ʻōpio more kuleana in maintaining the learning sites. For instance, the loʻi at ʻAihualama or the waʻa *Kānehūnāmoku* are living beings, and the Projects allowed the ʻōpio to develop long-term relationships with them. As Kumu Bonnie Kahapeʻa-Tanner, captain of *Kānehūnāmoku*, puts it, "They have these relationships to return to for the rest of their lives. No one can take that away from them."

During the middle years of the school's first decade, the Projects came to drive the schedule entirely. Two full days were spent in the field, in outdoor learning sites such as Heʻeia fishpond, and two days were spent on campus in the classrooms or computer lab. The weekly schedule was purposefully made flexible to give a Project's teaching team the autonomy to determine when the students would focus on any given subject (see Figures 6A and 6B). A lead teacher documented evidence that students were spending a balance of time in the core subjects and that they were addressing state-determined content standards in those areas. Students began each day with hula and/or Hawaiian language, and these classes mixed ʻōpio from various Project groupings together. For several years ʻōpio received hula and Hawaiian-language instruction at least three days a week. Fridays were set aside for physical education, health, guidance, and arts and cultural playshops.

Early HKM teachers and administrators hypothesized that students would learn better if they were given ways to connect book learning with applied learning on the ʻāina. If we could get students excited about developing the skills needed to sail on a waʻa, then perhaps that excitement would spill over into studying reef monitoring through observations made on or near the canoe. If students could feel motivated by their connection to Hawaiian genealogies and epic stories, then perhaps they could see parallel themes in their studies of Greek or Egyptian histories and mythologies or vice versa. If the skill sets and literacies valued and required by the state could be embedded within assignments that had meaning to the students and their communities, then perhaps we could keep them engaged and excited about being in school in the first place. If their previous schools were culturally alienating, we could instead expose them to the wealth of Hawaiian knowledge evident in our communities, environment, and literature so that they might see themselves as authors, leaders, thinkers, navigators, and masters of their own destinies.

I do not pretend that the program was ideal or perfect, yet numerous personal and collective successes were witnessed over the years. More students enjoyed coming to school. Throughout HKM's first decade, students averaged a 93 percent attendance rate, and each year we would collect responses like the following in parent surveys that told a similar story: "Before, my daughter hated school. Now she goes everyday and actually wants to learn. It's amazing."[30] "Our keiki are actually more willing to come to school. When sick, they refuse to stay home. They've really blossomed."[31] This blossoming was witnessed when a thirteen-year-old boy who first came to HKM wearing his hair over his eyes, constantly looking at the floor, and only hesitantly speaking to adults became a confident young man who repeatedly presented testimony at the state legislature about how his school had positively impacted his own and his family's life. It was witnessed in the graduate who after spending six years at HKM, decided to return as an instructional aide in the hope of becoming a Hawaiian-language teacher. It was witnessed when a girl who for three years constantly complained about getting muddy planted her own garden at home. It was witnessed in the group of students who were able to get on the wa'a and sail for miles with no help from their kumu.

Settler-Colonial Constraints: How NCLB Impacted the Educational Program and Inscribed a Safety Zone

As outlined at the beginning of this chapter, contemporary settler states like the United States adopt strategies for containing and minimizing potentially threatening Indigenous cultural difference. NCLB has functioned as a way to reign in Hawaiian sovereign pedagogies, to limit the conditions of possibility within which Indigenous education can occur and be transformative. During the first period of my research, the top hurdle to practicing self-determination cited across the board by HKM staff was the lack of a permanent home for the school, a central site where people could put down roots. By the time I had completed my PhD and began working as the school's Alakaʻi Hoʻomohala (program director), which I did from 2005 to 2007, that was beginning to shift. The lease for a long-term site was coming into view, yet the school's ongoing challenges with math were continuing to result in an inability to meet Adequate Yearly Progress (AYP) as defined by NCLB. HKM was following a larger system-wide trend, as almost every other secondary-level school in Hawaiʻi (save those in more affluent districts) was at the time moving down the path to restructuring. Variously characterized as a "sanction" or a "remediating intervention," restructuring is the federally mandated and state-enforced process through which any U.S. public school must go should its test scores fail to meet AYP. The intent of restructuring is to stimulate major changes in school governance and curriculum.

Math or, more specifically, student achievement on standardized math tests had consistently been an area of weakness for HKM. The school had a higher than average rate of students qualifying for special education services (approximately 25 to 35 percent of students each year over the ten-year period I studied) and an even higher rate of students whose family income was low enough to qualify them for the free and reduced lunch program (an average of two-thirds of the student body each year). Both of these groups historically perform lower on standardized tests than students without special needs and students from middle- and upper-class families. These structural inequalities were coupled with the problems that qualified math teachers were hard to recruit and retain, that students entering (usually between seventh and ninth grades) already were bringing along major deficiencies in math knowledge, and that owing to the lack of a state provision for land or facilities, the campus was forced to move four times.

In 2007–8, the very year the school finally moved into its present permanent campus of modular space structures (trailers), HKM entered Planning for Restructuring status, as per NCLB. Having finally overcome the major hurdle of securing a stable home, the school was immediately confronted with the pressures of restructuring. For the fourth year in a row, the school had not met the AYP math target, which at that point required that 46 percent of the students tested perform at grade level on the Hawai'i State Assessment test. Faculty members began to see and talk about NCLB as the most important factor impacting the educational program.

In contrast to the hundreds of volunteers who assisted with the move to the new campus—a move that symbolized hope for the future and the planting of permanent roots—we could barely get anyone to the open meetings of the school board's committee on restructuring. As a board member, I was appointed to chair the Restructuring Committee when the school entered Planning for Restructuring status. For Hawai'i schools entering restructuring at that time, there were a few options. Noncharter schools had to relinquish their decision making to the complex area superintendent (CAS)—an upper-level regional administrator—who then took control of personnel decisions, curriculum and instruction, and budgetary matters. The CAS could choose to (1) directly manage the restructuring process, (2) select and hire a restructuring provider to handle the process, or (3) allow the school community to apply for conversion to a charter school.[32] For charter schools decision-making authority was retained by the local school board (LSB). As long as the steps LSBs took toward restructuring were deemed acceptable by the state's Charter School Review Panel, a charter school could either self-restructure (that is, the LSB could lead the restructuring process), showing comprehensive change in governance, curriculum, and instruction, or the school could hire an external provider to manage the restructuring process.

In 2005 the Hawai'i State Department of Education created a process for hiring outside providers that significantly influenced the way most schools chose to restructure. Applications from ten aspiring vendors were reviewed, and three were approved, those for America's Choice, Edison Learning, and Educational Testing Services. In their 2009 report on how school restructuring was rolling out in Hawai'i, Hess and Squire explain, "State officials streamlined procurement by writing state-wide contracts and meet quarterly with complex area staff and comprehensive providers to review their performance."[33] As a result of the centralized contracts, of the first twenty-four Hawai'i schools that went into restructuring, twenty began the process under one of the three U.S. firms, at an annual cost of about $400,000 per year per school. As of 2009, "forty-four of Hawaii's 92 restructuring schools—a significantly higher percentage than in mainland states—currently partner with one of these three state-approved comprehensive providers."[34]

As we considered our options at Hālau Kū Māna, we met with representatives from various comprehensive restructuring and educational management organizations, including the large aforementioned firms. The teachers, parents, and other board members who comprised the committee could not reconcile, however, the school's vision and mission with turning management over to such a company. We felt such a move would negate the whole purpose of having a school like ours; it would be incommensurable with our understandings of educational self-determination. So we made the difficult decision to restructure the school ourselves. In order to avoid the settler-colonial logic of elimination, we faced the corresponding logic of containment.

Two veteran teachers, Bonnie Kahapeʻa-Tanner and Koalani Lagareta, and I led the brainstorming process about how we could reorganize the staffing, curriculum, and schedule to strengthen our math program, as well as the cultural foundations of our school, which at the time we saw as hula, loʻi, waʻa, and ʻōlelo. We hoped that we could turn the process into something that allowed us to renew the school's commitment to rigorous Hawaiian place-based and project-based learning while also improving test scores within a year or two. That ideal proved elusive.

Our hopes fell flat as the actual implementation at the program level was complicated by major leadership changes (not all of which were directly related to the official restructuring process). Between the 2007–8 and the 2010–11 school years, HKM had three different executive directors and four different Poʻo Kumu (principals or instructional leaders). In the meantime, a core of faculty members stayed on board and articulated growing concern that the reaction to the pressures of restructuring was causing HKM to look more and more like a mainstream school in terms of its weekly schedule, the emphasis on test scores, the imposed definition of what made a teacher highly qualified, and the need to demonstrate alignment to settler state–determined curriculum content standards and credit systems. No one disagreed with the goal of improving the school's math program so that students could strengthen their math abilities and perform better on math assessments. In fact, faculty regularly strategized about ways everyone could support such improvement in math teaching and learning. But they also continued to point out the ways the school was moving toward a conventional organization of the day and division of subjects.

Charts comparing sample student schedules prior to restructuring and following restructuring illustrate one of the fundamental shifts that took place: a change from project-based learning being the foundation and organizing force of the curriculum to Projects being compartmentalized as off-campus field trip days (see Figures 6 and 7). Classes were also then divided into discrete subjects taught by faculty members who had been state certified in that particular subject area. Kumu who had advanced graduate degrees, were highly skilled practitioners of the cultural knowledges that undergirded the Projects, and had significant experience and success as teachers of Hawaiian youth were told that if they did not pass the standardized state-mandated PRAXIS test, they could not be considered highly qualified and could lose their jobs. In daily language, people talked less about Project teams as the locus of integration and collaboration and more about going out on Projects. The imposed testing regimes reified a binary framing that associated Western learning with academics, indoor classroom time, and abstract and quantifiable knowledge in discrete subject areas. Hawaiian or Indigenous learning was simplified as cultural practice that was practical, as opposed to intellectual, and took place outdoors through hands-on work. Not only was NCLB's assessment regime functioning as a mechanism for assuring that Indigenous epistemologies and practices would remain subordinate to other fields of knowledge deemed core within the hegemonic educational discourses of the settler state and society, but the very binary framing of Western versus Hawaiian—often represented as academics versus culture—functioned to inscribe a safety zone and limit the possibility of deeply transformative school reform.

On the ground this meant that Projects came to represent the place and time in which Hawaiian culture was happening, and regular classes came to represent where core academic learning was taking place. The amount of time ʻōpio actually spent on the ʻāina diminished. If standards-based academic learning was assumed to be happening in the classroom, not the field, then preparation for high-stakes testing

Kaikaina

HOLA	Pōʻakahi	Pōʻalua	Pōʻakolu	Pōʻaha	Pōʻalima
8:15–9:15	Hula	ʻŌlelo Hawaiʻi	Hula	ʻŌlelo Hawaiʻi	Hula/ʻŌlelo Hawaiʻi
9:20–12:15	Project Off-campus day	Project Classroom day	Project Off-campus day	Project Classroom day	9:30–11:30 Ola Kino (PE and Health)
12:15–12:45pm	LUNCH				11:30–12:00 LUNCH
12:45–2:50	Project	Project	Project	Project	12:00–1:30pm Arts/Culture Electives

Kuaʻana

HOLA	Pōʻakahi	Pōʻalua	Pōʻakolu	Pōʻaha	Pōʻalima
8:15–9:15	ʻŌlelo Hawaiʻi	Hula	ʻŌlelo Hawaiʻi	Hula	Hula/ʻŌlelo Hawaiʻi
9:20–10:20	Project Classroom day	Project Off-campus day	Project Classroom day	Project Off-campus day	9:30–11:30am Ola Kino
12:15–12:45pm	LUNCH				11:30–12:00 LUNCH
12:45–2:50	Project	Project	Project	Project	12:00–1:30pm Arts/Culture Electives

FIGURE 6. *These are sample student schedules from the Kaikaina (middle school) and Kuaʻana (high school) levels, respectively, for the 2005–6 school year. Taken from HKM's end-of-the-year report, the schedules show the way culturally driven projects organized student learning in both on- and off-campus settings in the years prior to restructuring under NCLB. Hawaiian names for days were used, and hula and the Hawaiian language were foundational cores within the curriculum.*

was prioritized in the limited number of hours in a school week. Time in the field slowly shrank from every other day to twice a week to once a week. As of this writing, students get about half a day per week at their outdoor learning sites. For example, a student in the Waʻa Project now spends only forty-five minutes per week on the canoe, whereas on some days he or she receives math or English-language arts instruction twice a day.

Even the language of the school's end-of-the-year (EOY) report began to change. In the years prior to restructuring, the section on the school's educational program opened with statements that affirmed the centrality of Hawaiian culture as an organizing force and emphasized

7th grade schedule

	A-day	B-day	C-day	D-day	E-day
Opening 7:55–8:10					
Period 1 8:15–9:25	Earth science	Tech	Literacy circle	Project day	7th gr math
Period 2 9:30–10:40	Hawaiian history	Language Arts	Hula		Hula
Period 3 10:45–11:55	7th gr Math	7th gr math	7th gr math		Hawaiian history
LUNCH					
Period 4 12:30–1:40	Language arts	Olelo Hawaiʻi	Earth science		Language Arts
Period 5 1:45–2:50	Olelo Hawaiʻi	Hawaiian history	Olelo Hawaiʻi		7th gr math
Hookuʻu 2:55–3:05					

11th grade schedule

	A-day	B-day	C-day	D-day	E-day
Opening 7:55–8:10					
Period 1 8:15–9:25	Olelo Hawaiʻi	Hula	Olelo Hawaiʻi	Math practice	Project day
Period 2 9:30–10:40	US History	Literacy circle	US History	Hula	
Period 3 10:45–11:55	Language Arts	US History	Language Arts	Tech	
LUNCH					
Period 4 12:30–1:40	Math–Algebra II	Math–Algebra II	Math–Algebra II	Math–Algebra II	
Period 5 1:45–2:50	Transition planning (guidance)	Chemistry	Chemistry	Language Arts	
Hookuʻu 2:55–3:05					

FIGURE 7. *These sample student schedules from the 2008–9 school year reflect the changes following NCLB restructuring of the school. Note key changes from the prerestructuring schedules: periods organized by subject, a reversion to a standard grade level rather than multiage grouping system (i.e., "7th grade" versus "Kaikaina"), and the minimization of Projects to once-a-week hands-on field days, as opposed to the centerpiece of the curriculum.*

the equal importance of community and individual ʻōpio, as in the following excerpt from the 2005–6 EOY report:

Since HKM focuses on Hawaiian culture for its educational foundation, curriculum, instruction, assessment, educational philosophy, and school structure are all guided by Hawaiian values and epistemology, especially the core values of HKM. Through the unique approach of community-based Hawaiian education, students at HKM develop a positive and healthy sense of themselves, others, and their communities. We are committed to providing an educational opportunity that incorporates Native Hawaiian values, traditions, and teaching/ learning styles, along with the best in modern educational ideas. In meshing the two, we emphasize project-based learning, authentic assessment, team-teaching, and collaborative performance-based learning and evaluation.[35]

In contrast, as soon as HKM entered restructuring Hawaiian culture became referenced as a secondary purpose, distinct from core academics, and the focus was more on individual development. As the 2008–9 EOY report states:

HKM's instructional goals are to meet all our students' lifelong achievement needs through rigorous knowledge and skill based learning. We are committed to meet and help our students pursue personal career goals which will provide them the wherewithal to live successfully in this global world. Toward this end, we must prepare our students for post-secondary schooling and this means that the Hawaiian culture, as well as the core academics need to be learned and demonstrated with competence.[36]

Many teachers highlighted the fundamental tension that a school formed with the purpose of perpetuating Indigenous knowledge and empowering students and their local communities was operating within a system in which the standards for learning were determined by someone else. Some even described those external settler state authorities in adversarial terms—the same historical authorities who seized control of the lands, government, and public education system from the independent Hawaiian government and then systematically wiped the Hawaiian language and Hawaiian perspectives of history from the curriculum. One former teacher, Willy Kauai, talked specifically about how his work was diverted from the movements and vision that brought him to HKM in the first place. He described his hopes that Hawaiian education would help develop the collective capacity of the younger generations to exercise economic and political independence as a country and then remarked:

> We are being held to regulations and standards that are created by the movement's opposition. In order for our school to stay open, we have to pass the tests that the opposition created. That is the time when I feel like I have to conform . . . in order for the movement to survive one more day.[37]

His comments represented the sentiments of many—that we needed to play the game to survive, even when we did not want to lose the core of ourselves and our mission. As Gramsci points out, hegemonic social formations require the production of consent among those who are not positioned to benefit from the prevailing relations of power.[38] In order to continue functioning as a school, HKM educators took on the process of self-restructuring and as a result began reverting to an outdated and destructive language of "infusing" Hawaiian culture into an educational program structured by the core fields defined by state and federal curriculum content standards. Native educationalists have critiqued the cultural infusion model for years, and HKM founders attempted to push beyond it when envisioning the school in the first place. Yet NCLB made it even more difficult to get out from under the discursive weight of the hegemonic common sense of what counts as valuable knowledge within schools.

Kai Nui Project, January 13, 2011

The sky was overcast as I drove out to Ka'alaea, an ahupua'a that sits right in the middle of the lands that surround Kāne'ohe Bay. It's about a forty-minute drive from HKM's primary campus to the satellite site that is home to *Kānehūnāmoku*. Numerous fallen branches, signs of the previous day's storm, lined the windward highway leading out to Kumu Kahape'a's house along the shore. Kahape'a has opened her family home to HKM 'ōpio for several years, allowing the Wa'a Project to meet and conduct regular classes there.

I arrived just before the ʻōpio were dropped off by the school's minibuses. About twenty ninth and tenth graders disembarked and demonstrated their familiarity with the opening protocol. Still chatty from the bus ride, they placed their bags next to the steps leading up to Kumu Kahapeʻaʻs lanai and then quieted down as they formed a single line along a retaining wall at the water's edge. They stood as still as the waʻa kiakahi (single-masted double-hulled canoe) sitting forty to fifty feet out in the water as they faced her and chanted her genealogy.

After Kumu Kahapeʻa provided a brief summary of the day's tasks ahead, the students split into their designated watches—small working groups led by a watch captain and first mate. I joined one of the watches, following them through each of their three forty-five-minute rotations. By the middle of the first rotation, two ʻōpio had already caught my attention. The group of six sat at a round picnic table on the lanai with their kumu and me. They had been asked to memorize part of a chant from the *Wind Gourd of Laʻamaomao*, which they read the previous quarter. The focus of the lesson was a section listing specific wind names in each ahupuaʻa of the larger Kona district. The two I noticed were performing at opposite ends of the spectrum. Keaka, a tall, lanky boy who had impressed me when I overheard him reciting obscure old-school hip-hop lyrics during the breaks between tasks, immediately told the teacher it was too hard and that he couldn't memorize it. As Kumu Uʻi read aloud and had the ʻōpio repeat back the various lines in unison, he slumped forward and rubbed his eraser against the table. One of the teachers later told me that Keaka had been experiencing some difficult times at home and had become less motivated about coming to or staying in school.

Exactly across from him at the table, Mālie, a tenth grader who has attended HKM since she was eleven, picked up the chant quickly. She quietly repeated it to herself during lulls in the group's momentum. When the ʻōpio were set free to work on it independently, Mālie noticed some of her crewmates weren't doing much, so she asked, "What do we need to do to help you guys learn it?" In firm but encouraging tones, she took control and led them in a recitation. "There you go!" she told one of the boys when he got through several lines on his own. She had clearly been a watch captain in a previous quarter, but I could also see that because her ʻohana had raised her in the paddling and waʻa communities since she was a young girl, she brought a confidence and ease with her to this class.

In the second rotation, Kumu Kristi, the science teacher, instructed the group on the three ways they were expected to record observations of their environment. First, they partnered up, and using an anemometer and their senses, they recorded data on maximum and average wind speed, wind direction, air temperature, humidity, dew point, air pressure, estimated cloud cover, and predominant cloud type. Eager to learn to use this new instrument, the pairs walked around the yard with their anemometers and clipboards in hand. Mālie and her partner moved through the assignment quickly, and although Keaka was more engaged than in the previous rotation, his partner had gotten distracted, so they had a difficult time keeping up with the pace of the other two pairs. For the second part the students broke off individually and completed written observations in which they were prompted to describe what they noticed about the waves, the tide, the animals, the plants, or their feelings. By the third step Keaka was as engaged as Mālie, both of them sketching with pastels their perceptions of the sky over the waters in which *Kānehūnāmoku* sat. "Pay attention to the subtle shades of color," Kumu Kristi told them as the clouds shifted overhead. "I think I'm in love with pastels," Mālie remarked as she lay a wash of light grey over her page. Keaka was quiet, engrossed in his drawing, going back several times to highlight brownish spots with the lightest of blues. It was not until the drawings were complete and their kumu was spraying the sheets with a fixative to keep the images from smearing that Keaka affirmed out loud, but to no one in particular, "That was fun!"

On the waʻa for the third rotation, Keaka came alive completely, as though someone had raised a shade and rays of sunlight were pouring out of him. The crew had to work in unison to raise and lower the canoe's rig, remove the sail bag, and open and then reclose the sail again. Captain Kahapeʻa left little space for any of us to get off track, and Keaka took leadership in guiding the rig up and, later, lowering it in case another storm blew through. His kumu praised him for his participation, and they had a brief conversation in which he asked why they couldn't come on the waʻa more often. "We should do this every day," he mused.

FIGURE 8. *Science teacher Kristi Descuacido with HKM students at their Kaʻalaea outdoor learning site on Kāneʻohe Bay, Oʻahu. As part of the Kai Nui Project, students use multiple quantitative and qualitative methods to systematically observe and collect data on weather patterns throughout the year. Photograph by the author.*

In the closing circle before the ʻōpio got back on their buses, Kumu Kahapeʻa reaffirmed that the various watches did well during their rotations on the waʻa, although some got more done than others. "If you folks can maintain this focus, you should be able to take *Kāne* out for a sail within a few more visits." She also reminded them to take their good behavior with them into the classroom until she saw them again the following week. "This is why charter schools were created, so that you can get excited about the hands-on stuff, about being on the waʻa, and then you can translate that into the classroom, as well."

When the kids had gone, we sat on her lanai, talking about her statement to the ʻōpio. I asked her about the impacts she saw now that students were at her hale only once a week for three hours and on the waʻa for only forty-five minutes a week. This was a huge change in the amount of time they used to spend out in the field before the imposition of restructuring status. She emphasized that what had changed wasn't the kids' desire to get on the wa'a but their skill level and the way they related to *Kānehūnāmoku*.

> The last few years [since restructuring,] the kids want to sail, but they don't talk about the wa'a in the same way. They don't have the same relationship. The previous years' 'ōpio—the ones who spent two or three days a week at the wa'a—even today when they come back [now that they've graduated], when they talk about the wa'a, it's like they're talking about their grandma. It was a deeper, spiritual relationship.

She recalled that various classes throughout the years had their own strengths and learned different aspects of sailing and navigation. One year's crop of wa'a students were great sailors; they could take *Kāne-hūnāmoku* out and sail her across the bay to the sandbar, Ahuolaka, without any help from their kumu. Another group knew more than any other about weather and the stars used for navigating. But in her estimation as a teacher who had been at HKM since year one, as the restructuring years ate into wa'a time the 'ōpio became less and less proficient at the skills, behaviors, and values learned through the wa'a. A little over a month later, when I heard that Keaka had dropped out of school, I wondered if he would have stayed had he been able to touch the wa'a and the ocean more regularly, as had previous cohorts of HKM students.

"We Won't Lose Our 'Ike; We Will Grow Our 'Ike": Aspects of Self-Determination in Educators' Discourse

As an instance of the fundamental tensions of expressing Indigenous self-determination within the constraints of settler state institutions, this chapter focuses on the ways Hawaiian charter school operators struggle to practice contemporary Hawaiian culture–based education in the age of NCLB. Even though the settler state's law includes sections aimed to support Native Hawaiian, Indian, and Alaska Native self-determination, the No Child Left Behind Act functions as a reassimilating force. The testing regimes and definitions of highly qualified teacher status have served, for example, as a means of surveilling safety zones, of monitoring the extent to which self-determined Indigenous educational initiatives diverge from the dominant settler-colonial discourse of what a school should look like and do. Perhaps more important, NCLB reinscribes the settler state's authority to determine the measures of success. The effect is that Indigenous cultural knowledges are marked so as to contain, subordinate, or eliminate them.

For Hawaiian charter school educators, working within a settler state school system has both provided the possibility to implement Indigenous public schooling and structured the conditions of possibility for those schools. At HKM even when school leaders took on the restructuring process fully conscious that we were doing so as a way to survive—"to conform in order for the movement to survive one more day"—it was impossible to fully escape the discursive force of NCLB and the attendant definitions of educational success. Yet kumu and haumāna have continued to find holes in the safety zones' fences. Just as the students with whom I opened this chapter found gaps in and places of temporary respite away from the disciplinary structures of their former high school, HKM educators and teachers found ways to keep their students connected to the ʻāina and to cultivate such land-based relationships. Teachers and students acted creatively as agents without full autonomy.

In this concluding section I explore articulations of self-determination consistently iterated in HKM teachers' daily practice and conversations over the course of HKM's first ten years. Drawing on practices of community, sovereignty, learning, and aloha ʻāina, HKM teachers' formulations showed the ways their understandings exceeded the U.S. settler state's formulations of Indigenous self-determination. Some of these aspects included intergenerational efforts to strengthen Kanaka Maoli health and well-being, to redevelop economic self-sufficiency and ecological sustainability on our lands, to increase literacy in Hawaiian language and history, and to regain recognition of Hawaiian political sovereignty. As Kumu Kāwika Mersberg—who has been a teacher and/or alakaʻi at HKM since the school's opening—puts it:

> I really do believe our school is part of the movement for self-
> determination. By having this type of school, we're making
> our people even stronger. Being that we live on an island, our

resources are limited. So it's very important to help out the movement that we not only understand our history and what happened to our people but that we also know our lands and what we need to do to survive into the future. . . . We give back to the sovereignty movement by providing a nest where we feed these young birds to get them ready to leave the nest and fly away. And hopefully one day, they can return to the nest and nurture the next egg that's ready to hatch.[39]

The sense of being part of an intergenerational struggle to maintain and develop ancestral practices remained a fundamental aspect of HKM educators' understandings of self-determination. This genealogical awareness sustained many kumu and allowed them to persevere despite countless challenges. From a teacher's perspective, it was not easy to address the needs of a class in which students' reading levels spanned second grade to post–high school levels while teaching in a classroom dark and dank enough to be called the Batcave, all the while fearing that the school could be shut down if students' test scores were not high enough to meet AYP. Kumu Kaleilehua Maioho, who has taught Hawaiian language from the school's fifth year of operation to the present, articulated her motivation to persist amid such conditions. She talked about her role in a larger collective movement and her dual obligations to predecessors and future generations:

My work is *definitely* part of a movement. Charter schools are a movement: it's bigger than you, bigger than us. That's what I think keeps me here right now. It's not the pay, not the stress, the sacrifices. I think of my kūpuna before who sacrificed their lives. I think of the big battles, like Kekuaokalani and his wife, Manono. They went to battle because they felt that the ʻAikapu system should not be overthrown. Sometimes, I feel *that* entrenched in things: we will die for what we believe in. Or live for it, as long as we can. *Live* for what we believe in, as long as it keeps us alive, or until it kills us.[40]

Kumu Kaleilehua situated Hawaiian charter schools within a genealogy of those who fought to perpetuate ʻŌiwi knowledge and belief systems, specifically citing the two aliʻi famous for leading and losing their lives in the 1819 battle to maintain the social and religious practices expressed through the ʻAikapu, or sacred eating.[41] Kānaka Maoli of Kekuaokalani and Manono's time were afflicted by foreign-introduced infectious diseases, which Hawaiian historian Lilikalā Kameʻeleihiwa argues caused the ruling chiefs of Hawaiʻi Island to consider alternative ways of restoring and maintaining pono.[42] Against those aliʻi who supported abandonment of the ʻAikapu, Kekuaokalani and Manono fought to protect the ancestral ways.

When asked to elaborate on the aims of this contemporary movement, of which she saw Hawaiian charter schools as a part, she explained that a primary goal was

> to get our people out of those dangerous statistics that we talk about. . . . Our teachings will go across and help everyone, but I really think our people need the help. Looking at the statistics, we're not doing so well as far as health, prison, drugs. All that is directly related to education. . . . When you think about all our social problems, it comes back to being educated.

Here, Kumu Kaleilehua refers to a different set of diseases afflicting twenty-first-century Kānaka Maoli, socially driven conditions that Hawaiian educators have long argued can be addressed, in part, by educating Hawaiian youth in the cultural bases of strength that have sustained Kānaka ʻŌiwi for generations. Her own work has been based on the idea that Indigenous language and moʻolelo (stories/histories) are central to self-determination. This ʻike (knowledge, way of seeing) brings health. She further emphasized that Hawaiian education was not "just preservation" and replication of old knowledge but the development and renewal of ancestral ʻike in new contexts. Kumu Kaleilehua described twenty-first-century Hawaiian education as "the continuance of our ʻike, our people. . . . It is the actual *hana*, to see that our people will be healthy and thrive. We won't lose our ʻike; we will *grow* our ʻike." Such a statement stands in stark contrast to the model of education reinforced by NCLB testing regimes, which emphasize mastery of multiple-choice tests and do not encourage students to learn how to frame questions, to pursue different lines of inquiry, to value multiple possible answers, or to think critically about the questions themselves.[43]

Consistently throughout HKM's existence, kumu have talked about how the school should ground students in understanding that the health of the people and the land are directly linked. Mālama ʻāina, or the "actual hana" of caring for the land, in HKM's project-based curriculum has helped kumu and haumāna live the connections between personal and collective self-determination and well-being. (In the next chapters I offer more detailed portraits of how this plays out in the curriculum.) Kumu ʻĪmaikalani Winchester reflected on the relevance of mālama ʻāina and ea (sovereignty, breath) to his teaching practice as an educator who had taught Hawaiian and American history, Hawaiian and English language, and kalo cultivation since 2004. In the following, he specifically speaks of the lessons learned in restoring loʻi, or wetland taro fields:

> Project-based learning at the loʻi is about producing food and being self-sustainable. . . . It is the idea of taking care of the entire system instead of just your own parcel. The idea of being accountable to more than just one person—oneself. I think these are all values that are critical in the pursuit of ea or independence, not only within the political context but also as a personal statement to oneself. When we develop an understanding that Hawaiʻi and its people can live . . . without the support or constant intervention by outside forces, Hawaiians can be out there saying, "We have the ability to take care of ourselves. We are not wards of the state. Our traditions have meaning, and they have purpose. They have power, and they have wealth."
>
> Ea, I think, is the full realization that our purpose here is greater than owning material wealth, that our purpose needs to be aligned with aloha, with pono, with mālama ʻāina, with finding some sort of balance in our interactions between ourselves and nature, between ourselves and one another. I believe that mālama ʻāina reinforces and reinvigorates that idea of personal sovereignty and collective sovereignty and moves us

away from individualistic thought.... The basic principle of
farming is to feed, and I think that in itself—to feed, to allow
something to live—is a lesson learned on many levels working ʻāina.... The push toward sovereignty and independence
is as much about *interdependence* and the realization of it. The
emphasis that we place on individual success is going to start to
become overshadowed by the need for interdependent cooperation. And we see interdependence in action every time we are
working ʻāina.[44]

Kumu ʻĪmaikalani's perspective illustrates the ways many, though not
all, kumu at HKM understood self-determination and the work of
the school as directly connected to political and economic sovereignty.
His description of such sovereignty also shows that an ʻŌiwi Hawaiʻi
notion of sovereignty based on aloha ʻāina and mālama ʻāina has as
much to do with proliferating and nurturing relationships in balanced interdependence as it does with asserting autonomy and being
self-sufficient.

Moreover, in centering mālama ʻāina in their sovereign pedagogies,
HKM kumu pushed against the kind of individualist-oriented forms
of learning and assessment reinforced by NCLB. The learning goals of
realizing interdependence, seeing one's connection to and impact on
the natural environment, and finding one's responsibilities to the collective health of all those around one were emphasized by Kumu ʻĪmai:

For a sixteen-year-old kid who knows nothing else other than
living downtown some place, if they can get out and experience
some different things, return to their past, they can actually
breathe that life—that ea—into our culture and traditions again.
So it's not relics of the past but rather a living and breathing
function of who we are as people. Then [they see] why we need
to be connected to this place, why we need to take care of our
water, why we need to take care of our lands, why we need to
take care of our beaches and reefs, why we need to take care
of one another.... Hawaiian education is carrying the heavy
kuleana of introducing collectivist ideas into a very individualist
world, where private property, capitalism, and the free market

runs or guides most decision making and policies. I think one of the responsibilities of a charter school in Hawaiian education is to *change* that thought process, to make mālama ʻāina common knowledge, common sense. Environmental steward-ship? Second nature. It would make us better people. Not just Hawaiians but everyone who lives here needs to understand, needs to have the respect, needs to care for what is found here and nowhere else in the world.

Like Kaleilehua, ʻĪmaikalani saw it as particularly important to foster a new sense of health and connection to ʻāina among Kanaka Maoli youth, but he also articulated the belief that Hawaiian education could reach and benefit students of all backgrounds. It is impossible to change the relations of settler colonialism, racism, and imperialism without engaging a diversity of people in the effort.

Perhaps, the most effective way to loosen the powerful structuring influence of settler-colonial institutions like NCLB and to transform settler-colonial relations is to rebuild the Indigenous structures that have historically allowed for sustenance and the kind of balanced interdependence about which ʻĪmaikalani and other HKM kumu have spoken. Chapters 3, 4, and 5 offer portraits of the ways HKM educators have organized their sovereign pedagogies around the building and care of three Hawaiian vessels that have the potential to help create such transformation: the ʻauwai, the waʻa, and the leo. These kuleana have remained foundations for school members' practice of Hawaiian culture–based education in the face of the pressures and limits of NCLB. Through the articulation of ethical knowledge practices of kuleana and aloha ʻāina, kumu and haumāna have been able to maintain and grow Hawaiian cultural kīpuka without being reduced to safety zones. Chapter 3 takes up some of the complexities of engaging teachers and students of diversely gendered and genealogical positions in the revitalization of mahiʻai kalo (taro cultivation).

THREE

Rebuilding the Structures That Feed Us

'Auwai, Lo'i Kalo, and Kuleana

> *What I've come to understand as the whole idea of the lo'i
> and the importance to our youth and our future is [a] sense of
> place . . . particularly when you become nurtured by that sense of
> place, that is what really creates the identity, the connection, the
> spirituality. . . . . All of that comes when you're eating from it . . .
> what I owe that place, what I owe my people who came from that
> place and gave me this heritage, and then what I am going to give
> my children. Eating makes the circle complete. The food is impor-
> tant to us; it has a relationship to us.*
>
> ■ Kumu Danny Bishop, educator and Mahi'ai Kalo

Entering 'Aihualama, 2011

The marginalization and suppression of Indigenous knowledges has
gone hand in hand with the transformation and degradation of Indigenous economic systems and the ecosystems that nourish us. Con-
versely, settler-colonial relations might be transformed by rebuilding,
in new ways, the Indigenous structures that have historically sustained
our societies. As a foundational part of Hālau Kū Māna's educational
program, teachers and students work together to revitalize lo'i kalo and
the 'auwai (irrigation ditch systems) that enrich them. Since HKM's
early years, kumu have been building curriculum and engaging students in restoring 'auwai and lo'i within an ahupua'a saturated by global
corporate capital.

O'ahu, the most populated and overbuilt of the Hawaiian Islands,
has a landscape glutted with fast food-chains, big-box stores, and
U.S. military installations. Standing on Kalākaua Avenue, the main
thoroughfare in world-famous Waikīkī, tourists and locals alike find

themselves surrounded by the most recognizable brand names of consumer capitalist culture—Chanel, Hilton, Starbucks, Nike, Sheraton,
Tiffany, and McDonalds, to name a few. A twenty-minute drive mountainward from Waikīkī Beach brings one, however, to what seems a
completely different world from Kalākaua's glitzy tourist district.
There, at a small parcel of land called ʻAihualama in upper Mānoa valley, a group of HKM high school students and their teachers are restoring an ancestral ʻauwai and loʻi system, working to transform more
than a century's worth of social and ecological change. Under an agreement and partnership with the University of Hawaiʻi's Lyon Arboretum, they model and practice a different kind of economy, culture, and
lifestyle than that apparent along the famous Waikīkī strip. They cultivate a relationship to the land based on lineal connection, subsistence,
and collective work, thus disrupting the dominant mode of education
practiced in the public school system, the paradigm of preservation
historically practiced at the arboretum, and the hegemonic notion that
only a globalized market economy dominated by transnational corporations can provide for our needs.

In the first decades after ʻāina was privatized under the Hawaiian
Kingdom government as part of an effort to stave off imperial encroachment and blend older cultural values with the trappings of European-
style government, most of the parcels in Mānoa were controlled by
Hawaiian aliʻi.[1] By the late 1800s many parcels had been sold to
wealthy haole settlers. Under the U.S. Territory of Hawaiʻi's government, the Hawaiʻi Sugar Planters Association (HSPA) purchased the
largest swath of upper Mānoa valley in 1919 for use as a field experiment station. As the research arm of the islands' sugar industry, the experiment station came to be the center of decision making for production policies and practices across the plantations, and its development
supported the sugar agencies in maintaining supremacy in Hawaiʻi
land use, finance, and agriculture throughout the territorial era.[2]

After sugar was phased out of the area in the 1940s, Minnesota-
born plant pathologist Dr. Harold Lyon convinced the HSPA to con-
vey what had become a water conservation initiative and arboretum to
the University of Hawaiʻi. Although Lyon's project successfully reestab-
lished a watershed, the arboretum also became the point of introduction for thousands of foreign and invasive species.[3] Loʻi and ʻauwai were

filled to create space for these transplants.[4] Residents of the ahupua'a were strictly prohibited from gathering and using or selling any plants growing in the arboretum's territory, a model of conservation that directly contradicted Hawaiian customary practice. At the beginning of the twenty-first century, Hālau Kū Māna and Lyon Arboretum began a partnership that aimed to rebuild Indigenous Hawaiian structures and practices and, thus, to transform over one hundred years of non-Indigenous approaches to land use and the production of knowledge.

HKM's Papa Lo'i—the eleventh- and twelfth-grade Lo'i Project class—maintains one of only two fully functional kalo-growing complexes in the valley. HKM staff and students plant, harvest, use, eat, and trade the kalo and other plants grown within their lo'i. I visited 'Aihualama several times during the years I worked with Hālau Kū Māna, but I spent the most consistent time with 'ōpio and kumu of Papa Lo'i during spring 2011 as I completed my final phase of research for this book. I accompanied the teaching team and the eleventh and twelfth graders responsible for these lo'i kalo on their weekly field days to 'Aihualama.

The group's entry into 'Aihualama is framed by a set of protocols, chants composed in antiquity and in recent years, intended to remind everyone present—students, kumu, unseen ancestors, and the land itself—of their relationships to one another. Each Tuesday, the 'ōpio's voices ring through the lush, broad valley, aptly named Mānoa.[5] A senior haumāna from among them, almost always a kāne (man/male), issues the opening call, and then all join in:

Eia ae na kauouo, na oha o Haloa
Ua awa, ua pae i ta ua Tuahine
Linohau Luahine a ta puu Manoa[6]

On their first day back after winter break in the 2010–11 school year, twenty 'ōpio stood with backs upright as the valley's walls and arms paused at their sides, calling to the place and weaving themselves into a genealogy of those who have cared for the lo'i here. A rough translation of the chant is, "We are the descendants of Hāloa, young offshoots of the kalo, and we ourselves have grown roots in this 'āina nurtured here in the back recesses of the valley by the rain called Tuahine. Luahine and Pu'u Mānoa are beautifully adorned."

Standing in two rows—wahine (women/female) on the left, kāne on the right—they drew the syllables of the word Mānoa out as long as the space between the ridges on either side of us and then deeply inhaled before recounting more than a dozen significant wahi pana (place names) and aliʻi of the island. In the early years of Papa Loʻi, each student had to recount his or her own personal genealogy before crossing ʻAihualama stream to enter the loʻi. The protocols later evolved, largely in the interest of time, so that they could collectively reintroduce themselves to the ʻāina and ask for entrance. The ʻōpio are always joined by at least two or three other kumu who teach different subject courses. The intent is for those teachers to better integrate what is happening at the loʻi with what the students are doing when they are back in class at the main campus, a fifteen-minute drive away in the next valley. I stood at the back of the wahine line, alongside science teacher Trevor Atkins and language arts and math teacher Richard Kuewa, who rounded out the kāne line.

With our final collective exhale, Kumu ʻĪmaikalani Winchester, a social studies and Hawaiian-language teacher who has led HKM's restoration work at ʻAihualama for the past four years, chanted a welcoming response from the other side of the stream. The students have also been taught to pay attention for signs from the ʻāina itself that it is okay to enter. I noticed a few of them pausing to look around before moving further. A soft breeze rustled the tops of the trees across the stream, and we gathered our belongings in preparation for the day's work ahead. Descending the small hill, one of the kāne students took his usual place on a stone midstream to help others across. Upon arriving at the other side, the group circled up for another set of oli, asking for protection and honoring the akua, ʻaumākua, and kūpuna. After all the opening chants had been completed, Kumu ʻĪmai invited the ʻōpio to take five minutes to walk around and silently observe changes in the landscape since they were last there. I walked over to a couple of wāhine who were standing on the kuāuna (bank) carefully examining one of the lower loʻi.

"This is ours," one of the ʻōpio told me, unprompted. The need for clarification must have been written on my face because the second young woman added, "This one is the juniors' loʻi, and the one below it is the seniors'. We planted ours just before the break." Their sense of

FIGURE 9. *Students in HKM's Papa Loʻi, or eleventh- and twelfth-grade loʻi restoration Project, begin their regular visits to ʻAihualama with observation and then spend time fortifying the puʻepuʻe (mounds) in which the kalo grow. According to Kumu ʻImaikalani Winchester, this style of planting is conducive for educational loʻi because the roots are more protected within the puʻepuʻe, thus allowing the students to get into the loʻi regularly and interact with their plants without damaging the root systems. Left to right: Kaleilehua Kaʻeo-Okimoto, Angelique Gamundoy, Panaleʻa Morita, and Dariane Kaʻuhane. Photograph by the author.*

personal connection and ownership came through in the words offered to me, as well as in their nonverbal communication with the loʻi itself as they crouched down close to the ground, pulled weeds growing along the edge, and reshaped a few of the puʻepuʻe (mounds) within the loʻi.

When the short reorientation period ended, Kumu ʻĪmai instructed the group in Hawaiian that they would be divided by class (eleventh and twelfth grades), each group tending their own loʻi while observing a kapu ʻōlelo Hawaiʻi, a period in which they could speak only Hawaiian. The students generally come from English-speaking homes, so this mandate was a challenge obviously welcomed by some and seemingly tolerated, though not ignored, by others. Some ʻōpio remained relatively quiet. Others used Hawaiian sentence patterns peppered with English words and asked each other or their kumu how to say different things. English continues to be the dominant language of instruction at HKM, but ʻAihualama has become a place where the students can learn and practice language through their teacher's instructions and through informal conversation as they work. As I helped weed alongside the juniors, one told me it was her goal to be fluent in Hawaiian before she graduated and to raise her own children in the language one day.

Showing the students his own willingness to learn alongside them, their science teacher used as much of his limited Hawaiian as he could when he pulled out small groups to gather data for their science research projects. Each pair, triad, or individual was collecting observations and measurements related to an investigation of one part of the loʻi system: for example, the flow rate in the stream above the loʻi's poʻowai (intake) versus the rate below its hoʻiwai (return), a survey of the populations of invasive versus native stream animals, and comparative methods of mulching kalo. Kumu Trevor offered each group instruction based on his observation of their specific needs. For one group he emphasized the importance of using a consistent method of data collection. For a student working independently, he asked her to consider what external factors might be impacting the variation she noticed in her measurements from week to week. For a third he prodded the students to think about the implications of their observations of specific behaviors exhibited by the invasive crayfish they had caught. How could they share their important findings with their classmates, families, and larger communities?

For a second part of the day, Kumu ʻĪmai split the ʻōpio into two groups divided by gender: kāne and wahine. The task was to complete the building of two walls in the lowest terraces, which had been opened by students, families, and a larger coalition of taro farmers and supporters called ʻOnipaʻa Nā Hui Kalo (ONHK) earlier in the fall. The kāne-identifying group was engaged in helping remove and rearrange the large pōhaku (rocks or boulders) that would comprise the base and the mass of the wall. The wāhine were sent over to the stream to collect two different sizes of small stones and pebbles, hakahaka and ʻiliʻili, which would fill in the spaces between the pōhaku. Without these smaller stones, water could leak out more easily from the terraces. The kumu emphasized that each kuleana, or responsibility, was as important as the other. The division of labor was not unique to that day but reflected a typical assignment of heavy work to the kāne and less physically demanding labor to the wahine.

As I sat with the young female-identifying students in the stream, gathering 'ili'ili not larger than the palm of my hand, I felt it hard to see this work as equally challenging and significant to the structural construction of the lo'i walls. Although I was bothered by the presumption that only kāne possessed the physical strength to efficiently move the large stones and boulders, I also noticed that two students who seemed to be exploring gender identifications that did not fit neatly into a two-gendered frame were free to choose either work group. Watching the groups labor, I thought about the importance of rebuilding the ancestrally influenced structures that sustained balanced life in these islands for centuries. I also thought about the ways this reconstructive process of restoring kuleana to 'āina both muddied and, at times, resolidified colonial logics and binaries. This chapter fleshes out some of the particular complexities of rebuilding Indigenous structures in the context of this school and their lo'i.

Hāloa (the kalo plant) is both elder sibling and, historically, the primary staple food of Kānaka Maoli. E mālama iā Hāloa (care for Hāloa) is the central ethic and framework for HKM's multidisciplinary Papa Lo'i Project. The work of rebuilding the 'auwai and lo'i that carry water to and shelter Hāloa aims not only to ground learning in math, science, social studies, and language but also to root students in an ethics of kuleana—a notion of responsibilities, authority, and rights that are tied to one's positionality in relation to place, genealogy, and effort put forth in knowledge acquisition/production. The process of finding and restoring kuleana is a powerful method of inquiry, teaching, and learning in contemporary Hawaiian education. By centering collective responsibilities to restore specific 'āina (as kuleana), Indigenous and settler students and educators together open possibilities of transforming settler-colonial relations on at least three levels. First, the Project takes up the material practice of rebuilding physical structures that feed people. Dislodging overdependence on a corporate-dominated transnational market economy for basic nutritional needs is an important aspect of realizing sustainable self-determination. Second, by placing living ʻāina at the center, the reconstructive labor and the stories told about those efforts help to create epistemological space, providing sources of theory, metaphor, and multidisciplinary, cross-cultural inquiry. The notion of rebuilding ʻauwai, restoring the channels through which knowledge can flow to nurture land, youth, and their communities, helps us reconceptualize Indigenous education in ways more productive than hackneyed and harmful images like "teaching students to walk in two worlds."[7] Third, the emphasis on personal and collective kuleana rather than on identity allows students and teachers to productively engage in Indigenous cultural revitalization projects together without losing sight of positionality and power. Yet the final section of this chapter also takes up the ways kuleana for the loʻi is sometimes divided along limiting and biologically determinate notions of gender.

Restoring the Capacity to Feed: Subsistence Practices as Sustainable Self-Determination and Community Cultural Wealth

Structures of settler colonialism have inflicted a fundamental violence on the relationship between Kānaka and ʻāina; they have eroded our ability to feed ourselves from the land. Over the past two hundred years, the total area of land planted in kalo has shrunk by 98 percent to fewer than four hundred acres in the first decade of the twenty-first century (about 0.2 percent of total planted cropland in the islands).[8] Unlike the population of Kānaka Maoli, which has rebounded since the massive collapse of the 1800s, our elder sibling Hāloa continues to decline. It can be argued that this is a condition of genocide. To be sure, it is at the very least a major cultural and economic shift with profound consequences. From an Indigenous ʻŌiwi cultural perspective, being unable to feed yourself and your ʻohana is not only dishonorable but, as preeminent twentieth-century scholar of Hawaiian culture Mary Kawena Pukui describes it, outright "humiliating."[9] And yet that is the situation in which Hawaiʻi finds itself today. The vast majority of its food is imported.

The development of the Hawaiian Islands as a consumer market for food and other goods produced through a transnational corporate capitalist economic system has decreased Kanaka Maoli dependence on our own ʻāina for food and the intimacy that such dependence fosters. The dislocation from ʻāina and ancestral food systems deeply undermines the capacity for resilience among our communities against shocks to and failures of the market economy. Moreover, American consumerist values and practices have stigmatized subsistence practices. HKM's kalo cultivation Project is one example among a growing group of school- and community-based educational initiatives that seek to restore the kuleana relationships between ʻāina as source of food and the people who live on it.

Kumu Danny Bishop, who was a key visionary in HKM's loʻi restoration Project at ʻAihualama and who has taught student groups from various Hawaiian charter schools at his own kalo farm in Waiāhole, remembered the ways dominant discourses shaped his own views about farming as a youth. Like many who grew up in the years after the 1959 establishment of the State of Hawaiʻi, Kumu Danny was raised to see farming of any kind as a low-class job. This was in part a result of the hegemony of industrial plantation agriculture. People came to associate farming with working on the plantations.

> My grandma worked pineapple plantation. So her whole thing was, "Go school and get an education so you can get a good job." My dad's idea of a good job was go be a civil servant. "Go be a clerk because it's job security, it's retirement!" So my brother's a mailman; I'm a fireman; and my sister works for Hawaiian Tel[ephone]. . . . That was the whole mindset back then: Farmer? No way![10]

He observed that many families actively encouraged their kids to completely invest themselves in a growing service-oriented market economy. As a result mahiʻai kalo and other forms of farming, whether subsistence or commercial, were marginalized. Young people have not been encouraged to imagine kalo cultivation as a part of their own or Hawaiʻi's potential futures. Earlier in his own life, Kumu Danny would not have imagined becoming a crucial actor in loʻi restoration efforts.

He discovered his passion for kalo farming after his wife, Meaala

Bishop, brought him into the struggles to restore water to Waiāhole and other windward streams. Kumu Danny became one of the key Kānaka caring for Mauka Loʻi in Waiāhole. It was here that he learned some key differences between Indigenous planting methods and the forms of industrial plantation agriculture he and his elders had grown up alongside and thus associated with farming. For one,

> the loʻi-style agriculture system is basically a low maintenance with a high yield agricultural system. So it gave the Indigenous people here more free time to practice their arts, to pay attention to their environment. They didn't have to have their head down all the time toiling. They *had* the free time to *play* or explore or refine.

He noted that several anthropologists have correlated the high level of refinement in traditional Hawaiian arts with the sophistication and productivity of the forms of agriculture and aquaculture developed in the islands prior to recorded Western contact.[11]

He further explored with students the pragmatic benefits of what he calls "taro patch economics." Tracking the number of hours required to maintain one loʻi, they estimated the number of hours of human labor required to produce one crop of kalo. "It's amazing, 150 hours for two tons per crop cycle." Spread out over the average life cycle of different varieties of kalo, this might mean only fifteen to twenty-five hours of labor per month, leaving a lot of time for other pursuits. Kumu Danny emphasized the quality of life and well-being that Hawaiian methods of farming kalo enabled. Thus, he argued that restoring these Indigenous structures would allow for improved cultural, spiritual, and economic health.

Restoring the ability to feed ourselves is an important aspect of what Tsalagi (Cherokee Nation) scholar Jeff Corntassel calls "sustainable self-determination."[12] As Corntassel writes, "The freedom to practice indigenous livelihoods [and] maintain food security . . . which includes the transmission of these cultural practices to future generations," is essential to sustainable self-determination.[13] Since the transmission of cultural practices to future generations takes place through education, it is important to include the teaching of sustainable, Indigenous food production within our educational initiatives. Feeding ourselves from our own lands is foundational to self-determination and health.

HKM kumu who teach the cultivation of kalo and other Hawaiian food plants seek to reinvest value in subsistence practices, sometimes drawing on their own familial experiences and what critical race educationalist Tara Yosso calls "community cultural wealth." Yosso posits community cultural wealth as a way of resisting deficit-oriented modes of thinking about students of color and their communities.[14] Against that grain, she defines community cultural wealth as the arrays of knowledges and networks communities of color use to survive and thrive amid oppressive forces, and she identifies the following six forms of capital: aspirational, navigational, social, linguistic, familial, and resistant.[15] Though students bring such assets to the classroom, these skills and abilities are largely unrecognized in mainstream schools. My interviews and observations of educators at HKM show that knowledge and experience with land-based subsistence should be added to this list, as well. Such abilities continue to be important for many Indigenous and working-class communities yet marginalized in mainstream schooling.

Subsistence forms of community cultural wealth are particularly important because they cultivate interdependent relationships between people and our natural environments. Formally trained as a kumu hula and a special education teacher in his adulthood, Kumu Kāwika Mersberg drew heavily upon his childhood experiences with an ʻohana who "lived the culture day to day" in fueling his commitment to implement land-based practices into the curriculum. As a youth growing up in the 1970s and 1980s in Waiʻanae, Oʻahu (a predominantly Kanaka Maoli and rural community), reverence for and intimacy with the ʻāina was imbued in him through familial practices of fishing, hunting, gathering, and enjoying simple pleasures like ti-leaf sliding.

> My dad is a hunter and a fisherman. So almost every day after school we were at the beach. We were learning how to fish, dive, lay net, patch nets, and so forth. If not [at the coast], every weekend we're either up in the mountains hunting for pig or learning how to gather plants from the forests, like ti-leaves or kalo that just grow wild to make laulau. . . . I'm very, very

thankful for my parents. . . . I was very lucky to learn how to live off the land.[16]

It was through regular practices such as these that Kāwika says he "learned how to appreciate nature" and became familiar with all the water resources in the valleys of the Waiʻanae mountain range. This was the kind of familiarity he wanted his students to learn, as well as the epic stories, legends, and genealogies that imbued the material and subsistence practices with deeper meaning. Ancestral Hawaiian subsistence practices like growing kalo or fishing sustained hundreds of generations of Kānaka Maoli on the islands in centuries past. These have been joined by more recent introduced practices like hunting deer or pig, and families have been able to use these practices to mitigate the immediate effects of corporate capital expansion.

In my interviews at HKM, it was not only the Kanaka Maoli teachers who found value in ʻāina-based subsistence practices but also non-Hawaiian teachers who recognized the cultural, economic, and political stakes of drawing nourishment directly from the land rather than being wholly dependent on large corporations. Kumu Consuelo Gouveia—a Filipina who grew up in a largely Hawaiian and Japanese rural community on Lānaʻi island—was teaching the sixth-grade multidisciplinary Ahupuaʻa Project when I interviewed her. They had spent the previous semester restoring a small loʻi kalo near the HKM campus. Consuelo had transferred to Hālau Kū Māna after spending seven years teaching in a mainstream public school on Oʻahu. She reflected on how she was drawn to its focus on ʻāina-based learning that validated her own community's cultural wealth, and she could use expertise she had developed as a youth:

> When I came to HKM, I felt like I was home. I felt like this was where I needed to be. [We] grew up as a hunting family. My dad was an avid hunter and ʻopihi picker on Lānaʻi. So I learned how to hunt. I learned how to pick ʻopihi. . . . My mom loved to fish for halalū. So when halalū season would come, we would go and get bucketfuls, and that would sustain us for the rest of the year until the next season. We just learned how to live off of the land. We always had goats in our yard. We

learned how to slaughter pig. My dad was the town butcher, so he taught me how to cut meat, how to skin deer.... We raised chickens. We raised everything. Everything that I see here at the school is what I did—lived off of the ʻāina. The only things that came from the store was milk and bread. Everything else came from the land. So I grew up that way.[17]

In her community's case, ʻāina-based subsistence practices were as much about class as they were about perpetuating Hawaiian culture. She specifically pointed out that living off the ʻāina enabled her family and others a certain level of autonomy because it made them less dependent on what she called "the corporation." Lānaʻi island is owned by a single landowner who is also the primary employer on the island. In previous generations most jobs were on pineapple plantations and, more recently, in the two hotels on the island. She remembered times when people were afraid to speak out against decisions the corporation made that they did not agree with. But if a family could feed themselves, they might feel more comfortable voicing opposition when necessary. Thus, subsistence practices can provide a material basis for autonomy and self-determination. "My brother and I, when we were younger, were like, 'We're poor!' Now that I'm older, no, 'We lived rich.' We were rich when we were growing up," Kumu Consuelo reflected.

Despite the redisciplining of HKM's curriculum under NCLB, teachers found creative ways to use project-based pedagogies focused on the community's cultural wealth of kalo cultivation while also employing more staid modes of test prep. Hired the year that HKM went into restructuring under NCLB, Kumu Trevor Atkins was brought on to teach math and to help develop strategies for raising student scores on the Hawaiʻi State Assessment (HSA)—the state's primary instrument for determining Adequate Yearly Progress. He remembered:

By my second year, I had realized that you are gonna run into problems if you try to marry studying for the HSA and running a project-based math curriculum.... So of our five hours that we needed to meet for math, I dedicated four to classroom-, textbook-, and worksheet-based HSA prep and another hour to Project math. The idea was that for at least one hour a week, the math could be integrated with what people are doing in the field.[18]

With the limited space he was able to carve for project-based math within his assigned classes, Kumu Trevor designed a yearlong word problem–based math curriculum that explored the issue of sustainable food production.

> Each day we had a new word problem to solve, starting with, How much land would we need to dedicate to kalo production to feed ka paeʻāina o Hawaiʻi?[19] From there we moved into, How much water do we need? How many huli do we need? If we've got kalo, then how many fishponds do we need? How much fresh water needs to run into each of those fishpond? And we started to zoom out to the bigger picture of, Can we sustain ourselves?

Over the course of the year, students concluded that it would be possible to sustain Hawaiʻi's current population if 1.6 percent of the crown lands, or roughly 16,000 acres across various islands, could be put into kalo production.[20] This analysis required the ability to mobilize difficult algebra and geometry concepts in a sustained inquiry over time. It also required an understanding of the history of U.S. occupation and land tenure, as well as the contemporary legal and political issues surrounding competing claims to land and sovereignty in the islands, which had been developed through the social studies aspect of the Papa Loʻi Project by Kumu ʻĪmaikalani. The students' inquiry also underscored the significance and meaning of the physical and intellectual labor they were doing in learning to cultivate kalo. In Kumu Trevor's words, they came to see that the land would not be productive of ʻāina without the mahiʻai to "make use of the land the way it was once made use of. That was heavy [for us], *and* it was math."[21]

By including kalo cultivation in their curricula, HKM kumu were not necessarily aiming to prepare all students to become full-time farmers. Rather, they worked against the hegemonic notions that drawing sustenance from the ʻāina was backward, a sign of poverty, or low class. On the contrary, teaching students how to grow food sustainably in their own environments opens the possibility of restored reliance on local landed and social resources. In collectively rebuilding Indigenous agricultural structures, relationships between Kānaka and 'āina are renewed. In the coming generations, fossil fuel supplies will continue to wane, and Hawai'i's overdependence on imported foods and other manufactured goods will likely become increasingly untenable. Thus, providing youth with the ability to use subsistence practices to supplement their livelihoods provides them with more choices and offers a safety net in uncertain ecological and economic futures. Moreover, the revaluing of cooperative engagement in food production offers students a way to challenge dominant, capitalist value systems. In my interviews and observations at HKM, I saw wealth reframed in terms of community cooperation and ecological richness rather than in terms of the accumulation of manufactured possessions. As one graduate remarked about her experiences at HKM, "Prior to Hālau Kū Māna, everything was so materialistic, like, 'Oh, I have the newest watch,' or, 'Your jeans aren't more expensive than mine.' Or it was all about keeping up with MTV and the latest music videos. And then getting into Hālau Kū Māna, it was like, 'This is what it's about!'"

Reestablishing Kuleana for Living 'Āina

HKM's involvement in restoring 'auwai and lo'i are examples of Indigenous educational projects that make material intervention in the relations of settler colonialism by rebuilding, maintaining, and using physical structures that have enabled Indigenous health and well-being for generations. Such land-based practices can also be sources of metaphor and theory—tools to help clear and reclaim the epistemological space that allows Indigenous knowledge to flow and to grow. In recounting their stories of 'Aihualama's reopening and engaging their students in caring for the place, kumu pushed hegemonic epistemological boundaries and established pathways by which living 'āina was made the foundation of multidisciplinary inquiry.[22] They literally and figuratively rebuilt and maintained 'auwai, vessels that bring life-giving water and knowledge to the kalo kanu o ka 'āina.[23]

The story of Hālau Kū Māna community members' reestablishing kuleana at 'Aihualama speaks back to colonial histories and present

FIGURE 10. *The trunk of a large albizia tree was cut and then chopped into smaller pieces, allowing water to flow through the 'auwai system rebuilt at 'Aihualama. In this photo Kanaloa Bishop, member of 'Onipa'a Nā Hui Kalo, works to assure a clear and unobstructed pathway for the water to flow into lo'i kalo (just outside the frame of this image). The intellectual and physical labor of clearing invasive structures and rebuilding Indigenous ones provides a metaphor for the kind of work that Indigenous education can do. Photograph by the author.*

realities that are written upon the land itself.[24] Prior to HKM's restoration work at 'Aihualama, the area was covered in a dense canopy of different types of banyans and albizias brought into the valley in the 1920s and 1930s by Dr. Lyon and his staff. These trees are notoriously difficult to take down. By the beginning of the twenty-first century, the albizias had reached peak heights of over one hundred feet, with trunks six to eight feet in diameter, and the banyans had fully developed their characteristic aerial roots, which drop from the branches and anchor into whatever ground they touch, growing thick enough to appear like trunks themselves and extending a single tree over hundreds of feet of ground.

Despite daunting circumstances, the kumu who first envisioned the restoration project were encouraged by the clarity with which the original loʻi walls were defined, despite the dense overgrowth. "You could see the walls and terraces easily, without even imagining. . . . The walls are real straight, real big, real clear."[25] The walls were seen not as faint traces of an ancient, forgotten society but as clear instructions from the kūpuna and the ʻāina itself. Kumu interpreted the visibility of the walls in an area of prolific rain and plant growth as the ʻāina calling them to revitalize kalo cultivation in the area.[26] "This is one of the first places that I actually really started believing . . . ʻāina is alive," Kumu Kamuela Yim mused, recounting the story several years later as we sat near one of the springs that fed the restored loʻi. He described ʻAihualama as someone whose friends had disappeared for so long that it had grown depressed, wondering and longing for the return of caring companions. Through various hōʻailona, ʻAihualama communicated its desire to play again.

A team of arborists cut down some of the large trees to open space for loʻi at ʻAihualama in 2004. That year, the first group of HKM students moved thousands of pounds of chopped wood with little more than their bare hands. Although the students were also able to cut back large swaths of the undergrowth, several of the biggest trees were left blocking sunlight and creating safety hazards. The Arboretum leadership decided, however, that no further trees could be cut back. Without the removal of these invasive trees, it seemed that the Project would stall or be permanently stunted. Then, as teachers retell the story to new groups of ʻōpio each year, the kūpuna and ʻāina intervened.

During the second year of the Project, heavy winds blew through Mānoa. For more than a week, the class had not been able to go up to ʻAihualama, because of extreme weather conditions. When they came back, all of the trees that needed to be cut down had been blown over. Moreover, Kumu Kamuela recalled that they had all fallen *away* from the existing clearing for the envisioned loʻi rather than toward it. Kumu Kāwika Mersberg summarized it this way: "Through akuas [godʻs/gods'] hands . . . through the natural elements and through our pule [prayers] . . . our kūpuna came in and helped us out, guided us in that matter."[27] He described the winds as hōʻailona, affirmation that HKM was indeed meant to take on the kuleana of caring for this place. It was a signal offered only because of the prayers, intentions, and demonstrated commitment of the kumu and ʻōpio who were rebuilding relationships with the place. Kumu Kāwika described the generous winds as affirmation of the cultural protocols that they had been consistently practicing: "I look at those years as the beginning of instilling in our kids that, no matter what, we still keep doing our pule and our oli, and we goin' rely on our kūpuna to take care and handle the stuff that we physically no can handle." The winds were a means for ancestors to give direction about their kuleana, in response to HKM teachers' and students' cultural expressions of their intentions on the ʻāina. Thus, Kāwika, the school's kumu hula and senior cultural source on the faculty, understood this event as solidifying HKM's foundational protocols that continued with the opening and closing of each school day and with each entry into the loʻi.[28]

In these practices of storytelling, restoration, and cultivation, HKM kumu have articulated the central epistemological point that ʻāina is not *something* but *someone*. Their pedagogies of aloha ʻāina exceed models of environmental or place-based education that focus on examining and studying phenomena of the natural world without allowing students to cultivate deep relationships with those places and powers. Using ʻāina-based pedagogies, HKM kumu have taught their students that the chants, hoʻokupu, and hana offered to ʻAihualama and other ʻāina they work and visit are a means of conversing, acknowledging that the ʻāina is alive, listening, and actively communicating. Correspondingly, they have sought guidance from the daily, weekly, and seasonal hōʻailona (signs) that the ʻāina and kūpuna offer. Caring for and deepening that relationship has therefore become the centerpiece of their multidisciplinary learning.

In one of the first years of the Loʻi Project, students conducted an intensive stream study that blended Indigenous and introduced knowledge systems and met state content standards across various disciplines, including geography, biology, language arts, math, physical education, performing arts, and technology. The central goals included deepening students' knowledge of the valley's natural resources and raising awareness about the health of the stream system among the wider community of Mānoa residents. Kumu led their students through all the major trails and the main streambed within the valley, and the students learned the Hawaiian names of countless features and read

FIGURE II. *From the vantage point on a ridge above ʻAihualama—the site of Hālau Kū Māna's ongoing multidisciplinary kalo cultivation Project—the lower half of the restored loʻi kalo complex is visible. The roots of an invasive tree that had been previously blocking sunlight can be seen in the left foreground of the photo. Photograph by the author.*

and reenacted traditional moʻolelo associated with the area. While hiking more than three miles of the waterway, the ʻōpio also conducted a stream survey using methods of Western science to examine stream life and the water's quality, depth, and speed. As a form of authentic assessment, students prepared a final comprehensive report that included literary and scientific description and analysis, drawing on Hawaiian and mainstream American educational forms of inquiry and composition. The report was presented to community residents and decision makers.

Over the next few years, HKM students and teachers worked together to redig loʻi following the footprint of old terraces and to redesign the irrigation system, which could not follow the ancient path, because of the growth of introduced trees in its way. Because ʻAihualama has an abundance of natural springs and rain, the ʻauwai system was designed to divert very little from the stream and to maximize the

movement of spring and surface water from the lowest point of a slop-
ing ridge, through the loʻi, and then outward to the stream. Every step
of the way, students were engaged in the planning, decision making,
and hard labor of preparing the loʻi, digging the ʻauwai, moving huge
pieces of the felled trees, and finally planting. It is important to point
out that ʻauwai are technological innovations that Kānaka Maoli developed to allow for sustainable, prolific wetland taro cultivation, feeding Kānaka and the kupuna species living in the surrounding oceans
and streams. According to Hawaiian customary practice, water that
courses through the ʻauwai and feeds loʻi kalo remains in the watershed
and is always returned back to the stream. Whereas the sugar ditches
that historically drained and replaced ʻauwai centralized water flow,
wealth, and authority, traditional ʻauwai systems prioritized ecological health, equitable distribution of wealth, and the localized knowledge of practitioners.[29] HKM students learned and applied these
principles while using tools and construction materials that were un-
available in ʻŌiwi Wale Nō times, such as PVC piping and machetes.

HKM graduate Pōmaikaʻi Freed talked about how the work of
hoʻokahe wai (to cause the waters to flow) was one of her favorite parts
of working at ʻAihualama, in part because it served as an embodied and
metaphorical healing practice. "The thought behind hoʻokahe wai is to
prepare," she explained as she talked about cleaning the leaves, rocks,
and branches that inevitably collect within a flowing, natural waterway.

> Even before you do the work to open up loʻi, you have to make
> sure the water that will feed you has a steady flow. I believe in
> that process is where you make those sacrifices, so that one day
> you may reap the benefits. Every day you walk up that stream
> to go clean a little bit further, a little bit further, so that one day
> you can build the ʻauwai and watch water flow into your work.
> To hoʻōla. To bring that mana into it. . . . Hoʻokahe wai is also to
> do that within yourself so that your own mana can flow better,
> in a more pono way. To have your own mana flowing better,
> you have to face some things within yourself, so you can clear
> the blockages that we slowly set up. It's definitely a process, but
> we come out stronger for it.[30]

She explained that moving upstream to clear the stream paralleled the process of journeying deeper and deeper into oneself to deal with the emotional and physical blockages caused by old wounds and unresolved tensions. After assuring that water, or mana, could flow properly, then healthy growth could occur.

In 2006, under the light of a full moon, HKM students made their first planting of kalo in their restored lo'i. Since then, subsequent Papa Lo'i classes have opened approximately one new field per year, and they have learned and practiced all phases, from putting huli in the ground to putting 'ai (food, especially pounded kalo) on their families' and friends' tables. They have erected three stone altars—pōhaku o Kāne—at which they regularly place ho'okupu of their own making, and they have built kahua (stone foundation) and lele (lashed wooden altar) for Makahiki, a season of celebrating agriculture and harvest. Through their visits to other lo'i and exchange with other farmers, they have planted over thirty distinct varieties of kalo at 'Aihualama, as well as 'uala (sweet potato), niu (coconut), lā'ī (ti leaf), 'ōlena (turmeric), 'awa (kava), hō'i'o (a native fern), and kō (sugar cane). 'Ōpio have also carved papa (boards) and pōhaku (stone pounders) for their families so that poi can be pounded in the traditional style at home. In all of these practices, they have used modern tools to accomplish traditional tasks associated with subsistence based on the 'āina. Each year, students learn the Hawaiian and Western scientific names for all parts of the kalo. They also memorize the defining characteristics and common usages of fifteen to twenty different varieties of kalo.[31] I recall sitting in one class session in which students could not leave until they recited the names and characteristics of their assigned set of cultivars. One student picked up a ukulele and composed a song on the spot as a mnemonic device. By the end of the period, he and five of his friends could each sing the song to their kumu as their exit tickets to finish the day.

When I interviewed her in 2011, three years after her graduation, Pōmaika'i ruminated on the most important things she took away from the three years she spent working at 'Aihualama:

What I value the most is connection to 'āina that was found within that process and the appreciation for the hana ma'a mau. It's when I realized that I could and would love to [work with 'āina] every day. By the time I raise children, I would like to raise them on food from the land we live on.

By cultivating a familial relationship with living 'āina, Pōmaika'i found lasting personal healing and began to see her own capacities to heal others. As she cared for the place, 'Aihualama became a foundational, nurturing presence in her life. "For me, I never grew up with physical kūpuna. My grandparents were not around. The circumstances that we were raised into, I definitely turned inward, to extreme measures. But I found that quiet acceptance from the elements." She went on to talk about how she learned to pay attention to the hō'ailona and the ways that the 'āina spoke to her and her classmates: "Like when we were standing on the hill, chanting and looking over at the lo'i . . . from 'Aihualama, I learned that our oldest kupuna are the winds, the rains, the elements."

I thought back to the changes I had witnessed at 'Aihualama that were due to the work students like Pōmaika'i and dozens of others had put in. On a recent visit I had been cleaning out the 'auwai, taking pleasure in seeing and hearing the subtle changes in the water's flow as debris was removed from the channel. One of the fallen albizias that had been lying across the back of the area had finally been cut into smaller pieces. The huge tree was among those that had blocked out sunlight, inhibited the growth of native plants, and prevented the flow of water through the 'auwai to the lo'i kalo. The youth and adult caretakers of 'Aihualama, using cross-sections of the tree's trunk, had formed a set of steps alongside the 'auwai system. The steps made it much easier to access and maintain the waterway along its steeper sections, particularly when the grass was high.

The albizia was, like dominant disciplinary formations within education such as mathematics and English, destructive when the environmental context was organized around *it* as a fixed and rooted structure, drawing resources toward itself for its own survival. When the invasive tree was cut, decentered, and ordered around the central goal of caring for the Indigenous social and ecological landscape, however, its usefulness became apparent. Similarly, thinking about Indigenous education in terms of rebuilding and maintaining the Indigenous structures that can sustain balanced life—such as ʻauwai and loʻi—makes it easier to think about how to repurpose knowledges, skills, and materials from various cultures and lineages in projects of Indigenous survivance and resurgence. If transformative, meaningful Indigenous culture–based education is about changing the context rather than just the content of education, then taking the long-term kuleana to care for living lands like ʻAihualama provides powerful opportunities for changing the culture of schooling.[32]

Indigenous and Settler Kuleana

Thus far, I have looked at ways that transformative Indigenous education is enlivened by rebuilding Indigenous structures that provide life to people while also contributing to the health of the natural environment. One of the goals of critical Indigenous education and broader Indigenous resurgence projects is to engage diverse people in unmaking the social relations that characterize settler colonialisms. As I have discussed, at HKM both Indigenous and settler educators participate in this process together. As a publicly funded institution, it is assured that people of all racial, ethnic, gender, class, and religious backgrounds can be students, faculty, or staff at the school. Over the first decade HKM's student body primarily consisted of Kānaka Maoli, and almost all students had mixed racial and ethnic heritages. Though a majority of those who worked at HKM over the first decade were ʻŌiwi, many teachers were not Native Hawaiian.[33] The project at ʻAihualama, like the school itself, was generally Kānaka led, with non-Hawaiian teachers and administrators often playing important supporting or facilitating roles. Participants' access to ʻAihualama was and continues to be mediated by the settler state; teachers and students are able to mālama that place regularly because they are part of a public school working in conjunction with a state university's arboretum.

Both settler and Indigenous people must take part in dismantling the structures that prohibit sustainable Indigenous self-determination and caring for lands upon which all depend for life. But what are some of the complexities of such work? For instance, how might settlers express attachment to place without ignoring history and eliding Kanaka Maoli genealogies? What issues arise when settlers take on kuleana for the lands on which they reside when Indigenous people still do not have collective access to or political control of their land bases? How did HKM educators address these issues in ways that might be relevant for other schools? The notion of kuleana has been an important one within HKM's school culture because it shifts people's thinking away from static identity categories (who is or isn't Hawaiian) and toward more subtle, context-based responsibilities and positionalities. This section discusses the following three key aspects of kuleana that were manifested in HKM pedagogies and that may be useful to others considering the dynamics of Indigenous–settler collaboration in projects of Indigenous resurgence and education: (1) genealogical connection to place, (2) active commitment and contribution to the community, and (3) self-reflexivity and the desire to learn.

In HKM's Lo'i Project and other classes, lessons about Hāloa often emphasized the point that genealogy was a central factor in determining one's kuleana. One finds and fulfills his or her own kuleana by considering his or her relation to history/genealogy, to place, and to the other people with attachments to that place.[34] As discussed in chapter 1, kuleana is often translated as "rights, responsibilities, and authority," but it also fundamentally implies genealogy and place. Noted Hawaiian scholar Samuel Kamakau similarly underscores the significance of lineage in determining one's kuleana, not only in this life but also in the afterlife. Over centuries of living in a place, one's 'ohana becomes genealogically tied to the land itself. One's spirit resides in those places or becomes transformed into the bodily forms of things (animals, plants, thunder) from which they are lineal descended. Kuleana can be the relationship between a person or family and their 'āina, and it can be that 'āina itself. In the same way, HKM students talked about 'Aihualama or specific lo'i that they tended within that area as their kuleana. In HKM's case, because students came from various parts of the island and because 'Aihualama had been under the settler state and HSPA's control for so long, none of the Lo'i Project participants came with a direct genealogical connection to that specific piece of 'āina. In studying the mo'olelo of Hāloa, however, they recognized the distinct genealogical connection between Kānaka and Hāloa. Still, all Lo'i Project participants, both 'Ōiwi and not, were encouraged to introduce themselves as caretakers of 'Aihualama by acknowledging the genealogies they brought with them. No overt distinctions were made between Hawaiian and non-Hawaiian students.

In my observations at the lo'i and other HKM classes in which kumu talked about significant figures in Hawaiian history and culture, inclusive language was the norm. When 'Ōiwi teachers like Kumu 'Īmaikalani or Kumu Kaleilehua Maioho spoke to their haumāna, Hāloa was called "*our* elder sibling" (ko *kākou* kua'ana). Similarly, in lessons about the Kanaka forebears who developed various techniques of kalo production over centuries, kumu of Hawaiian ancestry referred to them as "*our* kūpuna." Thus, non-Hawaiian students were given the message that they too had a connection to Hāloa and to kūpuna Hawai'i. In my interactions with and observations of students, whether Kānaka Maoli or not, they generally replicated similar inclusive, possessive language. The non-Hawaiian students who stayed at the school for a number of years essentially assimilated and wove themselves into the genealogy. Those who had a difficult time fully committing to the school's cultural values and aims simply chose to move to other schools. In day-to-day learning contexts, action and behavior mattered more than identifying which students were Hawaiian and which ones were not.

Practice and commitment to the community were the more salient markers and aspects of kuleana. Kumu never called students to identify themselves as Hawaiian or non-Hawaiian, Indigenous or settler, and for the most part this possible division rarely seemed to be an issue among the students themselves, either. One graduate recalled learning only after years together that two of her peers were not Kānaka 'Ōiwi. She had always assumed otherwise.

> At first, it tripped us out. We were like, "Why are you here? Why did you sign up for this school?" But it didn't matter, because they appreciated and perpetuated just as hard as we did, as people with the blood. . . . It didn't matter. It just mattered how much we respected [Hawaiian culture] and pushed each other to respect the culture just as much as the next person, to appreciate it, to *practice* it. . . . What mattered was we go to this school, we're *in* Hawai'i; learn about where you're living. Learn about the values and culture of the place you call home.[35]

Her comment underscored what seemed to be the prevailing belief that all people in Hawai'i have some kuleana to learn about the Hawaiian culture and people. Each person's kuleana differs, however, and this was more apparent among the faculty.

Non–Kanaka 'Ōiwi teachers who stayed at HKM for any significant length of time, such as Kumu Consuelo, made it a point to signal to their colleagues and students that they were not of Hawaiian ancestry. Teachers I interviewed who went by Hawaiian names, were born and raised in the islands, and could have passed as Kānaka by appearance made it a point to tell me that they were not Hawaiian. Each of them talked about how they loved Hawai'i, felt an affinity for Hawaiian culture, and had Hawaiian children or partners but still recognized that they did not need to take on Hawaiian identity in order to do their work. In this way they modeled the point Beniamina makes about knowing the limits of one's kuleana. For some it was important to explicitly model for their students the value that non-'Ōiwi residents of Hawai'i should respect and support Indigenous Hawaiian culture and education.

For some non-'Ōiwi teachers, it was not necessary to explicitly verbalize that they were not Indigenous. A descendant of European and Japanese settlers to Hawai'i, science and math teacher Trevor Atkins's name and fair complexion read as haole to most people on the islands. His childhood experiences of being raised in a rural community on Hawai'i Island by parents who propagated native plants and who conveyed to him a deep "love and loyalty to Hawai'i" were more difficult to see on the surface. Trevor recalled that while the veteran HKM faculty members (almost all of whom were Kanaka Maoli) accepted him rather quickly, the students took more time to assess his membership in the community. Trevor learned firsthand about the process of earning trust and kuleana by sticking around. He reflected on his first couple of years at the school:

> For the students it was very cut and dry. At first I wasn't [Hawaiian]. And then I was. One eighth grader, who at first called me an effin' haole, now won't let me tell him I'm not Hawaiian. Some of them are not ready to understand the ways in which we can and can't be Hawaiian . . . the difference

between genealogy, nationality, aloha, the cultures in which we grew up. . . . When necessary [to distinguish Hawaiians from non-Hawaiians], I draw the line at moʻokūʻauhau, genealogy.

As a kumu, he had earned standing among his students by demonstrating his commitment to their individual successes, to the school community, to sharing his knowledge of Hawaiian plants, and to increasing his own knowledge of Hawaiian language and history. But he also complicated and resisted being fully included as "Hawaiian." Allowing such inclusion would collapse differences in positionality, genealogy, and ultimately, kuleana. For him such distinctions were important because of the different kuleana between one who has a four-generation connection to Hawaiʻi versus one who has a millennia-long genealogical connection. Speaking about how he navigates these tensions between wholeheartedly committing to being part of the learning community and remaining distinct as a settler, he returned to the issue of inclusive language:

> *Our*, that word gets used a lot, and I have made the mistake of using it. I call it a mistake because I don't feel that's my place. But it's funny because [HKM is] soʻohana, so kākou.[36] So at times I'll be talking to the ʻōpio like, "Well, *our* people . . ." [his voice trailed off]. I don't wanna say, "*Your* people . . . ." So it ends up being, "The people of this land . . . ." That's really what its about. . . . The ʻāina decides where you are. I can talk about the ʻāina as something that I love, and that's how I tie into the moʻokūʻauhau, but its different, and I think it's important to make that difference. . . . Certainly, I would prefer settlers like myself to learn the language and learn the winds and rains, not just the names of them but what they feel like—not to put themselves in disguise [passing as Hawaiians], as I've seen done before, but to actually want to give back to this ʻāina and simultaneously recognize that there's other people who have been giving to this ʻāina a *lot* longer. So it's kinda like just getting in line. If somebody's passing out kalo and there's a thousand years' worth of people in line . . . I rather just stand at the back of the line and wait my turn.

His reflections on struggling to find the right words highlights a central tension for many non-Indigenous people who aim to participate in the unmaking of settler colonialisms. On the one hand, he felt a deep connection to Hawai'i, its lands, its history, and its people, but on the other, he did not want that attachment to eclipse or minimize the distinct relationships between Kānaka Maoli and our 'āina, particularly when Hawaiian sovereignty continued to be suppressed. By repositioning land at the center and being attentive to the various relationships that others had with the 'āina, he found a place from which to work. He could act out of his aloha for the land and the people of it while also recognizing his genealogical difference by reckoning his family's history of settlement, complicity with colonialism, and later mālama 'āina. Perhaps, such a positioning might be thought of as a *settler aloha 'āina* practice or kuleana.[37] A settler aloha 'āina can take responsibility for and develop attachment to lands upon which they reside when actively supporting Kānaka Maoli who have been alienated from ancestral lands to reestablish those connections and also helping to rebuild Indigenous structures that allow for the transformation of settler-colonial relations.

Kumu Trevor's process of coming to understand his kuleana as a settler ally for sustainable self-determination and Hawaiian political independence exemplifies the idea that Indigenous methods of knowledge production (including pedagogy and research) require that one attend to the stakes of one's positionality in relation to Indigenous lands and communities and that one uphold the related ethical practices with respect to those lands and communities.[38] It also underscores the point that kuleana can be a concept that drives learning when posed as a question (what is my kuleana?) and when the learner is open to deep self-reflection. In Trevor's case, his process included enrolling in professional development courses focusing on Indigenous politics and Hawaiian language, engaging in conversations about the stakes of Indigenous and settler coalitions, and actively listening to feedback from 'Ōiwi peers about the impacts of his identifying as a Hawaiian national without first recognizing his white privilege. In these ways he worked to consciously avoid the problems Hawaiian scholars No'eau Warner and Julie Kaomea point out when they write about instances in which Hawaiian language and cultural education programs have sometimes become sites in which non-Hawaiian people try to speak for and wield power and authority over Kānaka 'Ōiwi.[39]

Kaomea provides the following useful set of questions that non-Indigenous participants in Indigenous educational programs might ask themselves: "What is my place in this setting? What is my role or kuleana here? Is this the time and place for me to step forward ... to step back ... or to step out?"[40] To these I would add that each member of the learning community, both Indigenous and settler, teacher and student, might ask, Given my and my family's relationship to history, to this specific 'āina, and to the other people who exist here, what is my kuleana?

It perhaps is this space of questioning that held the most productive power in pedagogies of kuleana at HKM. The goal was not to find finished answers but to continue asking the questions in each new context and moment. By placing the question, what is my kuleana? at the center, HKM community members moved beyond unproductive oppositions between settler and Indigenous participants without collapsing difference or leaving the importance of positionality behind. That is, kuleana was seen as a process of discovery rather than a prescription. Thinking and talking about kuleana became a way to open up discussions about Indigenous and settler collaboration in projects of Hawaiian knowledge revitalization and Kanaka Maoli survivance. In the next section I discuss the ways physical and intellectual labor at the lo'i was gendered in ways that sometimes ascribed rather than opened questions of kuleana.

Gender, Labor, and Kuleana

Although HKM kumu emphasized Indigenous or settler positionality as social practice, kuleana—when defined as specific, daily tasks—were often dispensed along gendered lines that assumed gender to be a fixed, biologically determined category rather than a social practice. For example, as described earlier, it was typical for wāhine to be assigned the kuleana of gathering small stones as filler for the organizing structure that the kāne were building as they moved heavier, larger pōhaku. As we were gathering 'ili'ili one day in the stream I asked one student who was completing her second year with the Project how she felt about the division of labor at the lo'i. She remarked, "'They assume that us girls don't want to do hard labor. I wouldn't mind. Sometimes, I would like to get in there and lift the heavy stuff. It's not like I don't *want* to do it." A similar division of labor was often doled out when community groups came to support the restoration efforts. When the Project was preparing for fundraisers or other events, the wāhine would far more frequently be asked to keep track of various supplies, set and implement event budgets, and track sales, whereas kāne more frequently were spokespersons or chant leaders. In this section I briefly discuss some of the ways in which pedagogies framed gender as a biologically determined reality and highlight opportunities for seeing gender in more fluid terms. It is important for those of us engaged in projects of Indigenous resurgence and freedom to think critically and self-reflexively about these issues. Otherwise, we risk replicating the gendered hierarchies that are at the core of settler-colonial logics and systems of power.[41]

In restoring the ʻauwai and loʻi at ʻAihualama, gendered kuleana tended to be based upon teacher-perceived natural strengths that in many ways aligned with Western gender categories. Kāne were assumed to be physically stronger and more capable of hard labor, and wāhine were seen as more attentive to detail and, thus, better at administrative tasks such as keeping inventory or documenting Project activities through photos and writing.[42] What was problematic was the fixed association of particular strengths with particular bodies. When such tasks are never exchanged, then each group of students never gets to practice and develop the particular strengths that they are observed and assumed not to possess. I am not arguing that there should be no spaces where kāne and wāhine work in single-gender settings. Educational researchers have shown the value of single-gender spaces for learning when students are expected to learn the same content, and Kānaka Maoli are rediscovering the importance of refashioned spaces such as the Hale Mua and the Hale Peʻa in contemporary cultural life. But if wāhine are not challenged to feel the psychological empowerment associated with the expression of their bodily strength and kāne are not given equitable practice in valuable administrative skills such as budgeting and organizing, then there is a danger of replicating a sort of biological determinism about appropriate kuleana that is limiting for ʻōpio of either gender.

To understand some of the complexities embedded in this gendering of kuleana at the loʻi, it is important to know that in the generations prior to recorded Western contact, kalo cultivation and food preparation was largely the kuleana of men. Contemporary practitioners and educators who are perpetuating the practices of mahiʻai kalo are rearticulating these practices in a time where it has become acceptable for people of all genders to grow and cook kalo and to make poi. I specifically use the word *rearticulating*, as the lens of articulation theory allows us to see that all cultures and traditions are constantly being refashioned under particular historical and political contexts. As James Clifford puts it, "Traditions articulate, selectively remember and connect pasts and presents."[43] At ʻAihualama, just as in any cultural practice, certain aspects of older practices are used while others are left behind. Tengan has shown how contemporary Hawaiian identities have been articulated through the ritual performances of specific moments or eras of Kanaka ʻŌiwi history, such as in reenactments of Hawaiian warriorhood of the ʻAikapu era and, more specifically, the generation and events leading up to Ke Aliʻi Kamehameha I's unification of the islands on the cusp between the eighteenth and nineteenth centuries.[44] Similarly, kumu in charge of HKM's work at ʻAihualama look to the ʻAikapu era as informing some of the gender regulations within the Project. As Tengan describes, the ʻAikapu was

> a religiopolitical set of laws that separated men and women during eating periods. More important it separated the classes of aliʻi (chiefs) from makaʻāinana and imbued the class of specialists known as kāhuna with powerful ritual authority. . . . On all levels, the responsibility for feeding both the family and the gods fell on the shoulders of men. They prepared food in separate imu (underground ovens) and built separate eating houses: the hale mua (front or first house) for the men and the hale ʻaina (eating house) for the women and children.[45]

The gendering of twentieth- and twenty-first-century loʻi work often draws on some but not all aspects of these gendered divisions.

Drawing on what he was taught by the kumu who trained him in mahiʻai kalo, Kumu ʻĪmaikalani Winchester enforced the restriction

FIGURE 12. *Several men, including HKM students, teachers, and community volunteers, work together to move a large boulder during the restoration process of one of the loʻi at ʻAihualama. Although kāne, wāhine, and māhū participate in the regular care of this place, including regular visits and special workdays such as this one, tasks requiring significant physical strength are typically given to the kāne. Photograph by the author.*

at ʻAihualama that women having their maʻi (menstruating) were not able to step into a loʻi, although they could work along the banks and do less demanding tasks. During their time of the month, they were similarly restricted from cleaning and pounding the cooked taro. But unlike the ʻAikapu restrictions of old, separate ovens or eating areas were not used at HKM nor in the wider Hawaiian community, nor were particular foods restricted to only men or only women. The ʻAinoa (freed eating) enacted by Kamehameha II, Kaʻahumanu, and Keōpūolani ended these kapu. But selected elements of the separate spheres of kuleana for kāne and wāhine have been recast at ʻAihualama and many other loʻi. Kumu ʻĪmaikalani explained, both to his students and to me in conversation, that there were both pragmatic and spiritual elements to these rules. On a pragmatic level, he related that any bodily fluids, whether due to open sores or to menstruation, should not be near something that would later be eaten. It is further considered rude to step over someone, including Hāloa. On a spiritual level, he expressed that the regulation was about respecting the sanctity of the kalo, understood as a male plant, by not introducing the "different kind of sacredness" of a woman menstruating.[46] In their process of restoring kuleana, many twenty-first-century loʻi revitalization projects take the period of the ʻAikapu as a point in the Hawaiian past by which to index contemporary gender practices. Gendered kuleana may have been different, however, in times before the ʻAikapu.

At ʻAihualama a clear line between kāne and wāhine was established from the moment students approach the loʻi, as they were asked to stand in separate lines when they called for entrance to the place. (As discussed in chapter 4, this gendering of protocol was not standard across the realms of different cultural practices within the school.) These entrance protocols mirrored the school's ritual opening of the school day, when students stood in kāne and wahine lines entering the piko (center) of the hālau simultaneously, but as distinct groups, and then coming together to form nested circles in which everyone was joined and faced one another, comprising a whole. The daily opening and closing were strongly influenced by the ritual protocols taught by Kumu John Keolamakaainanakalahuiokalaniokamehamehaekolu Lake, who served as a spiritual, cultural, and educational advisor to HKM from its founding until his passing in 2008. The joining of the two lines in a circle represented a balanced wholeness created in the joining of kāne and wahine spheres, reflecting the balanced dualism important in many understandings of Hawaiian culture.[47] At ʻAihualama the students similarly came together in a circle to complete their opening protocols before dividing out into different work groups. But in contrast to the broader community of oli practitioners, kāne students within the Loʻi Project were more often the ones to begin and lead chants. (Unlike some Indigenous Pacific Islander cultures, Kānaka Maoli do not have a tradition where men only or predominantly are orators or chanters.)

In the field one day, I asked one of the non-Hawaiian teachers why he thought kāne tended to be the ones leading oli within the Project. He observed that for the past three years there had been few wāhine in the senior class from year to year. There tended to be a much heavier representation of kāne among the ninth through twelfth graders enrolled at the school. Another issue was the predominance of kāne teachers in Papa Loʻi. But he also felt it had to do with the personal ʻano (nature, disposition, character) of the few wāhine who had been among the graduating seniors over those years; they had not been confident enough to step up into cultural leadership roles, such as being lead voice for the oli or actively mentoring younger students in proper behavior during protocol. Pushing further, I asked if there were specific arenas or places where the wāhine were given opportunities to lead or to shine. Upon reflection, he acknowledged that there weren't explicit spaces and mused about whether the school was "creating these ʻano through socialization" or if girls simply "came like this" to the school.

Noelani Duffey-Spikes graduated from HKM prior to the beginning of the ʻAihualama restoration, and she was a former student whom many kumu and students in subsequent classes remembered as a strong wahine leader. So I asked her about how any differences in kuleana for kāne and wāhine students during the first four years of HKM's operation might have impacted her. Similar to the experience of more recent students, she remembered that the places in which she saw a clear division of kuleana between kāne and wāhine were in hula and in doing physical labor on the ʻāina. Despite those distinct spaces, she felt she had been pushed to challenge her own physical capacities through mālama ʻāina work, and she reflected on how she valued those aspects of physicality in her education. In addition to successfully completing the intellectual labor of attending college and earning a bachelor's degree in political science, she also emphasized that in various jobs she held throughout her college years, employers had prized and praised her willingness to engage in more difficult physical labor as well as clerical and administrative work.

> It was a *big* deal that as a female I wasn't afraid to do whatever it took to get the job done . . . having that instilled in me in school that as a female, yeah, I can do office work, but I can also get down and dirty, and if I break a nail, so be it. . . . [For example] in the athletics job I had, other women would opt to just tape up posters, and I was the only female with a group of six guys

who was willing to try and move this fat 500-pound table. That
type of thing, being willing to do the job no matter what we
come across, that was a big, big thing.[48]

It was liberating and empowering for her to know that she could take
on all types of kuleana, and importantly, she developed this embodied
sense of her own capacities, in part, through her physical engagement
with the 'āina as part of her HKM education.

The presence of students who were questioning or moving between
the categories of kāne and wahine presented the opportunity for challenging rigid gender determinism. Kumu allowed such students to decide which gendered grouping they would want to work with on any
given day. These 'ōpio were not forced to pick one group and stick with
it all the time, indicating that there was at least some acceptance and
acknowledgement that gender is a practice rather than a physically determined, stable identity category. This also reflected the Hawaiian cultural recognition of māhū, third or transgendered individuals, as valuable members of our 'ohana and communities. Drawing on her research
in Hawaiian mo'olelo, mele, oli, and other forms of literature, Leilani
Basham describes the category of māhū as

a very broad, flexible space that includes those who are "her-
maphrodite" or what is now being called intersex, as well as
those who choose to alter their gender or what is now called
transgender. While māhū is an identity label, it is not necessarily an indicator of sexual preference and activity. There are
mo'olelo that describe māhū as having the genitals of both or
neither male or female. Māhū were integrated and honored
within Hawaiian contexts. They were the heroes of mo'olelo,
revered as coming from a spiritual place, and some were even
Mō'ī (Rulers), while others were Akua (Gods).[49]

Moreover, she argues that the lack of gender marking within Hawaiian-language pronouns and naming practices demonstrates the relative
unimportance of gendering people or positions in the first place. In
relation to this discussion of kuleana, Basham's insight underscores
the point that kuleana was not necessarily gendered uniformly across

the Hawaiian past. This is reflected, for example, in the fact that the names of roles such as aliʻi, kahuna, and mahiʻai were not ascribed or fixed to kāne or wāhine. Gendered kuleana also varied from island to island.[50] Pukui further describes classes of women who were trained as warriors—nā koa wāhine—and as priest-prophets—nā kāula—and wore clothing like men, whether they menstruated or not. Of the warriors, she writes:

> These were women trained in warfare. They went with their men, and when the men were fighting, the women prepared their food, though cooking was usually man's work. . . . They asked to become *nā koa wāhine* and then men trained them. . . . They were just like other women. When the fighting was over they came back home and took care of their children.[51]

These examples demonstrate that even when kuleana was gendered, it was not tied only to female or male bodies.

What is important with a Hawaiian understanding of gender is the work to achieve balance rather than to maintain hierarchy. Tengan has noted that the contemporary Kānaka Maoli often talk about Kū and Hina, ancestral figures symbolizing masculine and feminine energies. He argues that the desire to balance these forces does not mean there is an already agreed upon consensus as to what such a balance might look like. But he also observes that within the ritual spaces he studied, Kū and Hina came to be equated with men and women, "rather than masculine and feminine qualities that both may possess."[52]

This understanding of Kū and Hina as *energies* or *qualities* that could both be contained in a single body was sometimes communicated by HKM teachers in their explanations of Hawaiian understandings of gender, even if not always reinforced through the assignment of specific kuleana. For example, Kumuʻīmai explained to students on various occasions that in a Hawaiian worldview each person is comprised of kāne and wahine elements. The left side of the body is seen as female, and the right side, as male. The challenge for each individual is to find the right balance between the kāne and wahine energies within themselves. In that endeavor it may be just as useful, as Tengan begins to suggest, that we look beyond the Kū and Hina metaphor and also think about the dualistic pairings of Kū and Lono or Kāne and Kanaloa, who were often seen as male deities but all of whom had female forms, and of Pele and Hiʻiaka, sisters who embodied the complementary powers of creation and destruction, nurturing and violence, and strength and gentleness. Perhaps by looking at these diversely gendered pairings, it would be easier to loosen hegemonic, colonial notions of gender.

Rather than giving instructions about what it means to be a man, woman, or third-gendered person and how that shapes what an individual can be expected to do, educators can make room for open questions like, What is my kuleana as a wahine, a kāne, or a māhū on this ʻāina? In the process of discovering their own kuleana, the answers students find may be surprising. I asked HKM graduate Hōmai Luteru what his five years at HKM taught him about what it meant to be a Hawaiian kāne. He turned to the issue of leading chants and cultural protocols at the school. Though he did not want to lead oli until the ending of his senior year, he remembered closely observing the students who did take this leading cultural role. He recalled an instance when a wahine classmate opened and led a chant that one of his male peers normally started:

> I saw the boys like, "Huh? She's doing it?" with that look. . . . I didn't speak much [in class], but that time I did. I told them, "Why can't she do it? She's doing it better than most people right now. . . . She's willing to take the initiative, and she knows what she's doing. So of course, she can do it! She's equal like anybody else, if not sometimes she's *better* than most of us guys."[53]

A normally quiet and reserved student, he felt it his kuleana as a kāne to speak to defend the space of wahine leadership in a realm that was typically kāne dominant. "[HKM] taught me respect for women," he added.

"He Hāloa Au. Hānai ke Kalo."

In this chapter I have explored the kuleana HKM teachers and students took to restore and care for Hāloa, including rebuilding the structures that nurture both kalo and Kānaka: ʻauwai and loʻi. By making this restorative, land-based work foundational within their pedagogies, HKM teachers and their students created material and epistemological value for their communities. I have also looked at the ways that a focus on kuleana as practice and process worked to both disrupt and reinforce colonial binaries. I conclude with a brief story about how 'ōpio assumed this kuleana and continued to open the physical and epistemological space for ever-evolving forms of Indigenous education. With their feet firmly planted into lo'i of their own making, they named their kuleana in ways that productively muddied gendered divisions.

When I visited 'Aihualama with the students on their first day back to school in January 2011, their kumu bestowed the responsibility of naming the two new lo'i that they had opened earlier that fall with the assistance of 'Onipa'a Nā Hui Kalo. Each class—juniors and seniors— would name their own lo'i. Over the course of that quarter, as they visited Uncle Danny Bishop's Waiāhole farm, He Hawai'i Au (I Am Hawai'i/Hawaiian), and tended to the 'auwai, kuāuna, and kalo within their own lo'i, they contemplated different names. Whereas the senior class was composed of a kāne majority, the junior class was composed of eight wāhine and only one kāne. As I worked alongside them from week to week, the junior women considered Mana Wahine (Women's Power), and a couple of the seniors jokingly suggested Keolamaikalo'i in honor of one of their classmates. By the time they returned from spring break, they had finally decided.

Speaking for the junior class, two wāhine, Haumea and Donna, who had attended HKM since their sixth-grade year announced their chosen name, He Hāloa Au (I Am Hāloa), a name both honoring the influence of Uncle Danny and his lo'i as kumu and a name expressing the inseparable connection between kalo and Kānaka. In their explanation to Kumu 'Īmai, they recalled the 'ōlelo no'eau he had taught them: "Hāloa, ke kalo. Hāloa, ke Kanaka." (Hāloa, the plant. Hāloa, the person.). This predominantly wāhine class had chosen a name that directly identified themselves as Hāloa, whom they had always been taught was a male plant and ancestor. Yet they explained that as their kumu had always taught them, the connection between themselves and the kalo was so strong that they were like one.

The kāne-dominant senior class chose a name that emphasized the

FIGURE 13. *At the last Lā ʻOhana before his 2011 graduation, Kaleo Correia guides Laʻilaʻikūhonua Kaʻōpua-Winchester in planting a huli (taro stalk), the primary method of propagating kalo. These quarterly events allow HKM students to share their knowledge with other ʻohana members. Photograph by the author.*

nurturing aspect of their work at ʻAihualama over the two years they had spent in Papa Loʻi. Asked by their kumu, "E ka papa ʻumikūmālua, ʻo wai ka inoa o koʻoukou loʻi?" (Seniors, what is the name of your loʻi?), Hanohano, a senior who had attended HKM since his seventh-grade year, responded for his class, "Hānai Ke Kalo."[54]

"No ke aha mai?" (Why [did you chose that name]?), Kumu ʻĪmai prompted.

"Because we raise kalo, generation after generation it will continue; we will continue. If we take care of it, then it feeds us," Hanohano explained.

Their choice highlighted the recuperation of care, feeding, and planting as being as much masculine as it was feminine. Caring for Hāloa would be an ongoing kuleana for their cohort, comprised of ʻōpio from multiple racial backgrounds and multiple genders. Through the cultivation of kalo, under the malu of their kumu, they had made this kuleana their own.

Together, both classes' chosen names reflect an inversion of typical Western gender characterizations. These inoa and their stories will continue to reside with the ʻāina, to be passed on and recounted by new groups of haumāna who will continue to cultivate kalo and kuleana and to extend the genealogy of mahiʻai kalo. Genealogy has been a central way for HKM kumu and ʻōpio to think about their kuleana in class and beyond, and chapter 4 takes up that theme more fully. Just as Hāloa, as a kāne form, exhibits the reproductive and nurturing capacities often associated only with the feminine within Western gender frameworks, the chapter begins with *Kānehūnāmoku*, a waʻa recognized as wahine by her captain and those students who sail her but bearing the nickname *Kāne*. Under the care of her captain, Kumu Bonnie Kahapeʻa-Tanner, and crew, she travels the ocean and serves as a source for learning about the heavens, often seen as a realm of Wākea (Sky Father).

FOUR

Enlarging Hawaiian Worlds

Wa'a Travels against Currents of Belittlement

> The kūpuna are always trying to show us stuff, but half the
> time we probably never even see. . . . The canoe takes away
> all the barriers . . . and allows our ancestors to come in and
> show us and teach us. The canoe is a vehicle that takes the kids
> to another place so that they can also see beyond what is just
> in front.
>
> ▪ Kumu Bonnie Kahape'a-Tanner, December 4, 2004

Indigenous Pacific Islanders' senses of self are created as much in travel as in continuous residence upon particular lands.[1] We are both routed and rooted.[2] As Native Pacific cultural studies scholars Diaz and Kauanui write, "The land and sea constitute our genealogies and, not surprisingly, they lie at the heart of the varied movements to restore native sovereignty and self-determination. Land and sea are ways by which peoplehood is fashioned."[3] Along similar lines, this chapter balances chapter 3's focus on rootedness to 'Aihualama by exploring the routes of HKM's interdisciplinary wa'a education program and the Project's emphasis on learning through the preparation for and practice of sailing, including the genealogical mo'olelo that guide and give those practices deep meaning. Understandings of self and community in relation to the natural world are produced in movements across the ocean. Such travel requires no less detailed an understanding of place and kuleana than that of the more rooted practice of kalo cultivation.

Against knowledge regimes that cast the Pacific Islands as tiny, isolated "islands in a far sea" and Native islanders as backward and isolated from centers of economic and intellectual production, Epeli Hau'ofa calls us to look to "our sea of islands" as an expansive source of strength:

If we look at the myths, legends and oral traditions, and the cos-
mologies of the peoples of Oceania, it will become evident that
they did not conceive of their world in such microscopic proportions. Their universe comprised not only land surfaces, but the
surrounding ocean as far as they could traverse and exploit it, the
underworld with its fire-controlling and earth-shaking denizens,
and the heavens above with their hierarchies of powerful gods and
named stars and constellations that people could count on to guide
their ways across the seas. Their world was anything but tiny. They
thought big and recounted their deeds in epic proportions.[4]

This shift toward a strengths-based perspective brings attention to the
movements, trading patterns, and stories by which islanders have established "new resource bases and expanded networks for circulation"—to
the ways our people are enlarging their worlds.[5] In this chapter I attend to the ways Hālau Kū Māna's waʻa program enables processes of
world enlargement against limiting and belittling views of Indigenous
cultures and peoples. By seeing the waʻa as a living teacher herself and
using the social and spiritual relations developed with and through
her as opportunities for learning, HKM educators recenter Hawaiian
genealogical connection to a vast oceanic network.

Each time HKM students approach *Kānehūnāmoku*, their waʻa, or
enter their Waʻa Project class, they offer her the following genealogical
chant:

ʻO Hōkūleʻa ka wahine, ʻo Mau ke kāne
Noho pū lāua a loaʻa mai ʻo Makaliʻi
He keiki, he kiakahi
Holo pū ʻo Makaliʻi i ka moananuiākea
A loaʻa mai ʻo Kānehūnāmoku
Ka pulapula, he kiakahi
Kia aku ka maka i ka ʻalihilani
A ʻōili mai ka moku la
ʻO Kualoa ka ʻaina, ʻo Kānehoalani ka pali nāna e hiʻi
I ke ala pono e holo aku ai a hoʻi mai
Me ka ʻike o kō mua e kau mai nei
E mau mai ka ʻike a mau loa e![6]

Within HKM discourse the school's twenty-nine-foot wa'a kaulua kiakahi (double-hulled, single-mast canoe) *Kānehūnāmoku* is gendered feminine, as are the other wa'a within her genealogy. At first blush this language may seem to mirror the patriarchal gendering of both Western and Satawalese maritime traditions. Such language is evident in the first line of the genealogical mele written for *Kānehūnāmoku* by HKM students, with the assistance of Hawaiian singer-songwriter Kainani Kahaunaele. The chant begins by recognizing the female ancestor *Hōkūle'a*, the wa'a kaulua that ignited the resurgence of Hawaiian long-distance voyaging, and her first navigator, Mau Piailug, the Satawalese master of noninstrument celestial navigation who enabled the rebirth of open-sea canoe travel throughout Hawai'i and Polynesia by sharing his knowledge with a new generation of Hawaiian voyagers. In the mele, their heteronormative pairing produces the child wa'a *Makali'i*.

In this chapter I read beyond the initial apparent similarities to patriarchal gender systems in HKM's gendered language about the wa'a. By closely attending to the pedagogical practices within HKM's wa'a program, we see more fluid, nonbiologically determinate gender practices that emphasize balance over hierarchy. As one reads further into the genealogical mele the narrative disrupts dominant gender binaries. The second-generation wa'a *Makali'i* produces *Kānehūnāmoku* not through a heteronormative pairing with a male progenitor but through her travels across the vast ocean (ka moananuiākea). Following *Kānehūnāmoku*'s birth, the chant honors the lands that care for her. Within that dualistic pairing of kāne and wahine energies, it is the male element, Kānehoalani, who holds the young wa'a lovingly ("ka pali nāna e hi'i"), as a parent would a baby.

These more open gender practices can be seen as a form of world enlargement. Kāne and wāhine both can be leaders as navigators or captains or supporters as crew members. They can both be nurturers as mākua and kumu or those who are nurtured as students. The presence of a wahine captain and kumu, Bonnie Kahape'a-Tanner, and her longtime assistant, Pualani Lincoln, has been profoundly influential in this regard. The teachers portrayed in this chapter also build on a long legacy of wahine 'ōiwi voyagers.[7] Moreover, kumu and haumāna speak of *Kānehūnāmoku* not as an empty or inert vessel waiting to be directed by the masculinized energy of a navigator but as an active force who teaches and transports them, revealing knowledge and ways of seeing, thinking, and being that would not otherwise be possible.

Sailing against Legacies of Belittlement

It was Hoaka—an early, waxing moon—on the first day the mixed sixth- and seventh-grade class began their venture into the world of the waʻa during the 2010–11 school year. I pulled into the parking lot, with my two daughters in tow, just before the Hālau Kū Māna bus arrived carrying the group of fifteen ʻōpio across the Koʻolau mountain range forty-five minutes from their campus to the shores of Kualoa beach park. Their three primary teachers had decided to open the semester by bringing them to this site where, as science and language arts teacher Kuʻuleianuhea "Anu" Awo-Chun explained, "the waʻa of our generation began. From this beach, *Hōkūleʻa* first touched the water."[8] Later, social studies teacher Māhealani Treaster added that Kualoa was also the place where *Kānehūnāmoku* first launched in 2002. The visit not only allowed the ʻōpio to touch the one hānau (birth sands) of these two waʻa and the educational movements they continued to carry but also invited them to begin seeing themselves in the context of an intellectual moʻokūʻauhau of Indigenous Pacific navigators and voyagers. By drawing on the lessons and guidance of earlier generations of wayfinders, they might contribute to the intergenerational development of knowledge about place, self, and community through ka hoʻokele ʻana (travel, especially sailing). The students called to those teachers of times past who remained present but required careful observation to perceive:

> ʻAuhea wale ʻoe, kamaliʻi o ka pō?
> Eia hoʻi au, kamaliʻi o ke ao.
> E aʻo mai. E aʻo mai.[9]

> Where are you, child of the night?
> Here I am, a child of the day.
> Teach me, teach me.

As the opening protocols closed, the kumu asked their haumāna to engage in a practice common to navigators past and present: obser-

FIGURE 14. *HKM students and teachers launch* Kānehūnāmoku *from the shores of Kualoa, beginning a day of training on the waters of Kāneʻohe Bay. Captain Bonnie Kahapeʻa-Tanner (wearing sunglasses) is visible behind the waʻa. Kualoa was also the site of the first launching of* Hōkūleʻa, *a genealogical prede-cessor of* Kānehūnāmoku's *and the waʻa that relaunched Hawaiian sailing and wayfinding practices in the twentieth century. Photograph courtesy of Hālau Kū Māna New Century Public Charter School.*

vation of the natural forces around them. "During this ten-minute grounding activity, I want you to especially focus on the plant life and the geographic features around you," Kumu Anu instructed.

One ʻōpio drew and wrote about the "majestic mountains" of the steep Koʻolau range rising above. The northern most ahupuaʻa of the Koʻolaupoko moku (district) on the windward side of Oʻahu, Kua-loa is characterized by the ridge named Kānehoalani. Kānehoalani juts out from the main range and lies at the head of Kāneʻohe Bay, the largest sheltered body of water in the islands (approximately 12.7 kilometers/7.9 miles from farthest northwest and southeast points and about 4.3 kilometers/2.7 miles wide).[10] Another ʻōpio depicted the calmness of the ocean that day. In addition to the surrounding mountains, Kāneʻohe Bay contains one of the only barrier reefs in the Hawaiian Islands, and it is within these protected waters that HKM students, led by Captain Bonnie Kahapeʻa-Tanner, have done most of their waʻa training over the past decade. Additionally, the two natural channels, one at each end of the bay, make it an excellent place for launching and landing vessels such as large double-hulled sailing canoes. Prior to the heavy impact of suburban residential development in the post-1959 era, numerous streams and other fresh water outlets into the bay created an extremely diverse ecological and productive aquacultural environment.[11] The abundance of food and water was important for provisioning waʻa for long voyages.

Earlier in the year, the seventh graders had also learned that Kualoa was a key site of political power on the island when Indigenous systems of governance were still intact. Despite the fact that the Hawaiʻi state curriculum content standards for the seventh-grade course History of the Hawaiian Kingdom does not include Oʻahu chiefly traditions, Kumu Māhealani taught her students about eighteenth-century Oʻahu Island chief Kahahana. "How do we do this place-based learning if we're not connected to Oʻahu first?" she asked rhetorically as we talked about her reasoning for including that series of lessons even though they were not within the settler state's required curriculum. "I had to take it back [before the unification of the islands under Kamehameha]."[12] Thus, she told her students about Kahahana's refusal to relinquish control over Kualoa to Kahekili, Maui Island's ruler and Kahahana's hānai (adopted) father. Kahahana's advisors had assured him that giving up Kualoa would have essentially meant relinquishing his authority over the whole of Oʻahu.[13] Kumu Māhealani had made a conscious decision to depart from state benchmarks in order to align with HKM's foundational commitment to place-based pedagogies. Moreover, it was important for the ʻōpio to know that Kualoa has long been a place for raising leaders and a crucial site of seeking and maintaining sovereignty.

After our initial greetings to each other and to the ʻāina of Kualoa, the students, their teachers, my daughters, and I gathered around an ahu (shrine) protected by a hedge of naupaka. Affixed upon the ahu were stones representing several waʻa from across the groups of islands anthropologists (mis)named Polynesia. In the centuries prior to European and American imperialism in the Pacific, our sea of islands had long been connected by voyaging canoes and the crews that sailed them. For instance, Kualoa had been a home of Laʻamaikahiki, the stories of whose travels between Hawaiʻi and Tahiti approximately thirty generations ago remain in circulation despite colonial attempts to discount the great seafaring traditions of Kānaka. Earlier in the year, the seventh graders learned about another famous voyager, Hiʻiakaikapoliopele, who left her mark at Kualoa when she battled and defeated a powerful moʻo named Mokoliʻi. The great lizard's fin formed an islet just off the shore from where we stood that day. The ʻōpio had photographed and written poetry about Mokoliʻi and Hiʻiaka's feat in an integrated social studies and language arts project. Both teachers considered that project the most successful of all the assignments that year, and yet the content did not fit into the state's detailed social studies benchmarks. In mainstream public schools middle schoolers take two semester-length courses in the seventh grade, History of the Hawaiian Monarchy and The Pacific Islands. In such courses students learn *about* Hawaiians' and Pacific Islanders' cultures instead of experiencing and becoming producers within dynamic and relational Indigenous systems of knowledge production.

In contrast, we stood at the ahu honoring a network of twentieth- and twenty-first-century canoes that comprised part of the contemporary extended waʻa/waka family made possible when Satawalese master navigator Mau Piailug began sharing his knowledge with contemporary Hawaiian navigators such as Nainoa Thompson and Milton "Shorty" Bertelmann in the 1970s.[14] More than a just a successful scientific experiment, *Hōkūleʻa* became a symbol of Hawaiian ingenuity and intelligence. For Kānaka throughout Hawaiʻi, it represented a sort of undeniable, in-your-face redemption against the racist narratives saturating daily life, including especially those taught in schools. Its success spoke back to systems and individuals who demeaned and discounted Native knowledge (and people) as worthless, feeble, and anachronistic.

The simple sight of the waʻa entering bays and harbors across the islands provoked emotional responses and revelations that would be indelibly marked upon the naʻau and the minds of many Kānaka for the rest of their lives. *Hōkūleʻa* and its travels became living evidence that the racist stereotypes of Hawaiians as uneducated and incapable, which many Kānaka had internalized, were false. When I interviewed wahine aloha ʻāina Loretta Ritte about her involvement in the movement to stop the bombing of Kahoʻolawe beginning in the late 1970s, she immediately connected it to the symbolic power of *Hōkūleʻa*'s travels. Remembering her childhood and adolescence, she recounted the messages that had been repeated to her over and over: "Everybody told me Hawaiians were stupid, Hawaiians were lazy, Hawaiians were good for notin'. That's how I grew up, raised on Kauaʻi. That's what they told us Hawaiians."

These narratives shaped her own aspirations and identity as a youth. It was against this backdrop of racism that the vision of the *Hōkūleʻa* approaching the island of Molokaʻi, to which she had moved in her young adulthood, refreshed and inspired Auntie Loretta.

> When the *Hōkūleʻa* came and you see this magnificent ship coming in and [her voice slowed and dropped to a hush] there's no engine, there's no noise, only Hawaiians—hoooooh [she shook her fist above her head then opened her palm over her heart, patting it several times]—it was awesome. . . . [It was] a strong opening of the eyes of who we were as people.[15]

The year *Hōkūleʻa* first voyaged to Tahiti, Auntie Loretta was one of four individuals who crossed the channel between Molokaʻi and Kahoʻolawe to make the second landing in protest of the U.S. Navy's destruction and desecration of the island.[16] She observed that what "opened peoples' eyes" was the synergy of ostensibly purely cultural initiatives, like the *Hōkūleʻa*'s voyages, with movements viewed from the outside as simply political, such as the Protect Kahoʻolawe ʻOhana (PKO). As Tengan describes the interconnection of these two movements, "The *Hōkūleʻa*'s voyage and the activism of the PKO thus became the primary cultural and political catalysts for the development of the cultural nationalist movement."[17] Together, these currents triggered a deep recognition that far from worthless or irrelevant, the ʻike of our kūpuna were priceless treasures to be nurtured generation after generation. Important to note, both included ocean travel and the crossing of colonial and imperial boundaries. *Hōkūleʻa*'s voyages inspired similar efforts in Tahiti, Aotearoa, and the Cook Islands, as well as the building of more waʻa kaulua in Hawaiʻi, just as the PKO's activism linked Kānaka with demilitarization, denuclearization, and independence movements throughout the Pacific.[18]

On the sands of Kualoa, the HKM ʻōpio read a short narrative about Hōkūleʻa's first voyage. Kumu Māhealani asked them to think about the range of emotions that arose in the process of that first journey after a several hundred years' pause, from the joy of the 17,000 Tahitians who came to greet the waʻa in Papeete to the anger that flared as members of the crew fought among themselves. She gave two specific examples. In the first instance, the rebirth symbolized by Hōkūleʻa's arrival prompted so much excitement that the many children who had jumped up on the canoe nearly sank the stern.[19] In the contrasting second example, navigator and teacher Mau Piailug was so upset with the fighting and factionalism that had developed between the haole scientists and the Kānaka on board that he abruptly returned home from Tahiti, leaving only tape-recorded instructions for the crew's return to Hawaiʻi. Several students whispered their recognition of the teacher's supreme discontent with his students.

Kumu Māhealani went on to describe that conflict as a struggle provoked by distinctly different ways of viewing the purpose of the voyage. The white scientists on board, she explained, saw the voyage as an experiment, a way to provide evidence for the theory that Polynesia could have been settled in a purposeful manner with wooden canoes and noninstrument navigation. For the Kānaka on board, the voyage was a way to reconnect with ancestors and to restore Hawaiian pride. Her retelling of the story emphasized the importance of working together as a crew, even when people disagreed.

But embedded in the story was another implicit critique that could have been highlighted: Indigenous people have struggled for our knowledges, then and now, to be valued and seen as legitimate without being filtered through white, academic authorities. Although the successful voyages of the Hōkūleʻa and successive canoes have conclusively disproved earlier, racist anthropological theories that assumed Indigenous Pacific Islanders were incapable of making long-distance voyages for settlement and trade, belittlement of Indigenous knowledge and the kumu who carry that knowledge continues.

The struggles and successes of HKM's waʻa program illustrate the ways educators work against multiple forms of belittlement, demonstrating the depth and rigor of contemporary Hawaiian seafaring as a valid form of educational excellence. The fight for what counts as valuable knowledge and teaching authority continues to this day, and the impacts of NCLB and state-designed curriculum content benchmarks function as forms of belittlement in a variety of ways. For example, though the Waʻa Project persists as one of the most effective aspects of HKM's educational program, in the wake of NCLB restructuring, students' work with the canoe counts toward earning credit *only* insofar as that time can be attached to state-determined content standards in one or more of the four core areas (language arts, math, science, and social studies) and the assessments are graded by a teacher who is deemed to be of highly qualified status. That is, waʻa learning cannot stand on its own merit as a complex, legitimate knowledge field.

As I mention, teachers must make conscious decisions to teach outside the state's social studies benchmarks in order to include moʻolelo Hawaiʻi that precede known Western contact. The State of Hawaiʻi's content requirements for secondary-level social studies do not prescribe *any* inquiry of Hawaiian history and society prior to the unification of the islands under Kamehameha in the last decade of the 1700s and first decade of the 1800s. The K–12 Hawaiian studies curriculum is problematically periodized, privileging Captain Cook's 1778 arrival such that students study precontact Hawaiʻi only in the fourth grade. In other words, the state curriculum benchmarks structurally exclude upper-level study, for sixth through twelfth graders, of the vast majority of Kanaka Maoli existence. They leave out an immense field of storied and place-based knowledge that includes the voyagers of old. This represents a significant erasure and a violent disconnection of ʻŌiwi youth from their ancestral past, as well as a huge missed opportunity for all students in Hawaiʻi's schools to learn from the storehouses of social, scientific, historical, and literary knowledge contained within Hawaiian moʻolelo. Moreover, measuring student and school success by standardized multiple-choice tests constitutes knowledge as superficial and individually held. Finally, the NCLB definition of what constitutes a highly qualified teacher (HQT), coupled with the state's process for certifying teachers, excludes masters of Indigenous knowledge. In HKM's case the wa'a program's most experienced and well-trained master teacher has been structurally marginalized due to this failure to recognize Indigenous knowledge authorities. These examples represent ongoing discursive belittlement, and the sections that follow both elaborate and contest those master narrative structures. Simultaneously, I discuss the ways pedagogies associated with building, maintaining, navigating, and sailing wa'a provided students ways to traverse those currents of belittlement and rediscover Indigenous structures that allowed for world enlargement.

Voyaging to Become Kumu of Navigation

A founding HKM teacher, Bonnie Kahape'a-Tanner came to Hālau Kū Māna by way of Kawaihae on Hawai'i Island and then Satawal in the Federated States of Micronesia. It was through these travels that a wa'a called her back to her home to establish HKM's sailing and navigation program. In the ensuing years, she has captained and cared for *Kānehūnāmoku*, teaching dozens of youth and fellow teachers to sail. Kahape'a began her wa'a training with *Makali'i*, an educational voyaging canoe based on Hawai'i Island, in the mid-1990s. While working as a teacher and administrator in both English- and Hawaiian-language based settings, Kahape'a flew back and forth between O'ahu and Hawai'i islands every weekend over a four-year span to train with the *Makali'i* crew based in Kawaihae. At the time the training was not directly related to her job, so the time and money she spent came out of her own personal commitment. Her story of coming to see and practice Indigenous Oceanic traditions of sailing and navigation as complex knowledge and social systems is an example of the power of wa'a travel.

In 1999 the *Makali'i* crew took their teacher, Papa Mau Piailug, back to Satawal. It was the first time, after almost thirty years, that Hawaiian navigators and sailors whom he trained honored Piailug by sailing him home westward across the Pacific on a Hawaiian canoe. Unable to take leave, Kahape'a quit her job in order to serve on the crew and to learn from Mau in his own homeland. Describing that trip, she repeatedly spoke of his profound effect on her and the larger wa'a family in Hawai'i.

The journey informed her thinking about waʻa pedagogies, Indigenous Oceanic education, and its rootedness/routedness in a broader cultural system.

> If you talk about real traditional education, we got a really good glimpse of it when we did that trip because we got to see Mau in his own environment. See, he's been coming to teach in Hawaiʻi for thirty years, but [until 1999] no one had ever gone to learn from him in his own environment: how his people treat him, his own language, the clothes he wears, the foods that we ate with him. . . . I got a good glimpse of what traditional education really is, and it's all observation. It's observation and hard work. . . . He sees you working hard, and you go ask him something, he gon' tell you. But if he sees that you're just one lazy person that just wants information but you're not gonna do anything with it, then he won't even.

This experience solidified Kahapeʻa's commitment to the Indigenous principle that knowledge must be earned through the demonstration that one has the capability to be responsible for that knowledge. She also witnessed, through her own experience and the stories of her teachers, a strong emphasis on the pedagogical approach described in Hawaiian as ma ka hana ka ʻike (one learns by working or doing). "When Mau taught Shorty [Bertelmann] . . . it was like, you ask a question, he tells you the answer and then that's it. Don't ask that question again. . . . You watch what I'm doing, and then *you do it.*"

She distinguished these teaching practices from Western forms of collaborative learning in that the relationship between teacher and student mirrored the structure of authority on the waʻa. "When you're on the canoe, you listen to the captain. And if you have someone on your crew that's gonna be yapping and trying to tell other people what to do, it's like, that's not gonna work out." Similarly, in waʻa pedagogies, though the teacher and learners work together toward a common goal, the captain determines the scope of the collective work, divvies out tasks, and assures those assignments meet the teacher's high standards. Anything less could threaten life and safety at sea, which is the ultimate kuleana of the captain. "That's the sense of the kumu role to the

haumāna," Kahapeʻa explained. These experiences provided a foundation for her pedagogical practice, in which Indigenous knowledge is
understood to be created in mutual exchange and obligation that must
be lived daily.

Seeing the canoe and the navigator's authority woven into the social fabric was transformational for Kahapeʻa as a young voyager and
educator. I asked her what it was like as a female student of navigation
working with a teacher in whose culture navigational practice was then
reserved for men.

> He never made it a problem for us. In fact, he says—and its
> on YouTube—that the first navigator was a woman. I think
> she was from Majuro or somewhere in the Marshall Islands.
> And she was a female! So he would always say, "For Hawaiian
> women, its no problem." But then if you ask him about Micro-
> nesian women, he would say, "No. No." So it was funny, you
> know, he could make that stretch, too, right? "For *you* women
> its okay." Because since he had been here [in Hawaiʻi] this
> whole time, women were a part of it. All along. So it's okay
> for you guys over here, but not for them. It still is not okay for
> [women in Satawal] to do that. But it's never been a problem
> [for me]. Never. Not at all. I think that Mau would've taught
> anyone that would ask him a question. He was really open. It's
> just that people would never really ask him too many questions,
> like beyond the first [initial questions]. . . . But who [was] going
> [to] go back and actually interact with him on a regular basis?
> There are only a handful of people that did that.

Her response highlighted that in coming to Hawaiʻi, Mau had to change
to accommodate our Indigenous gender practices, which differed from
his at the time. And yet the difference was also explained by recalling
an earlier moment within his own people's navigational genealogies, in
which a woman initiated navigation.

The knowledge of such stories, as well as the oceanic and heavenly
currents and patterns observed by generations of navigators, has been
largely excluded from the dominant, formal educational institutions
throughout both Hawaiʻi and Micronesia. Because of these shared

contexts, one message Papa Mau shared with the crew during their stay in Satawal particularly stuck with Kahapeʻa:

> He said that our kuleana was to teach what we learned and share what we experienced. That was his only wish for those of us that were able to take him back to his island. . . . "You just keep your culture strong." It's so simple, yeah? You just keep doing it. Just keep doing it.[20]

This message, a clear instruction from her kumu about her kuleana, guided the next decade of her life and her teaching career. No matter what the personal, institutional, and systemic obstacles, restoring the practice of ocean travel and the relationships cultivated would thereby become a responsibility she could not deny.

Shortly after Kahapeʻa returned from Satawal and unsure of her next move, she met Keola Nakanishi at the Heʻeia fishpond a few months before Hālau Kū Māna was scheduled to open. HKM developers had just received a federal curriculum development and teacher training grant under the Native Hawaiian Education Act focusing on Hawaiian navigation and astronomy, or Kilolani. Though such a grant would not pay for the acquisition of property or the construction of facilities—two things that start-up charter schools sorely needed—grant writer Adam Kahualaulani Mick was able to argue that it was necessary to build a canoe for the field-testing portion of the grant. Crucial, authentic assessments of student learning entailed actually being able to sail and navigate. To demonstrate the ability to *apply* the principles of Hawaiian astronomy and navigation, students would need to get on a waʻa. For HKM, a school with no permanent facilities or land, the waʻa became its first floating moku (piece of land).

The waʻa became the constant as staff navigated the tumultuous waters of operating a Native Hawaiian community-based charter school. Although the canoe was not finished and functional until midway into the school's second year, the project of developing curriculum that could be used on the waʻa provided critical funding support and intellectual momentum in an environment of fiscal inequity and deep suspicion of Hawaiian culture–based schooling as a serious academic

FIGURE 15. *Hālau Kū Māna students sail in Kānehūnāmoku's home waters of Kāneʻohe Bay. Kānehoalani, the prominent ridgeline of Kualoa that is mentioned in Kānehūnāmoku's oli moʻokūʻauhau, rises up behind them. At the hoe uli (main steering paddle) are Kanaʻi Chock and Maika Motas. The additional crew members visible are Sanoe Sexton and Brandon Turk. Photograph courtesy of Bonnie Kahapeʻa-Tanner of Kānehūnāmoku and Mana Maoli.*

endeavor. At the outset of HKM's first year, we were informed that charter schools would be receiving $5,700 per student, which was well below equity with the already underfunded mainstream public schools. Then, three months into the school year, charter school administrators received word from the state that our schools would be given only $2,997 per pupil and zero funding for special education students. For HKM this amounted to an almost 70 percent decrease in expected state allocations the first year, after budgets had already been set, teachers had been hired, and students were attending class. Such a drastic, unexpected budget cut would have likely led to HKM's closure had it not been for the Kilolani grant. "It literally kept us afloat," Nakanishi remembered.

FIGURE 16. *HKM students crew* Kānehūnāmoku *as she sails the open waters
off the Kona coast of Hawai'i Island. Photograph courtesy of Bonnie Kahape'a-
Tanner of* Kānehūnāmoku *and Mana Maoli.*

For Kahape'a the grant and construction of a sailing canoe provided
an opportunity that allowed her to fulfill her kuleana to her teachers,
her kūpuna, and future generations.

> It was unheard of . . . to get paid, which is necessary, but to do
> something that is your kuleana at the same time! That hardly
> ever happens. You don't usually get paid to do your kuleana. . . .
> Hālau Kū Māna has been able to allow many of us to fulfill our

kuleana or, at least, try 'um out and see if you can hang tough
and last. The school allows students and staff to find it.... Had
I gone into teaching in a mainstream school, it would not have
allowed me to keep practicing and sharing this kuleana in a
school setting on a daily basis.

In fulfilling this kuleana, over the years Kumu Kahapeʻa has used a pedagogy that fosters gender balance. When students arrive at the waʻa,
they line up in a single mixed-gender line facing Kānehūnāmoku for
their opening chants. This differed from the opening protocols at the
Loʻi Project and for the school as a whole at the beginning of the each
school day, when students stood in two lines according to biologically
determined sex. Throughout the year, students in the Waʻa Project
were divided into small groups, called watches, mimicking the ways
a waʻa crew on a long journey were divided into smaller subunits to
attend particular duties for set periods of time. The watches were typically constituted as mixed-gender groupings. The kumu consciously
appointed both kāne and wahine students as watch captains, thus allowing all students to develop leadership skills through these rotat-
ing positions and also getting the ʻōpio maʻa (accustomed to) working
under leaders of various genders. As a consequence, over the years it
was just as likely that certain wahine or kāne students would rise up as
exceptional leaders and waʻa practitioners.

In 2004 I spoke with Captain Kahapeʻa just as the three-year Kilolani grant came to completion; she was envisioning an expansion of the
waʻaʻs role as a full-time classroom and an expanded curriculum. "Right
now [the waʻa] is only used two days a week, sometimes only one day,
which is not enough," she shared. Though HKM's program structure
for the next two years allowed for some of that expansion, the limitations imposed by NCLB restructuring soon circumscribed those visions. As detailed in previous chapters, time at the outdoor field sites
was steadily eroded. By the 2010–11 school year, students in the Waʻa
Project were able to spend only half a day at the waʻa site, and any given
ʻōpio would have only forty-five minutes of direct contact time with
the canoe (with the remaining time spent at onshore stations focused
on science or social studies and led by HQT-status teachers in those
disciplines).

Besides the schedule, Kumu Kahapeʻa became ineligible to employ as a full-time teacher because she did not meet HQT requirements according to NCLB regulations. It is hard to imagine a more qualified teacher to blend Indigenous and Euro-American marine-based knowledges in a project-based school environment. Kahapeʻa was trained and sanctioned to teach by internationally recognized masters of Indigenous navigation Mau Piailug and Clay Bertelmann. There is only a small number of Kānaka who have earned *and* continue to exercise the kuleana of captaining a Hawaiian voyaging canoe. In addition, she holds a captain's license through the U.S. Coast Guard-Merchant Marines. Kumu Kahapeʻa also earned two master's degrees (one in counseling psychology and the other in transformative learning and change) from Western universities, and she had more than fifteen years' experience working as a teacher and an administrator in both Hawaiian- and English-language settings when she was disqualified by the HQT definition. More important, she was recognized by her peers as one of the most effective and rigorous teachers at HKM. Yet despite these qualifications across a range of cultural contexts and institutions, she could not be deemed HQT, because she had not participated in a state-sanctioned teacher certification program and had not taken the PRAXIS exams.[21] Such regulations may be useful in assuring that teachers come into schools with some basic level of training. Scholars of Native education have critiqued, however, the notion of what constitutes being highly qualified and the mechanisms for enforcing it. At best these imposed definitions of authority and qualification are epistemologically incompatible with Indigenous knowledge systems, and at worst they serve as a barrier to Indigenous educators entering teaching as a profession and an affront to the self-determination of Indigenous nations.[22]

When I reinterviewed Kumu Kahapeʻa in 2011, she had been forced to find creative ways to continue upholding her kuleana as a teacher of Indigenous Oceanic voyaging. She was working on a part-time contract basis at HKM, and the days students spent at the waʻa had to include certified teachers in science or other core academic areas in order to legitimize the amount of time spent there. I thought back to something Kahapeʻa had told me seven years earlier. Speaking about how she responded to close friends and family members who were telling her she needed to have a job that paid more money, she stated matter-of-factly:

> I don't think so. Maybe I gotta do something else on the side, but I'm not willing to not teach kids on the canoe. *Kānehūnāmoku* is not something you can just walk away from. It's hard, but it's definitely my kuleana.[23]

Her kuleana included a commitment to place-based and genealogically rooted knowledge practices that required a lifetime of relational obligation. At the time, she had no idea of how hard that would become in the wake of NCLB restructuring and the redisciplining of the curriculum.

In order to continue teaching waʻa postrestructuring, Kumu Kahapeʻa cobbled together income from her part-time work at HKM, sought opportunities to run short-term waʻa camps on the private market, provided free waʻa training on weekends to interested HKM teachers so that they could integrate those experiences into their own classrooms, and ran another federal curriculum development grant, which was about to expire when we talked in 2011 (leaving her without full-time employment). What had kept her committed despite the structural remarginalization of Indigenous knowledge was Kahapeʻa's obligation to her kumu, among whom she included not only Papa Mau and Uncle Clay Bertelmann but also the waʻa as a living entity and kūpuna (ancestors) of generations past. It was through them that she came to fully understand and trust the power of Indigenous knowledge systems to stand as educational foundations in their own right. The waʻa's name, *Kānehūnāmoku*, reflects the kind of deep and extensive intergenerational, empirical knowledge that has often been marginalized as simply myth. Yet it is the basic revaluation of these wells of knowledge that has undergirded the success and longevity of the Waʻa Project despite these various challenges.

Kānehūnāmoku: Revealing Hidden Islands and Ancestors

Kānehūnāmoku—the waʻa HKM ʻōpio sail—has served as a vehicle for crossing temporal and epistemological oceans and, thus, enlarging the worlds to which teachers and students have access. Her name

and the story of her naming represent the ways the waʻa allows recon-
nection and rediscovery of ancestral knowledge from which Kānaka
have been alienated. The story also shows that Hawaiian names such
as *Kānehūnāmoku* are themselves vessels for intergenerational knowledge about changes in the natural environment over time. In short, this
knowledge resides in stories and in names. By seeing the capabilities of
ancestors, HKM kumu also hope that ʻōpio will come to recognize their
own intelligence and worth. As Kumu Kahapeʻa told her colleagues at
one faculty retreat with the waʻa, "Look at *Kāne*. She embodies us as a
people. She is a reflection of our kūpuna and their brilliance."[24]

As construction on the waʻa was being completed, Kumu Kahapeʻa
and others had been contemplating a name for the vessel. In early
fall 2002, Kahapeʻa was chosen to participate as an educator aboard
a thirty-day trip to Papahānaumokuākea, also known as the Northwestern Hawaiian Islands (NWHI), as part of a coral reef ecosystem
reserve expedition sponsored by the National Oceanic and Atmo-
spheric Administration. Through a process that included detailed and
consistent observation of the natural environment, quiet reflection,
familiarity with ancestral stories, and intellectual exchange with peers,
Kānehūnāmoku revealed itself to her.

On the voyage Kumu Kahapeʻa was in conversation with her colleague Kekuewa Kikiloi, an ʻŌiwi anthropologist who was researching
ancestral names and stories of these lesser-known islands lying north-
ward of the human-populated Hawaiian Islands. They began referring
to this part of the archipelago as the "kūpuna islands," both because
the NWHI were geologically older than the eight major islands and
because they were also believed to be places where spirits of the ancestors went after death.[25] During their trip up the island chain, they read
through the literature Kekuewa had brought along.

Writing of our shark ancestors, nineteenth-century historian Samuel Kamakau lists Kānehūnāmoku among the foundational gods, the
manō kumupaʻa who traveled between Hawaiʻi and the faraway lands
of Kahiki:

O na mano kupupaa. O Kanehunamoku, o Kamohoalii, o
Kuhaimoana, o Kauhuhu, o Kaneikokala, o Kanakaokai, a me

kekahi poe mano e ae. . . . Nolaila, ua hoike kino mai ma—na
akaku a ma na hihio, a ua hoike mai i ke ano o ke kino, he
mano kekahi kino oʻu, he pueo, he hilu, a he moo, a pela aku a
nui loa ke ano o na kino i lahui ia.[26]

These divine beings took many bodily forms, including shark, owl, lizard, and human, and they revealed themselves in dreams, visions, and
trances, sometimes as reflections and as sounds in the wind. As Kamakau's description of the ʻaumakua Kānehūnāmoku suggests, knowledge
lives and changes shape, requiring multiple reading practices to grasp
its many dimensions. Several texts also describe Kānehūnāmoku as
a mythical paradise, "the hidden islands of Kāne," set up in the heavens and appearing only occasionally.[27] Such understandings of Kānehūnāmoku signal the importance of prayer, patience, and revelation.
Even then, not all will come to see the hidden islands. In the *Kumulipo*, a Hawaiian cosmogonic origin chant, Kānehūnāmoku is a concrete physical place, too. It appears in the third wā (time period) as the
lands to which the birds of the sea flocked soon after their creation.[28]
It was to and among these kūpuna islands, frequented by the birds of
the sea, that Kahapeʻa and Kekuewa traveled.

They talked at length about the story of the hidden islands of
Kānehūnāmoku. They made daily observations about the patterns
they noticed in the ocean and sky. Finally, the ship they were on paused
at the northernmost of the Northwestern Hawaiian Islands, whose
traditional name Westerners obscured when they called it Kure after a
Russian explorer. Through his reading and interpretation of ancestral
stories and chants, Kekuewa believed the proper name of the island
to be Hōlanikū. There at Hōlanikū, Kahapeʻa placed all the lei in the
water that her students had made for her to take as hoʻokupu. It was
in this context of being saturated with information from their shared
readings, conversations, and observations of the typical rhythms of the
environment, as well as offering thanks and honor to the area, that
Kānehūnāmoku revealed itself to Kahapeʻa and Kekuewa. She described the moment on their return back down the archipelago, after
they had left Hōlanikū and were near an island widely known as Lisian-
ski but whom contemporary Kānaka have renamed Kapoukumau.[29]

One night, we slept out on the deck. . . . I had woken up before the sun rose. Right on the top of the deck, I sat up in my
lawn chair. I looked out over the railing, and I could see all
these islands! I mean, all the islands over there are so flat you
can barely see them even when you're just a mile away; they're
just like pancakes. But these were like big, high, rocky-looking
islands. I was just like, "Whoa! Where are we, 'cuz this is not
where we were when we anchored?!" But we were anchored the
whole time. I looked up and still had stars up, so I was trying to
figure out north, south, east, west, [trying] to figure out where
everything was and I thought, "This is nuts!" Then Kekuewa
came to wake me. He walked up the ladder, and I was like,
"Kekz, check this out!" Both of us just stood there like, "Holy
shit!" We counted, and there were twelve islands. We kept
going, "No, count again, count again!" All the things he brought
to read said there were these twelve islands; twelve islands,
Kānehūnāmoku.

Kahapeʻa shared this story with her students immediately upon her
return, and together, they agreed that *Kānehūnāmoku* was the appropriate name of the new waʻa. Kumu Kahapeʻa's story also emphasized
the importance of research, observation, and the revelatory aspects of
Hawaiian perspectives of knowledge. Kūpuna reveal ʻike to learners
that have been actively seeking it. In the naming process, Kahapeʻa and
her fellow learners used multiple literate practices to seek understanding of ancestral ways of relating to place through names and stories.

Kekuewa's further explanation of the name Kānehūnāmoku underscores the ways that such names carry concrete and complex understandings of the natural environment developed by Kānaka ʻŌiwi over
generations. In his blog written during the trip, he describes the natural phenomenon explained within the Kānehūnāmoku "myths":

Kānehūnāmoku and the twelve sacred islands represent a concept that is tied to real processes that have been observed for
generations by our ancestors. Over time the concept has become layered, and embellished with color and flavor. . . . What
this process directly translates to is the relationship between

tidal changes and moon phases, and the disappearance and reappearance of low lying landforms. As the moon reaches different phases with the Earth, it changes the gravitational pull of the planet, and thus creates changes in currents, and the level of our oceans. Islands that are sensitive to these changes can disappear, and become "hidden" by the god *Kāne*. These traditions and ancient stories of Hawai'i have many levels of meaning to them. They teach us important lessons in life, based on thousands of years of observation and learning. It is important to maintain the integrity of these stories, so that these fundamental lessons don't get "hidden" or "lost" themselves.[30]

What is perhaps most significant about this explanation is that the phenomenon described by the name Kānehūnāmoku was observed over time, across generations. That is, the kind of knowledge embedded in the name is developed intergenerationally. Thus, the name itself becomes a vehicle for transmitting knowledge across generations, for crossing temporal oceans.

In the chapter-opening epigraph, Captain Kahape'a describes Kānehūnāmoku as a vehicle for connecting students with ancestors typically veiled in our rushing through daily life—our world filled with unending distractions from the natural forces around us. With Kānehūnāmoku as the centerpiece, knowledge is framed as both spiritual and empirical, both revelatory and observable, developed over generations yet also deeply personal. The next section illustrates an example of this kind of Hawaiian-knowledge transmission in the contemporary era. In so doing, kumu and haumāna move between different cultural lenses for describing natural phenomena, and intellectual rigor is encouraged by making genealogical connections explicit.

Genealogy: Providing Direction, Depth, and Accountability

"You ever had your parents tell you you not the center of the universe?" Kumu Kahape'a asked the kaikaina (middle schoolers) who sat in a circle on her lawn. Sitting among them, I noticed a few chuckles and nodding heads. "Well, in the mana'o of the navigator, you are. *You* are the piko."[31] Talk about student-centered learning, I thought to myself.

This was not, however, an individualistic brand of student-centered learning. Rather, students were encouraged to understand themselves in relation, particularly in genealogical relation. For it is only in understanding relationships that a navigator is able to direct her or his course, perceiving the movements of celestial bodies in relation to one's location.

The ensuing lesson focused on the Satawalese and Hawaiian star compasses that Kahapeʻa and other contemporary Hawaiian navigators use and that are introduced to every new class of sailors at HKM. The compasses are introduced through diagrams, but ultimately, a navigator must internalize these tools for perceiving the surrounding environment. Each navigator calibrates her perception not to a universal instrument or standard of measurement but to the dimensions of her own body in relation to the waʻa, the sea, and the sky. The intellectual conversation I observed during this lesson illustrated the kind of interdisciplinary and intercultural fluencies that waʻa learning could enable, in contrast to the shallow accountability of standardized-testing regimes. As the kumu moved between languages and epistemes, students mirrored this behavior. She encouraged the learning process by giving her students tangible and genealogical proximity to an acknowledged master and source of knowledge. (By genealogical proximity I mean both lineages of intellectual exchange and the ways those intellectual connections are made familial and spiritual through the relationships between kumu, haumāna, and the knowledge practiced.) From an ʻŌiwi perspective, by invoking one of her kumu, the teacher created a context demanding excellence and, thus, accountability for learning. By explicitly calling students' attention to genealogical connections, they could better understand the stakes of their learning in a larger context. Self-direction, from each of their metaphorical waʻa at the center of their worlds, would be framed by this collective context.

From a small bag beside her, the kumu, whom the students simply called Aunty Kahaz, pulled out some simple objects that opened a series of complex lessons about two related star compasses: a Satawalese compass developed over centuries, taught to her by Mau Piailug, and a Hawaiian derivation, designed through the intellectual exchange and cultivation of lifelong relational obligations between Indigenous Oceanic peoples—between Papa Mau and one of his Hawaiian students.[32]

FIGURE 17. *Satawalese master navigator Papa Mau Piailug gifted his way-finding knowledge to several Hawaiians and encouraged those sailor-educators to pass on the skills and understandings. This compass (paafu) was made by Papa Mau using coral from Kualoa, and it is used as a tool for teaching the movements of celestial bodies in relation to each other and to a canoe in motion. It was given to Hālau Kū Māna and the crew of Kānehūnāmoku for training. Kānehūnāmoku sits on the waters of Kāneʻohe Bay in the background. Photograph courtesy of Bonnie Kahapeʻa-Tanner of Kānehūnāmoku and Mana Maoli.*

Kumu Kahapeʻa explained to her rapt audience, "Kūkulu o ka lani [the Hawaiian star compass] was Nainoa's modern creation, blending an old, old, old, old tool for using the heavens with the abstract kind of math normally taught in school." It used the Hawaiian names for various forces within our distinct natural environment. She explained that although the ideas behind Mau's compass came from far across the ocean, the physical materials in front of them were gathered by Papa Mau at Kualoa beach, a few ahupuaʻa down the coast. "He gave them to HKM and *Kānehūnāmoku*, so you gotta touch [the compass] before you leave! It was literally made by a grand master, a rare master in the entire world." The compasses exemplified the ways Hawaiian navigational knowledge had been produced in Indigenous intellectual exchange.

Sitting on the grass with her students circled around the map, she pointed to the various coral pieces with a stick and introduced their names. I imagined Kahapeʻa sitting like this as a student with her teacher. She told her haumāna that the compass was a tool for navigating waʻa as well as for directing oneself through life. It would soon become evident to her students that such navigation used multiple cultural fluencies, required a detailed understanding of the natural environment, and developed a clear and purposeful sense of self in relation. The compass provided a framework for visualizing oneself as the piko and situating oneself in relation to complex movements within the environment.

In these lessons about the star compasses, Kumu Kahapeʻa moved fluidly between the terms and orientations used in different languages—Hawaiian, Satawalese, and English. She pulled out two pieces of sennit cord with coral pieces tied to each end. "These four coral pieces indicate the cardinal directions: ʻākau, hema, hikina, komohana," she said as she pointed to each with a long stick. The ʻōpio repeated the names after her, also drawing diagrams into their notebooks. After teaching the names of the four quadrants, she added two more kaula (cords), dividing the circle into eight, and then added three more loose coral pieces into each space around the circumference to designate each house. The ʻōpio were expected to memorize both Hawaiian and Satawalese names for these star houses. Looking together at the compass on the grass in the middle of the circle, Kumu Kahapeʻa fired a series of questions at the ʻōpio.

"How many pieces of coral are there total?"

"32," the group answered quickly.

"What shape is this?"

"A circle."

"How many degrees are in a circle?"

"360."

"So how many degrees are in each house?"

This question met with silence.

"What is 360 divided by 32?" Kumu Kahapeʻa prompted. After a couple of close guesses, she provided the answer, "11.25. 11.25 degrees in each house. How many miles are represented by one degree?"

FIGURE 18. *Kumu Bonnie Kahapeʻa-Tanner teaches students about the movements of stars through various houses on the horizon, using a compass (paafu) made by Papa Mau Piailug. Photograph by Akoni Tacub. Courtesy of Bonnie Kahapeʻa-Tanner of Kānehūnāmoku and Mana Maoli.*

More silence.

"60 miles," she stated.

"Hoooo!" some of the ʻōpio responded.

Drawing on their awe, she continued, "On the waʻa you use your hand to measure. One finger is two degrees, which is 120 miles." She held up her hand in front of her, as though standing on a canoe gauging direction and distance.

"Papa Mau's island is only a half mile across. If you were off by just a finger's width, you would never even see the island, night or day! Even our own islands, if you were only two fingers off, you could totally miss Hawaiʻi. This is how skilled our kūpuna were! The navigator has to be precise. Every move is purposeful."

Students were expected to demonstrate mastery of the foundational idea that celestial bodies rise and set in different houses at the horizon, and they had to name the various houses in both languages. With that basic knowledge, the following lesson focused on the movement of the sun and a few primary constellations. Kumu Kahapeʻa added two long, thin sticks across the compass. "This is Ke ala polohiwa a Kāne, also known as the Tropic of Cancer, and this is Ke ala polohiwa a Kanaloa, also known as the Tropic of Capricorn."[33] These mark limits of the sun's movements in relation to us. Kahapeʻa used her familiarity with their learning site—her home—to point out how to observe the movements of the sun in one's own environment:

"Each day, the sun rises in a slightly different place. It moves a little until it hits that blue roof house near those coconut trees," she said, pointing across the bay. "Then, it turns around and moves all the way to between those two hau trees."

"This is like a science!" one of the boys blurted out in amazement.

"Exactly, it is a science," their kumu responded, encouraging them to notice the points at which the sun rose and set in relation to their own homes or at the school campus.

"So if you live above Ke ala polohiwa a Kāne, sometimes you never see the sun?" one girl asked.

In the discussion that ensued, the students' comments and questions mirrored the kind of movement between languages modeled by their teacher, speaking as comfortably about lines of latitude as about nā ala polohiwa or using the names Hōkūpaʻa, Wuliwulifasmughet, and the North Star interchangeably to refer to the same body in the sky. Yet the kumu also illustrated that the differences in these cultural names for the same celestial body were important, not to be collapsed. She returned to the example of the two compasses, the orientation of each relating to the prominence of particular stars in the Hawaiian or Carolinian night sky.

> In the Hawaiian compass, the primary orientation is to ʻākau, the north, because of the permanence of Hōkūpaʻa is always in our night sky. Mau's compass is oriented to the east because of the importance of the star Mailap. For our cousins in Aotearoa, the Southern Cross goes in circles [throughout the year] above their heads, but for us it goes like this [she drew a small, low-lying arc over the horizon with her finger].

Kumu Kahapeʻa emphasized that whether on a canoe or not what matters most was one's relationship to these bodies. Understanding the relationships was crucial to self-directed travel. Whether becoming the navigator of a waʻa or of one's own life, she explained, each of them needed to develop their awareness of the surrounding forces and movements as dependent upon the seasons and their location.

Genealogy was presented, then, as a way to understand relationality. In another class session, when students were learning the names and functions for various parts of the waʻa, Kahapeʻa explicitly pointed to the signs of the intellectual and familial genealogy of which the canoe and students were a part. Standing on the deck of the waʻa, she directed students' attention toward the kumu kia—the foundational piece that secured the mast to the deck. This part of Kānehūnāmoku's body was named Heiau.

"We call it Heiau because of genealogy. There are two kumu kia on Hōkūleʻa, one named Heiau. When Makaliʻi was born, its kumu kia was also named Heiau."

These naming practices mirrored the ways significant names were passed from one generation to another within Kanaka families. Kumu Kahapeʻa further emphasized the importance of genealogy as marked on Kāne as she explained the significance of the designs on each hatch cover of the two hulls. The patterns on the two rear covers signified two kūpuna, recently deceased, who were influential in the early years of HKM's waʻa program: ʻAnakala Eddie Kaanana and Captain "Cap" Clay Bertlemann.[34] And as Kahapeʻa taught about the parts of the canoe, she told stories about these elders. In this way, a seemingly utilitarian lesson about the parts of the canoe became a vehicle for transmitting genealogical narratives. Like kākau (tattoos), the patterns on Kāne's body reminded the ʻōpio that the kūpuna were always present with them. This is a form of both motivation and accountability—excellence is demanded by the presence of master teachers. She can continue to tell students year after year about how each of these figures contributes to the knowledge and practices they are learning. The weight and meaning of that kind of genealogical accountability was most apparent in authentic situations for assessing and demonstrating student's knowledge, such as the week-long trips the Waʻa Project completed at least once a year.

Throughout the school year, a significant amount of the Waʻa Project's learning time took place at the canoe's docking site. Even when students were spending four hours, three days a week at the site, the time and the number of students who could be on Kānehūnāmoku at any given time limited the extent to which they could sail weekly. Additionally, it was difficult to learn how to use the stars (other than the sun) to find direction when class was held during the daytime. In order to work around these limitations, over the past ten years Kahapeʻa and her teaching team regularly conducted week-long camps at which the ʻōpio did intensive waʻa training. These required camps were held both in and around Kānehūnāmoku's home waters in Kāneʻohe Bay, as well as along the west coast of Hawaiʻi Island with the Makaliʻi crew based in Kawaihae.

The camps provided a means of authentic assessment. Did all members of the group demonstrate the mastery of skills required to board the waʻa? Could each watch (small group) work together to create and execute a sail plan? Could students correctly identify important constellations in the night sky? Could the watches successfully work together to execute community responsibilities on land? They also minimized distractions. For instance, no electronic devices or mobile phones were allowed at camp, so students were unplugged the entire time. This allowed the ʻōpio focus on the waʻa, the natural environment, and each other.

Though the tasks and schedule varied based on the camp location and other conditions, many elements remained relatively constant over the years, mimicking the routines of a long-distance deep-water voyage. The whole group typically awoke before dawn to observe stars and weather patterns. Journaling and breakfast preceded a land-based lesson, in which the crew might be studying the compasses, sail theory, or navigational charting. Throughout the day each watch sailed a leg on the waʻa to practice what they had learned while watches on shore participated in small-group activities led by a science, social studies, Hawaiian-language, math, or language arts teacher. Just as the waʻa time at camp allowed for synthesis and practice of what students had learned about sailing throughout the semester or year, the land-based rotations also provided an opportunity for synthesis, analysis, and application of knowledge from the various fields of study. For example, in 2011 students had been taking weekly measurements of temperature, dew point, and humidity and documenting their qualitative observations about clouds and other weather phenomena through writing and drawing. At the spring camp, they compiled and analyzed this data against their earlier hypotheses about the relationships of different weather variables. They were also able to make predictions about how the forces they observed in the early morning sessions might affect weather patterns throughout the day and into the evening. Evening sessions allowed students to debrief about their sails, talk story with community visitors, and observe the stars in their late-evening positions.

Particularly when the camps brought HKMʻōpio together with the larger waʻa ʻohana (as Kumu Kahapeʻa and her haumāna referred to the crew members of other canoes throughout the islands), they provided a much deeper and more meaningful form of assessment and accountability than the testing regimes to which students were more frequently subjected. HKM alumni Noelani Duffey-Spikes recalled one camp that had a profound impact on her, in which the waʻa crews from Hālau Kū Māna and two other Hawaiian charter schools came to fulfill a commitment made between their elders. Noe was a senior when she helped crew the journey to sail ʻAnakala Eddie to his home in Miloliʻi. She called it the three generations' sail.

FIGURE 19. Kānehūnāmoku *crew member and instructional assistant Chastity Oilila'a supervises Maluhia Moses (HKM class of 2013) in learning to properly use the lines to manipulate the sail before taking* Kānehūnāmoku *out on the open water. Photograph by the author.*

There was *Kāne*, *Makali'i*, and *Hōkūle'a*. Right there, that was three generations of canoes. But also Cap had already passed, and we were continuing his promise to 'Anakala [Eddie]. That was three generations, too. 'Anakala and Cap as one, and then there was Auntie Kahaz and Auntie Pomai [Bertlemann] guys, and then there was *us*. Three generations. We were in Kealakekua, and . . . had all the canoes in the bay [about to set sail]. . . . Then, pū everywhere; that's all you heard. They were just blowing the pū. If you weren't blowing one, then you were hearing it echo off the cliff. Then, everyone was chanting, . . . At that moment it was like, [Noe took a long pause and spoke slowly] it made it *real*. We have a *reason*. [Her voice quickened.] This is the reason we do what we do. The reason we try and continue to perpetuate as traditionally as we can at this point, but also as *strongly* as we can, to show everyone else, whoever is a spectator, we're still here! Hawai'i is all capitalized, colonized, militarized. But we're still here. We're still practicing this. It is still strong in us, in our blood, in our voices, and we're still going to pass it on. It's not dying; it's not going anywhere. . . . Those moments, they make all that work, all the hardships, all *worthwhile*—to continue what you believe.[35]

It was in seeing her position, at a piko, in relation to the members of these three generations of a familial and intellectual genealogy of voyagers that the meaning of Noe's learning became most clear to her.

Sailing as a Crew and 'Ohana: "He Wa'a, He Moku. He Moku, He Wa'a." (A Canoe Is an Island. An Island Is a Canoe.)

The Wa'a Project's emphasis on teamwork, collective well-being, and collaborative success is particularly vital to transforming the way we think about education in this current era dominated by high-stakes testing. At a time when student and school success is primarily measured by the performance of individuals on tests taken in isolation, where each question can have only one right answer, the Wa'a Project uses the social units of the crew and the watch to assure that no one is left behind. On the waʻa cooperation is a prerequisite to survival. The structure of the crew has been an important heuristic for teaching/learning teamwork, leadership, interdependence, and a more collectivist concern for the well-being of the whole group, both on *Kānehūnāmoku* and on land.

Each quarter, the students are divided into watches. These small groupings correspond to the ways a waʻa crew on a long journey would be divided into smaller subunits to attend particular duties for set periods of time. The students work in watches of four to seven students while on the waʻa, as well as on land and in their classrooms on campus. As Kumu Kahapeʻa told students arriving for their first day of waʻa camp:

> Think of us as one crew. Each watch is a minicrew within that. Think about your role, about how to stay together as a crew, as an ʻohana. Mau always said, "Stay together." How challenging, yeah? Yet so simple. This camp, we get to practice: How do we learn to live with each other? How *do* we stay together?

Although collaboration in problem solving is among the skill sets identified by prominent national educational organizations as crucial to twenty-first-century literacies, the dominant assessment systems do not encourage team-based, collaborative learning.[36] The requirements of No Child Left Behind, for instance, *base school and student success solely on individual performance and thus marginalize the importance of cooperative and inquiry-based learning.*

A watch captain is assigned to each group, and this responsibility rotates to a different person each quarter. The watch captain bears responsibility for the safety of their group and assures that their collective tasks get completed properly. The watch captains also make sure that each member of their group sufficiently masters certain skills so that the whole group can progress. In many cases this means that if one person does not understand or demonstrate mastery of a skill, the entire watch cannot sail. For example, observing land-based rotations at the waʻa, I saw watch captains work side by side with peers having a difficult time learning the knots used on *Kāne*. If a single member of the watch could not complete the tasks, the whole group would stay on shore.

On another occasion, during these land-based rotations, one sopho-
more watch captain impressed me as she led and tutored the members
of her group. They were committing to memory a chant listing nearly
twenty winds of Oʻahu. Two of the boys were not putting forth much
effort.

"What do we need to do to help you guys learn it?" she asked them.
No response.

"Ok, I'll say it, and then you repeat after on your own." They began
to follow her lead, quietly at first. But with each line of the chant
gained, she acknowledged and encouraged their progress. "There you
go! That's how!"

From the very beginning of each year, kumu encourage this kind of
initiative and repeatedly emphasize the importance of a watch working
as one. In the swim test held the first week of each year, a watch is required to move together in the water. The group members can swim no
faster than the slowest swimmer in their group. This assures the safety
of each member of the watch and puts the emphasis on all members
successfully completing the test as a group.

In addition to using the structures of the crew and the watch on
the canoe, kumu also translate these relationships into the classroom.
In contrast to the kind of individualism cultivated by the culture of
high-stakes testing, Kumu Kahapeʻa explained that the interdependent relationships forged through the experience of being a crew were
transformative for many students who had not previously experienced
schooling as collaborative. Speaking in 2004, she explained:

> [The waʻa] makes them feel like they're a part of something, so
> they're willing to take more risks, academically and socially. . . .
> We can openly talk in our group about kids that are failing
> other classes. The kids don't get shame about it, because we
> try and put it out there like they each have to take care of each
> other. So if Laka's getting straight As and brother over here is
> getting straight Fs, we *all* need to do something about it. We
> not just gonna leave him over here, and Laka's not jus' gonna sail
> outta here with her straight As. Everyone has to work together.
> The more you get the kids real with each other and working as a
> crew, then they can function better in class and out of class.[37]

At the time she cited the specific example of a student who had come to HKM with "a thick file" cataloging disciplinary problems from his previous school, his flippant attitude toward education evidenced in actions like blowing smoke in his former teacher's face. When he came to HKM, he "just want[ed] to be able to go to the canoe," Kahapeʻa remembered. That desire, the structure of working cooperatively as a crew, and the sense that everyone was working toward a shared goal kept him motivated and eventually made him, in Kahapeʻa's words, a "shining star."

> He told us, "It feels like someone's got your back every day," and that's so important for them. . . . Kids are afraid to let others know about their vulnerability. We try and break down those barriers. When you're on the canoe, everyone's just there to take care of each other.

When I interviewed her again seven years later, Kumu Kahapeʻa cited numerous examples of the ways her students had responded positively to this cooperative approach (as opposed to one based on individualized reward and punishment) that also included a clear leadership structure.

I saw this reflected in the ways she cultivated such qualities in her watch captains. Captain Kahapeʻa stood on the deck as one of the watches and I boarded *Kānehūnāmoku*. "Where is Meahilahila?" she asked Moana, who was relatively new to the role of watch captain. We all looked back to see Meahilahila on the shore, unwilling to walk through the water to the canoe. As Moana explained her crewmate's hesitancy, her kumu directed her back to shore. "You gotta go back and get her. She's gonna get a class cut if she doesn't come out here."

On the canoe success demands caring for each other. The structure and metaphor of the crew or watch mirrors a larger collective understanding of the school as an extended family, which is iterated over time and by all segments of the school community as foundational to the school's success. These metaphors provide important counterpoints to the factory or business models that have historically pervaded American-style schooling.

With the canoe as a context for learning, students must attend to group dynamics, thus teaching them to work together and to look out for one another. The structure of the watch provides an embodied and immediate experience in the importance of successful interdependence. Each person is valuable. Everyone's survival and well-being is dependent upon each person's ability to carry her or his kuleana. As Captain Kahapeʻa explained:

> There's a sense of urgency that we like to stress, because if you don't do what needs to be done, someone's gonna get hurt. That's a reality . . . on the water. In the classroom the kids can go do something stupid, and maybe it's not gonna hurt anyone. But on the canoe the reality is that, yeah, you do something stupid, and you're either gonna endanger yourself or someone else. Its like, you *gotta* do it. You can't choose to not pull on the sheet line. You need to do it now! And you need to do it right. So it's natural that the canoe provides that sense of urgency and risk. Teenagers love that because they like to be on the edge of life.

This message of working together, of acting in synchronicity for shared purpose, pervaded much of the experiential learning and authentic assessment that took place in the Waʻa Project.

Seeing a Piko, Enlarging a World

The deep learning experiences *Kānehūnāmoku* has allowed over the years includes students' ability to simultaneously see themselves as the piko, a self-directed center, and as a piko, one point within an interconnected web of genealogy. Pōmaikaʻi Freed was twelve years old when *Kāne* was first launched from the shores of Kualoa. She and her three siblings were among the first students of Hālau Kū Māna, and she and her older brother Lahapa were a part of *Kāne*'s first crew. Reflecting on the years she spent learning from the waʻa and her kumu, Pōmaikaʻi described the experiences of being both rooted and routed on the canoe, which helped her enlarge her own world beyond the day-to-day challenges in her life. Of the waʻa, she said:

She just stays steady, a real constant. I was telling Auntie
Kahaz that it is good just knowing that the waʻa is there at all
those points through life. To have an opportunity to go on the
ocean and *exhale* anything that might be troubling my mind
at the time. It was beautiful, and it definitely preserved my
sanity.[38]

What would stay with her far longer than any standardized test scores
were the stories and lessons of her experiences. Through her training
to become part of *Kāne*'s first crew, she learned the value of "what it's
like to dedicate yourself to something, to sacrifice, to work after school
and on weekends." Through her participation in putting together and
carrying *Kānehūnāmoku*, she learned the value of "everybody working
together, one speed." Through the stories she was told and brief periods she got to spend with Papa Mau Piailug, she learned to value the
"in-tuneness that comes through constant daily observation." Through
her participation in the blessing before *Kāne*'s first launch, she saw
her first hōʻailona and thus learned to value purposeful ceremony and
attentiveness to the unseen kūpuna who will respond. And through
her study of the stars, she gained the sense that "if I just look up into
the sky and recognize a constellation and know what the name is and
maybe what the story is, I feel I know where I am." This is the kind of
world enlargement allowed by the restoration and use of Indigenous
life-giving vessels like the waʻa.

FIVE

Creating Mana through Students' Voices

*So it comes down to this: Does political action belong in a school
environment? I'll give you a simple answer. Hell, yes! ... If in
schools the teachers do not take political action or discuss politics
and recent issues, all they're doing is graduating ignorant fools. ...
Make sure that the political actions around the world aren't hidden from our youth, because forgotten knowledge is useless. Make
sure the youth are not ignorant to the world around them.*

▪ Kalani L.D. Aldosa, HKM graduate, class of 2007

*There is no doubt in my mind that the strongest leo is that of the
haumāna. I strongly believe that political issues belong in school
because it is the future of the students that most of today's disputes
will affect.*

▪ Dustin No'eau Pā'alani, HKM graduate, class of 2009

In this book I explore the tensions between asserting Indigenous educational self-determination and working within a settler state school
system. While HKM educators have tried to establish and maintain
cultural kīpuka (stands of continued Indigenous cultural growth),
they have been pressured by forces aimed at constraining the school as
a safety zone—a state-sanctioned space in which Indigenous culture
can be practiced as long as it remains unthreatening to settler society. In previous chapters I show how the pressures of NCLB, state
and federal standards, and dominant notions of settler education have
worked to fence such a zone, minimizing Kanaka connections to ʻāina,
to Indigenous knowledge authorities, and to moʻolelo. Yet at the same
time, those fences have not prevented kumu from finding holes and
open spaces. By using those spaces to rebuild Indigenous vessels that

carry wealth, meaning, and power, members of an educational community can restore collective and personal health and self-determination.

Chapter 1 establishes that this tension between functioning as kīpuka or safety zones was embedded in Hawaiian culture–based charter schools from the start, given that they were produced out of the intersection of two distinct movements: a Hawaiian (cultural and political) nationalist movement and a U.S.-based educational reform movement grounded in school choice. In chapter 2, I show how restructuring under NCLB worked to reinscribe HKM's educational program within mainstream American notions of what schooling should look like and do, stemming some of the early visions for liberatory forms of education. In other words, NCLB worked as a disciplining and re-assimilating force. The contradictions between Hawaiian nationalist aims and dominant settler regimes of accountability manifested as educators navigated between the often conflicting goals of preparing students for required state standardized tests and following the school community's founding educational framework grounded in inter-disciplinary, place-based, and project-based learning. Chapters 3 and 4 explore the ways 'āina-based curricula allowed kumu and haumāna to continue cultivating their kuleana and enlarging their worlds. Their sovereign pedagogies resisted and challenged confinement within the boundaries of settler state–inscribed safety zones by focusing on re-building and actively using generative Indigenous structures that both rooted us in and routed us through our lands and waters.

In this final chapter I circle back to the opening emphasis on social movement, focusing on the ways HKM's kumu and haumāna have explicitly engaged in Hawaiian social movement and cultural practice as political expression over the school's first ten years. Students have taken field trips to directly witness Kanaka families fighting state eviction from their ancestral homes in Kahana, independence activists protesting U.S. legislative efforts to limit Hawaiian sovereignty claims under the framework of U.S. federal recognition, and coalitions of University of Hawai'i students, faculty, and other supporters speaking out against the creation of a U.S. Navy applied research laboratory, the University Allied Research Center. In addition to observing such activism, HKM students have studied and been provided with options to participate in actions calling for funding equity for charter schools, a moratorium on the genetic modification and patenting of kalo, and the legal protection of various Hawaiian lands and entitlements. Kumu have posited these pedagogical engagements with contemporary Hawaiian politics as part of a holistic practice of aloha ʻāina.[1]

Though some people may argue that politics do not belong in schools, I believe, as made clear in previous chapters, that all schooling is political. By allowing students to confront controversial social issues head on, the unmarked politics of mainstream schooling have become more transparent. Moreover, students have begun to more clearly see the larger relations of power in which their lives are embedded and to transform themselves in the process of pushing for wider social change. In many cases students have developed critical analyses that would have been elusive without direct interaction with communities in struggle. If Hawaiian social movement precipitated the emergence of Hawaiian charter schools, continued articulation with such movements will sustain and extend the kīpuka, thus allowing the forest to grow.

More than previous chapters, this one foregrounds the words of HKM graduates rather than teachers. They have offered reflections on how their active engagement with politics produces meaningful learning. In order to highlight the point that cultural practice is always political, this chapter includes moments when HKM ʻōpio have performed diverse forms of cultural expression as acts of political expression. Coming to see their own voices and bodily actions as powerful and valuable has been a crucial part of cultivating personal and collective self-determination. Whereas chapters 3 and 4 focus on efforts to rebuild external vessels—the ʻauwai and the waʻa—this chapter looks at the ways HKM pedagogies have cultivated an internal vessel: the voice, or leo. I illustrate the multiple registers in which students have voiced and embodied their beliefs: testimonies, presentations, marches, conversations, and poetry, as well as chant and dance. Through these expressions, students have pushed the imposed bounds of settler safety zones that are manifested both around and inside us.

One way the cultural/political work of challenging safety zones can be described is with the Hawaiian term hoʻomana. Hoʻomana can mean "to honor" or "to invest with power." In many ways it is about creating mana (power) or assuring that mana can flow. If safety zones constrict the flow of mana, then cultural acts of hoʻomana can work toward rebalancing flows of power. Although the term is also translated as "religion," that one-to-one translation is insufficient and misleading when taken out of context, as the words are not exactly commensurate. Hoʻomana emphasizes a practice—an act of moving mana back and forth within a relationship—whereas religion typically denotes an institution that holds power. When I use the term *hoʻomana*, I invoke it to specifically communicate the idea of practices that open the mutual flow of mana within a relationship—cultural practices that work toward pono (justice/balance).

Ea: Collective Voice and the Breath of Sovereignty

In the first few years of HKM's existence, a handful of non-Hawaiians residing in the islands made a barrage of legal attacks against organizations that had provided social services—such as housing, education, business support, and holistic health care—for Kānaka Maoli. The flurry began when Harold Rice challenged the constitutionality of Hawaiian-only voting in Office of Hawaiian Affairs elections. The plaintiff, the U.S. Supreme Court's majority opinion, and the suits that followed in its wake all framed Hawaiians as a racial minority rather than as an Indigenous people or a national group with collective rights.[2] In the wake of that decision, several more lawsuits appeared, many led by the same attorneys and aimed at eroding Hawaiian-serving institutions such as the state's Department of Hawaiian Homelands and the Kamehameha Schools (KS). ʻĪlioʻulaokalani, a coalition of hula master teachers and practitioners, responded by spearheading a series of marches under the banner "Kū i ka Pono."[3] Representatives of the various institutions were joined by Kānaka Maoli from throughout the archipelago in making a unified call for "Justice for Hawaiians."

For the HKM students who voluntarily participated in these marches, accompanied by mākua from their families and school, the actions allowed them to experience the power of collective political voice. As Noelani Duffey-Spikes, who graduated from HKM in 2005, put it:

The biggest things I remember were marches—just knowing that you were supporting or against something that was bigger than you, bigger than just you and your school or you and your neighborhood. It was an island-wide or nation of Hawaiʻi–wide response to something that was so oppressive.[4]

Upon reflecting on their memories of these marches, several former students talked about the importance of being able to see, hear, and feel the mana of a living nation, the lāhui Hawaiʻi. Graduates also talked about how attending kūʻē (to oppose, resist, or stand apart) actions deepened their sense of kuleana to add their leo and mana to that collective Hawaiian voice. Oli and mele provided one way to join their voices together with other Kānaka calling for pono and ea.

In September 2003, hundreds of Kānaka Maoli walked from Maunaʻala, the royal mausoleum and resting place of several of our nineteenth-century aliʻi nui, to the ʻIolani Palace, built by King Kalākaua as the residence for the head of state and as a representation of Hawaiian national modernity and independence.[5] The relatively solemn procession, held on King Kalākaua's 167th birthday, followed a few months after the more visible and highly publicized march through the streets of Waikīkī.[6] Both brought people together in solidarity against the mounting legal attacks on Hawaiian entitlements and private estates, but this second procession and overnight vigil served a more intimate and internally focused purpose. Organizers emphasized that this event was more about honoring and connecting with the mana of kūpuna, aliʻi, ʻaumākua, and akua in the company of fellow Kānaka than about mobilizing masses of people in front of tourists and news cameras. People came together to offer prayers and hoʻokupu at Maunaʻala in hopes of a favorable decision in the state supreme court's ruling on the *Doe v. Kamehameha Schools* case scheduled to be released the following day. In the case four unidentified non-Hawaiian plaintiffs challenged the private school's century-old admissions policy that gave preference to Native Hawaiians, per the will of its founder, Princess Bernice Pauahi Bishop.[7]

Pōmaikaʻi Freed, who was among the first students to go all the way through HKM from sixth to twelfth grade, remembered an example of her schoolmates' embodied expression of their commitment to the lāhui Hawaiʻi that day. I interviewed her a few years after her graduation. She was training to become a health and healing practitioner, and we sat in the Waimānalo living room of her kumu lomilomi. She

FIGURE 20. *Many Hālau Kū Māna students and parents chose to march alongside thousands of other Kānaka Maoli and supporters of Hawaiian rights and institutions in the 2005 Kū i ka Pono march through Waikīkī. Kumu Hula Kāwika
Mersberg, who has taught at HKM since the opening year, stands at the far right.
Photograph courtesy of Hālau Kū Māna New Century Public Charter School.*

laughed recalling that day of the second Kū i ka Pono march in which
she had participated as a student:

> The boys were like, "I'm gonna be Hawaiian and not wear my
> slippers!" [She chuckled.] And then we get to ʻIolani Palace,
> and everyone in the whole school was [each] just wearing one
> slipper ʻcuz everyone was sharing with the people who didn't
> wear slippers. Yeah, they were either hopping or we were just
> walking in with one slipper. As we walked into ʻIolani Palace
> [grounds], this uncle comes rushing up and gives us some
> slippers: "Here, take these; just give ʻum back latah." [We gig-
> gled.] See, you gotta be smaht Hawaiians; make your ti-leaf
> slipper first![8]

Her classmates' self-imposed hardship was evidence that students not only attended such actions of their own free will but in fact went out of their way to demonstrate their presence through body and voice. Pōmaikaʻiʻs recollection spoke not only to the boys' desire to show their Hawaiianness by being tough enough to walk barefoot over two miles of hot concrete but also to the kuleana that their peers and other fellow marchers felt to share in their (unanticipated) pain and to offer them respite.

The procession eventually entered the ʻIolani Palace grounds from the oceanside gate, each group approaching the foot of the palace steps to make offerings of chant and dance before moving off toward the bandstand. In honor of Kalākauaʻs birthday, the palace was festooned in white, red, and blue—the colors of the Hawaiian flag—and two enormous flags draped down two stories alongside the palace doors. The Hālau Kū Māna students were the final group, walking beside Kealiʻi Gora, an HKM alakaʻi (leader), and Professor Lilikalā Kameʻeleihiwa, then director of the Kamakakūokalani Center for Hawaiian Studies (KCHS) and a member of HKM's local school board.[9] The group carried a KCHS banner, and to the ordinary passerby, there were no signs that they were associated with Hālau Kū Māna. Yet, together, they chanted oli they had learned in school, their collective voices rising up toward the palace. Though the doors and windows of the building were closed and locked, it felt as though the spirits of our kūpuna and aliʻi were listening from places unseen.

I had arrived earlier and stood under a nearby tree, hurriedly fumbling through my backpack to find my camera in hopes of catching a photo of the HKM students in front of the palace. But before I could raise my head, a guitar riff made popular by the Sunday Mānoa's 1971 rendition of the song "Kāwika"—a mele honoring Kalākaua—backed by synthesized rhythm, blasted over from the sound system at the bandstand. The beat filled the palace grounds. *Da da da da, dun, dun, da dun dun. Da da da da, dun, dun, da dun dun.*

An MC's voice called out, "To all my people, tell me what you want!"

"Ea!" voices from the crowd shouted along with another amplified voice.

"Hawaiians, tell me what you need!"

"Ea!"

I looked up but was too slow. The ʻōpio were already sprinting over to the bandstand to watch Sudden Rush, a Hawaiʻi Island–based group that popularized nā mele pāleoleo (Hawaiian rap) in the 1990s and early 2000s.[10] No one else had gotten up to dance yet, but the HKM ʻōpio did not hesitate. No longer chanting an ancestral piece, the students lifted their voices to lyrics issued forth in a newer style:

Hawaiians, tell me what you want
Ea!
Kānaka Maoli tell me what you need
Ea!
We must nevah foʻget what our kūpuna taught
Ea, even if ʻah have to bleed.[11]

They had seamlessly made the transition from oli to rap in less than the time it took me to reach into my bag and pull out a camera. And in both instances of cultural expression, they asserted ea—life, breath, sovereignty.

The ʻōpio participated in raising a collective Hawaiian voice not only by reciting memorized chants and lyrics but also by sharing information and discussing the substantive issues to which the marches were trying to bring attention. A few months after the walk from Maunaʻala, HKM ʻōpio invited their fellow youth from multiple islands to join the collective conversation. At the annual Kuʻi ka Lono conference, organized by the Nā Lei Naʻauao alliance of Hawaiian charter schools, HKM students presented what they were learning in school to peers, teachers, and leaders from other schools and agencies. One of their groups specifically chose to talk about current political issues they were studying in their moʻolelo (social studies) class.

First, two girls, each representing a different side, detailed opposing arguments regarding the Native Hawaiian Government Reorganization Act. More popularly known as the Akaka Bill, this piece of legislation has been circulating in the U.S. Congress since 2000, without a hearing held on Hawaiʻi Island, where the students were presenting, or any island, besides a single hearing on Oʻahu. The next pair spoke about a proposed city council measure that would repeal forced lease-to-fee conversion, a policy that heavily impacted the Kamehameha

Schools, as it required the school's nonprofit trust to sell off its ownership of leasehold residential lands. As I listened from the audience I was particularly struck by one of the student's emphasis on explaining and asking us to consider how this would impact *us*.

In the year or two preceding her presentation, I had attended countless hearings, meetings, demonstrations, and vigils surrounding issues related to both Hawaiian charter school issues and the Kamehameha Schools. I had seen a more consistent physical presence of charter school students and teachers at the public marches and demonstrations supporting Kamehameha in the *Doe v. Kamehameha* case than I had KS teachers and students. Several of the HKM students presenting had applied and been denied admission to Kamehameha, yet they still articulated a clear investment in the school's success as a place for Hawaiians. It was about "us." While I was interviewing and observing KS teachers and leaders as part of my dissertation research, I rarely if ever heard them talk about Hawaiian culture–based charter schools in the language of "us," and I had never seen any of them at hearings on charter school–related bills.

As I reflected on this lack of political engagement in my own experience as a Kamehameha alumna and a researcher examining cultural change at that school the fifteen-year-old boy who was wrapping up the HKM presentation reeled my attention back. Looking out and making eye contact with several of his peers in the crowd, he asked the audience filled with students from other Nā Lei Na'auao schools, "Why should we as 'ōpio be at the forefront of the movement?" This was, in his words, their "kuleana to lead our people into the future." For me, his self-description of him and his peers as leaders of Hawaiian movements also captured the essence of what I had seen in the students' sharing of their learning through chanting, marching, singing, dancing, and presenting. These were acts to ho'omana lāhui, to increase the collective mana of the Hawaiian people/nation.

Kumulipo: Our Genealogies Are Political

For Kānaka Maoli, moving toward the future involves looking to the past. The practice of hula and oli has been one important way to retell stories from the past in the present. Native American writer Thomas

King's insight that "the truth about stories is that that's all we are" is in many ways a truth that holds for Kānaka Hawaiʻi, too.[12] Within Kanaka Maoli historical practice, our genealogies have long been a way to hoʻomana—to remember and reconstitute ourselves through the renewal of ancestral connections.

HKM's kumu hula, Kāwika Mersberg, has taught hula and oli at the school since it opened.[13] When I interviewed him in 2003, he talked about the purpose of daily hula practice within the school's pedagogies. In contrast to the "flashy and touristy" ways hula had been appropriated, Kumu Kāwika emphasized that the primary intent of learning hula and oli at Hālau Kū Māna was to honor the kūpuna by dancing in their footsteps, singing their songs, and telling their stories. He told me, "On any given day, there are at least sixty of us here [at Hālau Kū Māna] still doing what our kūpuna did hundreds of years ago, and it's really nice to pass on that tradition and to see it continue."[14] His intended purpose was to hoʻomana kūpuna. Within a Kanaka Maoli worldview, we see our kūpuna in broad terms. Grandparents, aliʻi of times past, ancestral deities, respected elders in the community, islands, and various beings and elements of our natural world can all be referred to as beloved kūpuna, those who adorn and strengthen us.

In spring 2003, the school's second year of operation, HKM ʻōpio undertook a two-year-long process of learning and performing the only full-length Hawaiian cosmogonic genealogy still in existence—the *Kumulipo*. When printed, the *Kumulipo* runs over two thousand lines long. When chanted from start to finish, it can easily extend over an hour of continuous recitation. The narrative is divided into two acts: pō, or night, and ao, or daylight. Similarly, the HKM performance of the *Kumulipo* was divided into two parts, with the pō section recounted in 2003 and the ao section recounted in 2004. At the time they were the first known school group to attempt this feat of collective oratory in the past century. In the process of offering their mana to the ancestors named in the genealogy, mana also flowed back to haumāna and their kumu, families, and communities. In order to understand how such a cultural performance was a form of political engagement, it is necessary to understand the background of the *Kumulipo*'s persistence in Kanaka Maoli life over the past century despite the ravages of colonialism on Indigenous knowledge.

As scholar of Hawaiian genealogies and professor of Hawaiian studies Lilikalā Kameʻeleihiwa explained in her introduction to HKM's hōʻike, the *Kumulipo* offers one view of the creation of the universe and all the beings of the Hawaiian natural world. It was once one among many genealogical chants that traced chiefly lineages all the way back to the world's origin. The *Kumulipo* survived the decimation of the ʻŌiwi population after the introduction of foreign diseases, making its way to the late nineteenth century, when it was documented and published under King Kalākaua. In addition to recognizing it as a moʻokūʻauhau of the aliʻi Lonoikamakahiki also known as Kalaninuiʻīamamao or Kaʻīʻīamamao, Kānaka Maoli of the present see the chant as offering a genealogy of us all, linking us to the birth of all beings.[15]

Noenoe Silva argues that the *Kumulipo* must be seen as "a political text because of how it figures in the national consciousness of the lāhui."[16] She describes the collection and transcription of the *Kumulipo* by Kalākaua's Papa Kūʻauhau Aliʻi o Nā Aliʻi Hawaiʻi (the Board of Genealogy of Hawaiian Chiefs) in the 1880s as an act of anticolonial resistance that validated Native leaders, systems of governance, and knowledge while rebutting assertions that only Western foreigners produced real knowledge, whether through science or Christian dogma.[17] The *Kumulipo* also affirmed Kalākaua's position as Mōʻī and head of state as a descendant of Lonoikamakahiki. Later, Queen Liliʻuokalani worked on her translation of the genealogical epic during her imprisonment by the haole men who had conspired against her and called in U.S. military forces to aid in their coup against her, the lawful head of state. Her version was published in 1897, a year before the United States claimed control of the islands under a military occupation. Silva further argues that the *Kumulipo* was part of the Native narrative strategy that worked against colonial discourses characterizing Hawaiians as savage and incapable of self-rule; the perpetuation of this genealogy was a form of "anticolonial nationalism . . . bridging the present to the past and providing a basis for self-definition of the lāhui as those who are connected to the ʻāina genealogically."[18] Hālau Kū Māna's 2003 and 2004 performances of the *Kumulipo* can be seen within this same trajectory, as evidenced by the fact that the hōʻike directors dedicated the show to Queen Liliʻuokalani and her brother, King Kalākaua.

The house lights of Hawai'i Theatre dimmed and a single spot-
light at midstage illuminated a young male student who had attended
Hawaiian-language immersion schools before coming to HKM. He
sounded the pū (conch shell) five times, preparing the audience and
making the way for chanters, who ascended upon a rising stage from
the orchestra pit. Sounds of raging winds filled the theater. Then, as
they waned, Kumu Kāwika Mersberg and Keali'i'olu'olu Gora, adorned
in lei and kīhei, opened the epic chant with booming voices:

O ke au i kahuli wela ka honua
O ke au i kahuli lole ka lani
O ke au i kukaiaka ka la.
E hoomalamalama i ka malama
O ke au o Makalii ka po
O ka walewale hookumu honua ia
O ke kumu o ka lipo, i lipo ai
O ke kumu o ka Po, i po ai
O ka lipolipo, o ka lipolipo
O ka lipo o ka la, o ka lipo o ka po
Po wale hoi
Hanau ka po
Hanau Kumulipo i ka po, he kane
Hanau Poele i ka po, he wahine . . .

Finishing their last line—in which the female Pō'ele is born—the two
kumu moved off to the side as a group of five young women took their
place at the front of the stage and began recounting the births of all the
creatures of the reefs. Unaccompanied by dance or musical instrument,
the 'ōpio wahine orated the first half of the wā. Midway through, two
male students came forward, inserting their voices such that the chant
modulated back and forth between wahine and kāne voices.

Pōmaika'i Freed was a seventh-grade kaikaina among the group
that chanted the first of eight wā (time periods) performed that night.
Reflecting back three years after her graduation, she told me, "It was
truly epic just being able to visit that and have kumu who would urge
us to go through that process." The process included learning up to 130

lines of text in each of their various sections, more than she had ever been asked to memorize.

> Going through the process of memorizing, seeing the different ways we went about memorizing, and watching how other people would kind of struggle through it, it was really amazing. Throughout learning the actual lines in our wā, we were also learning about what the *Kumulipo* was, who it was written for, and what was going on in our wā.... Going to HKM in general has really helped with my memory.[19]

But beyond helping with the skill of faithfully committing information to memory, which was even more highly prized and perfected among Kānaka of earlier times, Pōmaikaʻi further explained that the process sparked within her a deep desire to learn more:

> I didn't realize the full scope of what we were doing at the time. I thought it was cool that we were chanting a 2,000-line chant of creation! But I definitely didn't realize what was going on.... Not until years later, like in the last two or three years, has it really set into me what we were doing. Going through the *Kumulipo* more now and trying to understand, there's so much hidden manaʻo in it. The kaona . . . I really like to get into the deeper layers of what we're talking about, why the chant might have been written, and what it's speaking about. I feel that essentially, especially, that experience of going through the *Kumulipo*, that's what sprouted within me the most—that desire to explore the field of oli.

Importantly, she came to recognize Hawaiian chant as a broad and deep *field* of knowledge and a way of connecting with kūpuna. This realization and her desire to continue to be a lifelong learner of the obscured meanings and wisdom within oli were particularly salient in light of the context in which, as indicated in chapter 4, the *Kumulipo* and all traditional moʻolelo were marginalized by the state's curriculum content standards and benchmarks. Had Pōmaikaʻi been a seventh grader in any other school within Hawai'i's mainstream settler state system, it is more than likely that she would have never even been exposed to the *Kumulipo*, let alone asked to participate in a collective performance of it.

Against that wall of ignorance, the second wā began with the sounds of crashing waves. Three kāne and three wāhine walked to the front of the stage, chanting together the names of saltwater and freshwater fish. One by one, three older students emerged from the line, taking short solos until falling into a rhythm of chanting back and forth between kua'ana and kaikaina, between the two trios of older and younger students. The kumu had clearly constituted each group to include a diversity of students, a mix of stronger and weaker chanters, but importantly, all students in the school participated. Birds chirped as the third wā began with students soaring into a line of seven standing side by side. Other 'ōpio danced as flying creatures behind the chanters, and the wā came to a close through call and response. As with each successive wā, the refrain "pō nō" reminded the audience that it was "indeed night," the time before the creation of Kānaka. But also resounding as the word "pono," the students' collective voices reflected the importance of balance—balance of female and male, land and sea, elder and younger, broad and narrow. Such balance creates mana and, perhaps, justice.

As the eighth wā of the *Kumulipo* came to a close, day broke (ua ao). All the 'ōpio came together on stage to perform hula they had learned over the course of the school year. Their dance performances opened with a medley for Kalākaua and Lili'uokalani. Standing shoulder to shoulder in a tight rectangular formation, the kāne danced the first line of the mele, "Kāwika," while the wāhine stood in rows between them with hands on hips and eyes fixed outward. Then the boys knelt, giving way to the wāhine, who honored the queen in "Lili'u E." Line by line they continued: kāne dancing for the king, and wāhine dancing for the queen, remaining in a strong, fixed configuration. As the 'ōpio moved, modulating back and forth between kāne and wahine energies, their mana expanded until at last they called out together, "He inoa no Lili'uokalani!" (In the name of Lili'uokalani!). Members of the audience audibly exhaled before bursting into applause, a flood of their mana flowing back to the 'ōpio.

Eight years later, I sat observing Kumu Kāwika teaching hula to another cohort of 'ōpio, some of whom were siblings or cousins of HKM students who performed the *Kumulipo* years earlier. These haumāna were just beginning to prepare for an event paying tribute to Prince Jonah Kūhiō Kalaniana'ole, the Kaua'i-born ali'i who actively fought the haole oligarchs who participated in the U.S.-backed coup against Queen Lili'uokalani and then later worked within the U.S. political system to fight for justice for Hawaiians.[20] The nearby Papakōlea Hawaiian Civic Club had invited HKM to dance, and Kumu Kāwika told his haumāna that this was "an honor and a privilege."

"Why do you think this might be an honor and a privilege?" he asked them.

"So we can show what we can do," one boy answered.

"Ok. Go deeper," he prodded.

"So we can show we mālama the kuleana of these hula," another ventured.

"'Ae, so we can mālama the kuleana of these hula, and one kuleana is to honor our kūpuna, like Prince Kūhiō and the kūpuna of Papakōlea," the kumu affirmed.

He proceeded to talk about Kūhiō's role as a founder of the Hawaiian Homes Commission and asked how many of the students lived on Hawaiian homelands. Several raised their hands. "See, today, one hundred years later, people are still benefitting from his work." The mana of this kūpuna still touched them, and the stories, hula, and mele Kumu Kāwika shared would be a way that the 'ōpio could ho'omana in return.

Confronting Blockages of Mana Within

The practice of hula and oli at HKM allowed students to connect with and ho'omana kūpuna through the performance of stories and genealogies. Thus, they challenged and pushed against external safety zone fences, such as state curriculum content requirements that left out mo'olelo such as the *Kumulipo*. But the practice also allowed some to do the personal, political work of confronting the blockages of mana that lay within. Hula, as a cultural form, has been represented as feminine by the intersecting discourses of U.S. imperialism and the corporate tourist and entertainment industries.[21] Kānaka Maoli have ourselves sometimes internalized these heteropatriarchal notions. For

instance, in Tengan's study of Hawaiian masculinity, he explains that
"many of the men in the Hale Mua still associated hula with women
and māhū."[22] At HKM the practice of hula and oli often provided an
opportunity to challenge such limiting notions, which I argue stem
the balanced flow of mana on societal, interpersonal, and individual
levels. The year of the first *Kumulipo* performance, two kāne—a kumu
and a senior about to graduate—separately shared with me their
intersecting stories about how they each came to rethink long-held
sexist reservations about hula and their own practices of culture and
gender.

Labeled as a delinquent and truant at his previous high school,
Alika Kaʻahanui came to HKM with a suspicion of schooling but an
unparalleled confidence in his athletic abilities and interpersonal and
social skills. He emerged as a leader early on in the two years he attended Hālau Kū Māna and remained so until his graduation. He had
a knack for keeping the younger students laughing while also keeping
them in line, and many of them looked to him as an elder brother figure. Whenever I took the seniors off campus, no matter where we went,
Alika was shaking hands with someone he knew and was saying aloha
to everyone else. We teased that he was like the mayor. But even as he
shed imposed and internalized representations of himself as a kāne
who proved his manliness through warrior-like acts such as physical
fighting he held memories of schools he had attended throughout his
life. When I interviewed him a few months before the *Kumulipo* con-
cert and his subsequent graduation, he recalled:

> They make Hawaiians feel stupid—all the time. They make
> Hawaiians think that we dumb, we lazy, we no can do nothing.
> If we no complete this, we not gon' be able fo' go anywhere. [At
> my old school] I would think of myself as a Hawaiian, but I
> wouldn't express myself as a Hawaiian. I would express myself
> as a [he took a long pause] a disobedient adolescent. I would
> just cut school because school was boring and they weren't
> teaching me what I wanted to learn.[23]

The memories he shared with me raised my ire such that I can only
imagine how much anger these experiences had provoked in him. He

spoke in a markedly different way about his experiences at HKM. Distinguishing between HKM and his previous school gave him a way to talk about the day-to-day experiences of racism and colonialism that impacted the way he understood manliness and Hawaiianness. In his stories I could see the work he had done to transform himself as he described how the practice of hula and oli "makes you a better Hawaiian and makes you look forward to *being* Hawaiian, not just *saying* you're Hawaiian." Alika elaborated on how his growing practice of Hawaiian culture, which he understood as necessarily including the range of practices such as hula, mahi ʻai kalo, chanting, and seafaring, opened space for him to shift his ways of thinking:

> I see more that Hawaiians can help out Hawaiians in time of distress, or war. They can make another Hawaiian feel welcome.... [With] my friends I feel more caring. I try help them out. I tell them, "We bettah than that, braddahs. We can do more than what dey tink we can do, and you can do more than what you tink you can do. It's better for you be more cool-headed and help each other out than having them label us as dumb Hawaiians and lazy."

His newfound practice of hula and oli was not only a tool for Alika's own self-development but an inspiration for one of his kumu to similarly reexamine his assumptions about Hawaiianness and masculinity and the blockages to balanced mana that resided within him.

During Alika's senior year, Kumu Dan Ahuna had come on board as a math teacher and curriculum coordinator. Raised in Papakōlea, one of HKM's primary geographic communities, Dan had been an outstanding athlete in his community and later in high school and college. He and Alika were cut from the same cloth: physically strong, playful, charismatic, and full of aloha. He remembered growing up, even though within a Hawaiian homestead community, strongly influenced by "a Westernized world, [in which] men have a macho image to uphold." With his friends it was "automatic" to make comments about men dancing hula: "Ho, look that guy, so gay!" In coming to HKM, he still had a difficult time accepting hula for kāne, but talking with Alika made him pause.

The one person that I could relate to was Alika, who loved to play sports, loved to go surfing. He was basically a manly type of guy. But when I saw him doing hula, I had to ask him, "How do you feel doing the hula?" And he told me, "You know, the first time I felt like it was gay and everything." But then he learned . . . about the cultural meaning of a circle. . . . He said everything we do in Hawaiian culture is like a circle. I'm not just talking about the physical circle but also the spiritual side. In the Hawaiian culture, there's hula, oli, you, our community, your parents, the kūpuna. Everybody's a part of this circle. You have a commitment and responsibility to each of these things in the circle, and you cannot just do one or two and leave the rest out because this circle, it runs continuous. If you stop at one, you cannot flow and you cannot be pono, and the whole message he was trying to tell me was about being pono. . . . Hula is part of it. Yeah, it's gonna be hard, but after you do it, you feel pono. You did your job as part of your responsibility to this circle. And it made sense to me. This was coming from a student, and this is something that I'm gonna remember for the rest of my life.[24]

Alika recounted the same conversation when I was asking him what challenges he had overcome in order to finish high school:

[Kumu Dan] was telling me that he didn't agree with dancing hula, and he would never get the courage to dance hula 'cuz he felt that it's not like "a man thing." But I told him, in order to make the circle work, you gotta tie in hula, oli, mele, 'ōlelo. Hula is one of the things that makes the circle complete.[25]

He talked about how important it had been to him that a kumu had listened to him, had been open to receiving his mana'o and mana. In return, months later when Alika was considering dropping out with less than a semester to go before graduation, his kumu directed that mana right back toward him and inspired him to finish.

I wouldn't have graduated. I was feeling like it was over already. I nevah like finish school, and he helped me out, for get me

through with that and get over my actions. . . . He grasped
upon what I had said, so I grasped upon what he said.

As Kumu Dan remembered, the guidance he gave Alika was simply
passing back the lesson Alika had taught him the previous year. Ultimately, "he didn't think it was pono to leave the circle. . . . I don't know
who was learning, him or me?"

Their conversation was powerful not only because it allowed each
of them to reconsider the role of hula in their lives but because this
instance of two kāne willing to openly confront and discuss their assumptions about masculinity and cultural practice ultimately allowed
the student to overcome internalized barriers that have too often led
boys like him to drop out of school without realizing their mana to
succeed in that academic realm. In both of these ways, this personal
work was also profoundly political.

"Fighting for Our School"

The collective liberation of a people from imposed safety zones is directly related to each individual's courage to challenge internalized
limits. Similarly, the development of a self-determined people's collective voice is interlinked with the cultivation of each person's individual
voice. This section describes ways political engagement in the legislative processes of state government provided opportunities for 'ōpio to
exercise their own singular voices, develop confidence, and realize the
power of their personal stories and actions.

By Pōmaikaʻi Freed's junior year in high school, she had attended a
variety of political events since entering the school as a sixth grader. On
several occasions throughout those years, she had gone to the Hawaiʻi
state capitol to argue before the legislature for equitable funding for
charter schools. Those visits had contributed, over time, to a shift in
her view of a place that once felt intimidating and foreign. Responding
that year to an in-class writing prompt, "Does political action belong
in a school environment?" Pōmaikaʻi wrote about a realization that
she, like many of her classmates, had come to *only* through the experience of visiting, chanting, speaking, and dancing hula at that center of
power and decision making several times during her education. She

wrote: "The State Capitol isn't something to fear, somewhere that feels forbidden. It's somewhere that represents the struggle we go through not only as Hawaiians, but as human beings, always fighting for what we deserve." For several HKM alums I interviewed, these acts of going to the state capitol and making their voices heard were formative learning experiences.[26]

In HKM's early years, the disparity in funding for charter schools in Hawai'i was more extreme than in the latter part of the ten-year span. Between 2001 and 2006, small groups of students accompanied then–executive director Keola Nakanishi as he went to the capitol to garner legislative support for funding equity. These students had the opportunity to meet legislators in their offices, as well as give public testimony at legislative hearings. Additionally, there were several occasions, usually at critical moments when charter school bills were up for hearings, that several charter schools (typically dominated by the Hawaiian culture–based schools) would bring their students down to the capitol to chant and dance in the capitol's rotunda. Among the HKM graduates I discussed these experiences with, many spoke to the ways they learned about government at a close level and, more important, came to know that they could make a difference. Students developed the confidence to speak publicly without being intimidated by an imposed hierarchy.

Noelani Duffey-Spikes remembered the process of preparing for and then going to the state capitol to express her political opinions and analysis through both speeches and songs. Reflecting back, she believed that "fighting for funding for our school" was an ideal issue for learning about government because of the direct connection to something she cared about in her daily life.

> Our teachers, at that time, went from the beginning, "OK, this is how government works." So we learned the background politics, how government is organized, and then after fully understanding it, we went. Being that we were just kids, that was like adult stuff for us. It was a big deal being able to understand [the issues] and go to the capitol. It wasn't like we were just kids out there saying, "Kūē!" [but] who don't even know what they're fighting for. We knew exactly what we were talking

FIGURE 21.   *Dustin No'eau Pā'alani (HKM class of 2009), then a student at HKM, made clear the inequity in funding between Hawai'i charter schools and mainstream public Department of Education schools at a rally near the state capitol in Honolulu, circa 2004. Photograph courtesy of Hālau Kū Māna New Century Public Charter School.*

about, why were fighting against or supporting a bill. We knew what we were talking about. We knew [she paused, finding the words and then stating emphatically] *what was at stake.*

She went on to talk about the multiple ways in which students had been taught and could then *practice* in a meaningful context expressing their voices:

> We learned how to write testimonies! I don't know kids that know how to write testimony.... Even those moments where we sang, or pule, in the rotunda—the middle part of the capitol. Getting that chicken skin feeling like, yeah, we're here for a bigger purpose. We're not just Hawaiians out there who are causing havoc. We're here for a reason, and we're not gonna shut up until you listen to us.

Throughout our conversation, Noe emphasized that her experiences at both the state capitol and in the Kū i ka Pono marches helped her develop the ability to thoroughly analyze a controversial political issue and the skills to articulate her opinion on the matter.

Kauʻi Onekea (HKM class of 2006) expressed similarly valuing such experiences, but she emphasized the ways she felt her kumu encouraged her to consult her own naʻau, the seat of intelligence and intuition in a Hawaiian epistemology, as a basis for discovering her own powerful voice:

> [Our teachers] didn't force us to be fighters or activists, but its something that is in your own naʻau. You are asked to think about what is pono. [For me] I was like, that's not fair, why are they gonna give us less money? If I go to a DOE school, then you would give that school more money? Why wouldn't you give this school the same amount of money for me as if I go to a DOE school? The teacher wasn't telling us, "This is wrong what they're doing." . . . It was like, "OK, this is the situation." And then on your own, you would write a testimony if you felt like it. When we went [to the legislature], you could actually go up to the mic and speak your manaʻo. That's on you. It's all you. We were never ever pushed to go and give testimony.

Kauʻi was one of the ʻōpio who chose to testify at the legislature on multiple occasions. She remembered feeling compelled to speak and to tell state decision makers about the funding inequities that were threatening the existence of charter schools like HKM:

> How can this even happen? How can you sit back and not do anything about it? To me, I love this school; this school has given me a lot. Why shouldn't I say something about it and explain to [legislators]? . . . Being given the opportunity to testify is something that is teaching you from the inside—not just your lolo, your brain, but your naʻau, feeling on your own what is pono and what isn't pono. And then being able to do something about it! Not be shy or be lazy or be like, "They're

not gonna listen to me anyway. I'm only fifteen years old. Why should they listen to us?" [My voice] makes a difference, when they can see the impact, see what Hālau Kū Māna is doing for students.

Her direct, personal experiences in speaking her own voice helped her to challenge imposed hierarchies that might otherwise devalue her opinions—as an ʻōpio, a woman, and a Hawaiian—as less important.

> I don't know how many schools can go down to the capitol and learn about legislation and give testimony, learn to speak from your naʻau. [Learn] public speaking in front of these people that make the ultimate choice. Even that is a big part of me now—not being afraid of saying what I feel and fighting for what I want, because we were put in that environment. You know, as kids you kinda feel intimidated by all these adults walking around in suits, and they all got their titles. But you know, you have a mouth, and you can use it. . . . That was amazing to be in that kind of environment but to be in school. . . . Before I used to be super scared to speak in public, especially on the mic, when everyone is silent. Everyone's listening to you, so it's your time. It's hard the first time, but when you understand what kind of impact you can have, I mean, you can *change* someone's mind by what you say, and that's important. I used to be so scared to speak, just to people. That's more power to you when you can get up and say what you feel and have no fear that people are staring at you and everyone's listening to you and you might mess up. Even now, sometimes I feel like I don't want to sit down. I wanna make sure I get everything out.

Kauʻi's experiences at the state capitol did more than cultivate the sort of citizenship ethic taught in many American civics courses. Rather, it taught her the value of speaking the truth of her experience. It taught her that her stories were valuable. She was able to realize the mana within her and see the importance of using her voice to let that mana flow, no matter what the setting.

Mālama iā Haloa: "Hell No, GMO!"

As the gap in state per pupil funding between charter schools and conventional public schools grew smaller over the next five years—also mitigated by supplemental funding for qualified schools provided by Kamehameha Schools and the Office of Hawaiian Affairs—HKM's survival became less tenuous and the focus of students' and teachers' political attention moved beyond protecting our own kīpuka. Kumu particularly looked out for issues that related to things with which students had already developed a pilina (close relationship). Teachers saw student engagement with social movements around such issues both as a form of assessment and as community development and networking. In this section I discuss the ways HKM school members participated in community actions mobilized around the ethic of mālama Hāloa (to care for the kalo) and in opposition to the patenting and genetic modification of this culturally significant plant.[27] By attending a series of political actions over the course of three school years, students learned through experience a number of things about power and critically reading the world. The graduates I interviewed talked about seeing power relations exposed, critically analyzing media representations, and witnessing multiple forms of kūʻē by which to intervene in conditions of injustice.

Hālau Kū Māna kumu and ʻōpio first became involved in efforts to stop the patenting and genetic modification of Hāloa in 2006. When a call went out to various Hawaiian organizations to become involved in this issue, HKM ʻōpio and kumu had already established relationships with kalo farmers on various islands through their participation in collaborative loʻi restoration efforts with the archipelago-wide coalition ʻOnipaʻa nā Hui Kalo. Thus, they had developed pilina with Hāloa and with a broad network of farmers from various islands. Many haumāna had been exposed to the full spectrum of taro cultivation, from clearing land to eating the fruits of their labor.

Kauʻi Onekea likened HKM's and other sibling Hawaiian charter schools' responses to the call to become involved in this issue to the way a family comes together when one member is in need:

> Whenever you get the call, you show up just like family! It's just like, so-and-so is in the hospital, and so everyone just shows

up. You put the call out, and everyone comes. I liked knowing that we weren't alone. . . . There were other people and [Nā Lei Naʻauao] students the same age as us learning about the same things. . . . We were the lucky ones that were able to learn about [Hāloa and GMOs].[28]

Her comments mirror a central Indigenous research ethic—that the production of knowledge is attentive to the needs of the community.[29] This is a very different orientation to curriculum and learning than the dominant approach within the settler state system, in which statewide standards and detailed quarterly benchmark maps are developed by a centralized group of professionals removed from Indigenous or local community concerns. Such a static curriculum makes it difficult to be responsive to important issues impacting communities as they arise.

At the time HKM became involved in the Mālama Hāloa movements, University of Hawaiʻi agricultural researchers were holding U.S. patents on three varieties of kalo that had been derived from the Hawaiian Maui Lehua variety through conventional cross-breeding methods (in other words, they were not genetically modified). As early as 2005, a number of kalo farmers—both ʻŌiwi and settler—had begun organizing their opposition to any form of ownership of taro cultivars. They believed the foray into patenting would fundamentally alter the centuries-old Indigenous practice of mahiʻai kalo freely exchanging and gifting the huli (the upper part of the root used for replanting) of different varieties. As Alapaʻi Hanapī asserted, "Ownership of taro is like slavery. . . . We [Kānaka Maoli] are the custodians who have guided the appropriate use of kalo for millennia as a benefit for all people of Hawaiʻi."[30] Cultural practitioners like Hanapī were concerned that university scientists had claimed intellectual property without consulting the Indigenous people who have successfully stewarded kalo for hundreds of generations. Additionally, non-Kanaka kalo farmers were crucial to the alliance. Chris Kobayashi, a female mahiʻai kalo from Kauaʻi, expressed her opposition as a farmer to the patenting of kalo or any other crop plant, asking, "How can anyone claim ownership of plants that have evolved and been selected or bred by farmers for specific environmental conditions and desirable properties over generations?"[31]

Community organizers and farmers also saw in any move to

commodify kalo connections to the encroaching forms of commercial agriculture practiced by large biotechnology corporations, including genetic modification and field testing in Hawaiʻi. The strong links between industrial agricultural producers supporting genetic modification and the university made such insights particularly salient. Long-time Hawaiian organizer and subsistence practitioner Walter Ritte articulates a Hawaiian critique of genetic modification as it is connected to patenting and commodification of food plants:

> On the island of Molokaʻi, Hawaiians have expressed their deep concern about genetic engineering by referring to this technology as mana mahele, which means owning and selling our mana or life force. Mana is the spiritual force that comes from our knowledge and intricate relationship with nature. Part of mana is what westerners call "biodiversity."[32]

Ritte was a key organizer of two events in which HKM students participated. Each of the events might be seen as representing a different side of a dualistic Hawaiian orientation to thinking about mana, symbolized by the akua Kū and Lono. As Kameʻeleihiwa describes, the two paths—one of confrontation and even violence and the other of celebrating peace and productivity—complement each other in the search for or creation of mana.[33] In the first instance, ʻōpio came together with farmers, university students, and other community members in a more aggressive Kū-like stance. Protestors purposefully yet spontaneously dismantled the stone garden outside the University of Hawaiʻi's central administration building.

Alakaʻi Kotrys, who was an eighth grader at the time, remembered that classes were cancelled so that the entire school could attend the march and protest on the University of Hawaiʻi campus. The central demand of the action was to call university administrators to get their faculty to relinquish the patents and approach research on kalo in consultation with Kānaka Maoli. Alakaʻi recalled that although he had been learning about the cultural significance of kalo in school, he didn't know anything about patenting or genetic modification until he began attending these Mālama Hāloa events. These actions exposed him to community experts who helped educate him and his classmates. When the haumāna arrived at Ka Papa Loʻiʻo Kānewai, a genealogical predecessor to HKM's loʻi kalo, they listened to several farmers and kūpuna speak in both Hawaiian and English about the cultural importance of kalo and the potential implications of patenting and genetic modification. Inspired by what they heard, some of the ʻōpio, Alakaʻi included, spontaneously "put all this mud on our bodies. [Then we] carried kalo all the way to the UH [central administration building] to do our chants." When asked that day about why they chose to adorn themselves in this fierce-looking manner, some of the students explained that it was an outward display of their connection to their ancestor, Hāloa.

Respected kupuna Eddie Kaanana led the procession from a truck guarded by younger Kanaka demonstrators. HKM students and staff chanted many of the oli we regularly did at opening or closing protocol each school day. The oli surrounded the few hundred people who walked behind ʻAnakala's truck from the loʻi to Bachman Hall, the center of decision making for the University of Hawaiʻi system. As Kauʻi remembered, "We walked down the road like it was a sidewalk." When the procession arrived, students and kumu from another Hawaiian charter school, Hālau Lōkahi, stood at the top of the entranceway in full traditional dress. They offered chants of greeting to us marchers and of resistance to university administrators who were refusing to speak to the crowd or to even come out of the building. The multitude of people packed around the square-shaped courtyard just outside Bachman's front doors. Students pressed up against the glass doors, a security guard posted to keep protestors from entering visible just on the other side. Organizers spoke from one corner, projecting their voices with a bullhorn. Alakaʻi recalled one speaker in particular:

> I sat there and listened to ʻAnakala Eddie talk ... [about] how we as Hawaiians think about kalo in general. And then it really hit me. It was just super crazy to hear all this new info about something that I had been learning about nonstop [in school] but never really *got* until he started talking. He was on the bullhorn—someone was holding it for him—and it was super soft, so you had to be super quiet to hear him. ... We came in screaming and yelling, and it didn't phase the people in the building at all, and then when Uncle Eddie starts talking,

FIGURE 22. *Alakaʻi Kotrys (HKM class of 2010) holds a picture of ʻAnakala Eddie Kaanana. HKM students were participating in a rally at the Hawaiʻi state capitol calling for legal protections of kalo against genetic modification. The rally followed an earlier event at University of Hawaiʻi at Mānoa's Bachman Hall, which had been led by ʻAnakala Eddie and had expressed discontent with university researchers' holding patents on specific varieties of kalo. In the time between the two events, ʻAnakala passed into the ao ʻaumākua (realm of the ancestors). Photograph courtesy of Hālau Kū Māna New Century Public Charter School and ʻĪmaikalani Winchester.*

everyone shuts up. All chanting is done. All yelling is done. All
anger is done. He just talks, and everybody just stops and lis-
tens. I think that's the craziest form of kūʻē I've ever seen. . . . I
remember him saying that there were Hawaiians in this building who didn't know what it meant to be Hawaiian . . . didn't
know what their kuleana was . . . that it's not about the money;
it's about the culture. He said something along those lines, but
I can't do justice to what ʻAnakala Eddie says.[34]

And yet while participants like Alakaʻi were listening to their elder,
what struck Kauʻi was the way in which university officials could simply shut out their voices. For her this was a moment when the relations
of power became very clear.

Being there and *seeing* UH lock us out and not want to hear
us. When you are *there*, then you can actually see for yourself
how other people can respond. I was like, "Why you gonna do
that? Why you not gonna talk to us? That's not pono! If you
have a pilikia, let's talk about it. We have a pilikia with you, and
we wanna talk about it." Just to see that [lock out] happen, you
understand why Hawaiians are so active in the political world.
Why sit down and be pushed and *shoved* to the side and not
heard? We are people! And we deserve a right to be heard. You
can't be changing our kalo! It's our life! You can't just be doing
whatever you want with our cultural history.[35]

The feelings of frustration at not being heard provoked Hālau Lōkahi
Kumu Hinaleimoana Wong Kalu to call everyone present to take
a stone from the garden in the courtyard. Before dispersing, people
stacked these stones in front of the glass doors as a statement of our
presence. Administrators who had not come out from their offices
would then be confronted with a physical reminder of all who had
been there that day.

In the following months, kumu from Hālau Lōkahi and Hālau
Kū Māna began talking about how this Kū-like event, which had included defacing the garden outside Bachman through the removal of
all those stones, would impact students if they did not see another

side to balance that action. Former Hālau Lōkahi teacher Kalaniākea Wilson spearheaded a second follow-up event, at which people would come together again to rebuild in the previous garden's place an ahu built of pōhaku from around the islands and surrounded by native plants. The intent of Lā Kūkahi (A Day to Stand as One) was to establish a permanent Hawaiian presence at Bachman Hall. Organizers decided, however, the tone and intention would be to hoʻoulu (nurture growth) and to hoʻomana kūpuna (to honor the elders and the ancestors). Kumu Kalani began traveling from island to island in search of pōhaku that would be the cornerstones of the ahu.[36]

HKM leaders planned the school's quarterly Lā ʻOhana (Family Day) around Lā Kūkahi, asking all students, families, and staff to participate. Joining with others, the HKM ʻohana lined up along the mile-long stretch of road between Kānewai and Bachman Hall and passed from hand to hand the stones that would fill the structure of the ahu.[37] Through this physical work, participants experienced kūkahi and lōkahi, coming together for a common purpose.

After the various Mālama Hāloa events, reflective journaling encouraged students to articulate for themselves the meaning of the experiences, responding to prompts such as:

- Was this event an expression of aloha ʻāina? Describe why or why not.
- Have your actions been executed with pono? Use specific examples.
- How has your participation helped your community, people, and/or āina?
- What difference do you feel you have made?
- What was the greatest lesson that you have learned through this experience?

It was through such writing assignments that students wrote, for example, "I believe that students and schools have a lot of power, in fact I know this. Just look at the Civil Rights movement. Many of those protestors and leaders were students in high school and college, and they made a world of a difference."

HKM teachers also used the students' participation in these events

FIGURE 23. *HKM students and teachers joined numerous other Hawaiian school groups and community members at the Hawaiʻi state legislature during the 2008 session. Organized by Nā Kahu o Hāloa, people gathered in support of a bill that would have put a ten-year moratorium on the genetic modification of Hawaiian varieties of kalo. Left to right: Kumu ʻĪmaikalani Winchester, Lolena Aldosa (HKM class of 2009), Anuhea Papaʻia (HKM class of 2009), Kaleialiʻi Baldwin (HKM class of 2008), and Kumu Kāwika Mersberg chant in the capitol's rotunda. Photograph courtesy of Hālau Kū Māna New Century Public Charter School and ʻĪmaikalani Winchester.*

and the local news media's regular coverage of the issues as an opportunity to practice critical media literacy. Students in the high school–level Loʻi Project watched, read, and talked about daily newspaper and television coverage of events at which they had been present. Kauʻi remembered that her direct involvement enabled a critical lens, which in turn motivated her to watch the news because she could watch it with an active, analytical gaze rather than as a passive listener.

You were actually there, so you can make your own decision.
Like when you hear the media, they only want to tell you what

they want to tell you and what they saw from their perspective. But everyone has their own eyes and can see. So it was good to be there. That's what I used to like, too, not just watching the news because we want to see ourselves on TV but to hear what they're actually sharing to the world and Hawai'i. Is it like, "Oh, crazy Hawaiians again at UH!" No, we're not crazy. We're upset because of what you're doing to us. You're the crazy ones. Just being able to make your own decision and to say that's not right. People might say, "Oh, these crazy Hawaiians, what's wrong with you now?" And its like, no, no, no. You show up for yourself, and you see what's wrong with this picture.

Additionally, haumāna read commentaries on perceived pros and cons for genetically modifying and patenting kalo, and they considered the different positionalities and investments of various commentators. With all of this information, the students wrote their own argumentative papers using the positions they had developed on the subject.

In June 2006, the University of Hawai'i voluntarily released its patents, turning them over to the collective Native Hawaiian community. Even after this victory, HKM continued to participate in community mobilizations aimed at getting the state legislature to pass a moratorium on the genetic modification of kalo. Students attended hearings and wrote testimonies on these bills, as well as performing hula and pounding poi in the capitol's rotunda. Additionally, the ahu still stands right outside the front doors of Bachman Hall to remind decision makers that the kūpuna Hawai'i are always present to provide guidance and accountability. As of this writing, HKM's Papa Lo'i continues to visit the ahu on occasion, in Kumu 'Īmaikalani Winchester's words, "to ho'omana with oli, pule, and ho'okupu" as part of their ongoing kuleana to mālama iā Hāloa.

Chants for Ea: A Ha'ina

In this chapter I show the ways HKM students used diverse forms of cultural expression to directly engage meaningful political issues at multiple levels. By creating mana in these ways, they resisted restriction by imposed and internalized safety zones, and they enacted ea. I close with a final example of the ways students purposefully *blended* cultural forms. In this case, two different styles of oratory—oli and spoken-word poetry—were combined in a practice of hoʻomana to empower self, kūpuna, and the Hawaiian nation.

I interviewed Alakaʻi Kotrys, a member of HKM's class of 2010, almost exactly a year to the day after his graduation. He had just returned home, having completed his freshman year at the University of San Francisco. As we sat under the mango tree next to Maunalaha stream and in front of HKM's main classrooms, I asked him why he initially came to the school as an eighth grader. He remembered that it was the chants that drew him. At family reunions he had heard his cousins Janelle, Jasmine, and Kaʻimi Hoʻohuli perform oli they practiced daily at Hālau Kū Māna. "I wanted to get into it," he continued. "So I told my mom that I didn't want to go to my school in Waipahu anymore and that I would make the trek all the way to Mānoa to go to school. She was fine with it." And so Alakaʻi began making the hour-long city bus ride each morning to get to the school of his choosing.

He got to oli alongside his cousins every morning to start the school day and every afternoon to close it. That year, he was also exposed to the art that would become the driving passion of his life—slam poetry. Hawaiʻi Youth Speaks mentor Travis Thompson was leading one of the Friday playshops taught by community volunteers, and although Alakaʻi could not remember ever having any interest or talent in writing poetry, he was drawn to Travis's description that they would "learn to tell stories and tell good jokes in the class." Encouraged by both Thompson and his language arts teacher, Kanoa Castro, Alakaʻiʻs love for poetry began to flourish, and his skills followed suit. By the time I interviewed him postgraduation, he had two youth slam team U.S. national championships under his belt, and he had just led the University of San Francisco's team to a solid finish in their first national competition as the team's captain.

That day, under the mango trees, he reminded me of the first piece he had ever written. It was a poem I heard him perform for the school when he was an eighth grader and that he later took to competitions. He described the origins and inspiration for the poem:

> I tied in an oli with my experiences of the first time we went to the state capitol—my first time. It was about how that whole

kū'ē felt to me that very first year I came here. So I would do
the chant in the beginning and then go off into the piece itself.

He titled the piece "Chants."[38] The oli he chose to use is one HKM students have given breath to every day at opening protocol since the school
first opened—"Pule Ho'ōla" (A Prayer to Bring Life)—given to Hālau
Kū Māna for its daily protocols by Kumu John Keola Lake. According
to the Pukui and Elbert Hawaiian dictionary, *ho'ōla* can also be understood as "to save, heal, cure, or spare." It is significant that he combined
an oli for life (ea) with a poem about fierce resistance. Pule Ho'ōla calls to
the 'aumākua, and so too begins Alaka'i's poem: "Na aumakua mai ka la
hiki a ka la kau ..." (To our ancestral deities, from the rising to the setting sun).[39] Alternating back and forth, he utters lines in Hawaiian that
speak directly to the ancestors and then spits English lyrics to describe
to the audience what it felt like when the mana of the kūpuna came together with his and his fellow students' energies in a moment of action.

> Eia ka pulapula a oukou
> armies of spirit people armed with spears
> suited for battle
> chanting, motionless
> we stood side by side
> with the army of transparent grandparents
> our kupuna took warrior form
> e malama oukou ia makou
> screaming, they mixed chants with battle cries
> words flowed, spewing from lips like lava from Kilauea
> the army turned toward us
> and charged with massive force
> unafraid, in formation we stood there
> chanting till we lost our voices
> with spears raised high in the air
> they rushed us full sprint
> and we clashed, combining our spirits
> using their voices within us

As the poem continues the synergy of past and present Kanaka Maoli
collective voice builds. His voice quickens and intensifies, and the

kūpuna respond in kind, letting nothing hold them back from joining with their moʻopuna. Having acknowledged them in all their places and urged the growth of the heavens, the earth, and the islands of Hawaiʻi, he asks to be granted specific abilities and qualities: ʻike (knowledge), ikaika (strength), akamai (intelligence), maopopo pono (understanding), and the following:

> E ho mai ka ike papalua
> grant us foresight
> so that with our clenched fists and open eyes we can create a
>   bond with our
>   people's previous lifetimes
> eternal
> with our kupuna

It is with that mana that he describes Kānaka as people:

> following the trails blazed by our akua
> living life to the fullest
> walking the paths our ancestors started
> binding our hearts with their spirits
> speaking the tongue of our native, greatest, grandest parents
> feeling the blood of our kupuna spreading through our bodies
> hearing the beauty of their voices travel through phrases of wit
> seeing the beauty of Hawaiʻi through the faces of our people
>   waking up!
> from the daydream that America cast upon us
> standing up, against the laws set by the U.S.
> fighting for the land our native roots were made in
> fighting for our sovereignty

The verse reaches its crescendo as he asks, in closing, for one final thing:

> E ho mai ka mana.
> Empower us.
> ke akua olelo ma ke kanaka
> the gods' language is in the people,
> and we have started listening.

The Ongoing Need to Restore Indigenous Vessels

As I was nearing the completion of my manuscript, sitting at my kitchen table and typing away one afternoon in the late spring of 2011, the familiar chime of my text message notification sounded. It was HKM's po'o kumu, Mahinapoepoe Duarte:

"Ua lanakila. We passed our math HSA test!!!"

Mahina had come on board that fall and led a relentless campaign to improve students' math scores on the Hawai'i State Assessment (HSA), as math had been the subject keeping HKM from meeting AYP targets. Absolutely determined to get the school out of NCLB restructuring status, the faculty, administration, and families together supported Saturday math tutoring, before- and after-school math enrichment, monthly pizza parties for the groups or students who spent the most time on their computer-based supplemental math program, and weekend-long intensive math camps, in addition to regular daily math instruction. Kumu Mahina made it a point to inform teachers, board members, students, and their families at every possible opportunity about the targets that needed to be met—how many students needed to pass in order to make safe harbor or to fully meet Adequate Yearly Progress targets. I texted Mahina back, "Hulō! Hulō! Mahalo nui for all your dedication and commitment to this goal. It's a huge day for HKM! Send my congratulations to all, and hug all the 'ōpio for me!"

Under the state's new testing protocols, students were allowed to take the computer-based Hawai'i State Assessment three times during a set window of time. As long as each student met the target score on one of these three attempts, they could be counted toward the school meeting AYP. With each administration the anticipation on campus built, and students' scores climbed. On the day of the final administration of the test, I had been observing hula classes. Even at a distance from the classrooms designated for the tests, the anxiety and excitement was palpable. Emotions were running high.

Several folks I had spoken with during the testing days told me that students who had previously said, "Screw this test!" were trying their best and using the full amount of test time allotted. Most of the ʻōpio expressed a desire to score well for themselves and for their school. As I watched from afar several exited the doors of the testing room final score in hand, jumping for joy, greeted by supportive teachers and peers waiting outside.

Over the course of the next day, I got more emails and phone calls from other members of the school community—teachers and board members—who were as jubilant as Kumu Mahina. Enough students had exceeded state targets on the test for the school not only to make safe harbor by showing incremental gains in comparison to the previous year but to exceed the math AYP goals outright! I shared their elation. For the first time in five years, the school was surpassing the state's math score targets. More important, students were making tremendous math gains, with many ʻōpio improving by two or more grade levels over the course of the year. There was collective relief that the school would survive another year under NCLB. (As this book went to press the preliminary results of the 2012 Hawaiʻi State Assessment were released, and Hālau Kū Māna was one of only two high schools on Oʻahu to be "in good standing, unconditional" under the stipulations of NCLB.)

I took a breath, exhaling before turning back to my computer and continuing to write. The sense of shared jubilation provoked a sudden flashback to the moment Keola and I celebrated the granting of HKM's charter as we stood in front of the state's board of education ten years earlier. The memory tempered my initial joy about the test results. "So according to the settler state's definitions, our students and school are *adequate*," I thought.

I opened the transcripts from my interview with math and science teacher Trevor Atkins, whom I had spoken with a few months earlier. He had told me about the tensions he and other math teachers felt between trying to implement project-based math curriculum (such as the curriculum he had designed on sustainable kalo production) and trying to "respond to the pressure from the state and federal governments" to meet AYP targets and the state's "very textbook math standards."

"It's a microcosm of the bigger picture," he stated flatly.

I asked him what he meant by "the bigger picture," and he lamented what felt like an increasing pressure to standardize, which seemed the very antithesis of Indigenous forms of place-based knowledge, teaching, and learning.

> I like to meet any challenge, even if its from an enemy . . . but it's not just the math program that's being standardized. It's a matter of centralizing and controlling education. It's the exact *opposite* of the Hawaiian charter school movement, the exact opposite of why we [Hālau Kū Māna] were created and why we go on Projects: to create a different story of education, a different pedagogy, a different curriculum. So math is simply just an anecdote.
>
> We jump over that bar, and we'll be looking at the next bar. And even if we meet all the bars they already have, there will be new bars, because it's not about the bars themselves. It's about the *control*, and this is just the mechanism of control, the vehicle of control right now—the HSA scores—but there's always a vehicle of control. So I think I've begun to assume the standpoint of many of the longtime teachers here: there's always gonna be resistance, and you should know that it is there, but you shouldn't drop everything and worry about beating one particular challenge, because it's just going to be challenge after challenge. You can't beat the state or federal government just by passing a test when they're actively colonizing or occupying a country.

His point closely mirrored Lomawaima and McCarty's analysis of a hundred years of Indian education in the United States; the strategies of maintaining safety zones have changed over time, but that impulse has never gone away. The tests, the instruments of measurement and control, change, but settler colonialism and its undergirding logics continue. As a non-Native teacher learning alongside his colleagues and students, Trevor also came to recognize that one of the most powerful ways to challenge the settler state and individual settler practices was to help make space for Indigenous-led communities to keep practicing and transforming ancestral knowledges on their own terms. As Papa Mau told Kumu Kahapeʻa about wayfinding and sailing traditions,

"You just keep doing it, keep doing it." Hawaiian-language and hula scholar and practitioner Kahikina De Silva put it this way:

> In many ways the indigenous person's most powerful weapon against further destruction and exploitation is simply *staying*. When the ultimate goal of colonization is to remove ʻōiwi from our land in order to access and suck dry the material and marketable resources our ancestors have maintained for generations, it follows that the stubborn, steadfast refusal to leave is essential to our continued existence as a lāhui.[1]

Trevor's insights also reflected the manaʻo that I have come to after a decade of working alongside Kanaka and settler aloha ʻāina teachers like him: the historically rooted educational inequalities (often called achievement gaps) that persist in Hawaiʻi and among most Indigenous nations will never be fully remedied without addressing the question of sovereignty and without ending colonial and imperial social relations. To see these inequalities through the lens of a racialized achievement gap that just needs more money or test prep to close is to reinvest in settler-colonial discourses. As Chickasaw scholar and critical Indigenous theorist Jodi Byrd has argued:

> The generally accepted theories of racialization in the United States have, in the pursuit of equal rights and enfranchisements, tended to be sited along the axis of inclusion/exclusion as the affective critique of the larger project of liberal multiculturalism. When the remediation of the colonization of American Indians is framed through discourses of racialization that can be redressed by further inclusion into the nation-state, there is significant failure to grapple with the fact that such discourses further reinscribe the original colonial injury.[2]

However well-meaning, discourses of educational equality aimed at narrowing achievement gaps—such as those that have animated multiple sides of debates about NCLB within the United States—perpetuate settler-colonial relations and do little to address the roots of the problem. For Kānaka Maoli, we have channeled a tremendous amount of time and energy into education reform as a major avenue for enacting change for our lāhui, our nation, and our people throughout my lifetime. Since the 1970s and 1980s, notable gains have been made in developing Hawaiian language and culture–based education within a settler state's public school system: Hawaiian studies programs in publicly funded K–12, tertiary, and enrichment education, Hawaiian-language immersion schools, and, within the past decade, Hawaiian-focused public charter schools. These kīpuka have nurtured kumu and haumāna who continue to do valuable work in various aspects of society. Yet our collective work, thus far, has not resulted in ending the deep inequalities of power, wealth, and well-being. Studies completed in the early 1980s, such as the Native Hawaiian Educational Assessment project and the Native Hawaiians Study Commission report, showed that Kānaka Maoli had the highest rates of family poverty, incarceration, academic underachievement (including drop-out and absentee rates), and various negative health indicators, including behavioral health such as suicide and depression.[3] For our people as a whole, data in the first decade of the twenty-first century show that these statistics remain largely unchanged thirty years later.[4]

These conditions force those of us who work within settler state educational systems to confront whether our attempts to carve space within those systems go far enough to create the kind of transformation necessary for the health and well-being of our lands and peoples. I have come to believe that cultural and language-based education will never be enough without autonomous control of land and the rebuilding of Indigenous systems that have allowed our peoples to thrive on those lands over centuries. Funding for Indigenous education without land and sovereignty will never fully alleviate the problems and the ongoing harms our youth endure.

My research and work with HKM over the years has also taught me that ʻŌiwi Hawaiʻi practices of sovereignty or, more appropriately, of ea and aloha ʻāina both include and exceed statist forms of sovereignty. To call the pedagogies I have described in this book "sovereign" is in some ways to acknowledge that they are constrained within the language and institutions, the discursive structures, of a state-based frame. Yet by grounding pedagogies in the theories and practices of aloha ʻāina, kuleana, and hoʻomana, Kanaka and settler educators are expressing forms of contemporary Hawaiian independence and sovereignty that are not solely based on Western statist models. Even without external recognition of Hawaiian political sovereignty, communities are organizing to meet social needs in spite of the lack of a functioning state apparatus to represent us at the present time. The pedagogies of aloha ʻāina explored in this book are just a few examples of the ways Hawaiians are enacting ea in ways that recognize that sovereignty is not just a political status but a way of living in relation to land and others. Thus, I have argued that Indigenous sovereign pedagogies include collaborative educational approaches, political engagement with issues that directly impact the communities of learners and their extended families, and opportunities to develop deep familial relationships with lands as living and active presences in our lives. Sovereign pedagogies cultivate land-centered literacies that attend to the health of the environmental systems of which we are a part. They create the space and give Indigenous and settler participants the intellectual tools to reckon their genealogies and positionalities in relation to history, land, and the diverse peoples with which one lives.

In the coming generation or two, it will be even more crucial to look to our ancestral storehouses of knowledge for how to relate in familial and mutually beneficial ways with our lands, waters, and nonhuman relatives. As we look toward the likelihood of massive environmental and economic changes on our planet, largely precipitated by the rise and growth of industrial and postindustrial empires and societies, we will need all the resources of our pasts and innovative capacities of our peoples to help us shape those transitions in ways that can bring us into preferred, nonimperial futures.

This is why I like to imagine Indigenous education as the process of rebuilding and maintaining ʻauwai. Groups of people come together to collectively reconstruct and care for the Indigenous channels that balance the human need for a life-giving resource, water, with the surrounding environment's need for that same mana. These structures sometimes follow ancient courses but are usually modified based on the current landscape. The metaphoric and actual practice of rebuilding ʻauwai also underscores the interconnection of educational, economic, and ecological systems, reminding us that restoration of one goes hand in hand with restoration of the others.[5]

If settler states and their educational systems have drained and diverted resources from the systems that sustained Indigenous societies for centuries prior to colonization, how can the balanced flows of
such resources be restored again? This is a central question that can
continue to animate Indigenous education in the coming generations.
In my conversations over the past several years, mahiʻai kalo Danny
Bishop put it best, "Water is important. Let's get the water back. Why
do we need the water back? So we can be the people that we are. So we
can raise our children to understand who we are."[6]

Notes

Preface

1. I use a number of terms interchangeably to refer to the Indigenous people of Hawai'i, people who are genealogically connected to Ka Pae 'āina 'o Hawai'i (the Hawaiian archipelago) since time immemorial: Kānaka Maoli, Kānaka, 'Ōiwi, 'Ōiwi Hawai'i, Kānaka Hawai'i, Hawaiian, and Native Hawaiian. Preference is given to Native terms. In my usage of any of these terms, I mean all people of 'Ōiwi ancestry, not restricted by blood quantum.

2. Charlot, *Classical Hawaiian Education*, 42; Schütz, *The Voices of Eden*, 173–74; Wist, *A Century of Public Education in Hawaii*, 23; Benham and Heck, *Culture and Educational Policy in Hawai'i*, 72.

3. Wist, *A Century of Public Education in Hawaii*; Schütz, *The Voices of Eden*; Benham and Heck, *Culture and Educational Policy in Hawai'i*.

4. Chapin, *Shaping History*; Silva, *Aloha Betrayed*.

5. Kroeber, "Why It's a Good Thing Gerald Vizenor Is Not an Indian," 25.

6. Vizenor, *Survivance*, 1.

7. The first family-run, private Hawaiian-immersion preschools, or Pūnana Leo, opened in 1984 on Kaua'i, with two more opening the following year on O'ahu and Hawai'i islands. The first publicly funded Hawaiian-language immersion program, Ka Papahana Kaiāpuni Hawai'i, was approved on a pilot basis for Keaukaha Elementary School in Hilo, Hawai'i, and Waiau Elementary School in Pearl City, O'ahu, in 1987. The Hawai'i State Board of Education approved permanent status for Ka Papahana Kaiāpuni Hawai'i in 1990.

8. Okamura reported that in the early 2000s only 10 percent of public school teachers were Native Hawaiian, as compared with 26 percent of the students. Okamura, *Ethnicity and Inequality in Hawai'i*, 65–66.

9. Wist, *A Century of Public Education in Hawaii*; Kuykendall, *The Hawaiian Kingdom*; Daws, *Shoal of Time*.

10. See "Political Caricatures of the Hawaiian Kingdom, circa 1875–1905," University of Hawai'i Kapi'olani Community College Library & Learning Resources website, accessed August 2, 2010, http://library.kcc.hawaii.edu/ ~soma/cartoons. These examples of imperialist cartoons depict Hawaiians, Filipinos, Puerto Ricans, African Americans, and Indians often in the same classroom being taught by the adult figure of Uncle Sam. Additionally, Noenoe

Silva discusses racist cartoon representations of Queen Liliʻuokalani, particularly highlighting the way American cartoonists drew on belittling stereotypes of blackness in their raced and gendered representations of the Hawaiian head of state. See Silva, *Aloha Betrayed*, 173–80.

11. Justice, Rifkin, and Schneider, "Introduction to Special Issue on Sexuality, Nationality, Indigeneity," 16.

12. Takayama, "Academic Achievement across School Types in Hawaiʻi." Takayama reports that 65 percent of students attending Hawaiian language and culture–based (HLCB) schools receive free or reduced lunch, as compared with 51.8 percent in similar-sized conventional public schools and only 26.5 percent in Western-focused charter schools. The rate of enrollment of students with a special education designation at Western-focused charters (5 percent) is less than half that at HCLB schools (12 percent) and small-sized conventional public schools (11 percent).

13. I am referring, for example, to the content and performance standards such as the Hawaiʻi Content and Performance Standards, the U.S. national Common Core State Standards, which Hawaiʻi has adopted, and the definitions of Adequate Yearly Progress (AYP) as defined and measured by the state and federal governments.

14. This has subsequently changed. In June 2012, Hawaiʻi State Governor Neil Abercrombie signed into law Act 106, which repeals the existing state law on charter schools and is intended to overhaul charter school governance. The law establishes the Public Charter School Commission, whose members are appointed by the state board of education. The commission is charged with monitoring and reporting on all charter schools in Hawaiʻi. As of this writing, the commission remains the single authorizing body for any new charters, having replaced the Hawaiʻi State Charter School Review Panel, but the new law also allows postsecondary institutions, state and county agencies, and nonprofit organizations to apply to the state board of education for charter-authorizing authority. The majority of existing start-up schools in Hawaiʻi were granted charters under the original state law.

Introduction

1. The term ʻŌiwi Wale, distinct from the term *precontact*, which privileges the encounter with European foreigners as a primary reference point for Pacific histories, was coined by Kanalu Young. Young, *Rethinking the Native Hawaiian Past*. Noenoe Silva points out that the more proper Hawaiian-language usage would be *wale nō*, since *wale* alone has the negative connotations of doing something without regard or cause. Personal communication with

the author, 2010. I add this small modification to Young's term while maintaining his intent.

2. McGregor, *Nā Kuaʻāina*, 7–8.

3. Kauʻi Onekea, interview with the author, May 2011.

4. Vizenor, *Survivance*, 1.

5. Warrior, *Tribal Secrets*, 91.

6. Ibid., 124.

7. Clifford, "Indigenous Articulations," 474.

8. Alfred, *Peace, Power, Righteousness*; Alfred, *Wasáse*; Basham, "Ka Lāhui Hawaiʻi"; Corntassel, "Who Is Indigenous?"; Holm, Pearson, and Chavis, "Peoplehood"; Meyer, *Hoʻoulu*; Smith, *Decolonizing Methodologies*; Wilson and Bird, *For Indigenous Eyes Only*.

9. Huli are the stalks of the taro plant, which are used for replanting. *Huli* also means "to turn" and can suggest revolutionary change. "Huli" was a slogan used by Kanaka activists, such as Kōkua Hawaiʻi in the 1970s.

10. Because the Hawaiʻi state public school system functions as a single district, its size can be compared against other public school districts in the United States. As such, the Hawaiʻi State Department of Education is the tenth-largest district system in the United States.

11. Lomawaima and McCarty, *To Remain an Indian*, 6.

12. Kanaʻiaupuni and Ishibashi, *Left Behind?*; Kanaʻiaupuni, Malone, and Ishibashi, *Ka Huakaʻi*; Kanaʻiaupuni and Ishibashi, *Hawaiʻi Charter Schools*; Kanaʻiaupuni, Ledward, and Jensen, *Culture-Based Education and Its Relationship to Student Outcomes*; Takayama, "Academic Achievement across School Types in Hawaiʻi"; Tibbets, Kahakalau, and Johnson, "Education with Aloha and Student Assets."

13. Wells, *Where Charter School Policy Fails*; Dingerson et al., *Keeping the Promise?*; Lubienski and Weitzel, *The Charter School Experiment*.

14. Jung, *Reworking Race*.

15. The song "Seventh Generation" was written by HKM students as part of an elective music project bringing students together with experienced and professional musicians. It was first released on the school-produced fundraiser compact disc *Mana Maoli: The Seventh Generation*, as well as on an album by Kupaʻāina. Chock et al., "Seventh Generation"; Kupaʻāina, *Simple Island People*.

16. Corntassel, "Who Is Indigenous?"

17. Demmert, "What Is Culture-Based Education?"; Kanaʻiaupuni, *A Brief Overview of Culture-Based Education and Annotated Bibliography*.

18. The No Child Left Behind Act of 2001 passed through the U.S. Congress with bipartisan support just months after the 9/11 attacks, and it was

signed into law by President George W. Bush. A reauthorization of the Elementary and Secondary Education Act (ESEA) first adopted in 1965, NCLB has been seen as both an evolutionary development and a radical departure from previous federal education policy in that it set a single nationwide timetable for meeting federally established targets and a prescriptive set of punitive or remedial measures for underperforming schools.

19. I capitalize the word *project* when I am referring to one of the yearlong place-based and project-based courses, which HKM faculty and staff refer to as Projects.

20. The Cherokee National Council set up a national school system comprised of eleven schools at roughly the same time as the Hawaiian national school system was being established. Similarly, the Choctaws set up a system of tribal schools in 1842. See Reyhner and Eder, *American Indian Education*, 55–56. These Indian and Hawaiian national educational initiatives contrast the passage of school laws by the U.S. Congress that imposed schooling on Indian nations. See Lomawaima and McCarty, *To Remain an Indian*; Lomawaima, "American Indian Education." Lomawaima, *They Called It Prairie Light*, 2–3.

21. Benham and Heck, *Culture and Educational Policy in Hawai'i*; Pickens and Kemble, *To Teach the Children*; Wist, *A Century of Public Education in Hawaii, October 15, 1840-October 15, 1940*.

22. The noun *hoa* can be modified by various verbs to further specify the relationship. For example, *hoa hānau* (peers in birth) refers to cousins.

23. Hawaiian-language scholar Kalani Makekau-Whittaker is currently conducting some of this work. When published, his research will be of great value in shedding more light on the politics of education in nineteenth-century Hawai'i.

24. Schütz, *The Voices of Eden*, 101.

25. Schools were not the first educational institutions in the islands. Native educational institutions based on apprenticeship, mastery, and community predated and survived the advent of Western-styled schooling in Hawai'i. The ways those institutional and personal relationships transformed and were transformed by schooling is beyond the scope of this chapter.

26. Wist, *A Century of Public Education in Hawaii*, 22.

27. Additionally, some missionaries did not stay, so all fifty-two would not have been in the islands at the same time. Hawaiian Mission Children's Society, *Missionary Album*.

28. Kuykendall writes, "As soon as a bright pupil (and there were many such) had acquired a little facility in reading, he was sent out, or went out on his own initiative, to teach a school of his own." Kuykendall, *Hawaiian Kingdom, 1854–1874*, 106.

29. Wist, *A Century of Public Education in Hawaii*, 27.

30. Within the next two decades, the corpus of Hawaiian schoolbooks and literature amounted to over 80,000,000 pages, as reported by the president of the board of education, Richard Armstrong, in 1852. Hawaiian Kingdom, *Report of the Minister of Public Instruction*, 37. Chapin and Silva have documented the centrality of newspapers in struggles for political and cultural power in the islands. Silva argues that newspapers in fact became *the* primary battleground for competing political discourses and interests. See Chapin, *Shaping History*; Silva, *Aloha Betrayed*, 54.

31. Pukui, ʻŌlelo Noʻeau.

32. Benham and Heck, *Culture and Educational Policy in Hawaiʻi*, 69.

33. There are conflicting interpretations of the intent and impact of the Chiefs' Children's School. Linda Menton's study emphasizes the violent, colonizing, and Americanizing aspects of the school. See Menton, "Christian and 'Civilized' Education." Kamana Beamer argues, however, that the intent of the school "was not to *Americanize* these keiki, it was to *Internationalize* them," preparing them as leaders for an increasingly internationally connected Hawaiʻi. Beamer, "Na Wai ka Mana?," 208. Keahiolalo-Karasuda connects the education of aliʻi at the Chiefs' Children's School with technologies of prosecuting and imprisoning Hawaiians in ways that have eroded political sovereignty. She argues that the school "largely resembled methods of disciplinary control and punishment often found in detentionlike settings." Keahiolalo-Karasuda, "A Genealogy of Punishment in Hawaiʻi," 154.

34. Beginning in 1846, the kingdom's government published laws in both Hawaiian and English, rather than in Hawaiian alone. When disputes arose and there were differences in the interpretation of the two versions, early courts recognized the Hawaiian-language version as the prevailing and controlling law. Lucas argues that the shift in 1859 toward using the English version as the authoritative one signaled the rise of a growing "English-mainly" movement, led by certain missionaries and their descendants. Lucas, "E Ola Mau Kākou i ka ʻŌlelo Makuahine," 3–4.

35. Benham and Heck, *Culture and Educational Policy in Hawaiʻi*; Wist, *A Century of Public Education in Hawaii*.

36. John Papa Iʻi also served as a teacher, trustee, and adviser of the Chiefs' Children's School, also called the Royal School. Allen notes that he was a teacher of the young Liliʻu, future queen of the Hawaiian Kingdom, and that he instructed the young chiefs in reading, writing, English grammar, arithmetic, and spelling. See Allen, *The Betrayal of Liliuokalani*.

37. Kuykendall, *The Hawaiian Kingdom, 1778—1854*, 347–48.

38. Arista, "Davida Malo." Numerous letters written by Davida Malo to

the kingdom's head of public education after Malo's tenure as luna, expressing his support for Native teachers and their adequate compensation, can be found in the records and correspondences of the Department of Education at the Hawai'i State Archives.

39. By that time, the governance of public instruction had been restructured so that the presidency of the board of education was the highest post in the kingdom. Starting in 1865, the president was also assisted by an inspector general.

40. It was under Armstrong's administration that the first government appropriation was made to support public education, in the amount of $22,000. Benham and Heck, *Culture and Educational Policy in Hawai'i*, 91.

41. Hawaiian Kingdom, *Biennial Report of the President of the Board of Education to the Hawaiian Legislature of 1866*, 2.

42. Kekūanāoʻa further expressed concern with the fact that the poll tax was not providing adequate funding for the common schools and called for increased funding of the schools serving the common people.

43. Lucas, "E Ola Mau Kākou i ka ʻŌlelo Makuahine."

44. Hawaiian Kingdom, *Biennial Report of the President of the Board of Education to the Hawaiian Legislature of 1864*. Also quoted in Kuykendall, *The Hawaiian Kingdom, 1874–1893*, 112.

45. In September 1876, Samuel Alexander secured rights to collect water from the slopes of Haleakalā to the east of Haiku Plantation. Alexander and Henry Baldwin, both of missionary families, organized and owned the Hamakua Ditch Company, now known as the East Maui Irrigation Company. In the 1870s, Samuel Alexander and Henry Baldwin began purchasing hundreds of acres for sugar. Their company, Alexander & Baldwin, is now a multinational transportation, real estate, and agribusiness corporation headquartered in Hawaiʻi.

46. In 1876 government funding for the select schools, some of which were also privately supported, amounted to $38,000 for 2,678 pupils, whereas funding for the common schools was only $13,000 for 4,313 pupils. The appropriations stayed about the same for the next biennium, and by 1883, just before Bishop's forced resignation, the difference in appropriation was $75,000 for the select schools and $10,000 for the common schools. See Hawaiian Kingdom, *Biennial Report of the President of the Board of Education to the Legislature of 1878*; Hawaiian Kingdom, *Biennial Report of the President of the Board of Education to the Legislature of 1884*.

47. From Hawaiian Kingdom, *Biennial Report of the President of the Board of Education to the Legislature of 1874*, 18. This passage is also quoted in Kanahele, *Pauahi*, 155.

48. Hawaiian Kingdom, *Biennial Report of the President of the Board of Education to the Legislature of 1878.*

49. As foreign minister under King Lunalilo (1873–74), Bishop was also one of the leading proponents of a reciprocity treaty that would cede Pearl Harbor to the United States for use as a naval port in exchange for duty-free trade of Hawaiian sugar into the United States. As minister of foreign affairs, he officially proposed that the Hawaiian Kingdom cede Pearl River—the place Kānaka ʻŌiwi named Puʻuloa—to the United States as an enticement to approving the treaty. The treaty was eventually negotiated under Kalākaua's reign granting exclusive use, rather than cession, of Pearl River to the U.S. Navy. The treaty triggered a boom in the sugar industry. It was during this rapid period of growth in the industry that Bishop became most adamant, and powerful, in pushing for manual education. It was also during this time that he worked with the private Hawaiian Immigration Society and as a member of the kingdom's board of immigration to secure foreign laborers for the growing plantation industry. As the kingdom's preeminent banker and a personal investor, he financially supported and profited from the growth of the sugar industry. For example, in 1876 he and four other investors incorporated to form the Hawaiian Agricultural Company, a plantation on Bishop's land in Kaʻū. By 1894 he had sold all of his stock in this company to C. M. Cooke, fellow trustee of Bernice Pauahi Bishop's estate, for a total of $166,455. Bishop also became the largest stockholder in C. Brewer and Co. in 1883 and served as a director of the board through 1892. For detailed information on Charles R. Bishop's ventures in the sugar industry, see Kent, *Charles Reed Bishop.*

50. Benham and Heck, *Culture and Educational Policy in Hawaiʻi*, 93.

51. Osorio, *Dismembering Lāhui.*

52. Schütz reports that the number of Hawaiian language–medium schools took a dramatic decline, from 150 schools in 1880 to zero in 1902, whereas English-medium schools increased from 60 to 203 in the same period. See Schütz, *The Voices of Eden*, 352. This was a direct result of the takeover by white businessmen backed by the U.S. government. The suppression of education in the Indigenous Hawaiian language and culture stifled the collective ʻŌiwi ability to define for ourselves what it meant to be a lāhui—a nation or a people—particularly as the sugar oligarchy and the U.S. federal government contested our ability to do so.

53. Wilson and Kamanā, "'For the Interest of the Hawaiians Themselves'"; Kawaiʻaeʻa, Housman, and Alencastre, "Pūʻā i ka ʻŌlelo, Ola ka ʻOhana."

54. Silva, *Aloha Betrayed*; Blaisdell, "Kanaka Maoli Self-Determination"; Kajihiro, "The Militarizing of Hawaiʻi"; Sai, "American Occupation of the Hawaiian State."

55. Trask, *From a Native Daughter*, 25.

56. Both Fujikane and Okamura include statistics demonstrating settler dominance in the public education system in Hawai'i, wherein Japanese residents comprise the largest percentage of teachers and administrators in the system. Fujikane writes, "If white settlers continue to dominate in economic and political institutions and in educational apparatuses like the University of Hawai'i, the figures here provide an overview of the degree to which Japanese and Chinese settlers have also come to command real power economically and politically. These last figures for the DOE provide some of the most visible illustrations of the complex interconnection between the materiality of state politics and the ideological production of knowledge." Fujikane, "Introduction," 25; Okamura, *Ethnicity and Inequality in Hawai'i*.

57. Trask, *From a Native Daughter*, 25; Wolfe, *Settler Colonialism and the Transformation of Anthropology*; Wolfe, "Settler Colonialism and the Elimination of the Native"; Smith, *Conquest*; Smith, "Queer Theory and Native Studies"; Kauanui, "Colonialism in Equality"; Fujikane and Okamura, *Asian Settler Colonialism*; Barker, "The Contemporary Reality of Canadian Imperialism"; Goldstein, "Where the Nation Takes Place"; Driskill et al., *Queer Indigenous Studies*.

58. Goldstein, "Where the Nation Takes Place," 835.

59. Recent scholarship on Hawaiian law and politics has proposed throwing out an analysis of colonialism, arguing that according to international law, the particular circumstances of the American takeover of Hawai'i are that of a prolonged military occupation rather than of colonization. This strand of Hawaiian scholarship asserts that Hawai'i is not a U.S. colony but an occupied state under international law. Its advocates emphasize the relevance of this distinction by asserting the continuity of the independent Hawaiian State and the agency of Hawaiian Kingdom leaders. See Sai, "American Occupation of the Hawaiian State"; Sai, "A Slippery Path Towards Hawaiian Indigeneity"; Beamer, "Na Wai ka Mana?" I believe this important legal clarification does not require dispensing with an analysis of colonialism, which is more than just a legal status but a set of discourses and social relations. In other words, I do not think critiques of prolonged U.S. military occupation and of settler colonialism in Hawai'i need to be mutually exclusive. I draw on Taiaiake Alfred's understanding of colonialism, which includes "the fundamental denial of our freedom to be Indigenous in a meaningful way, and the unjust occupation of the physical, social and political spaces we need in order to survive as Indigenous peoples." Alfred, "Warrior Scholarship," 89. Grande's definition of colonization is also useful in seeing it as a cultural/political/economic set of forces. She describes colonization as a historically produced

"multidimensional force underwritten by Western Christianity, defined by white supremacy, and fueled by global capitalism." Grande, *Red Pedagogy*, 19.

60. Kahakalau, "Kanu o ka'āina."

61. According to the 2000 U.S. Census, Native Hawaiians made up about 20 percent of the state's total population. The U.S. Census and the Hawai'i State Department of Education report different percentages of Native Hawaiian enrollment in the public schools that year, 32 percent and 25 percent, respectively. In either case, both figures are significantly higher than the proportion of Hawai'i's total population. Between 1980 and 2000, the number of Hawaiian students increased by 44 percent, whereas the number of Japanese and Caucasian students declined by more than 30 percent each. Ishibashi, *Hawaiian Population Update*, 21–24. As of the 2007–8 school year, Native Hawaiian students comprised 27.6 percent of total public school enrollment, representing a continuing, gradual upward trend. Kamehameha Schools, *Native Hawaiian Educational Assessment Update 2009*, 7.

62. From the 1996–97 to the 2007–8 school year, the percentage of Native Hawaiian students with a special education designation has exceeded the percentage among non-Hawaiian students by 4.8 to 7.6 percent, demonstrating a "significant and persistent over-representation of Native Hawaiians among students identified as needing special educational services." Kamehameha Schools, *Native Hawaiian Educational Assessment Update 2009*, 8.

63. "Restructuring" and "corrective action" are punitive action statuses that result from a school not meeting Adequate Yearly Progress standards as set by the U.S. federal government. In determining AYP for Hawai'i public schools, the instrument used to measure student achievement is called the Hawai'i State Assessment. Kana'iaupuni and Ishibashi, *Left Behind?*

64. The survey is part of the larger national U.S. Youth Risk Behavior Surveillance System, administered and funded by the Centers for Disease Control and Prevention. Lai and Saka, *Hawaiian Students Compared with Non-Hawaiian Students*; Kamehameha Schools, *Native Hawaiian Educational Assessment Update 2009*, 36.

65. Lai and Saka, *Hawaiian Students Compared with Non-Hawaiian Students*.

66. Smith, *Conquest*; Coulthard, "Subjects of Empire"; Wolfe, "Settler Colonialism and the Elimination of the Native."

67. Wolfe, "Settler Colonialism and the Elimination of the Native," 388.

68. Fujikane, "Introduction," 8.

69. Rafael, "White Love"; Rodriguez, *Suspended Apocalypse*; Byrd, *The Transit of Empire*; Aikau, *A Chosen People, a Promised Land*.

70. Smith, "Heteropatriarchy and the Three Pillars of White Supremacy," 67.

71. Leonardo, *Race, Whiteness, and Education*, 77.

72. Kahakalau, "Kanu o ka ʻāina," 51.

73. Ibid., 54.

74. Okamura, *Ethnicity and Inequality in Hawaiʻi*.

75. Driskill et al., *Queer Indigenous Studies*, 19.

76. Finley, "Decolonizing the Queer Native Body," 34.

77. Beyer, "Female Seminaries in America and Hawaii"; Beyer, "The Connection of Samuel Chapman Armstrong."

78. Finley, "Decolonizing the Queer Native Body," 34.

79. Grande, *Red Pedagogy*, 19.

80. Barnhardt and Kawagley, "Indigenous Knowledge Systems"; Kawagley and Barnhardt, *Education Indigenous to Place*; Harrison and Papa, "The Development of an Indigenous Knowledge Program"; Kahakalau, "Kanu o ka ʻāina"; Grande, *Red Pedagogy*; Smith, "Kaupapa Maori Theory"; Smith, *Decolonizing Methodologies*; Warner, "Kuleana"; Wong and Maaka, "Foreword for Ke Ala Hou"; Kaomea, "Indigenous Studies in the Elementary Curriculum"; Kaomea, "Reading Erasures and Making the Familiar Strange"; Gegeo and Watson-Gegeo, "How We Know"; Gegeo and Watson-Gegeo, "Whose Knowledge?"; Meyer, *Hoʻoulu*; Cajete, *Look to the Mountain*; Deloria and Wildcat, *Power and Place*; Villegas, Neugebauer, and Venegas, *Indigenous Knowledge and Education*.

81. Smith, "Building a Research Agenda," 94.

82. Coulthard, "Subjects of Empire," 456.

83. Corntassel, "Toward Sustainable Self-Determination."

84. Ibid., 118.

85. Coulthard, "Subjects of Empire," 456.

86. Maaka and Fleras, "Indigeneity at the Edge."

87. Fujikane, "Introduction," 8.

88. Horton and Freire, *We Make the Road by Walking*.

89. Both Kanaka Maoli historian Jonathan Kamakawiwoʻole Osorio and Cherokee author Thomas King remind us that in the face of powerful discourses that seek to fix Native identity, Native studies at its best holds the tension between proclaiming who we are and genuinely embracing the question, who are we? Osorio, " 'What Kine Hawaiian Are You?' "; King, *The Truth about Stories*.

90. Pukui and Elbert, *Hawaiian Dictionary*, 21.

91. Pukui, Elbert, and Mookini, *Place Names of Hawaii*, 268–69.

92. Silva, *Aloha Betrayed*, 11.

93. Kameʻeleihiwa, *Native Land and Foreign Desires*.

94. Naone, " 'O ka ʻāina, ka ʻŌlelo, and me ke Kaiāulu"; Oliveira, "Wahi a Kahiko"; Goodyear-Kaʻōpua et al., "Teaching amid U.S. Occupation."

95. McClintock, "'No Longer in a Future Heaven,'" 110.

96. See the articles collected in Smith and Kauanui, "Native Feminisms Engage American Studies."

97. Hall, "Strategies of Erasure," 278.

98. Handy and Pukui, *The Polynesian Family System in Kaʻū, Hawaiʻi*, 43.

99. Kameʻeleihiwa, *Nā Wāhine Kapu*; Hoʻomanawanui, "Pele's Appeal."

100. Hoʻomanawanui has similarly argued for an inclusion of ʻŌiwi knowledge practices in reframing literacy, referring to indigenous Hawaiian knowledge of the land as ʻIke ʻāina. Hoʻomanawanui, "ʻIke ʻāina."

101. Papakū Makawalu, a project of the Edith Kanakaʻole Foundation, conducts research, curriculum development, and teacher-training workshops that underscore this point. Their presentation that I was fortunate to see on July 31, 2010, in Kaʻū, Hawaiʻi, reminded me of this important point about the multiplicity of languages that our world speaks.

102. Meyer, "Our Own liberation"; Meyer, *Hoʻoulu*; Gegeo and Watson-Gegeo, "How We Know."

103. International Reading Association, "New Literacies and 21st-Century Technologies"; Coiro et al., *Handbook of Research on New Literacies*.

104. Australian literacy scholarship and practice seems to be ahead of U.S.-based literacy education in terms of articulating an Indigenous literacy that includes practices of reading the land. In her description of indigenous literacy as it emerged from the Building Bridges project of the Australian Early Childhood Association, Williams-Kennedy includes "speaking, listening, reading natural and man-made symbols, recording language in lore, stories, songs, dance, rituals and traditions and observing body and sign language, combined with intuitive and critical thinking. Religious and spiritual beliefs, values, customs and traditions are embedded within all of these elements." Williams-Kennedy, "Building Bridges between Literacies," 89–90. Also see the Indigenous Literacy Project at http://www.indigenousliteracyproject.org.au. There is, however, a long way to go before such broader understandings of literacies pierce mainstream literacy education in the United States, Australia, and other settler states. Thus, it is imperative for us to stake a claim within the field of literacy for these land-centered relational practices.

105. Street, *Literacy in Theory and Practice*. Luke, Iyer, and Doherty identify three contemporary paradigms that have framed literacy research, policy, and practice. The *development paradigm* focuses on "the spread of basic literacy and its economic and social effects." The *hegemony paradigm* focuses on "the ideological and cultural effects of 'official' versions of literacy formalized by schools, media and the state." It is this wing of the literacy research that has gone the farthest to elaborate literacy instruction as a social practice that

serves particular interests and relations of power. Finally, the *new literacies paradigm* focuses on "emergent cultures, identities and practices of multimodal and digital literacies." They recognize that print and digital literacies produce distinct pedagogical issues, and yet their relations to continued global inequalities of wealth and power are connected. They write, "New literacies and persistent lack of access to basic print literacy sit in close social, geographical and cultural proximity." Luke, Iyer, and Doherty, "Literacy Education in the Context of Globalisation," 2.

106. Luke, *The Social Construction of Literacy in the Primary School*, 6.

107. hooks, *Teaching to Transgress*; Freire, *Pedagogy of the Oppressed*.

108. Grande, *Red Pedagogy*, 5–6.

109. Kahn, *Critical Pedagogy, Ecoliteracy, and Planetary Crisis*, 18.

110. Basham, "I Mau ke Ea o ka'āina i ka Pono"; "Ka Lāhui Hawai'i"; "Mele Lāhui"; Silva, *Aloha Betrayed*; Trask, *From a Native Daughter*.

111. Silva, *Aloha Betrayed*, 11.

112. This mele was taught to me by Kumu Hula Leilani Basham in the context of her hālau hula. For the text, see Spencer, *Kaua Kuloko 1895*.

113. Silva, *Aloha Betrayed*, 11.

114. Ritte and Sawyer, *Na Mana'o Aloha o Kaho'olawe*; Trask, *From a Native Daughter*; McGregor, *Nā Kua'āina*; Kajihiro, "The Militarizing of Hawai'i."

115. Morales, "George Helm."

116. McGregor, *Nā Kua'āina*.

117. Morales, *Ho'iho'i Hou*, 73.

118. Ibid., 72.

119. Hale, *Engaging Contradictions*, 20.

120. Smith, *Decolonizing Methodologies*.

121. Speed, "Forged in Dialogue"; Slack, "The Theory and Method."

122. Colectivo Situaciones, "On the Researcher-Militant," 193.

123. Lawrence-Lightfoot and Davis, *The Art and Science of Portraiture*.

124. Lawrence-Lightfoot, *The Good High School*.

125. Hau'ofa, "Our Sea of Islands"; Kana'iaupuni, "Ka'akālai Kū Kanaka"; Yosso, "Whose Culture Has Capital?"

126. Lawrence, "The Word and the River"; Solorzano and Yosso, "Critical Race Methodology."

127. Chapman argues that portraiture and critical race theory (CRT) storytelling methods are compatible. "In portraiture, a researcher investigates and presents the multiple contexts and interactions that surround participants. In CRT, these contexts take into account political events, personal histories, societal norms, and laws and policies that affect the primary setting. Using portraiture and CRT, a researcher connects participants' experiential knowledge

as racialized subjects to the multiple ways in which people of color understand and navigate their communities, schools, and professional lives." Chapman, "Interrogating Classroom Relationships and Events" 137.

128. Yosso, "Whose Culture Has Capital?"

1. The Emergence of Indigenous Hawaiian Charter Schools

1. Cooper and Daws, *Land and Power in Hawaii*; Trask, *From a Native Daughter*; Fujikane and Okamura, *Asian Settler Colonialism*.

2. Okamura, *Ethnicity and Inequality in Hawai'i*.

3. Saranillio, "Seeing Conquest," 3.

4. Ibid., 5.

5. Sai, "American Occupation of the Hawaiian State"; Martínez, *Study on Treaties, Agreements and Other Constructive Arrangements*; Saranillio, "Seeing Conquest"; Fujikane and Okamura, *Asian Settler Colonialism*; Trask, *From a Native Daughter*; Kauanui, "Precarious Positions"; Vogeler, "'For Your Freedom and Ours.'"

6. Wolfe argues that control over knowledge and ideology is particularly central for Native resistance against settler colonialism. According to his analytic framework, dependent colonial economies rely upon Native labor, and thus the Native people can withdraw their labor as a form of resistance. Since settler-colonial economies are not primarily dependent upon Native labor but rather upon Native lands, he argues that Native resistance is waged primarily at the level of ideology, against the colonial project of eliminating the Native people's collective connection to land. "Where survival is a matter of not being assimilated, positionality is not just central to the issue—it *is* the issue." Wolfe, *Settler Colonialism and the Transformation of Anthropology*, 3.

7. The team conducted extensive quantitative and qualitative research on the educational and endowment aspects of the institution, and their final report included four volumes in sixteen chapters with a long-range plan for Kamehameha's future. See Booz, Allen and Hamilton, *The Kamehameha Schools Planning Survey*.

8. Ibid., 10.

9. Ibid., 12.

10. McGregor, *Nā Kua'āina*, 249.

11. Trask, "The Birth of the Modern Hawaiian Movement."

12. Ibid., 128.

13. Niheu is a graduate of the Kamehameha Schools. Kīhei Niheu, interviewed by the author, November 2009. Also see Trask, "The Birth of the Modern Hawaiian Movement," 139.

14. Trask, "The Birth of the Modern Hawaiian Movement," 151.

15. Pete Thompson, interviewed by Bernadette Gigi Miranda, 2009. Chinatown, Ota Camp, Waiāhole, Niumalu-Nāwiliwili, and Sand Island were just a few of the antieviction struggles Thompson listed as following in the wake of Kalama Valley. Pete Thompson is a graduate of the Kamehameha Schools.

16. Nakata, "The Struggles of the Waiahole-Waikane Community Association."

17. Sproat and Moriwake, "Ke Kalo Pa'a o Waiāhole," 252.

18. McGregor, Nā Kua'āina, 265.

19. Ibid., 272.

20. In HKM's early years, school leaders looked to Kumu John Keola Lake to help design daily protocols and teach appropriate chants. Kumu Lake was also one of the first board members of Hālau Kū Māna, and he presided over the school's opening ceremonies in 2001. Many years earlier, Kumu Lake had also been a teacher of PKO leader George Helm.

21. See the documentary film *Papa Mau: The Wayfinder* by filmmaker Nā'ālehu Anthony, released in 2010.

22. The Polynesian Voyaging Society's mission reads: "With a legacy of ocean exploration as its foundation, the Polynesian Voyaging Society is committed to undertake voyages of discovery (Holokai); to respect, learn from, and perpetuate through practice our heritage and culture ('Ike); and to promote learning which integrates voyaging experiences and values into quality education (Ho'ona'auao). We are committed to nurturing communities and the leadership therein that values learning and sharing knowledge in order to foster living well on islands." "Hawaiian Voyaging Traditions," Polynesian Voyaging Society website, accessed August 20, 2012, http://pvs.kcc.hawaii .edu/about_pvs.html.

23. Mower, *The Vision of Mo'ikeha*; *The Voyage to Tahiti*; Kapepa, *A Canoe for Uncle Kila*; Lindo, *A Resource Curriculum Guide on Polynesian Voyaging*; Lindo and Mower, *Polynesian Seafaring Heritage*; Menton and Stender, "Hōkūle'a Educational Resource Guide."

24. For example, the Hōkūle'a Education Program, based at the East-West Center and coordinated by the center's Asia Pacific Leadership Program, has allowed students from almost one hundred schools throughout the region to track the canoe and communicate with crew members via internet and satellite telephone hookups. Students become virtual crew members. See "Hokule'a Takes International Students under Her Sails," East-West Center website, http://www.eastwestcenter.org/news-center/east-west-wire/ hokulea-takes-international-students-under-her-sails.

25. Both of these schools are at the intersection of the immersion and charter movements. Of the twenty-two Hawaiian immersion schools or programs within schools in Hawai'i, two are stand-alone schools operating within the mainstream Department of Education system, fifteen are schools within larger mainstream department schools, and five are semiautonomous charter schools that use the immersion pedagogical approach. See Takayama, "Academic Achievement across School Types in Hawai'i," 255.

26. Kahakalau, "Kanu o ka 'āina."

27. Kauanui provides a detailed historical analysis of this fractionalizing 50 percent blood rule and the 1921 Hawaiian Homes Commission Act. Through a detailed analysis of the congressional hearings at which various versions of this measure were debated, she argues that the colonial project of racializing Hawaiians in the name of "rehabilitation" marginalized Kanaka Maoli entitlements to land and sovereignty. Kauanui, *Hawaiian Blood*.

28. It is important to note that the Hawaiian national lands, commonly and misleadingly referred to as the Ceded Lands, are designated by section 5(f) of the 1959 Hawai'i Admissions Act for five purposes. One of these purposes is public education.

29. Trask, *From a Native Daughter*.

30. Ku'ulei Maunupau, interviewed by the author, June 3, 2003.

31. Na Maka o ka 'āina, *Hui Na'auao*; Nā Maka o ka 'āina, *The Tribunal*; Nā Maka o ka 'Āina, *Act of War*; Osorio, *Dismembering Lāhui*; Trask, *From a Native Daughter*; Kame'eleihiwa, *Native Land and Foreign Desires*; Silva, *Aloha Betrayed*; Young, *Rethinking the Native Hawaiian Past*; Dudley and Agard, *A Call for Hawaiian Sovereignty*; American Friends Service Committee, *He Alo ā He Alo*.

32. Forman, "The Secret History of School Choice."

33. In their study of policy makers' motivations for supporting charter schools as an educational reform initiative, Wells and colleagues found that "the charter school concept has been embraced by a broad range of policy makers who would otherwise agree on very little, particularly in the area of educational reform. In several states, charter school legislation has broken through legislative impasses between reformers who seek to reconstitute the public education system through tuition voucher policies and those who strongly resist vouchers. In states where bitter and unsuccessful battles for voucher initiatives have been waged in the statehouse or ballot boxes, charter school legislation has emerged as a middle-of-the-road policy, creating more autonomous 'public' schools of choice that are purported to be free from state regulations and district oversight but still held accountable for student achievement." Wells et al., "Underlying Policy Assumptions of Charter School Reform," 514.

34. Wells et al., "Underlying Policy Assumptions of Charter School Reform," 515.

35. Budde, *Education by Charter*; Kolderie, *Ray Budde and the Origins of the "Charter Concept."*

36. Fine, *Chartering Urban School Reform*, 2.

37. Fuller, *Inside Charter Schools*; National Alliance for Public Charter Schools, "Public Charter School Dashboard."

38. The 2009 annual report on market share published by the National Alliance for Public Charter Schools notes that "the number of communities with at least a 20% market share has steadily climbed from six in 2005–06 to eight in 2006–07 to 12 in 2007–08 to 14 in 2008–09." Nicotera and Ziebarth, *Top 10 Charter Communities by Market Share*.

39. Buchanan and Fox, "To Learn and Belong," 2.

40. Koki, *School/Community-Based Management Revisited in the Pacific*; Erbes, "School/Community-Based Management."

41. Buchanan and Fox, "To Learn and Belong."

42. During the 2011–12 school year, 9,109 students attended thirty-one charter schools in Hawai'i, comprising 5 percent of all public school enrollment and a growth of over 900 students from the previous year. By comparison approximately 4.6 percent of Hawai'i public school students attended charters in 2010–11; 4.4 percent in 2009–10; and 4.1 percent in 2008–9. A pattern of modest but steady growth has persisted over the past few years. Over time the gains have been more marked. In 2004–5, the five-year point after initial charter legislation was passed in Hawai'i, charter schools comprised only 2.8 percent of all public school enrollment.

43. Nicotera and Ziebarth, *Top 10 Charter Communities by Market Share*.

44. Guy Kaulukukui, interviewed by the author, March 10, 2004.

45. Warner, "Kuleana"; Young, "Kuleana."

46. For example, he writes, "The persons who have a kuleana in Ka Lua o Pele are the direct descendants (pulapula pono'i) of Haumea, Kanehekili, Kaho'ali'i, Kanewawahilani, Kauilanuimakehaikalani, Nakoloilani, Kamohoali'i, Pele, Hi'iaka, and Namakaokaha'i. . . . Only through the blood lineage (koko i eweewe mai) of the ancestors does the *kuleana* come." Kamakau, *Ka Po'e Kahiko*, 66.

47. Andrade, *Hā'ena*; Lucas, *Dictionary of Hawaiian Legal Land-Terms*; Kame'eleihiwa, *Native Land and Foreign Desires*.

48. Blaich, "Mai Uka a i Kai," 64.

49. Ibid., 63–64.

50. Beniamina, "Tēnā," 16.

51. Ibid., 21.

52. Numerous Hawaiian educational scholars have strongly asserted that, considering legacies of colonialism, Kānaka Maoli should have the primary authority and leadership over educational projects of language and cultural revitalization. See Warner, "Kuleana"; Kaomea, "Contemplating Kuleana"; Meyer, *Ho'oulu*; Kahakalau, "Kanu o ka 'āina."

53. Shon, *A Charter School Story*, 123.

54. The thirteen Hawaiian schools that formed shortly following the passage of 1999 legislation include Kanu o ka 'āina, Ke Ana La'ahana, Kua o ka Lā, Ka 'Umeke Ka'eo, and Ke Kula 'o Nāwahīokalani'ōpu'u Iki Laboratory on the island of Hawai'i; Hālau Kū Māna, Hakipu'u Learning Center, Hālau Lōkahi, Ke Kula o Samuel M. Kamakau, and Ka Waihona o ka Na'auao on the island of O'ahu; and Kanuikapono Learning Center, Ke Kula Ni'ihau o Kekaha, and Kula Aupuni o Ni'ihau a Kahelelani Aloha on the island of Kaua'i. I say thirteen communities across four islands because of the role of the Ni'ihau community in forming two of the schools located on Kaua'i. Many of the 'ohana involved in these schools move back and forth between the two islands, even though the schools themselves are on Kaua'i.

55. Kahakalau, "Kanu o ka 'āina."

56. Ibid., 99.

57. Describing the urgency of this early period, Kahakalau writes, "Time was of the essence, since there were only 23 charter school slots available and competition from groups looking for alternatives in education was to be expected. In an effort to inform Hawaiian educators and communities about the tremendous potential of charter schools for Hawai'i's Native students, [I] organized a Liberatory Education Conference in June 1999, which inspired many current Hawaiian charter school operators to start up charter schools in their communities. In addition, [I] visited with numerous Hawaiian communities, community leaders and organizations on several islands to recruit them to become charter school developers. In the end, 13 of 23 applicants who received charter school start-up grants and were subsequently chartered have a Hawaiian focus." Kahakalau, "Kanu o ka 'āina," 18–19.

58. Kahakalau, "Kanu o ka 'āina," 29–30.

59. World Indigenous Peoples' Conference on Education, "The Coolangatta Statement on Indigenous Rights in Education."

60. *Rice v. Cayetano* (98–818) (146 F3d 1075, reversed). Kauanui points out that "Hawaiians were in a fraught position, with no direct voice in the case, even though it was central to Hawaiian concerns." See Kauanui, "Precarious Positions," 7.

61. Kauanui, "Precarious Positions," 7.

62. Charlotte "Coco" Needham, interviewed by the author, June 2, 2003.

63. HKM's initial start-up subgrant application cited various indicators, drawing on data available at that time in 1999: "Performance below national and statewide norms has been a persistent trend for Hawaiian students. For example, in 1991, on SAT scores in math, Hawaiian sixth graders scored in the 47th percentile compared with Filipinos in the 57 percentile, Caucasians 71st and Japanese 85th. DOE statistics show that across grades 3, 6, 8, and 10 the rank for Hawaiians averages the 30th percentile, while the statewide average is at the 40th percentile, and average rank among Caucasians and Japanese is at the 60th percentile. In reading achievement tests, fewer than 10 percent of Hawaiians scored in the 'above average' range.... In 1992, 18% of all Hawaiian secondary school students were considered excessively absent compared with 9% of non-Hawaiian students. In the 1997–99 school year, the DOE reported that one in four high school students of Hawaiian ancestry is absent, on average, one day each week. (Over the course of a 35-week school year, this would amount to missing *seven* weeks of school!)" As reported in the introduction, the picture has not significantly changed as of the second decade of the twenty-first century, as Hawaiian students continue to score lowest in standardized tests administered by the State Department of Education. In reading and math, Hawaiian students lagged behind total department scores by an average of eleven to seventeen percentiles (Kanaʻiaupuni and Ishibashi, *Left Behind?*; Kahakalau, "Kanu o ka ʻāina"). What had changed since then is that initial studies show that Hawaiian culture–based charter schools are doing a better job of helping the lowest scoring students move out of the well below grade-level category.

64. HKM's initial application for federal start-up grant funds drew on Hawaiʻi Legislative Reference Bureau statistics to show the specific conditions of urban Kanaka youth: "Indicative of the gravity of urban youths' disenchantment with mainstream public education is the fact that Honolulu has the highest drop-out rate of all districts on Oʻahu. All Honolulu district high schools, with the exception of Kalani, are experiencing an upward trend in drop-out rates. More importantly, it is the high schools in Hālau Kū Māna's targeted service area—McKinley, Roosevelt, Kaimukī and Farrington—that have the highest drop-out rates in the district."

65. These adjacent communities are neighbors to Maunalaha, but unlike Maunalaha, they are official homesteads administered under the Hawaiian Homes Commission. A Hawaiian community developed in Papakōlea, on the outskirts of downtown Honolulu, beginning in at least the late 1890s, but residents were constantly being threatened by corporate agriculture and the ruling white oligarchy.

66. Lee and Landau, *Papakōlea*.

67. Theone Kanuha was one of the leaders of the Kula initiative, and she also served as a member and as chair of HKM's local school board during the early years of the school's existence.

68. Nitta, "Native Hawaiians, Freedom and Education," 147.

69. In 1999, Kula leaders joined in forming an alliance called the Papakōlea Community Development Corporation (PCDC). The PCDC became successful in taking control of the Papakōlea Community Center, formerly administered by the City and County Department of Parks and Recreation. The center now serves as a full-service community center with a broad scope of culturally relevant services, including entrepreneurial opportunities, health and human services, and educational and recreational activities. This center has served as a site for Hālau Kū Māna meetings and classes from time to time.

70. The Spirit of the Earth: Sovereignty Symposium XII held in Tulsa, Oklahoma, June 7–9, 1999.

71. Keola Nakanishi, Personal interview, June 18, 2003.

72. Numerous people contributed to the early conversations that led to the founding of HKM. The initial subgrant application for federal start-up funds was written, however, by the following five primary authors: Keola Nakanishi, Noelani Goodyear-Ka'ōpua, Evan Beachy, Kalama Cabigon, and Coco Needham. The applicant group, named Mana Maoli, also included a steering committee comprised of those five authors, as well as the following individuals: Wanda Atkins, Mehana Blaich, Kyle Kajihiro, Malulani Orton, Mahina Paishon, Hoku Tibayan, and Kanalu Young. Two years later, after HKM received its charter, Mana Maoli formally transitioned to become a 501(c)(3) nonprofit organization supporting HKM.

73. The partnership between HKM and the Center for Hawaiian Studies was finalized under the center's then director Lilikalā Kame'eleihiwa.

74. Buchanan and Fox, "To Learn and Belong"; Buchanan and Fox, "Back to the Future"; Lubienski and Weitzel, *The Charter School Experiment*; Rofes and Stulberg, *The Emancipatory Promise of Charter Schools*.

2. Self-Determination within the Limits of No Child Left Behind

1. All names in this opening section are pseudonyms.

2. I use a pseudonym for the name of this school because it was not a primary subject of my research, so I did not secure permission to use its real name. I also realize that this portrait of it, sketched through the memories of a small group of its former students on a single day, provides only a limited and one-dimensional view of the school.

3. Hālau Kū Māna New Century Public Charter School, *Hālau Kū Māna, A New Century Public Charter School, Federal Sub-grant Application*, 2.

4. Kaomea, "A Curriculum of Aloha?"; Kaomea, "Reading Erasures and Making the Familiar Strange"; Warner, "Kuleana"; Kahakalau, "Kanu o ka ʻāina."

5. Kahakalau, "Kanu o ka ʻāina."

6. Bevir and Rhodes, *Interpreting British Governance*. I thank David Brier for introducing me to Bevir and Rhodes's work.

7. Nitta, "Native Hawaiians, Freedom and Education," 161.

8. Dehyle and Swisher, "Research in American Indian and Alaska Native Education"; Benham and Heck, *Culture and Educational Policy in Hawaiʻi*; Lipka, "Schooling for Self-Determination."

9. The Native Hawaiian Education Act is significant in that it was the first U.S. statute to specifically recognize in its findings that the Native Hawaiian people have "never relinquished its claims to sovereignty or our sovereign lands" (sec 7202, 12, A). The law further states that Native Hawaiians have "an ongoing right to self-determination and self-government that has never been extinguished" (sec 7202, 12, E, ii).

10. Beaulieu, "Native American Education Research and Policy Development"; Beaulieu, Sparks, and Alonzo, *Preliminary Report on No Child Left Behind*; McCarty, "American Indian, Alaska Native and Native Hawaiian Education."

11. Winstead et al., "Language, Sovereignty, Cultural Contestation, and American Indian Schools," 47.

12. Ibid., 49.

13. The 1893 coup and invasion by the U.S. military breeched Hawaiian and U.S. domestic laws, as well as the international treaties in force between those two countries, and was, thus, a breech of international law. Following the 1893 actions, President Grover Cleveland commissioned James Blount to complete a thorough investigation. Drawing on Blount's detailed report, President Cleveland addressed the U.S. Congress on December 18, 1893, stating in part, "But for the lawless occupation of Honolulu under false pretexts by the United States forces, and but for Minister Stevens' recognition of the provisional government when the United States forces were its sole support and constituted its only military strength, the Queen and her Government would have never yielded to the provisional government. . . . By an act of war, committed with the participation of a diplomatic representative of the United States without the authority of Congress, the Government of a feeble but friendly and confiding people has been overthrown." As quoted in Blount, *Foreign Relations of the United States, 1894*, 455–56; Trask, *From a Native Daughter*, 14–15.

14. Lomawaima and McCarty, *To Remain an Indian*, 6.

15. Ibid.

16. In Lomawaima and McCarty's definition of educational choice in the Native context, the individual and collective dimensions are referred to as "linked domains" that are inextricable from the personal and political sovereignty of Native people. Lomawaima and McCarty, *To Remain an Indian*, 9.

17. Aikau, personal communication, December 2, 2011.

18. Dehyle and Swisher, "Research in American Indian and Alaska Native education."

19. Hālau Kū Māna New Century Public Charter School, *End-of-the-Year Self-Evaluation Report 2005–06*, 3.

20. Even within the settler state's own organic laws, these lands, often called the Ceded Lands, are supposed to serve five purposes, two of which include support of public education and "the betterment of native Hawaiians."

21. The majority of state charter school laws do not include a provision mandating a particular composition of charter school boards. According to the National Resource Center on Charter School Finance and Governance's report *Creating and Sustaining High Quality Charter School Governing Boards* (2008), at the time Hawai'i was one of only four states that required both parent and teacher representatives on all local charter school boards. The law was changed in 2012 to professionalize charter school boards, as it has been in most other states.

22. Until 2012 Hawai'i's charter school law did not outline the way in which the representatives from the various stakeholder groups should be selected. In HKM's early years this was generally a self-selection process (e.g., a parent who volunteered to fill one of the parent representative seats could be confirmed without a broader vote). As the school matured, however, each segment began deciding upon their own selection processes. By the 2007–8 and 2008–9 school years, these practices were regularized and institutionalized. As of this writing, it remains to be seen how the new law will impact the selection of board members.

23. Traditionally, the Hawaiian language did not have words that directly correspond to the words *auntie* or *uncle* in English. The terms 'Anakē and 'Anakala are more recent additions to the language.

24. As a condition of enrollment at HKM, families are asked for sixteen hours of volunteer service to the school each year. This policy has not historically been strictly enforced, as there are no punitive measures if a family does not live up to this commitment. Despite this, the outpouring of kōkua has been overwhelming. At the time of this writing, the data on 'ohana kōkua hours was available for school years 2004–5 (when Micky Huihui began tracking), 2005–6, and 2006–7. In school year 2004–5, 62 families gave 2,920 hours (2,060 hours more than the required total and an average of 47 hours per family). In school year 2005–6, 70 families gave 3,145 hours (1,900 hours

more than the required total and an average of 45 hours per family). In school year 2006–7, 63 families gave 2,200 hours (860 hours more than the required total and an average of 35 hours per family). These numbers demonstrate a consistent pattern of families voluntarily giving more than twice the amount of service suggested by the school. See HKM's end-of-the-year reports for those years, respectively.

25. Lesley Micky Huihui, interviewed by the author, January 30, 2011.

26. Kaomea, "A Curriculum of Aloha?"; Warner, "Kuleana."

27. Hermes, " 'Maʻiingan Is Just a Misspelling of the Word Wolf,' " 53.

28. Hermes, "Complicating Discontinuity," 10.

29. I capitalize these terms to distinguish, for example, the yearlong Project courses, which involved interdisciplinary place-based inquiry, from projects in the usual sense of shorter-term assignments completed by individuals or small groups of students.

30. Hālau Kū Māna New Century Public Charter School, *End-of-the-Year Self-Evaluation Report 2002–03*, 12.

31. Hālau Kū Māna New Century Public Charter School, *End-of-the-Year Self-Evaluation Report 2006–07*, 10.

32. Tschumy, *Act 51, NCLB and Options for Restructuring*.

33. Hess and Squire, *"Diverse Providers" in Action*, 4.

34. Ibid.

35. Hālau Kū Māna New Century Public Charter School, *End-of-the-Year Self-Evaluation Report 2005–06*, 14.

36. Hālau Kū Māna New Century Public Charter School, *End-of-the-Year Self-Evaluation Report 2008–09*, 11.

37. Willy Kauai, interviewed by Zanette Johnson, October 8, 2008.

38. Gramsci, *Selections from the Prison Notebooks*; Hall, "Gramsci's Relevance for the Study of Race and Ethnicity."

39. Kāwika Mersberg, interviewed by the author, May 30, 2003.

40. Gina Kaleilehua Maioho, interviewed by Zanette Johnson, October 8, 2008.

41. Kamakau, *Ruling Chiefs of Hawaii*, 226–28; Kameʻeleihiwa, *Native Land and Foreign Desires*, 73–85; McGregor, *Nā Kuaʻāina*, 31; Tengan, *Native Men Remade*, 36.

42. Kameʻeleihiwa, *Native Land and Foreign Desires*.

43. About the hegemony of the standardized multiple-choice testing approach to assessment under NCLB, educational historian Diane Ravitch asks, "What happens to [students'] ability to think when they are never asked to consider the validity of the questions? What if the question is not the right question? Is there a different way to elicit a better response? What if there are

two right answers? Does this format over time teach students to think inside the box, quite literally? Does it punish divergent thinking? Does it squash creativity and originality?" Ravitch, "Let Your Voice Be Heard," 111–12.

44. Hayden J. ʻĪmaikalani Winchester, interviewed by Zanette Johnson, October 8, 2008.

3. Rebuilding the Structures That Feed Us

1. ʻAihualama was claimed by Pahau as Konohiki land under Land Commission Award 12. The award notes that ʻAihualama is a lele of the ʻili Kahaumakaawe. By the 1882 Hawaiian Kingdom government survey, the land had been split in half: the lower half sold to Kekūanāoʻa in 1863, and the upper half still in Pahau's control. Mahalo nui to geographer Donovan Preza for helping me find this information.

2. Jung, *Reworking Race*, 199.

3. See "History: Lyon Arboretum," Lyon Arboretum website, http://www.hawaii.edu/lyonarboretum/about/historyla.

4. The annual reports of Lyon Arboretum, made to the Hawaii Sugar Planters Association from the 1920s to the 1940s, detail the gradual change to the landscape as the arboretum established nurseries and then planted thousands of introduced plants. For example, as the 1926 report describes, "A series of drainage ditches has been cut through the ancient taro patches lying on the eastern side of Aihualama Stream. In digging these ditches, numerous, well-preserved stumps of large coconut palms were found buried in the muck, showing that coconuts once grew in this valley. It is proposed to drain this land to a point where it will no longer supply breeding places for mosquitoes, which have always been very plentiful in its vicinity. We shall eventually plant it up with trees and shrubs or use it for nursery purposes as our work in the Arboretum progresses." Mahalo to Ray Baker, longtime Arboretum staff member, for assisting me in looking through these reports.

5. *Mānoa* is an adjective meaning "vast" or "thick." Also, *manoa* (without the kahakō, or macron) means "numerous," which can suggest this valley's abundance of greenery and water.

6. These are the opening lines of a chant composed by Kamuela Yim, a former HKM kumu, specifically for the school and for the loʻi class. I do not use any diacritical marks in writing these few lines, because they were taught to me orally, not using a printed text, and because the addition of such marks would fix particular interpretations of the chant's meaning. I do not provide the full text of this or any other oli used at the school, because they are the kuleana of the practitioners at HKM. While some of the chants are widely

known and accessible elsewhere in print, many of them are unique composi-
tions of the kumu at HKM, and it is not my place to share them in an open
and public manner such as this book. For anyone who wants to learn any
of the oli used at HKM in their entirety, it would be proper to seek out the
kumu and make a face-to-face request. The kumu, in turn, may or may not be
willing to transmit that knowledge, depending on the person making the request and the intended usage. When I was taught oli during my time at HKM
as a researcher, employee, or board member, it was with the understanding
that I would use these chants in practice at the school or in my personal life
and that I might write about their use and general meaning but not publish
them in full.

7. A thorough critique of the "walking in two worlds" metaphor is beyond the scope of this chapter, and an excellent critique was already issued by
Henze and Vanett several years ago. They argue that this metaphor masks the
complexity of Indigenous lives and limits educational opportunities by ignoring systems of power. See Henze and Vanett, "To Walk in Two Worlds." I
would add that this metaphor is inadequate for Indigenous education because
it focuses only on the individual rather than on the kind of community and
land-based regeneration that is crucial for individual health and success. The
reoccurrence of this outdated and insufficient metaphor twenty years after
Henze and Vannet's trenchant critique points to the need for powerful alternative ways of conceptualizing Indigenous education.

8. Cho, Yamakawa, and Hollyer, *Hawaiian Kalo, Past and Future*, 4–5.

9. Pukui, Haertig, and Lee, *Nānā i ke Kumu*, 249.

10. Danny Bishop, interviewed by the author, January 19, 2009.

11. Kirch, *Feathered Gods and Fishhooks*; Kirch and O'Day, "New Archaeological Insights into Food and Status"; Ladefoged et al., "Opportunities and
Constraints for Intensive Agriculture in the Hawaiian Archipelago Prior to
European Contact"; Vitousek et al., "Soils, Agriculture, and Society in Precontact Hawai'i"; Kelly, "Dynamics of Production Intensification in Precontact Hawaii."

12. Corntassel, "Toward Sustainable Self-Determination."

13. Ibid., 118.

14. Yosso's work responds to the ways in which Bourdieu's notion of "cultural capital" has been used within deficit-oriented approaches to teaching
students in communities of color. She writes, "In addressing the debate over
knowledge within the context of social inequality, Pierre Bourdieu (Bourdieu
& Passeron, 1977) argued that the knowledges of the upper and middle classes
are considered capital valuable to a hierarchical society. If one is not born into
a family whose knowledge is already deemed valuable, one could then access

the knowledges of the middle and upper class and the potential for social mobility through formal schooling. Bourdieu's theoretical insight about how a hierarchical society reproduces itself has often been interpreted as a way to explain why the academic and social outcomes of People of Color are significantly lower than the outcomes of Whites. The assumption follows that People of Color 'lack' the social and cultural capital required for social mobility. As a result, schools most often work from this assumption in structuring ways to help 'disadvantaged' students whose race and class background has left them lacking necessary knowledge, social skills, abilities and cultural capital." Yosso, "Whose Culture Has Capital?," 70.

15. Ibid., 77.

16. Kāwika Mersberg, interviewed by the author, May 3, 2003.

17. Consuelo Goveia, interviewed by the author, February 15, 2011.

18. Trevor Atkins, interviewed by the author, February 22, 2011.

19. "Ka pae ʻāina o Hawaiʻi" refers to all the islands of the Hawaiian archipelago.

20. During the mid-nineteenth-century transition to a system of private property, the Hawaiian Kingdom's crown lands were set aside for the direct control of the Mōʻī (head of state). Approximately one million acres were included among the crown lands, and these lands were made inalienable, ineligible for sale, in 1865. Kānaka Maoli and other Hawaiian Kingdom nationals continue to assert a claim to these lands along with the Hawaiian Kingdom's government lands, both of which are currently controlled by the settler state. For a detailed history of the crown lands, see Van Dyke, *Who Owns the Crown Lands of Hawaiʻi?* Van Dyke makes clear that "Native Hawaiians have been deprived of their lands without compensation or their consent, and that these lands must be returned to them" (9).

21. Trevor Atkins, interviewed by the author, February 22, 2011.

22. The question of what it means to recognize land, deceased ancestors, and ʻaumākua as living and present and to honor them in ritualized ways that might be considered religious in the context of a public school is addressed in chapter 5.

23. "Kalo kanu o ka ʻāina" refers both to the kalo plant itself and to the people of the land.

24. The establishment of kuleana to the ʻāina includes learning ancestral moʻolelo and place names, as well as the creation and retelling of a new generation of stories and impassioned memories, what ʻŌiwi anthropologist Ty Kāwika Tengan calls "memory work." In *Native Men Remade* Tengan shows the ways narrative memory work—such as commemorative events, ritual practices, and the sharing of life stories—has been foundational to the reformulation

of Hawaiian nationalist subjectivities and Indigenous masculinities among men in the Hale Mua. He writes about how this group recuperates Indigenous masculinities in the context of legacies of colonial dislocation and the commodifying forces of corporate tourism. As Tengan writes, the narratives of memory work are not only "efforts at decolonizing the mind, but they are also acts of self-determination as community members seek to assert control over the destiny of the lāhui while defining the self (through group membership) as Hawaiians struggling with the burdens of history." Tengan, *Native Men Remade*, 67.

25. Kamuela Yim, interviewed by the author, January 26, 2009.

26. HKM Kumu who have contributed to this project over the last seven years include alaka'i (leaders) Kamuela Yim, Kawika Mersberg, Danny Bishop, Neil McCulloch, and 'Īmaikalani Winchester, as well as kāko'o (supporting teachers) Kaleilehua Maioho, Kapela Collins, Kawika Shizuma, Daniel Anthony, Richard Kuewa, Trevor Atkins, and Kristi Desuacido. Additionally, Lyon Arboretum staff Kaleo Wong, Kāwika Winter, and Līloa Dunn have been instrumental in initiating and continuing the partnership. HKM school leaders Keola Nakanishi and Micky Huihui also helped secure formal agreements between the two institutions, facilitating the project.

27. Kāwika Mersberg, interviewed by the author, January 23, 2009.

28. The school-wide protocols that open each day at Hālau Kū Māna were developed under the advising of Kumu John Keolamakaainanakalahuiokalaniokamehamehaekolu Lake and the leadership of former HKM director Keola Nakanishi, in conversation with numerous kumu, such as Kāwika Mersberg. These daily protocols in turn informed the development of HKM's specific place-based protocols at 'Aihualama. Tengan describes the role of Kumu Lake and his Nā Wa'a Lālani Kahuna in the recuperation of Pu'ukoholā heiau as a place of ceremony for the unification of the Hawaiian nation. Tengan, *Native Men Remade*, 93–123.

29. Jung, *Reworking Race*; Wilcox, *Sugar Water*.

30. Pōmaika'i Freed, interviewed by the author, May 1, 2011.

31. Different varieties of kalo can be recognized by the color, size, shape, and other characteristics of the leaf, corm, and petiole of each plant. Kānaka Maoli of old cultivated different varieties for all types of ecological conditions. For more information about kalo cultivars, see the Kupuna Kalo website at http://kupunakalo.com/index.php/kalo_varieties (commonly known as Bulletin 84); and Whitney, Bowers, and Takahashi, *Taro Varieties in Hawaii*.

32. Hermes, "The Scientific Method, Nintendo, and Eagle Feathers"; Hermes, "Complicating Discontinuity"; Meyer, "Our Own Liberation"; Sumida and Meyer, "T4 and Culture."

33. In the first ten years of Hālau Kū Māna's existence, an average of 85 to 90 percent of families enrolling their 'ōpio at the school identified them as Native Hawaiian. A majority of HKM's teachers also claimed some 'Ōiwi lineage, but the school did not keep specific records on the race or ancestry of its instructional and support staff. From my observations and conversations over the years, I estimate that Kānaka Maoli comprised well over half of the faculty in any given year and that the proportion of non-'Ōiwi teachers increased (but not to the point of becoming a majority) after the heavy enforcement of the highly-qualified teacher (HQT) requirements of NCLB.

34. It is important to remember here that divisive blood racializations are not the same as attention to genealogy. Whereas racialization in the United States tends to be about fractionalizing and focusing on difference, Hawaiian genealogical practices look for the ways people are *connected*. See Kauanui, *Hawaiian Blood*.

35. Noelani Duffey-Spikes, interviewed by the author, March 23, 2011.

36. *Kākou* is an inclusive plural pronoun referring to three or more people, meaning "all of us," including the speaker and everyone to whom she or he is speaking. In recent colloquial terms, it has been explicitly used to inclusively mobilize groups in action, as in the saying, "It's a kākou thing!"

37. I thank Candace Fujikane for our discussion about these issues of how to acknowledge the connections that non-Indigenous people cultivate with lands and Native communities without usurping Native identity or mana. It was in one such discussion that she posed the possible term *settler aloha 'āina* as a way that settlers might identify.

38. Mahalo to Hokulani Aikau for putting this so succinctly, in personal communication to the author, March 27, 2011.

39. Warner, "Kuleana"; Kaomea, "Contemplating Kuleana."

40. Kaomea, "Contemplating Kuleana," 95.

41. Smith, *Conquest*; Smith and Kauanui, "Native Feminisms Engage American Studies"; Driskill et al., *Queer Indigenous Studies*.

42. In considering this assumption that men are physically stronger than women, I could not help but think back to an instance when HKM was making its move to the current campus. The old offices had been completely cleared out, save for the largest and heaviest desk, which no staff or volunteer group had been able to move, including the boys' football team of a nearby local high school. Then, before professional movers were hired, the women of my canoe paddling team volunteered to help with the final stages of the move. Accustomed to lifting together canoes weighing about four hundred pounds, the women had no problem moving the desk, which only speaks to the role that training has in cultivating physical or other forms of strength.

43. Clifford, "Indigenous Articulations," 475.

44. Tengan, *Native Men Remade*.

45. Ibid., 35.

46. ʻĪmaikalani Winchester, in personal communication with the author, April 4, 2011. Also see the discussion on the origins of the ʻAikapu in Kameʻeleihiwa, *Native Land and Foreign Desires*, 19–49.

47. Kameʻeleihiwa, *Native Land and Foreign Desires*; Basham, "Awaiaulu ke Aloha"; Tengan, *Native Men Remade*; Pukui, Haertig, and Lee, *Nānā i ke Kumu*; Handy and Pukui, *The Polynesian Family System in Kaʻū, Hawaiʻi*.

48. Noelani Duffey-Spikes, interviewed by the author, March 30, 2011.

49. Basham, "Awaiaulu ke Aloha," 6. In the passage quoted, she also cites Pukui, Haertig, and Lee, *Nānā i ke Kumu*.

50. Pukui, Haertig, and Lee, *Nānā i ke Kumu*, 110.

51. Ibid.

52. Tengan, *Native Men Remade*, 157.

53. Homai Luteru, interviewed by the author, March 14, 2011.

54. The name Hānai Ke Kalo has a double meaning ("We Nurture the Kalo" and "The Kalo Feeds Us") that captures the reciprocal relationship between kalo and Kānaka.

4. Enlarging Hawaiian Worlds

1. Hauʻofa, "Our Sea of Islands"; Teaiwa, "Militarism, Tourism and the Native: Articulations in Oceania"; "Articulated Cultures"; Diaz and Kauanui, "Native Pacific Cultural Studies on the Edge"; Diaz, *Repositioning the Missionary*; Tengan, *Native Men Remade*; Aikau, "Indigeneity in the Diaspora"; Aikau, *A Chosen People, a Promised Land*.

2. I was first introduced to this metaphor of "roots and routes" by the work of James Clifford. In particular, see Clifford, *Routes*. Commenting on the significance of the intervention made by *Routes*, Friedman writes, "Clifford's stress on movement itself as the source of cultural production implies that it is people and things on the move that in themselves are agents of cultural creation as against the received view that culture is constituted in localized populations or communities." Friedman, "From Roots to Routes," 22.

3. Diaz and Kauanui, "Native Pacific Cultural Studies on the Edge," 318–19.

4. Hauʻofa, "Our Sea of Islands," 7.

5. Ibid., 11.

6. This genealogical chant for *Kānehūnāmoku* appears in its entirety through the permission of *Kānehūnāmoku*'s captain, Kumu Bonnie Kahapeʻa-Tanner.

7. Silva, *Aloha Betrayed*, 19.

8. The *Hōkūleʻa* is the waʻa kaulua (double-hulled sailing canoe) that launched the resurgence of Hawaiian seafaring practices. See Finney, *Sailing in the Wake of the Ancestors; Voyage of Rediscovery*; Kyselka, *An Ocean in Mind*.

9. These are the concluding lines of a chant composed by Kumu Kāwika Mersberg for Hālau Kū Māna.

10. Jokiel, "Jokiel's Illustrated Scientific Guide to Kaneʻohe Bay, Oʻahu," 18.

11. Almost all of the large fishponds that were built on Oʻahu by Kānaka Maoli in days past were filled for suburban development through the mid-twentieth century. In more recent years new generations of marine resource stewards have attempted to revitalize traditional Hawaiian fishponds and loʻi. Most notable among them is Paepae o Heʻeia, a nonprofit organization that was formed by a group of young Kānaka in the early 2000s to care for and revitalize the largest existing fishpond on Windward Oʻahu, the fifty-acre Heʻeia fishpond. Paepae o Heʻeia provided an outdoor learning site and science-based instruction to several Hawaiian-focused charter schools, including Hālau Kū Māna. See the Paepae o Heʻeia website at www.paepaeoheeia.org.

12. Māhealani Treaster, interviewed by the author, April 26, 2011. During this interview Kumu Māhealani made a point to say, "For the record, I am not Hawaiian." This was important for her to state explicitly, since she goes by a Hawaiian name, teaches Hawaiian language and history, and could pass as a Kanaka. She also explained that it was important to acknowledge her position to her students, as well as to me, so that they might see that non-Hawaiians also have a kuleana to learn and care about the histories, place names, and practices of the Kānaka ʻŌiwi and the ʻāina.

13. Kaʻōpulupulu advised Kahahana against giving Kualoa to Kahekili: "Oh Chief! If you give away these things your authority will be lost, and you will cease to be a ruler. To Kualoa belong the water courses of your ancestors, Kalumalumaʻi and Kekaiheheʻe; the sacred drums of Kapahuʻulu, and the spring of Kaʻahuʻula; the sacred hill of Kauakahi son of Kahoʻowaha of Kualoa." See Kamakau, *Ruling Chiefs of Hawaii*, 129.

14. The ahu at Kualoa includes stones representing these waʻa: *Hōkūleʻa* and *Hawaiʻiloa* of Honolulu, *Makaliʻi* of Waimea, *Te Au o Tonga* and *Takitumu* of Rarotonga, *Taiohae* of Nuku Hiva, *Eʻala* of Waiʻanae, and the Oʻahu Hawaiian Canoe Racing Association.

15. Loretta Ritte, interviewed by the author, June 2009. Video clips of this and other oral history interviews with early Kahoʻolawe activists can be found on the Moʻolelo Alohaʻāina project's website at http://moolelo.manainfo.com.

16. This landing included Loretta Ritte; her husband, Walter Ritte; his sister, Scarlet Ritte; and Noa Emmett Aluli. See Ritte and Sawyer, *Na Manaʻo Aloha o Kahoʻolawe*.

17. Tengan, *Native Men Remade*, 55.

18. For a listing, with detailed descriptions, of *Hōkūleʻa*'s voyages, see Nainoa Thompson, "Why We Voyage: Reflections on Rapanui and Hokuleʻa's First Twenty-Five Years," Polynesian Voyaging Society website, http://pvs.kcc.hawaii.edu/holokai/intro_holokai.html. For more on the Protect Kahoʻolawe ʻOhana and demilitarization movements in Hawaiʻi, see Blaisdell, "The Indigenous Rights Movement in the Pacific"; McGregor, *Nā Kuaʻāina*; Kajihiro, "The Militarizing of Hawaiʻi."

19. For more information and images related to the story of *Hōkūleʻa*'s 1976 arrival in Tahiti, see Nainoa Thompson, "Voyaging and the Revival of Culture and Heritage," Polynesian Voyaging Society website, http://pvs.kcc.hawaii.edu/ike/intro_ike.html.

20. Bonnie Kahapeʻa, interviewed by the author, December 13, 2004.

21. The PRAXIS tests are a series developed by the Educational Testing Service and widely used as part of the certification process required by many states and professional licensing organizations. Some studies have begun to show the uneven impacts this test has on teacher candidates of various ethnic and racial backgrounds. One study in Alaska shows that among teacher candidates only 30 to 50 percent of Alaska Native candidates passed the PRAXIS I exam, whereas more than 90 percent of white candidates passed. The authors argue that the test is "essentially a test of cultural assimilation." Hogan and Winebarger, "Decolonizing Education in Alaska." Bennett, McWhorter, and Kuykendall argue that the PRAXIS I is an inequitable admissions tool, based on their findings among Latino and African American applicants seeking entrance to the teacher education program at a Big Ten university. Bennett, McWhorter, and Kuykendall, "Will I Ever Teach?"

22. Watanabe, "Because We Do Not Know Their Way."

23. Bonnie Kahapeʻa-Tanner, interviewed by the author, December 4, 2004.

24. Hālau Kū Māna staff retreat, December 6, 2010.

25. Personal communication, September 2004.

26. *Ke Au Okoʻa*, April 14, 1870. The Hawaiian text can be found through Ulukau: Hawaiian Electronic Library's online Hawaiian newspaper archive, Hoʻolaupaʻi, at http://nupepa.org/gsdl2.5/cgi-bin/nupepa?l=en. The archive is searchable by title of newspaper, date or keyword search. The following English translation of the quoted segment is Mary Kawena Pukui's: "Kanehunamoku, Kamohoaliʻi, Kuhaimoana, Kaʻuhuhu, Kaneikokala, Kanakaokai, and some others were mano kumupuʻa. . . . They showed themselves in trances and visions in the forms they assumed as sharks, owls, hilu fish, moʻo and so forth. There were many forms that these ancestral gods, the ʻaumakua

kumupaʻa, such as Kamohoaliʻi and Kanehunamoku ma and other ancestral beings from the po (spirit world) assumed." Kamakau, *Ka Poʻe Kahiko*, 75.

27. Beckwith, *Hawaiian Mythology*; Rice, *Hawaiian Legends*; Gutmanis, *Na Pule Kahiko*.

28. Beckwith, *Hawaiian Mythology*; *The Kumulipo*.

29. Bonnie Kahapeʻa-Tanner explained that this name comes from what is believed to be the ancestral name of the island, Kapou, and "ku Mau," in deference to Papa Mau Piailug, who helped Hawaiian voyagers find their ways back to these islands by reclaiming voyaging traditions.

30. For Scott Kekuewa Kikiloi's full posting on *Kānehūnāmoku*, see "Where Kane Hides the Islands," Northwestern Hawaiian Islands Multi-agency Education Project website, September 30, 2002, http://www.hawaiianatolls.org/research/NOWRAMP2002/journals/kanehunamoku.php.

31. The word *piko* can refer to the navel. Kānaka Maoli recognize, however, several piko within each person. A piko is both a center within an individual being and a node or connector to generations that preceded or follow.

32. For diagrams of both compasses, see "Star Compasses," Polynesian Voyaging Society website, http://pvs.kcc.hawaii.edu/ike/hookele/star_compasses.html.

33. According to Kanahele mā, "Ke Alanui Polohiwa a Kāne and Ke Alanui Polohiwa a Kanaloa are nā Ao Polohiwa. The ao polohiwa are the boundaries of the sun's travels. Ao can be interpreted as realm, world, or space. Polohiwa means a dark space." These terms can also refer to the summer and winter solstices. For further explanation, see Kanahele et al., *Kūkulu ke Ea a Kanaloa*.

34. Uncle Clay Bertelmann is symbolized by the design *Makaliʻi* on the rear ākea side of the waʻa. ʻAnakala Eddie's design *Maka upena* sits on the rear ama side of *Kānehūnāmoku*.

35. Noelani Duffey-Spikes, interviewed by the author, March 31, 2011.

36. See, for example, the National Council for Teachers of English's "The Definition of 21st Century Literacies," the Partnership for 21st Century Skills' "Framework for 21st Century Learning," the National Council for Social Studies' "Principles for Learning," the Association for Career and Technical Education, the Consortium for School Networking, the National Council of Teachers of English, the National Council of Teachers of Mathematics, the National Middle School Association, and the National Science Teachers Association.

37. Bonnie Kahapeʻa-Tanner, interviewed by the author, December 4, 2004.

38. Pōmaikaʻi Freed, interviewed by the author, May 1, 2011.

5. Creating Mana through Students' Voices

1. Goodyear-Kaʻōpua et al., "Teaching amid U.S. Occupation."

2. *Rice v. Cayetano* (98–818) (146 F3d 1075, reversed). The Rice case is introduced and discussed at greater length in chapter 1.

3. The ʻIlioʻulaokalani coalition was formed in 1997. Kamahele provides an account of the origins of the ʻIlioʻulaokalani coalition in her article that describes hula as a fundamental expression of Hawaiian *national and Indigenous* culture. See Kamahele, "ʻIlioʻulaokalani."

4. Noelani Duffey-Spikes, interviewed by the author, March 31, 2011.

5. King Kalākaua had the ʻIolani Palace that stands today built to replace an older Hale Aliʻi, demolished in 1874. The new structure was outfitted with all of the most innovative technological advancements of the time, including indoor plumbing and, within years of their invention, electric lighting and a telephone system.

6. *Kū i ka pono* can be translated as "stand for justice." One of the march's organizers has written a brief history of this aspect of the Hawaiian movement. See Kaiama, "Kū i ka Pono Movement."

7. Judge Alan Kay ruled on *Doe v. Kamehameha Schools et al.* (Civ. No. 03–00316) on November 17, 2003, in favor of Kamehameha's preference policy. The primary reasons cited in his decision were (1) that Kamehameha Schools is a private actor that receives no federal or state funding and (2) that the admissions policy serves a remedial purpose. *Doe v. Kamehameha Schools* made its way to the Ninth U.S. Circuit Court of Appeals, which eventually found in favor of Kamehameha in 2006. Subsequently, both state and circuit courts ruled that the case could not proceed any further, as plaintiffs hoped, without the plaintiffs giving up their pseudonyms and anonymity. On August 18, 2003, Brayden Mohica-Cummings, through his mother, Kalena Santos, filed a lawsuit in a U.S. district court in Hawaiʻi claiming he was denied admission based on ancestry. Like the plaintiffs in *Doe*, Mohica-Cummings charged that Kamehameha Schools' admission policy violated the Civil Rights Act under Section 1981. Kamehameha Schools had accepted Mohica-Cummings based on his application, which claimed he was of biological Hawaiian ancestry. When the schools discovered the documentation was unverifiable, they withdrew their acceptance of the student. On August 20, 2003, U.S. district court judge David Ezra ordered the schools to temporarily admit Mohica-Cummings pending a court decision on the merits of the case. On November 28, 2003, the Kamehameha Schools' board of trustees announced that they would settle with the plaintiff, allowing Brayden Mohica-Cummings to

continue through graduation in exchange for dropping the lawsuit. The settlement was approved by U.S. district court judge David Ezra.

8. Pōmaikaʻi Freed, interviewed by the author, May 1, 2011.

9. As noted in chapter 1, the Kamakakūokalani Center for Hawaiian Studies at the University of Hawaiʻi at Mānoa served as HKM's main site for the school's first two years of operation.

10. Akindes, "Sudden Rush"; Hoʻomanawanui, "He Lei Hoʻoheno no nā Kau a Kau"; Kalyan, "Hip-Hop Imaginaries."

11. Sudden Rush, "Ea," on Ea (Kapolei, Hawaiʻi: Way Out West, 2002). A Sudden Rush–authorized music video of this song was produced by Jason Lau of Lau Vizion and Laulau TV. For the video, which uses footage of Hawaiian charter school students from Hālau Lōkahi and Hālau Kū Māna, see "Sudden Rush Ea," YouTube video, 4:31, posted on February 10, 2007, by RealRushMedia, http://www.youtube.com/watch?v=hgmOO5jiiqo.

12. King, The Truth about Stories.

13. Mersberg began his study of hula at the University of Hawaiʻi and took courses in chant and dance from Kumu Hula Noenoe Zuttermeister and Kumu Vicky Holt-Takamine. Later, he practiced with Hālau Kukunaokalā under Kumu John Kaʻimikaua and, finally, with Hālau ke Kiaʻi aʻo Hula under Kumu Hula Kapiʻolani Haʻo. It was Haʻo who "gave [him] permission to start teaching the basic hula fundamentals." Kumu Kapiʻolani has also been integrally involved with the annual concerts, as has former HKM kumu Kealiʻi Gora.

14. Kāwika Mersberg, interviewed by the author, May 30, 2003.

15. Kameʻeleihiwa, Native Land and Foreign Desires; Silva, Aloha Betrayed.

16. Silva, Aloha Betrayed, 97.

17. Ibid., 94–104.

18. Ibid., 98.

19. Pōmaikaʻi Freed, interviewed by the author, May 1, 2011.

20. A full description of Prince Kūhiō's role in advocating for a U.S. law that would establish the Hawaiian Homelands trust and commission can be found in Kauanui, Hawaiian Blood.

21. Trask, From a Native Daughter; Kamahele, "ʻĪlioʻulaokalani"; Tengan, Native Men Remade; Desmond, Staging Tourism; Imada, "Hawaiians on Tour"; Ferguson and Turnbull, Oh, Say, Can You See?; Halualani, In the Name of Hawaiians.

22. Tengan, Native Men Remade, 154.

23. Alika Kaʻahanui, interviewed by the author, April 15, 2003.

24. Dan Ahuna, interviewed by the author, April 8, 2003.

25. Alika Kaʻahanui, interviewed by the author, April 15, 2003.

26. Pōmaikaʻiʻs writing further expresses the idea that Hawaiians, like all human beings, deserve a high-quality public education. Just as a people's self-determination is interconnected with each individual's sense of their own power to create change, meaningful education for each person is a public good for all.

27. While the ethic and slogan of the pro-kalo, anti-GMO events has been articulated by organizers as "mālama Hāloa," I was reminded by Hawaiian-language scholar Keao Nesmith that the proper way to express care for Hāloa is to include the article *iā*. "Mālama iā Hāloa" refers to caring for Hāloa, whereas "Mālama Hāloa" refers to Hāloa who cares for us. I use the former as the title for this section but the latter in the text of this section, as it is the way that organizers of the movement expressed the sentiment.

28. Kauʻi Onekea, interviewed by the author, May 11, 2011.

29. Smith, *Decolonizing Methodologies*.

30. Ritte and Freese, "Haloa," 12.

31. Ibid., 13.

32. Ibid., 11.

33. Kameʻeleihiwa, *Native Land and Foreign Desires*, 44–45.

34. Alakaʻi Kotrys, interviewed by the author, June 9, 2011.

35. Kauʻi Onekea, interviewed by the author, May 11, 2011.

36. As a further example of the fluidity of Hawaiian gender roles and practices and their difference from Western heteropatriarchal gender practices, it is worth noting that it was Kumu Hina, a māhū wahine, who initiated the more Kū-like event and Kumu Kalaniākea, a kāne, who initiated the more Lono-like event.

37. The construction of the ahu was led by Molokaʻi Kānaka, Walter Ritte, Kalaniua Ritte, and Hanohano Naehu, with the assistance of many other hands.

38. Alakaʻi Kotrysʻs original composition, entitled "Chants," was performed as a team piece by Kotrys and Jamaica Osorio at the quarterfinals of the 2007 Brave New Voices International Youth Poetry Slam Festival in San Jose, California. This annual event is touted as the largest ongoing spoken word competition. While "Chants" is no longer available for viewing online, one can watch videos of the current year's competition at http://youthspeaks.org/bravenewvoices/blog. Other examples of Alakaʻi Kotrysʻs performance poetry can be viewed at http://uwhiphopvideos.blogspot.com/2009/11/tense-alakai-kotrys.html and http://www.youtube.com/watch?v=4_MuCU_vXic&feature=related.

39. Because this poem is typically offered as a performance piece rather than as a printed one, I do not include any diacritical markings in the Hawaiian-language lines, so as to leave space for multiple ways of interpreting

it. I have included only short sections from the piece here, as the composition was meant to be heard rather than read.

Conclusion

1. Kahikina De Silva, "Ka'ala, Molale i ka Mālie," 1.

2. Jodi Byrd, *The Transit of Empire*, xxiii.

3. Native Hawaiians Study Commission, *Native Hawaiians Study Commission*; Kamehameha Schools, *Native Hawaiian Educational Assessment Project Report*.

4. Kana'iaupuni, Malone, and Ishibashi, *Ka Huaka'i*; Kamehameha Schools, *Native Hawaiian Educational Assessment Update 2009*.

5. Noelani Goodyear-Ka'ōpua, "Rebuilding the 'Auwai," 46–77.

6. Danny Bishop, interviewed by the author, January 19, 2009.

Glossary

Definitions in this glossary draw from and expand upon those offered in the revised and enlarged edition of Mary Kawena Pukui and Samuel Elbert's *Hawaiian Dictionary*. This resource is now digitized, and readers can consult it at www.wehewehe.org. The definitions here do not include every possible meaning of each word, and readers should be aware that many of the words have layers of meaning that are not captured in full here. Some of the definitions reflect the specific ways community members of Hālau Kū Māna used and understood the terms.

'aelike. An agreement or contract. To agree together.
'aha. (1) Assembly or council. (2) Sennit or braided cord.
'aha'aina. Feast, banquet. Any large gathering that includes a meal. Popularly referred to as a lū'au.
ahu. Altar, shrine.
ahupua'a. A land division usually extending from the mountains to the ocean.
'ai. Food or food plant, especially vegetable food. Often refers specifically to pounded kalo, as in pa'i 'ai.
'āina. Land, particularly land in food production and land with which humans have an active, mutually beneficial relationship.
'ākau. (1) North or northern. (2) Right (not left).
akua. A general term for a god/goddess or other supernatural being.
alaka'i. Leader, guide, director. Used at HKM to refer to members of the school's leadership team.
ali'i. Chief/chiefess, officer, ruler, monarch, peer.
aloha. Love, affection, compassion, mercy, kindness. A loved one.
'anakala. Uncle.
'anakē. Auntie.
'ano. Variety, nature, character, disposition, manner.
ao. Light, day, daylight; to dawn; enlightened; to regain consciousness.

'aumakua ('aumākua, plural form). Family or personal god; deified
   ancestor who might assume the form of various animals, plants, or
   other natural phenomena.
aupuni. Government, kingdom, nation, or people under a ruler;
   national.
'auwai. Ditch; often refers specifically to the irrigation ditches that
   carry water within a watershed area to wetland kalo fields.
ea. Sovereignty, rule, independence; life, air, breath, respiration.
hālau. Meeting house; place of learning or meeting; can also refer
   to the people who make up a group of teachers and students, as a
   hālau hula; large, numerous.
hana. Work, labor, job, function, process, reason, action, deed, task.
   To do, behave, make, create, transact, perform, prepare, happen.
hānai. To raise, feed, nourish, rear. An adopted child.
hānau. To give birth; productive or prolific.
haole. Foreigner, specifically of European or American descent; white.
haumāna. Student or students.
heiau. A general term for Hawaiian structures used for worship,
   usually non-Christian and ranging in size and complexity.
hema. (1) South or southern. (2) Left (not right).
hikina. (1) East or eastern. (2) Coming or advent.
hoa. Friend, companion, peer, associate, colleague.
ho'i. To leave or come back; to cause to come back; to enter.
hō'ike. Performance, exhibition, proof, commencement.
ho'okele. To sail or navigate; the steersperson or navigator.
ho'okumu. To create, establish, initiate, found, originate.
ho'okupu. A tribute, ceremonial gift, or offering. To cause growth;
   to sprout.
ho'oponopono. A Hawaiian cultural, familial, and spiritual process
   for healing and maintaining harmonious relationships. Literally,
   to make right, to correct, or to make ready.
ho'oulu. To cause to grow or increase; to spread; to stir up, inspire,
   excite, taunt.
hui. Organization, group, association, team.
huli. (1) The stalk of a kalo plant, used to repropagate it. (2) To turn,
   reverse, curl over as a breaking wave, or change as an opinion or
   manner; to look for, search, explore, seek, study.

'iewe. Afterbirth or placenta.

'ike. To see, know, perceive, feel, experience, recognize; to receive revelation. Can also be used in noun form.

'ili. Skin; surface.

'ili'ili. (1) Pebble or small stone. (2) To pile or overlap.

imu. Underground oven.

iwi. Bone; carcass; core.

kahu. Honored attendant, guardian, keeper, administrator, or caretaker.

kahua. Foundation, base.

kahuna. Priest, master of skilled and spiritual practices; expert in any profession; historically used to refer to doctors, surgeons, etc.

kai. Sea, sea water, seaside.

kaikaina. Younger sibling, usually of the same gender. This term is used at HKM to refer to students of the middle school division.

kākau. To write, sign, or mark; tatoo.

kākou. We, inclusive of three or more people.

kalo. Taro, the primary staple food of Kānaka Maoli from time immemorial.

kanaka (kānaka, plural form). Person (without specific gender reference); subject; population; private individual or party as distinguished from the government; humanity. Kanaka also means Hawaiian person.

Kanaka Maoli. Native Hawaiian.

kāne. Man; male, masculine.

kanu. To plant or bury.

kapu. Prohibited; sacred; a restriction.

kaula. Rope or cord.

kaulua. Double canoe, pair, two of a kind; to yoke or harness together; to double in quantity.

keiki. Child, offspring.

kiakahi. Single mast, as on a canoe or ship; person of fixed purpose; in unison, with one accord or purpose.

kīkepa. Tapa, or bark cloth, worn usually by women under one arm and over the shoulder of the opposite arm; to cover one side.

kilolani. An expert observer of the sky, including navigators or seers; to do astronomy or observation of the heavens; an astronomer.

kīpuka. A variation or change of form, as a calm place in a high sea, a deep place in a shoal, an opening in a forest, openings in cloud formations, and especially a clear place or oasis within a lava bed where there may be vegetation.

koa. Brave, bold, valiant, courageous, fearless; a warrior or fighter, but also any fearless hero; the largest of the native trees in Hawai'i forests.

kōkua. To help or assist; assistant, helper, aide.

komohana. West or western.

kua'ana. Elder sibling, usually of the same gender. This term is used at HKM to refer to students in the high school division.

kuāuna. Bank or border of a kalo field.

kū'ē. To oppose, stand apart, resist.

kūkākūkā. Discussion, negotiation, consultation, deliberation.

kula. School.

kulāiwi. Native land, homeland; refers to the connection created when generations of ancestral bones lay buried in the earth.

kūlana. Rank, title; reputation; stance.

kuleana. Responsibility, privilege, authority, especially as tied to land, extended family, and community.

kumu. Teacher, intellectual, source; reason or cause.

kumupa'a. Firm foundation; ancient times; family god(s).

Kūpau. (1) Sixth day of the lunar month and last of the four days kapu to the god Kū. The moon appears about a quarter full. (2) Entirely finished.

kupuna (kūpuna, plural form). Ancestor; grandparent or one of the granparents' generation.

lā. Sun, solar; day, date.

lāhui. Nation, nationality; people; species; to assemble or gather together; to prohibit or proclaim a law.

laulima. Cooperation, joint action; literally, many hands.

lei. A garland, often of flowers, feathers, or shells. Figuratively refers to a beloved child or lover.

lele. (1) An altar or stand for tributes or offerings. (2) To fly, jump, disembark.

leo. Voice.

lo'i. Irrigated agricultural terrace.

lo'i kalo. Wetland taro field

loko i'a. Fishpond.

lomilomi. Massage.

lū'au. A contemporary term commonly referring to a large party including a feast. Literally, taro top.

luna. High, upper, above, up, over.

mahalo. Thanks, gratitude, appreciation, admiration, respect, praise.

mahi'ai. Farmer or planter; to farm or cultivate.

māhū. Commonly refers to transgendered persons; a person practicing gender beyond or outside the male/female or man/woman binary.

ma'i. Genitals; to menstruate.

maka'āinana. Common people, citizen, populace; refers to those who reside on and are of the land or who are, perhaps, the eyes of the land.

makawalu. Numerous, many. Often refers to the ability to see multiple perspectives or to proliferate; literally, eight eyes.

makua (mākua, plural form). Parent or one of the parents' generation.

mālama. To care for, attend, preserve, protect.

mana. Supernatural, spiritual, or divine power; life force or energy.

māna. A chewed mass; a trait aquired from those who raised a child; shortened term for haumāna, or student.

māna'ai. Food chewed by an adult for a child, or any mouthful of food.

mana'o. Thought, belief, idea, opinion, theory, thesis, intention, meaning.

maoli. Native, aboriginal; genuine, real.

mō'ī. Monarch, sovereign.

moku. (1) To be cut, severed. (2) A district or piece of land.

mokupuni. Island.

mo'okū'auhau. Genealogy, genealogical narrative, or chant; lineage or sucession.

mo'olelo. A mode of representing events of the past. Story, history, tradition, literature, chronicle, minutes as of a meeting, myth, essay, record.

mo'opuna. Grandchild or one of the grandchildrens' generation.

na'au. Intestines, guts; mind; heart. In Hawaiian philosophy the na'au is the seat of intelligence and emotion.

na'auao. Learned, intelligent, enlightened, wise; learning, knowledge, wisdom, science.

'ōiwi. Native.

'ohana. Extended family—a crucial institution within Hawaiian society, past and present.

'ōlelo no'eau. A proverb or wise saying.

oli. Chant that is not accompanied by a dance.

one hānau. Birth sands, figuratively refers to one's birthplace or homeland.

'ōpio. Young person, generally adolescent or preadolescent.

'opihi. A general term for limpets.

pa'a. Firm, solid, fixed, secure, steadfast, durable.

paio. To quarrel, argue, fight, or engage in battle.

palapala. Document of any kind.

papa. (1) Class, grade, or level. (2) A flat surface, such as a plain, reef, board, or floor.

piko. Navel; summit; crown of head; a common kalo of many varieties, also a part of the kalo plant where the stem and leaf blade meet.

pilina. Relationship; connection.

pō. Night, darkness, obscurity.

po'e. People; assembly or group of something.

pōhaku. Stone.

pono. Balance, equity, goodness, wellness, morality, excellence, integrity, justice, rights, correct or proper procedure; that which is necessary or needed.

po'o. Head; summit; director or head of an organization, such as a po'o kumu (principal).

pū. Large triton conch or helmet shell, *Charonia tritonis*, known for its characteristic sound that is often used to call people together or mark an event; to share food together; also refers to a cluster of several stalks, as of bananas or pandanus, or a topknot, as of rope or hair.

pu'epu'e. Hill or mound; to hill or mound up.

pule. Prayer.

puʻuhonua. Place of refuge, sanctuary, or asylum.

wā. Period of time, era, season, epoch, age.

waʻa. Canoe.

wahine (wāhine, plural form). Woman; female, feminine.

wai. Fresh water; liquid of any kind other than sea water, including juice, sap, and liquids discharged from the body; to flow like water, fluid.

Bibliography

Aikau, Hokulani. *A Chosen People, a Promised Land: Mormonism and Race in Hawai'i*. Minneapolis: University of Minnesota Press, 2012.

———. "Indigeneity in the Diaspora: The Case of Native Hawaiians at Iosepa, Utah." *American Quarterly* 62, no. 3 (2010): 477–501.

Akindes, Fay Yokomizo. "Sudden Rush: Nā Mele Pāleoleo (Hawaiian Rap) as Liberatory Discourse." *Discourse* 23, no. 1 (2001): 82–98.

Alfred, Taiaiake. *Peace, Power, Righteousness: An Indigenous Manifesto*. Ontario: Oxford University Press, 1999.

———. "Warrior Scholarship: Seeing the University as a Ground of Contention." In *Indigenizing the Academy: Transforming Scholarship and Empowering Communities*, edited by Devon Abbott Mihesuah and Angela Cavender Wilson, 88–99. Lincoln, Neb.: Bison Books, 2004.

———. *Wasáse: Indigenous Pathways of Action and Freedom*. Toronto: Broadview Press, 2005.

Allen, Helena G. *The Betrayal of Liliuokalani: Last Queen of Hawaii, 1838–1917*. Honolulu: Mutual Publishing, 1982.

American Friends Service Committee, Hawai'i Area Office. *He Alo ā He Alo: Face to Face*. Honolulu: American Friends Service Committee, Hawai'i Area Office, 1993.

Andrade, Carlos. *Hā'ena: Through the Eyes of the Ancestors*. Honolulu: University of Hawai'i Press, 2008.

Arista, Denise Noelani. "Davida Malo, ke Kanaka o ka Huliau." Master's thesis, University of Hawai'i at Mānoa, 1998.

Barker, Adam. "The Contemporary Reality of Canadian Imperialism: Settler Colonialism and the Hybrid Colonial State." *American Indian Quarterly* 33, no. 3 (2009): 325–51.

Barnhardt, Ray, and Angayuqaq Oscar Kawagley. "Indigenous Knowledge Systems and Alaska Native Ways of Knowing." *Anthropology and Education Quarterly* 36, no. 1 (2005): 8–23.

Basham, Leilani. "Awaiaulu ke Aloha: The Ties that Bind Hawaiian Gender, Sexuality and Marriage." Paper presented at the University of Illinois, Urbana-Champaign, 2009.

———. "I Mau ke Ea o ka 'āina i ka Pono: He Puke Mele Lāhui no ka Lāhui Hawai'i." PhD diss., University of Hawai'i at Manoa, 2007.

———. "Ka Lāhui Hawai'i: He Mo'olelo, he 'āina, he Loina, a he Ea Kākou." *Hūlili: Multidisciplinary Research on Hawaiian Well-Being* 6 (2010): 37–72.

———. "Mele Lāhui: The Importance of Pono in Hawaiian Poetry." *Te Kaharoa* 1 (n.d.): 152–64.

Beamer, B. Kamanamaikalani. "Na Wai ka Mana?: 'Ōiwi Agency and European Imperialism in the Hawaiian Kingdom." PhD diss., University of Hawai'i, 2008.

Beaulieu, David. "Native American Education Research and Policy Development in an Era of No Child Left Behind: Native Language and Culture during the Administrations of Presidents Clinton and Bush." *Journal of American Indian Education* 47, no. 1 (2008): 10–45.

Beaulieu, David, Lilian Sparks, and Marisa Alonzo. *Preliminary Report on No Child Left Behind in Indian Country.* Washington, D.C.: National Indian Education Association, 2005.

Beckwith, Martha W. *Hawaiian Mythology.* Honolulu: University of Hawai'i Press, 1977.

———. ed. *The Kumulipo: A Hawaiian Creation Chant.* Honolulu: University of Hawai'i Press, 1981.

Benham, Maenette K. P., and Ronald H. Heck. *Culture and Educational Policy in Hawai'i: The Silencing of Native Voices.* Mahwah, N.J.: L. Erlbaum Associates, 1998.

Beniamina, Jean Ilei Keale. "Tēnā: A Learning Lifestyle." *Hūlili: Multidisciplinary Research on Hawaiian Well-Being* 6 (2010): 9–23.

Bennett, Christine I., Lynn M. McWhorter, and John A. Kuykendall. "Will I Ever Teach? Latino and African American Students' Perspectives on PRAXIS I." *American Educational Research Journal* 43, no. 3 (2006): 531–75.

Bevir, Mark, and R. A. W. Rhodes. *Interpreting British Governance.* New York: Routledge, 2003.

Beyer, Carl Kalani. "The Connection of Samuel Chapman Armstrong as Both Borrower and Architect of Education in Hawai'i." *History of Education Quarterly* 47, no. 1 (2007): 23–48.

———. "Female Seminaries in America and Hawaii during the 19th Century." *Hawaiian Journal of History* 37 (2003): 91–118.

Blaich, Mehana. "Mai Uka a i Kai: From the Mountains to the Sea, 'āina-Based Education in the Ahupua'a of Waipā." Master's thesis, University of Hawai'i at Mānoa, 2003.

Blaisdell, Kekuni. "Kanaka Maoli Self-Determination and Reinscription of

Ka Pae'āina (Hawai'i) on the U.N. list of Non-self-governing Territories." *In Motion Magazine*, November 22, 1998. http://www.inmotionmagazine. com/ngo2.html.

———. "The Indigenous Rights Movement in the Pacific." *In Motion Magazine*, May 25, 1998. http://www.inmotionmagazine.com/pacific.html.

Blount, James. *Foreign Relations of the United States, 1894: Affairs in Hawai'i.* Report of the Commissioner to the Hawaiian Islands to the 53rd Congress of the United States. Washington, D.C.: United States Government Printing Office, 1895. http://libweb.hawaii.edu/digicoll/annexation/ blount/br0443.html.

Booz, Allen and Hamilton. *The Kamehameha Schools Planning Survey Prepared for the Trustees of the Bernice P. Bishop Estate.* Honolulu: Kamehameha Schools/Bernice Pauahi Bishop Estate, 1961.

Buchanan, Nina K., and Robert A. Fox. "Back to the Future: Ethnocentric Charter Schools in Hawai'i." In *The Emancipatory Promise of Charter Schools*, edited by Rofes and Stulber, 77–106. Albany: State University of New York Press, 2004.

———. "To Learn and Belong: Case Studies of Emerging Ethnocentric Charter Schools in Hawai'i." *Education Policy Analysis Archives* 11, no. 8 (2003): 1–23.

Budde, Ray. *Education by Charter: Restructuring School Districts. Key to Long-Term Continuing Improvement in American Education.* Andover, Mass.: Regional Laboratory for Educational Improvement of the Northeast and Islands, 1988.

Byrd, Jodi A. *The Transit of Empire: Indigenous Critiques of Colonialism.* Minneapolis: University of Minnesota Press, 2011.

Cajete, Gregory. *Look to the Mountain: An Ecology of Indigenous Education.* 1st ed. Skyland: Kivaki Press, 1994.

Chapin, Helen Geracimos. *Shaping History: The Role of Newspapers in Hawai'i.* Honolulu: University of Hawai'i Press, 1996.

Chapman, Thandeka. "Interrogating Classroom Relationships and Events: Using Portraiture and Critical Race Theory in Education Research." *Educational Researcher* 36, no. 3 (2007): 156–62.

Charlot, John. *Classical Hawaiian Education: Generations of Hawaiian Culture.* Lā'ie, Hawai'i: The Pacific Institute, Brigham Young University–Hawai'i, 2005.

Cho, John J., Roy A. Yamakawa, and James Hollyer. *Hawaiian Kalo, Past and Future.* Honolulu: College of Tropical Agriculture and Human Resources, University of Hawai'i at Mānoa, 2007.

Chock, Shari Kapua, Lei Freed, Ka'apuni Asaivao, and Kaleiali'i Baldwin.

"Seventh Generation." On *Mana Maoli: The Seventh Generation*. CD. Hono-lulu: Hālau Kū Māna and Native Sounds of Da Underground, 2003.

Clifford, James. "Indigenous Articulations." *The Contemporary Pacific* 13, no. 2 (2001): 467–90.

———. *Routes: Travel and Translation in the Late Twentieth Century*. Cambridge: Harvard University Press, 1997.

Coiro, Julie, Michele Knobel, Colin Lankshear, and Donald Leu, eds. *Handbook of Research on New Literacies*. New York: Routledge, 2008.

Colectivo Situaciones. "On the Researcher-Militant." In *Utopian Pedagogy: Radical Experiments against Neoliberal Globalization*, edited by Mark Cote, Richard F. Day, and Greig de Peuter, 186–200. Toronto: University of Toronto Press, 2007.

Cooper, George, and Gavan Daws. *Land and Power in Hawaii: The Democratic Years*. Honolulu: University of Hawai'i Press, 1990.

Corntassel, Jeff. "Toward Sustainable Self-Determination: Rethinking the Contemporary Indigenous-Rights Discourse." *Alternatives: Global, Local, Political* 33 (2008): 105–32.

———. "Who Is Indigenous?: 'Peoplehood' and Ethnonationalist Approaches to Rearticulating Indigenous Identity." *Nationalism and Ethnic Politics* 9, no. 1 (2003): 75–100.

Coulthard, Glen S. "Subjects of Empire: Indigenous Peoples and the 'Politics of Recognition' in Canada." *Contemporary Political Theory* 6, no. 4 (2007): 437–60.

Daws, Gavan. *Shoal of Time: A History of the Hawaiian Islands*. Honolulu: University of Hawai'i Press, 1974.

Dehyle, Donna, and Karen Swisher. "Research in American Indian and Alaska Native Education: From Assimilation to Self-Determination." *Review of Research in Education* 22 (1997): 113–94.

Deloria, Vine, and Daniel R. Wildcat. *Power and Place: Indian Education in America*. Golden, Colo.: American Indian Graduate Center and Fulcrum Resources, 2001.

Demmert, William. "What Is Culture-Based Education? Understanding Pedagogy and Curriculum." In *Honoring Our Heritage: Culturally Appropriate Approaches to Indigenous Education*, edited by Jon Reyhner, Willard Sakiestewa Gilbert, and Louise Lockard, 1–9. Flagstaff: Northern Arizona University, 2011.

De Silva, Kahikina. "Ka'ala, Molale i ka Mālie: The Staying Power of Love and Poetry." Colloquium presentation presented at the Reclaiming CELANEN: Land, Water, and Governance, University of Hawai'i at Mānoa, October 28, 2011.

Desmond, Jane. *Staging Tourism: Bodies on Display from Waikiki to Sea World.* Chicago: University of Chicago Press, 1999.

Diaz, Vicente M. *Repositioning the Missionary: Rewriting the Histories of Colonialism, Native Catholicism, and Indigeneity in Guam.* Honolulu: University of Hawaiʻi Press / Center for Pacific Islands Studies, 2010.

Diaz, Vicente M., and J. Kehaulani Kauanui. "Native Pacific Cultural Studies on the Edge." *The Contemporary Pacific* 13, no. 2 (2001): 315–42.

Dingerson, Leigh, Barbara Miner, Bob Peterson, and Stephanie Walters, eds. *Keeping the Promise? The Debate over Charter Schools.* Milwaukee, Wis.: Rethinking Schools, 2008.

Driskill, Qwo-Li, Chris Finley, Brian Joseph Gilley, and Scott Lauria Morgensen, eds. *Queer Indigenous Studies: Critical Interventions in Theory, Politics, and Literature.* Tucson: University of Arizona Press, 2011.

Dudley, Michael Kioni, and Keoni Kealoha Agard. *A Call for Hawaiian Sovereignty.* Honolulu: Nā Kāne O Ka Malo Press, 1993.

Erbes, Kristen M. "School/Community-Based Management: Discursive Politics in Practice." PhD diss., University of Hawaiʻi at Mānoa, 2003.

Ferguson, Kathy E., and Phyllis Turnbull. *Oh, Say, Can You See? The Semiotics of the Military in Hawaiʻi.* Minneapolis: University of Minnesota Press, 1999.

Fine, Michelle, ed. *Chartering Urban School Reform: Reflections of Public High Schools in the Midst of Change.* New York: Teachers College Press, 1994.

Finley, Chris. "Decolonizing the Queer Native Body (and Recovering the Native Bull-Dyke): Bringing 'Sexy Back' and out of the Native Studies' Closet." In *Queer Indigenous Studies*, edited by Driskill et al., 31–42. Tucson: University of Arizona Press, 2011.

Finney, Ben R. *Sailing in the Wake of the Ancestors: Reviving Polynesian Voyaging.* Honolulu: Bishop Museum Press, 2004.

———. *Voyage of Rediscovery: A Cultural Odyssey through Polynesia.* Berkeley: University of California Press, 1994.

Forman, James, Jr. "The Secret History of School Choice: How Progressives Got There First." *Georgetown Law Journal* 93 (2005): 1287–319.

Freire, Paulo. *Pedagogy of the Oppressed.* 30th ed. New York: Continuum International Publishing Group, 2000.

Friedman, Jonathan. "From Roots to Routes: Tropes for Trippers." *Anthropological Theory* 2, no. 1 (2002): 21–36.

Fujikane, Candace. "Introduction: Asian Settler Colonialism in the U.S. Colony of Hawaiʻi." In *Asian Settler Colonialism*, edited by Fujikane and Okamura, 1–42. Honolulu: University of Hawaiʻi Press, 2008.

Fujikane, Candace, and Jonathan Y. Okamura, eds. *Asian Settler Colonialism:*

From Local Governance to the Habits of Everyday Life in Hawai'i. Honolulu: University of Hawai'i Press, 2008.

Fuller, Bruce, ed. *Inside Charter Schools: The Paradox of Radical Decentralization*. Cambridge: Harvard University Press, 2002.

Gegeo, David Welchman, and Karen Ann Watson-Gegeo. "'How We Know': Kwara'ae Rural Villagers Doing Indigenous Epistemology." *Contemporary Pacific* 13, no. 1 (2001): 55–88.

———. "Whose Knowledge? Epistemological Collisions in Solomon Islands Community Development." *Contemporary Pacific* 14, no. 2 (2002): 377–409.

Goldstein, Aloysha. "Where the Nation Takes Place: Proprietary Regimes, Antistatism, and U.S. Settler Colonialism." *South Atlantic Quarterly* 107, no. 4 (2008): 833–61.

Goodyear-Ka'ōpua, Noelani. "Rebuilding the 'Auwai: Connecting Ecology, Economy and Education in Hawaiian Schools." *AlterNative: An International Journal of Indigenous Peoples* 5, no. 2 (2009): 46–77.

Goodyear-Ka'ōpua, Noelani, Willy Kauai, Kaleilehua Maioho, and 'Īmaikalani Winchester. "Teaching amid U.S. Occupation: Sovereignty, Survival and Social Studies in a Native Hawaiian Charter School." *Hūlili: Multidisciplinary Research on Hawaiian Well-Being* 5 (2008): 155–201.

Gramsci, Antonio. *Selections from the Prison Notebooks*. New York: International Publishers, 1971.

Grande, Sandy. *Red Pedagogy: Native American Social and Political Thought*. Lanham, Md.: Rowman & Littlefield, 2004.

Gutmanis, June. *Na Pule Kahiko: Ancient Hawaiian Prayers*. Honolulu: Editions Limited, 1983.

Hālau Kū Māna New Century Public Charter School. *End-of-the-Year Self-Evaluation Report 2002–03, Submitted to the Hawai'i Charter School Administration Office*. Honolulu: Hālau Kū Māna New Century Public Charter School, 2003.

———. *End-of-the-Year Self-Evaluation Report 2005–06, Submitted to the Hawai'i Charter School Administration Office*. Honolulu: Hālau Kū Māna New Century Public Charter School, 2006.

———. *End-of-the-Year Self-Evaluation Report 2006–07, Submitted to the Hawai'i Charter School Administration Office*. Honolulu: Hālau Kū Māna New Century Public Charter School, 2007.

———. *End-of-the-Year Self-Evaluation Report 2008–09, Submitted to the Hawai'i Charter School Administration Office*. Honolulu: Hālau Kū Māna New Century Public Charter School, 2009.

———. *Hālau Kū Māna, a New Century Public Charter School, Federal Subgrant Application*. 1999.

Hale, Charles R., ed. *Engaging Contradictions: Theory, Politics, and Methods of Activist Scholarship.* Berkeley: University of California Press, 2008.

Hall, Lisa Kahaleole. "Strategies of Erasure: U.S. Colonialism and Native Hawaiian Feminism." *American Quarterly* 60, no. 2 (2008): 273–80.

Hall, Stuart. "Gramsci's Relevance for the Study of Race and Ethnicity." *Journal of Communication Inquiry* 10, no. 2 (1986): 5–27.

Halualani, Rona Tamiko. *In the Name of Hawaiians: Native Identities and Cultural Politics.* Minneapolis: University of Minnesota Press, 2002.

Handy, E. S. Craighill, and Mary Kawena Pukui. *The Polynesian Family System in Ka'ū, Hawai'i.* Honolulu: Mutual Publishing, 1998.

Harrison, Barbara, and Rahui Papa. "The Development of an Indigenous Knowledge Program in a New Zealand Maori-Language Immersion School." *Anthropology and Education Quarterly* 36, no. 1 (2005): 57–72.

Hau'ofa, Epeli. "Our Sea of Islands." In *A New Oceania: Rediscovering Our Sea of Islands,* edited by Eric Waddell, Vijay Naidu, and Epeli Hau'ofa, 2–16. Suva, Fiji: School of Social and Economic Development / University of the South Pacific, 1993.

Hawaiian Kingdom. *Biennial Report of the President of the Board of Education to the Hawaiian Legislature of 1864. Report of Mataio Kekuanaoa.* Honolulu, 1864.

———. *Biennial Report of the President of the Board of Education to the Hawaiian Legislature of 1866. Report of Mataio Kekuanaoa.* Honolulu, 1866.

———. *Biennial Report of the President of the Board of Education to the Legislature of 1874.* Honolulu, 1874.

———. *Biennial Report of the President of the Board of Education to the Legislature of 1878. Report of Charles R. Bishop.* Honolulu, 1878.

———. *Biennial Report of the President of the Board of Education to the Legislature of 1884. Report of Walter Murray Gibson.* Honolulu, 1884.

———. *Report of the Minister of Public Instruction Read before the King to the Hawaiian Legislature. Report of Richard Armstrong.* Honolulu, 1852.

Hawaiian Mission Children's Society. *Missionary Album: Portraits and Biographical Sketches of the American Protestant Missionaries to the Hawaiian Islands.* Honolulu: Hawaiian Mission Children's Society, 1969.

Henze, Rosemary, and Lauren Vanett. "To Walk in Two Worlds: Or More? Challenging a Common Metaphor of Native Education." *Anthropology and Education Quarterly* 24, no. 2 (1993): 116–34.

Hermes, Mary. "Complicating Discontinuity: What about Poverty?" *Curriculum Inquiry* 35, no. 1 (2005): 9–26.

———. "'Ma'iingan Is Just a Misspelling of the Word Wolf': A Case for Teaching Culture through Language." *Anthropology and Education Quarterly* 36, no. 1 (2005): 43–56.

———. "The Scientific Method, Nintendo, and Eagle Feathers: Rethinking the Meaning of 'Culture-Based' Curriculum at an Ojibwe Tribal School." *Qualitative Studies in Education* 13, no. 4 (2000): 387–400.

Hess, Frederick, and Juliet Squire. "'Diverse Providers' in Action: School Restructuring in Hawaii." Working paper, AEI Future of American Education Project, American Enterprise Institute, 2009.

Hogan, Maureen, and Caitlin Winebarger. "Decolonizing Education in Alaska: Animating the Praxis I Test as a Site of Cognitive Imperialism in Neoliberal Times." Washington, D.C.: AERA Online Paper Repository, 2011. www.aera.net.

Holm, Tom, J. Diane Pearson, and Ben Chavis. "Peoplehood: A Model for the Extension of Sovereignty in American Indian Studies." *Wicazo Sa Review* 18, no. 1 (2003): 7–24.

hooks, bell. *Teaching to Transgress: Education as the Practice of Freedom.* New York: Routledge, 1994.

Hoʻomanawanui, Kuʻualoha. "He Lei Hoʻoheno no nā Kau a Kau: Language, Performance and Form in Hawaiian Poetry." *Contemporary Pacific* 17, no. 1 (2005): 29–81.

———. "'Ike ʻāina: Native Hawaiian Culturally Based Indigenous Literacy." *Hūlili: Multidisciplinary Research on Hawaiian Well-Being* 5 (2008): 203–44.

Hoʻomanawanui, Sherilyn Kuʻualoha. "Pele's Appeal: Moʻolelo, Kaona and Hulihia in 'Pele and Hiʻiaka' literature (1860–1928)." PhD diss., University of Hawaiʻi at Mānoa, 2007.

Horton, Myles, and Paulo Freire. *We Make the Road by Walking: Conversations on Education and Social Change.* Philadelphia: Temple University Press, 1990.

Imada, Adria. "Hawaiians on Tour: Hula Circuits through the American Empire." *American Quarterly* 56, no. 1 (2004): 111–49.

International Reading Association. "New Literacies and 21st-Century Technologies: A Position Statement of the International Reading Association." May 2009. http://www.reading.org/Libraries/Position_Statements_and_Resolutions/ps1067_NewLiteracies21stCentury.sflb.ashx.

Ishibashi, Koren. *Hawaiian Population Update.* Policy Analysis and System Evaluation Report. Honolulu: Kamehameha Schools, 2004.

Jokiel, Paul. "Jokiel's Illustrated Scientific Guide to Kaneʻohe Bay, Oʻahu." Hawaiʻi Coral Reef Assessment and Monitoring Program, Hawaiʻi Institute of Marine Biology, n.d. http://cramp.wcc.hawaii.edu/Downloads/Publications/OD_JOKIELs_Scientific_Guide_to_K-Bay.pdf.

Jung, Moon-Kie. *Reworking Race: The Making of Hawaii's Interracial Labor Movement.* New York: Columbia University Press, 2006.

Justice, Daniel Heath, Mark Rifkin, and Bethany Schneider. "Introduction to Special Issue on Sexuality, Nationality, Indigeneity." *GLQ: A Journal of Lesbian and Gay Studies* 16, nos. 1–2 (January 2010): 5–39.

Kahakalau, Kū. "Kanu o ka ʻāina—Natives of the Land from Generations Back: A Pedagogy of Hawaiian Liberation." PhD diss., Union Institute, 2003.

Kahn, Richard. *Critical Pedagogy, Ecoliteracy, and Planetary Crisis: The Ecopedagogy Movement.* Studies in the Postmodern Theory of Education. New York: Peter Lang, 2009.

Kaiama, Manu. "Kū i ka Pono Movement." In *Ea: Hawaiian Movements for Life, Land and Sovereignty,* edited by Noelani Goodyear-Kaʻōpua, Ikaika Hussey, and Kahunawai Wright. Durham, N.C.: Duke University Press, forthcoming.

Kajihiro, Kyle. "The Militarizing of Hawaiʻi: Occupation, Accommodation, and Resistance." In *Asian Settler Colonialism,* edited by Fujikane and Okamura, 171–94. Honolulu: University of Hawaiʻi Press, 2008.

Kalyan, Rohan. "Hip-Hop Imaginaries: A Genealogy of the Present." *Journal for Cultural Research* 10, no. 3 (2006): 237–57.

Kamahele, Momiala. "ʻĪlioʻulaokalani: Defending Native Hawaiian Culture." In *Asian Settler Colonialism,* edited by Fujikane and Okamura, 76–98. Honolulu: University of Hawaiʻi Press, 2008.

Kamakau, Samuel Manaiakalani. *Ka Poʻe Kahiko: The People of Old.* Translated by Mary Kawena Pukui. Honolulu: Bishop Museum Press, 1991.

———. *Ruling Chiefs of Hawaii.* Rev. ed. Honolulu: Kamehameha Schools Press, 1992.

Kameʻeleihiwa, Lilikalā. *Native Land and Foreign Desires: Pehea Lā E Pono Ai?* Honolulu: Bishop Museum Press, 1992.

———. *Nā Wāhine Kapu: Divine Hawaiian Women.* Honolulu: ʻAi Pōhaku Press, 1999.

Kamehameha Schools. *Native Hawaiian Educational Assessment Project Report.* Honolulu: Kamehameha Schools Bishop Estate, 1983.

———. *Native Hawaiian Educational Assessment Update 2009: A Supplement to Ka Huakaʻi 2005.* Honolulu: Kamehameha Schools Research and Evaluation Division, 2009.

Kanahele, George S. *Pauahi: The Kamehameha Legacy.* 1st ed. Honolulu: Kamehameha Schools Press, 1986.

Kanahele, Pualani, Huihui Kanahele-Mossman, Ann Kalei Nuʻuhiwa, and Kaumakaiwapoʻohalahiʻipaka Kealiʻikanakaʻole. *Kūkulu ke Ea a Kanaloa: The Culture Plan for Kanaloa Kahoʻolawe.* Kahoʻolawe Island Reserve Commission, February 1, 2009. http://kahoolawe.hawaii.gov/downloads/ Kukulu%20Ke%20Ea%20A%20Kanaloa.pdf.

Kanaʻiaupuni, Shawn. *A Brief Overview of Culture-Based Education and*

Annotated Bibliography. Culture in Education Brief Series. Honolulu: Kamehameha Schools Research and Evaluation Division, 2007.

———. "Ka'akālai Kū Kanaka: A Call for Strengths-Based Approaches from a Native Hawaiian Perspective." *Educational Researcher* 34, no. 5 (2005): 32–38.

Kana'iaupuni, Shawn, and Koren Ishibashi. *Hawai'i Charter Schools: Initial Trends and Select Outcomes for Native Hawaiian Students.* Honolulu: Kamehameha Schools Policy Analysis and System Evaluation, 2005.

———. *Left Behind? The Status of Hawaiian Students in the Hawai'i Public Schools.* Policy Analysis and System Evaluation Report. Honolulu: Kamehameha Schools, 2003.

Kana'iaupuni, Shawn, Brandon Ledward, and 'Umi Jensen. *Culture-Based Education and Its Relationship to Student Outcomes.* Honolulu: Kamehameha Schools Research and Evaluation Division, 2010.

Kana'iaupuni, Shawn, Nolan Malone, and Koren Ishibashi. *Ka Huaka'i: 2005 Native Hawaiian Educational Assessment.* Honolulu: Pauahi Publications / Kamehameha Schools, 2005.

Kaomea, Julie. "Contemplating Kuleana: Reflections on the Rights and Responsibilities of Non-Indigenous Participants." *AlterNative: An International Journal of Indigenous Peoples* 5, no. 2 (2009): 78–99.

———. "A Curriculum of Aloha? Colonialism and Tourism in Hawai'i's Elementary Textbooks." *Curriculum Inquiry* 30, no. 3 (Fall 2000): 319–44.

———. "Indigenous Studies in the Elementary Curriculum: A Cautionary Hawaiian Example." *Anthropology and Education Quarterly* 36, no. 1 (2005): 24–42.

———. "Reading Erasures and Making the Familiar Strange: Defamiliarizing Methods for Research in Formerly Colonized and Historically Oppressed Communities." *Educational Researcher* 32, no. 2 (March 2003): 14–25.

Kapepa, Stanley. *A Canoe for Uncle Kila: No Kila ka Wa'a Kaulua.* Honolulu: Polynesian Voyaging Society, 1976.

Kauanui, J. Kēhaulani. "Colonialism in Equality: Hawaiian Sovereignty and the Question of U.S. Civil Rights." *South Atlantic Quarterly* 107, no. 4 (2008): 635–50.

———. *Hawaiian Blood: Colonialism and the Politics of Sovereignty and Indigeneity.* Durham, N.C.: Duke University Press, 2008.

———. "Precarious Positions: Native Hawaiians and U.S. Federal Recognition." *Contemporary Pacific* 17, no. 1 (2005): 1–27.

Kawagley, Angayuqaq Oscar, and Ray Barnhardt. "Education Indigenous to Place: Western Science Meets Native Reality." Alaska Native Knowledge Network, 1998. http://www.ankn.uaf.edu/curriculum/Articles/BarnhardtKawagley/EIP.html.

Kawaiʻaeʻa, Keiki K.C., Alohalani K. Housman, and Makalapua Alencastre. "Pūā i ka ʻŌlelo, Ola kaʻOhana: Three Generations of Hawaiian Language Revitalization." *Hūlili: Multidisciplinary Research on Hawaiian Well-Being* 4, no. 1 (2007): 183–237.

Keahiolalo-Karasuda, RaeDeen. "A Genealogy of Punishment in Hawaiʻi: The Public Hanging of Chief Kamanawa II." *Hūlili: Multidisciplinary Research on Hawaiian Well-Being* 6 (2010): 147–67.

Kelly, Marion. "Dynamics of Production Intensification in Precontact Hawaii." In *What's New? A Closer Look at the Process of Innovation*, edited by Sander Ernst van derLeeuw and Robin Torrence, 82–105. London: Unwin Hyman, 1989.

Kent, Harold Winfield. *Charles Reed Bishop, Man of Hawaii*. Palo Alto, Calif.: Pacific Books, 1965.

King, Thomas. *The Truth about Stories: A Native Narrative*. Toronto: House of Anansi Press, 2003.

Kirch, Patrick V., and Sharyn Jones O'Day. "New Archaeological Insights into Food and Status: A Case Study from Pre-contact Hawaii." *World Archaeology* 34, no. 3 (2003): 484–97.

Kirch, Patrick Vinton. *Feathered Gods and Fishhooks: An Introduction to Hawaiian Archaeology and Prehistory*. Honolulu: University of Hawaiʻi Press, 1997.

Koki, Stan. *School/Community-Based Management Revisited in the Pacific*. PREL Briefing Paper. Honolulu: Pacific Resources for Education and Learning, 1998.

Kolderie, Ted. "Ray Budde and the Origins of the 'Charter Concept.'" Education Evolving, June 2005. www.educationevolving.org/pdf/Ray_Budde.pdf.

Kroeber, Karl. "Why It's a Good Thing Gerald Vizenor Is Not an Indian." In *Survivance*, edited by Vizenor, 25–38. Lincoln: University of Nebraska Press, 2008.

Kupaʻāina. *Simple Island People*. CD. Honolulu: Kototama Productions, 2004. http://www.cdbaby.com/cd/kupaaina.

Kuykendall, Ralph S. *The Hawaiian Kingdom, 1778–1854: Foundation and Transformation*. Vol. 1. Honolulu: University of Hawaiʻi Press, 1953.

———. *The Hawaiian Kingdom, 1854–1874: Twenty Critical Years*. Vol. 2. Honolulu: University of Hawaiʻi Press, 1953.

———. *The Hawaiian Kingdom, 1874—1893: The Kalakaua Dynasty*. Vol. 3. Honolulu: University of Hawaiʻi Press, 1967.

Kyselka, Will. *An Ocean in Mind*. Honolulu: University of Hawaiʻi Press, 1987.

Ladefoged, Thegn N., Patrick V. Kirch, Samuel M. Gon III, Oliver A. Chadwick, Anthony S. Hartshorn, and Peter M. Vitousek. "Opportunities and Constraints for Intensive Agriculture in the Hawaiian Archipelago Prior to European Contact." *Journal of Archaeological Science* 36, no. 10 (2009): 2374–83.

Lai, Morris, and Susan Saka. *Hawaiian Students Compared with Non-Hawaiian Students on the 1997, 1999, 2001, 2003, 2005 and 2007 Hawai'i Youth Risk Behavior Surveys.* Hawaii Youth Risk Behavior Survey. Honolulu: Hawai'i State Departments of Education and Health, 2007. http://www.ksbe.edu/spi/PDFS/Reports/Demography_Well-being/yrbs.

Lawrence, Charles R., III. "The Word and the River: Pedagogy as Scholarship as Struggle." *Southern California Law Review* 65 (1992): 2231–98.

Lawrence-Lightfoot, Sara. *The Good High School: Portraits of Character and Culture.* New York: Basic Books, 1985.

Lawrence-Lightfoot, Sara, and Jessica Hoffmann Davis. *The Art and Science of Portraiture.* San Francisco: Jossey-Bass, 2002.

Lee, Edgy, and Saul Landau. *Papakōlea: A Story of Hawaiian Land.* DVD. Institute for Cinema Studies, 1993.

Leonardo, Zeus. *Race, Whiteness, and Education.* New York: Routledge, 2009.

Lindo, Cecilia Kapua. *A Resource Curriculum Guide on Polynesian Voyaging.* Honolulu: Polynesian Voyaging Society, 1977.

Lindo, Cecilia Kapua, and Nancy Alpert Mower. *Polynesian Seafaring Heritage.* Honolulu: Kamehameha Schools / Polynesian Voyaging Society, 1980.

Lipka, Jerry. "Schooling for Self-Determination: Research on the Effects of Including Native Language and Culture in the Schools." *ERIC Clearinghouse on Rural Education and Small Schools* (2002). http://www.ericdigests.org/2002-3/effects.htm.

Lomawaima, K. Tsianina. "American Indian Education: By Indians Versus for Indians." In *A Companion to American Indian History,* edited by Philip J. Deloria and Neal Salisbury, 422–40. Malden, Mass.: Blackwell Publishing, 2004.

———. *They Called It Prairie Light: The Story of Chilocco Indian School.* Lincoln: University of Nebraska Press, 1994.

Lomawaima, K. Tsianina, and Teresa L. McCarty. *To Remain an Indian: Lessons in Democracy from a Century of Native American Education.* New York: Teachers College Press, 2006.

Lubienski, Christopher A., and Peter C. Weitzel, eds. *The Charter School Experiment: Expectations, Evidence, and Implications.* Cambridge: Harvard Education Press, 2010.

Lucas, Paul F. Nahoa. *Dictionary of Hawaiian Legal Land-Terms.* Honolulu: Native Hawaiian Legal Corporation / University of Hawai'i Press, 1995.
———. "E Ola Mau Kākou i ka 'Ōlelo Makuahine: Hawaiian Language Policy and the Courts." *Hawaiian Journal of History* 34 (2000): 1–28.
Luke, Allan. *The Social Construction of Literacy in the Primary School.* South Melbourne: Palgrave Macmillan Australia, 1994.
Luke, Allan, Radha Iyer, and Catherine Doherty. "Literacy Education in the Context of Globalisation." In *Handbook of Research on Teaching of English Language Arts,* edited by Diane Lapp and Douglas Fisher, 104–10. New York: Routledge, 2010.
Maaka, Roger, and Augie Fleras. "Indigeneity at the Edge: Towards a Constructive Engagement." In *The Indigenous Experience: Global Perspectives,* edited by Roger Maaka and Chris Andersen, 337–60. Toronto: Canadian Scholars' Press, 2006.
Martínez, Miguel Alfonso. "Human Rights of Indigenous Peoples: Study on Treaties, Agreements and Other Constructive Arrangements Between States and Indigenous Populations." United Nations Commission on Human Rights, 1999. http://www.unhchr.ch/huridocda/huridoca.nsf/0/696c51cf6f20b8bc802567c4003793ec?opendocument.
McCarty, Teresa L. "American Indian, Alaska Native and Native Hawaiian Education in the Era of Standardization and NCLB: An Introduction." *Journal of American Indian Education* 47, no. 1 (2008): 1–9.
McClintock, Anne. "'No Longer in a Future Heaven': Gender, Race and Nationalism." In *Dangerous Liaisons: Gender, Nation, and Postcolonial Perspectives,* 89–112. Minneapolis: University of Minnesota Press, 1997.
McGregor, Davianna. *Nā Kua'āina: Living Hawaiian Culture.* Honolulu: University of Hawai'i Press, 2007.
Menton, Linda K. "Christian and 'Civilized' Education: The Hawaiian Chiefs' Children's School." *History of Education Quarterly* 32, no. 2 (1992): 213–52.
Menton, Linda, and Holoua Stender. "Hōkūle'a: A Guide to Educational Resources." Curriculum Research and Development Group, University of Hawai'i at Mānoa, 1990. http://www.eric.ed.gov/ERICWebPortal/detail?accno=ED369670.
Meyer, Manulani Aluli. *Ho'oulu: Our Time of Becoming: Collected Early Writings of Manulani Meyer.* Honolulu: 'Ai Pōhaku Press, 2003.
———. "Our Own Liberation: Reflections on Hawaiian Epistemology." *Contemporary Pacific* 13, no. 1 (2001): 124–48.
Morales, Rodney. "George Helm: The Voice and Soul." In *Ho'iho'i Hou: A Tribute to George Helm & Kimo Mitchell,* 10–33. Honolulu: Bamboo Ridge Press, 1984.

———. ed. *Hoʻihoʻi Hou: A Tribute to George Helm & Kimo Mitchell*. Honolulu: Bamboo Ridge Press, 1984.

Mower, Nancy Alpert. *The Vision of Moʻikeha: Ka Moeʻuhane o Moʻikeha*. Honolulu: Polynesian Voyaging Society, 1976.

———. *The Voyage to Tahiti: Ka Huakaʻi i Kahiki*. Honolulu: Polynesian Voyaging Society, 1976.

Nakata, Bob. "The Struggles of the Waiahole-Waikane Community Association." *Social Process in Hawaiʻi* 39 (1999): 60–73.

Nā Maka o ka ʻāina. *Act of War: The Overthrow of the Hawaiian Nation*. Documentary. Nā Maka o ka ʻāina in association with Center for Hawaiian Studies, University of Hawaiʻi at Mānoa, 1993.

———. *Hui Naʻauao: A Community Education Project*. Documentary, 1992.

———. *The Tribunal: The Proceedings of Ka Hoʻokolokolonui Kanaka Maoli Peoples' International Tribunal Hawaiʻi 1993*. Documentary, 1994.

Naone, C. Kanoelani. "ʻO ka ʻāina, ka ʻŌlelo, and me ke Kaiāulu." *Hūlili: Multidisciplinary Research on Hawaiian Well-Being* 5 (2008): 315–39.

National Alliance for Public Charter Schools. "Dashboard: A Comprehensive Data Resource from the National Alliance for Public Charter Schools." Accessed August 12, 2012. http://www.publiccharters.org/dashboard/home.

Native Hawaiians Study Commission. *Native Hawaiians Study Commission: Report on the Culture, Needs and Concerns of Native Hawaiians*. Washington, D.C.: United States Department of the Interior, 1983.

Nicotera, Anna, and Todd Ziebarth. *Top 10 Charter Communities by Market Share, Fourth Annual Edition*. Washington, D.C.: National Alliance for Public Charter Schools, 2009.

Nitta, Liela. "Native Hawaiians, Freedom and Education: Kula no na Poʻe Hawaiʻi, Native Self-Determination." EdD diss., University of Hawaiʻi at Mānoa, 1996.

Okamura, Jonathan Y. *Ethnicity and Inequality in Hawaiʻi*. Philadelphia: Temple University Press, 2008.

Olivera, Katrina-Ann. "Wahi a Kahiko: Place Names as Vehicles of Ancestral Memory." *AlterNative: An International Journal of Indigenous Peoples* 5, no. 2 (2009): 100–115.

Osorio, Jonathan Kamakawiwoʻole. *Dismembering Lāhui: A History of the Hawaiian Nation to 1887*. Honolulu: University of Hawaiʻi Press, 2002.

———. " 'What Kine Hawaiian Are You?': A Moʻolelo about Nationhood, Race, History, and the Contemporary Sovereignty Movement in Hawaiʻi." *Contemporary Pacific* 13, no. 2 (2001): 359–79.

Pickens, Alex L., and David Kemble, eds. *To Teach the Children: Historical*

Aspects of Education in Hawaii. Honolulu: Bernice Pauahi Bishop Museum, 1982.

Pukui, Mary Kawena. *ʻŌlelo Noʻeau: Hawaiian Proverbs & Poetical Sayings.* Bernice P. Bishop Museum Special Publication no. 71. Honolulu: Bishop Museum Press, 1983.

Pukui, Mary Kawena, and Samuel H. Elbert. *Hawaiian Dictionary.* Revised and enlarged edition. Honolulu: University of Hawaiʻi Press, 1986.

Pukui, Mary Kawena, Samuel H. Elbert, and Esther T. Mookini. *Place Names of Hawaiʻi.* Honolulu: University of Hawaiʻi Press, 1974.

Pukui, Mary Kawena, E. W. Haertig, and Catherine A. Lee. *Nānā i ke Kumu.* Vol. 2. Honolulu: Hui Hānai / The Queen Liliʻuokalani Childrenʻs Center, 2002. First published in 1972.

Rafael, Vicente. "White Love: Surveillance and Nationalist Resistance in the U.S. Colonization of the Philippines." In *Cultures of United States Imperialism,* edited by Amy Kaplan and Donald E. Pease, 185–218. Durham, N.C.: Duke University Press, 1993.

Ravitch, Diane. "Let Your Voice Be Heard: A Q&A with Academic Historian, Diane Ravitch." *Thought & Action* 27 (2011): 111–16.

Reyhner, Jon Allan, and Jeanne M. Oyawin Eder. *American Indian Education: A History.* Norman: University of Oklahoma Press, 2006.

Rice, William Hyde. *Hawaiian Legends.* Bernice P. Bishop Museum bulletin 3. Honolulu: Bishop Museum Press, 1923.

Ritte, Walter, and Bill Freese. "Haloa." *Seedling,* October 2006.

Ritte, Walter, and Richard Sawyer. *Na Manaʻo Aloha o Kahoʻolawe: Hawaiʻi Warriors Love for Land and Culture.* Honolulu: Aloha ʻāina o na Kūpuna, 1978.

Rodriguez, Dylan. *Suspended Apocalypse: White Supremacy, Genocide, and the Filipino Condition.* Minneapolis: University of Minnesota Press, 2009.

Rofes, Eric E., and Lisa M. Stulberg, eds. *The Emancipatory Promise of Charter Schools: Toward a Progressive Politics of School Choice.* Albany: SUNY Press, 2004.

Sai, David Keanu. "American Occupation of the Hawaiian State: A Century Unchecked." *Hawaiian Journal of Law and Politics* 1 (2004): 46–81.

———. "A Slippery Path towards Hawaiian Indigeneity: An Analysis and Comparison between Hawaiian State Sovereignty and Hawaiian Indigeneity and Its Use and Practice in Hawaiʻi Today." *Journal of Law and Social Challenges* 10 (2008): 101–66.

Saranillio, Dean Itsuji. "Seeing Conquest: Colliding Histories and the Cultural Politics of Hawaiʻi Statehood." PhD diss., University of Michigan, 2009.

Schütz, Albert J. *The Voices of Eden: A History of Hawaiian Language Studies.* Honolulu: University of Hawai'i Press, 1994.

Shon, Jim. *A Charter School Story: Hawaii's Experience in Creating a Charter School System.* Honolulu: Jim Shon, 2007.

Silva, Noenoe K. *Aloha Betrayed: Native Hawaiian Resistance to American Colonialism.* Durham, N.C.: Duke University Press, 2004.

Slack, Jennifer. "The Theory and Method of Articulation in Cultural Studies." In *Stuart Hall: Critical Dialogues in Cultural Studies,* edited by Kuan-Hsing Chen and David Morley, 112–27. New York: Routledge, 1996.

Smith, Andrea. *Conquest: Sexual Violence and American Indian Genocide.* Cambridge, Mass.: South End Press, 2005.

———. "Heteropatriarchy and the Three Pillars of White Supremacy: Rethinking Women of Color Organizing." In *The Color of Violence: The INCITE! Anthology,* edited by INCITE! Women of Color against Violence, 66–73. Cambridge, Mass.: South End Press, 2006.

———. "Queer Theory and Native Studies: The Heteronormativity of Settler Colonialism." *GLQ: A Journal of Lesbian and Gay Studies* 16, nos. 1–2 (2010): 41–68.

Smith, Andrea, and J. Kēhaulani Kauanui, eds. "Native Feminisms Engage American Studies." *American Quarterly* 60, no. 2 (2008): 241–49.

Smith, Graham Hingangaroa. "Kaupapa Maori Theory: Theorizing Indigenous Transformation of Education and Schooling." Paper presented at the Kaupapa Maori Symposium, a joint conference of the New Zealand Association for Research in Education and the Australian Association for Research in Education, Auckland, New Zealand, December 2003.

Smith, Linda Tuhiwai. "Building a Research Agenda for Indigenous Epistemologies and Education." *Anthropology and Education Quarterly* 36, no. 1 (2005): 93–95.

———. *Decolonizing Methodologies: Research and Indigenous Peoples.* New York: Zed Books, 1999.

Solorzano, Daniel G., and Tara J. Yosso. "Critical Race Methodology: Counter Story-Telling as an Analytical Framework for Educational Research." *Qualitative Inquiry* 8, no. 1 (2002): 23–44.

Speed, Shannon. "Forged in Dialogue: Toward a Critically Engaged Activist Research." In *Engaging Contradictions,* edited by Hale, 213–36. Berkeley: University of California Press, 2008.

Spencer, Thomas P., ed. *Kaua Kuloko 1895.* Honolulu: Bishop Museum Press, 2000.

Sproat, D. Kapua'ala, and Isaac Moriwake. "Ke Kalo Pa'a o Waiāhole: Public Trust as a Tool for Environmental Advocacy." In *Creative Common Law*

Strategies for Protecting the Environment, edited by Clifford Rechtschaffen and Denise Antolini, 247–84. Washington, D.C.: Environmental Law Institute, 2007.

Street, Brian V. *Literacy in Theory and Practice*. Cambridge: Cambridge University Press, 1984.

Sumida, Anna Y., and Meleanna Aluli Meyer. "T4 and Culture: Pedagogy of Transformation." *Hūlili: Multidisciplinary Research on Hawaiian Well-Being* 5 (2008): 343–70.

Takayama, Brennan. "Academic Achievement across School Types in Hawai'i: Outcomes for Hawaiian and Non-Hawaiian Students in Conventional Public Schools, Western-Focused Charters, and Hawaiian Language and Culture–Based Schools." *Hūlili: Multidisciplinary Research on Hawaiian Well-Being* 5 (2008): 245–83.

Teaiwa, Teresia. "Articulated Cultures: Militarism and Masculinities in Fiji during the Mid-1990s." *Fijian Studies: A Journal of Contemporary Fiji* 3, no. 2 (2005): 201–22.

———. "Militarism, Tourism and the Native: Articulations in Oceania." PhD diss., University of California–Santa Cruz, 2001.

Tengan, Ty P. Kawika. *Native Men Remade: Gender and Nation in Contemporary Hawai'i*. Durham, N.C.: Duke University Press, 2008.

Tibbets, Katherine, Kū Kahakalau, and Zanette Johnson. "Education with Aloha and Student Assets." *Hūlili: Multidisciplinary Research on Hawaiian Well-Being* 4, no. 1 (2007): 147–81.

Trask, Haunani-Kay. *From a Native Daughter: Colonialism and Sovereignty in Hawai'i*. Rev. edition. Honolulu: University of Hawai'i Press, 1999. First published by Common Courage Press in 1992.

———. "The Birth of the Modern Hawaiian Movement: Kalama Valley, O'ahu." *Hawaiian Journal of History* 21 (1987): 126–53.

Tschumy, Ruth. *Act 51, NCLB and Options for Restructuring*. Perspectives on Act 51, Reinventing Education. Honolulu: Hawai'i Educational Policy Center, March 7, 2005.

Van Dyke, Jon M. *Who Owns the Crown Lands of Hawai'i?* Honolulu: University of Hawai'i Press, 2008.

Villegas, Malia, Sabina Rak Neugebauer, and Kerry R. Venegas, eds. *Indigenous Knowledge and Education: Sites of Struggle, Strength, and Survivance*. Cambridge: Harvard Education Press, 2008.

Vitousek, P. M., T. N. Ladefoged, P. V. Kirch, A. S. Hartshorn, M. W. Graves, S. C. Hotchkiss, S. Tuljapurkar, and O. A. Chadwick. "Soils, Agriculture, and Society in Precontact Hawaii." *Science* 304, no. 5677 (June 2004): 1665–9.

Vizenor, Gerald, ed. *Survivance: Narratives of Native Presence*. Lincoln: University of Nebraska Press, 2008.

Vogeler, Stephen Kūhiō. "'For Your Freedom and Ours': The Prolonged Occupations of Hawai'i and the Baltic States." PhD diss., University of Hawai'i at Mānoa, 2009.

Warner, Sam L. No'eau. "Kuleana: The Right, Responsibility, and Authority of Indigenous Peoples to Speak and Make Decisions for Themselves in Language and Cultural Revitalization." *Anthropology and Education Quarterly* 30, no. 1 (1999): 68–93.

Warrior, Robert Allen. *Tribal Secrets: Recovering American Indian Intellectual Traditions*. Minneapolis: University of Minnesota Press, 1995.

Watanabe, Sundy. "'Because We Do Not Know Their Way': Standardizing Practices and Peoples through Habitus, the NCLB 'Highly-Qualified' Mandate, and PRAXIS I Examinations." *Journal of American Indian Education* 47, no. 1 (2008): 118–35.

Wells, Amy Stuart, ed. *Where Charter School Policy Fails: The Problems of Accountability and Equity*. New York: Teachers College Press, 2002.

Wells, Amy Stuart, Cynthia Grutzik, Sibyll Carnochan, Julie Slayton, and Ash Vasudeva. "Underlying Policy Assumptions of Charter School Reform: The Multiple Meanings of a Movement." *Teachers College Record* 100, no. 3 (1999): 513–35.

Whitney, Leo, F. A. I. Bowers, and M. Takahashi. *Taro Varieties in Hawaii*. 1939. Reprint, Honolulu: University of Hawai'i, 1997.

Wilcox, Carol. *Sugar Water: Hawai'i's Plantation Ditches*. Honolulu: University of Hawai'i Press, 1996.

Williams-Kennedy, Denise. "Building Bridges between Literacies." In *Early Childhood Education: Society and Culture*, edited by Angela Anning, Joy Cullen, and Marilyn Fleer, 80–92. London: Sage, 2004.

Wilson, Waziyatawin Angela, and Michael Yellow Bird. *For Indigenous Eyes Only: A Decolonization Handbook*. Santa Fe, N.Mex.: School of American Research Press, 2005.

Wilson, William H., and Kauanoe Kamanā. "'For the Interest of the Hawaiians Themselves': Reclaiming the Benefits of Hawaiian-Medium Education." *Hūlili: Multidisciplinary Research on Hawaiian Well-Being* 3, no. 1 (2006): 153–81.

Winstead, Teresa, Adrea Lawrence, Edward J. Brantmeier, and Christopher J. Frey. "Language, Sovereignty, Cultural Contestation, and American Indian Schools: No Child Left Behind and a Navajo Test Case." *Journal of American Indian Education* 47, no. 1 (2008): 46–63.

Wist, Benjamin Othello. *A Century of Public Education in Hawaii, October 15, 1840–October 15, 1940.* Honolulu: Hawaii Educational Review, 1940.

Wolfe, Patrick. "Settler Colonialism and the Elimination of the Native." *Journal of Genocide Research* 8, no. 4 (2006): 387–409.

———. *Settler Colonialism and the Transformation of Anthropology: The Politics and Poetics of an Ethnographic Event.* London: Cassell, 1999.

Wong, Laiana, and Margaret Maaka. "Foreword for Ke Ala Hou: Breaking Trail in Hawaiian Research and Development." *AlterNative: An International Journal of Indigenous Peoples* 5, no. 2 (2009): 6–13.

World Indigenous Peoples' Conference on Education, Task Force. "The Coolangatta Statement on Indigenous Rights in Education." *Journal of American Indian Education* 39, no. 1 (Fall 1999): jaie.asu.edu/v39/V39I1A4.pdf.

Yosso, Tara J. "Whose Culture Has Capital? A Critical Race Theory Discussion of Community Cultural Wealth." *Race, Ethnicity and Education* 8, no. 1 (2005): 69–91.

Young, Kanalu G. Terry. *Rethinking the Native Hawaiian Past.* New York: Garland Publishing, 1998.

———. "Kuleana: Toward a Historiography of Hawaiian National Consciousness, 1780–2001." *Hawaiian Journal of Law and Politics* 2 (2006): 1–33.

Index

academics: binary between culture and, xiv, iii, ii4, i80; broadening definition of, i2; culture-based environmental education and, 27, 71

achievement gap, 9, 244

Adequate Yearly Progress (AYP), i08, i09, i2i, 24i, 242. *See also* No Child Left Behind Act of 200i

'Aha Pūnana Leo, 57. *See also* Hawaiian language: contemporary Hawaiian immersion schools

Ahuna, Dan, 22i–23

ahupua'a, 54, 66; as foundation for curriculum, i05, ii6, i28–29, i38

'Aihualama, i06, i27–29, i45, 27ini, 27in4; HKM protocols at, i30, i44; restoration of lo'i kalo at, i4i–34, i45, i56–57; as venue for 'āina-based education, i32, i46–48, i64–66

Aikau, Hokulani, 9i

'āina: xvi, 2, 42, 84, 87, iii, i23–25, i28, i29–30, i33–34, i4i, i50, i53–54, i60, i66; and food, i35, i37–39, i40; as living being, i43, i44, i48; struggles to protect against overdevelopment, 53–54, 58

'āina-based education, 5, ii, i2, 33, 39, 72, i03–7, i20, i23–25, i37, i38, i40, i4i, i44, i47, 206, 234. *See also* land-centered literacies

Akaka Bill. *See* Native Hawaiian Government Reorganization Act

Aldosa, Kalani, 205

Aldosa, Kipeni, 3

Aldosa, Lolena, 235

Alencastre, Makalapua, 57

Alfred, Taiaiake, 256n59

aloha 'āina, xvi, 5, i2, i4, 42, 47, 54–55, i20, i24–25, i44, i74, 207, 234, 244–46; as basis for non-patriarchal nationalism, 33–34; as ethical practice, 3i–39; in late nineteenth- and early twentieth-century resistance to U.S. seizure of Hawai'i, 36–37; as multiplicity of literacies, 3i–39; settler practices of, 35, i54, 275n37, 277ni2; in twentieth-century Hawaiian movements, 37–39, 48–59

Armstrong, Richard, i8, 253n30, 254n40

articulation theory, i3, 48, i57, 207

Asaivao, Ka'apuni, i

Atkins, Trevor, i30–32, i39–40, i52–54, 242–43

autochthonous, 5

'auwai, i2, i25, i27, i63–64, 207; rebuilding 'auwai irrigation systems, i28, i33–34, i4i–49, 246

Awo-Chun, Ku'uleianuhea, i70–7i

safety zones, 7–8, 11–13, 25, 29, 83, 87–91, 111, 120, 125, 205–7, 219, 223, 236, 243. *See also* logic of containment

Saranillio, Dean, 48

school choice, 12, 64–65, 81, 206, 269n16; progressive history of, 60–62

school governance, 9, 22, 59, 61–64, 66, 95–96, 108–9, 250n14

Schütz, Albert, 15

self-determination, 5, 12, 47–49, 67–69, 91–101, 119–25, 139, 206–7; educational, xi, xviii, 8, 59, 87–88, 110, 184, 205, 282n26; epistemic, 29; Hawaiian movements for, 67, 80; sustainable, 29–30, 134, 136–37, 149, 154; U.S. policy on, 89–90

settler colonialism, 23, 27, 134; alternatives to, 31, 133–34; Asian settlers in Hawaiʻi, 2, 9, 31, 47, 256n56; and infantilizing discourses, xiv; role of settlers in Native education, 7, 149, 152–55, 244; settler–Indigenous relations, 7, 11, 22, 30–31, 149–50; settler practices, 23, 25, 243; structures of, xii, 25. *See also* logic of containment; logic of elimination

settler state: educational systems, xii, 7, 23–24, 25; emergence of in Hawaiʻi, 14, 22; recognition frameworks, 26, 29, 90, 120, 206, 246; working within settler state structures, xii, 7. *See also* State of Hawaiʻi

"Seventh Generation," 1, 10–11, 251n15

Sexton, Sanoe, 181

Shanker, Albert, 61

Shon, Jim, 66–67

Silva, Noenoe K., 32, 36–37, 215

Sixkiller, Ardy, 10

Smith, Linda Tuhiwai, 29

sovereign pedagogies, 6, 12, 29, 31, 108, 124–25, 206, 246

sovereignty, 13, 26, 33, 91; Hawaiian, 21–22, 47, 49, 54, 57–59, 68, 70, 88–91, 94, 120–21, 123–24, 140, 154, 172, 206, 212, 239, 244–46; intellectual, 6; sovereign practice, 5, 245. *See also* ea

standardized tests, 12, 108, 111, 176, 190, 204, 206, 241–43, 266n63, 270n43. *See also* No Child Left Behind Act of 2001

State of Hawaiʻi, 9, 12, 23, 26, 58, 70, 90, 93, 95, 135

student voice. *See* leo

subsistence practices, 137–39, 147

Sudden Rush, 212, 281n11

sugar ditch irrigation systems, 18, 20, 23, 53, 146, 254n45

sugar industry, 17–18, 20–21, 128, 255n49, 271n4

survivance, xii, xvi, 2, 5–6, 28, 31–32, 34, 79, 149, 155

taro. *See* Hāloa; kalo; loʻi kalo

Tengan, Ty Kāwika, 157, 162, 174, 220, 273n24, 274n28

Thompson, Nainoa, 56, 173, 191

Thompson, Pete, 51–53

Thompson, Travis, 237

Tjibaou, Jean-Marie, 6

tourism, 50–51, 214

Trask, Haunani-Kay, 23, 36, 51–52

Treaster, Mahealani, 170, 172, 175, 277n12

Tui, Aaron, 3
Turk, Brandon, 181

unions. *See* labor unions
U.S. occupation of Hawaiʻi, xi,
    22–23, 37–38, 58, 140, 215,
    256n59, 268n13

Vizenor, Gerald, xii
voice. *See* leo
voyaging, 4, 45, 56–57, 77, 169, 173,
    175, 176, 177–85, 197–99. *See also*
    Bertelmann, Clay; Kahapeʻa-
    Tanner, Bonnie; Piailug, Mau

waʻa, 4, 12, 45, 168, 171, 173–75,
    185, 198, 199–203, 203–4. *See
    also Hōkūleʻa; Kānehūnāmoku;
    Makaliʻi*
Waiāhole, 53–54, 135–36, 164,
    262n15
Waiāhole-Waikāne Community
    Association, 53
Waikīkī, 105, 127–28, 209–10

Warrior, Robert Allen, 6
water, 32, 39, 128, 181, 182, 246–47;
    diversion of, 18, 20; and edu-
    cation, 39, 105, 117, 124, 138,
    140, 145–47, 171–72, 196, 201,
    203, 246–47; Indigenous
    Hawaiian waterways, 34, 133,
    141–42, 148, 246–47; struggles
    for, 53–54, 136
Wells, Amy Stuart, 60, 263n33
white supremacy, 9, 20, 24–25, 27,
    48
Wilson, Kalaniākea, 234
Winchester, ʻĪmaikalani, 123–25,
    130–32, 140, 151, 157–58, 162,
    164–65, 236
Wist, Benjamin, 15
Wolfe, Patrick, 24, 261n6
Wong-Kalu, Hinaleimoana, 233,
    282n36
world enlargement, 13, 168–69, 177,
    204

Young, Kanalu, 79–80, 250n1

Noelani Goodyear-Kaʻōpua is associate professor of political science at the University of Hawaiʻi at Mānoa.